From Blue Ridge to Barrier Islands

From Blue Ridge to Barrier Islands

An Audubon Naturalist Reader ⌒

Edited by

J. KENT MINICHIELLO

and ANTHONY W. WHITE

The Johns Hopkins University Press

Baltimore and London

© 1997 The Johns Hopkins University Press
All rights reserved. Published 1997
Printed in the United States of America on acid-free paper

Johns Hopkins Paperbacks edition, 2000
9 8 7 6 5 4 3 2 1

The Johns Hopkins University Press
2715 North Charles Street
Baltimore, Maryland 21218-4363
www.press.jhu.edu

ISBN 0-8018-6531-X (pbk.)

Library of Congress Cataloging-in-Publication Data
will be found at the end of this book.

A catalog record for this book is
available from the British Library

frontispiece: David Johnson "The Natural Bridge of Virginia"
1860 from *An American Perspective*, p. 19

For our wives, Marcia and Trina

Contents

Preface and Acknowledgments

THIS ANTHOLOGY celebrates nature in the Central Atlantic region. It is inspired by the centennial of the Audubon Naturalist Society, formerly the Audubon Society of the District of Columbia. ANS, the nation's second-oldest Audubon society, is an independent environmental organization whose roots lie in the turn-of-the-century crusade to end the commercial slaughter of birds. Its one hundred–year history typifies the maturing of the American conservation movement, for its concerns broadened beyond bird protection to encompass all that is summarized by Vice President Al Gore's slogan: The central organizing principle for civilization must be the rescue of the environment.

To see the Central Atlantic from the Audubon Naturalist Society's perspective is to view it from Washington, D.C.—halfway between the ocean and the heart of the Appalachian Mountains—an hour's drive from the Blue Ridge or the Chesapeake Bay. This is a region of great natural diversity and surprising beauty. That beauty can be as subtle as a shell-pink November sunrise through clouds over the Chesapeake Bay, as startling as a moccasin flower nestled among loblolly pine needles, or as sublime as the blue blaze of frost on a West Virginia cranberry bog. It can also be grand. Autumn anoints the mountain forests with vibrant color; maples and black gums flame crimson in a landscape painted with a wash of ochre by hickory, sassafras, and oak. Autumn concentrates migrating raptors along the ridges and down the coast. This avian spectacle draws birders from far and near to Hawk Mountain Sanctuary in Pennsylvania and to Kiptopeke State Park on Virginia's Eastern Shore. On the coastal bays, as on the Chesapeake, flocks of wintering geese, ducks, and swans are as much a marvel today as they were to the first English colonists.

Washington itself remains remarkably wooded and diverse; its natural character is preserved in many national and city parks. From the outer suburbs into the city's heart, Rock Creek Park maintains a wild aspect; near the creek, a night-heron rookery crowds the denizens of the National Zoo, and, in spring, the veery calls in deep tributary ravines. The Chesapeake and Ohio Canal National Historical Park protects the Potomac's east shore for 180 miles upstream from Washington to Cumberland, Maryland. National parks also protect both sides of the Great Falls of the Potomac.

Located just below the falls, Washington stands astride the meeting place of two major physiographic provinces—the coastal plain and the piedmont plateau. This location doubles the biological richness that writers from John Burroughs to Louis Halle and Roger Tory Peterson have acclaimed. Scientists from the Smithsonian Institution and government agencies have also responded to this richness by making local natural history their avocation; the result is 150 years of close study that is unsurpassed in quality. From among these writers and scientists have come some of the Audubon Naturalist Society's best-known leaders. Political Washington has also made its contribution. C. Hart Merriam, first head of the Biological Survey, and Assistant Secretary of the Navy Theodore Roosevelt were two of the society's founders; Justice William O. Douglas, who was instrumental in creating the C & O Canal Park, and Rachel Carson were more recent members. All four thought and acted both globally and locally in defense of nature. Their examples are an inspiration to the new generation of environmentalists whose challenges are as diverse as the region's natural history.

Editorial Methods and Objectives

Our primary objective in choosing selections was to provide complete essays of high literary quality and significant interest. We have included, however, several short pieces that relate important natural history information. In a few selections, we extracted material on a single subject from an article that deals with a variety of topics. In these cases, we have preserved authors' sentences unaltered, allowing their words to provide the link between paragraphs that may be separate in the original text. All such editing has been indicated by ellipses at the end of paragraphs. In a very few instances, we have deleted a phrase or sentence from the text of a selection when it refers to matters outside the context of the selected material and when retention would have been both confusing and irrelevant. These omissions are marked by ellipses. We have not changed any author's spelling, punctuation, or choice of words, nor have we indicated errors in the original texts.

With three exceptions, all bracketed inclusions are our editorial comments. The three exceptions are: the translator's interpolations in William Byrd's *The Natural History of Virginia*; the interpolations of Frost and Musselman in Fernald's text; and Ogburn's interpolation in a quotation in "Down the Coast to Assateague."

Acknowledgments

We are indebted to Louis Halle for suggesting this project to the Johns Hopkins University Press. We are grateful for the editorial help and patience of Robert J. Brugger, at Johns Hopkins, and Lesley Yorke. Shirley Briggs suggested many improvements in the introduction and lent us original works from her personal library. We thank Shawneen Finnegan for her illustrations, which enhance the appearance of the book. We also thank Marcia and Lisa Minichiello, who entered many of the selections on disk and proofread the entire manuscript. We appreciate the support of Katherine White throughout the editing and writing.

From Blue Ridge to Barrier Islands

Introduction

Kent Minichiello

Aｍｅｒｉｃａ's ｌｅｇａｃｙ of literature about nature is a cultural treasure to be valued with the nation's other arts. It is part of the history of the development of our unique American character; and the record of a people's relation to the land is as significant a measure of character as is the record of its politics and wars. The chronicle of love and stewardship and of waste and abuse tells much about the maturing of a nation, and its prospects. Nature helped to mold American culture and attitudes; the frontier experience, credited by some for our democratic institutions, was part social and part environmental.

The Central Atlantic region has had a preeminent role in the evolution of our society, and it enjoys a major share in the legacy of nature literature. Lacking the topographic extremes of the western states, the area between the Allegheny Plateau and the Atlantic Ocean is nonetheless rich in natural and environmental history. It required over two hundred years for the frontier to cross this biologically diverse and scenic landscape; after another two hundred years, the exploration of its flora and fauna is still incomplete.

Regional character, as distinct from national character, is created out of a unique natural base. In the Central Atlantic, the perception of nature has been, from the beginning of its settlement, quite different from that of climatically more extreme places. This difference accounts, in part, for the appreciation that people here have for the land: That the Chesapeake Bay country is called "the land of pleasant living" is an ecological reality rather than a cultural artifact; that West Virginia is "almost heaven," is more a scenic truth than a song lyric. The region's residents are proving their commitment to the land through the implementation of the Chesapeake Bay Program, the nation's first bioregional attempt to establish a sustainable way of life.

These laudatory words are not written in a chauvinistic spirit, but to define the variety of written responses to nature that this anthology contains. Not limited to the traditional personal nature essay in the "I came, I experienced, I emoted" style, they cover the full range of human interactions with nature and are spaced more or less evenly through time. The temporal distribution and broad range of subject matter help expose the cultural and environmental matrix in which the writings were produced. In particular, selections from the colonial period introduce the ecological foundations of regional culture, attitudes, and literature. From among often neglected genres come many interesting and entertaining works: journals of exploration and settlement, early scientific exposition and speculation, a nineteenth-century fishing story and a hunting guide, travelogues, ruminations on country living, and even a poem. The authors are as diverse as the topics; they range from such figures of national prominence as Captain John Smith, Thomas Jefferson, Theodore Roosevelt, and William O. Douglas, to men obscure in their own day. Many of the nation's greatest nature writers lived and worked in the region: John Burroughs, Rachel Carson, and Annie Dillard each, for a substantial time, made the Central Atlantic their home. The early selections have not been included at the expense of fine modern writing; in the past forty years, regional writers have won two Pulitzer Prizes and seven John Burroughs Medals for excellence in nature writing. The selections touch, with informing insights, each natural province and nearly every current environmental issue.

As is fitting in a book inspired by an Audubon society, birds have a prominent, but not a dominant, place. The attention paid them here is their due, in light of the importance of their role in making conservation an accepted part of our national character. Birds are the vehicle we have chosen to explicate the relationships among literature, science, and conservation. In this introduction, we compare four authors, each of whom wrote about birds but whose primary works run the gamut from pure literature to pure science: Walt Whitman, John Burroughs, Florence Merriam Bailey, and Elliott Coues.

Other material in the introduction and the head notes places the selections and their authors in cultural context. While the range of writing is broad, many nature-related genres have been omitted, among them fiction, the nineteenth-century woodcraft and nature hobby fads, and current popular scientific exposition.

The Colonial Period

The colonial period's nature-related literature chronicles the change from a European curiosity about exotica to the emerging nation's pride in its landscape and biota. The southern colonies' share of this literature displays attitudes toward nature different from those usually attributed to New England, significant among them being "love of wilderness."

The impressions of the first European explorers of the Central Atlantic are as lost to us as are those of their paleo-Indian predecessors. Neither Verrazano, who entered the Chesapeake Bay, nor Cabot, who skirted the coast, recorded what he found. Nearly one hundred years passed before the first description by an Englishman was published: Thomas Hariot's 1588 account from the Roanoke colony, *A briefe and true report on the new found land of Virginia*. His annotated list of plants, animals, minerals, and soils described their uses by the natives and their prospective value to the colonists. There is, however, a disinterested aspect in Hariot's report. He was a trained scientist and mathematician, and he accompanied John White, the colony's professional artist and surveyor, who painted illustrations of snakes, lizards, fish, and especially birds. Although Hariot's and White's main business was promoting the colony's success, they delighted in nature and sought to satisfy the English public's curiosity about the New World. Naturally, the colonists recognized their dependence on their new environment; consequently, Hariot's book and other early regional reports are surprisingly modern in their holistic, ecological approach.

Captain John Smith was in a unique position to reach a large public with his comprehensive and useful appraisal of the colonial environment. In 1609, living again in England and at odds with his former employer, the London Company, Smith was at liberty to be honest and objective, at least about nature. In 1612, defying company prohibitions, he published *A Map of Virginia. With a Description of the Countrey, the Commodities, People, Government and Religion*. Smith's very first analytical remark is an insight whose full import was not understood until the recent work of environmental historians: "The temperature of this countrie doth agree well with the English constitutions being once seasoned to country."[1] This comment highlights the single most important factor in European expansion throughout the world's temperate areas: Europeans were biologically preadapted to the climate; that is, the climate so suited them that it maximized their overall health and thereby minimized susceptibility to disease. Smith had been the man on the spot in Jamestown, knew the high mortality, and correctly foresaw that it would abate with improved living conditions. His statement contradicted the generally held opinion that what was believed to be the southern climate of Virginia would be fatal to northern Europeans.

In fact, the climate, topography, and biota fostered the English colonial

1. John Smith, *A Map of Virginia. With a Description of the Countrey, the Commodities, People, Government and Religion* (Oxford: J. Barnes, 1612), 1.

enterprise and produced a colonial society unique to the region. The climate's strong but balanced seasonality epitomized the temperate zone. Despite hotter summers and colder winters than in England, northern European crops, domestic animals, weeds, and people flourished. The topography was as welcoming as the climate. The coastal plain broadens southward from New York to a width of one hundred miles at Richmond. Cutting this fertile province in two is the Chesapeake Bay, the nation's largest estuary and seasonal home to immense numbers of waterfowl, fish, and crabs. The shellfish harvest was for a time the largest in the world. Even more significant than this resource base was the sheltered access which the bay and its tidal tributaries gave to oceangoing ships. Ease of access dispersed settlement, delaying the development of commercial centers and manufacturing and so cities and literature, but it provided cheap water transport for agricultural and forest products. East of the bay, the land lies nearly flat; west, it is gently rolling. Both topographies permitted effective farming of relatively large tracts, once a profitable crop was found. And a native crop was at hand. In 1613, John Rolfe—Pocahontas's husband—crossed the hardy native tobacco plant with the more flavorful Caribbean species and so produced the hybrid that became the staple of the colonial economy. From the natural base of flora, topography, and climate rose the plantation society that populated Delaware, Maryland, and Virginia in the seventeenth century and created the wealth to expand into the piedmont uplands and beyond in the eighteenth.

The colonial attitude that developed under this benign regime was quite different from that often attributed to the New England settlements, in which historians find a biblically and culturally based hostility toward wilderness—*the howling wilderness* of Michael Wigglesworth and Cotton Mather. These words were more a rhetorical device than a metaphoric phrase and still less a description of physical realities; nevertheless, they are sometimes seen to embody the whole Puritan relationship to nature. The South's lack of a well-known early literature and the northern cultural ascendancy after the Civil War permit this view to be projected onto the entire nation. In fact, both North and South shared a generally positive attitude. An example of this common attitude is the earliest of our champions of nature, James Fenimore Cooper's New York Leatherstocking, who is not usually recognized as the fictional alter ego of John Filson's southern Daniel Boone. Boone's Pennsylvania birth and Quaker childhood predisposed him to an open-minded response to the Virginia-Carolina-Kentucky frontier. Filson and Boone collaborated on a ghost-written autobiography in which Boone forgoes his simple, backcountry diction and speaks through Filson's grandiloquent prose of the beauties and bounty of nature, not of an enemy to be overcome.

"Practical interest" best summarizes the early Virginia colonists' attitude toward their environment, which was certainly not viewed as *hostile* wilderness. As John Smith's writings reveal, they well knew that they were entering a fertile and already occupied land. They emulated its native peoples and, as William Byrd's writings make clear, were knowledgeably using Native American land-clearing and seeding methods one hundred years after first contact. As frontier men and women learned the Native Americans' woodcraft as well as agriculture, a pioneering spirit emerged that combined the explorer's wanderlust with the husbandman's desire to settle new lands. The result was a rugged appreciation of wild nature typified by Boone and Leatherstocking but present in the southern colonies from nearly the beginning.

One of the earliest explorers, John Lederer, learned the pleasures of woodland travel so well that he might be credited with the first (non-native) expression of the attitude that we now call love of wilderness. In 1669, he and three Indian companions made the first recorded journey to the summit of the Blue Ridge. The yarns in Lederer's narrative would have made any frontier storyteller proud: a rattlesnake charming squirrels out of the trees, a wildcat clinging onto the back of a doe, and, of course, the awe-inspiring view from the summit.

Only two years after Lederer's exploration, Robert Fallam and two other white men set out to find an overland route to the Pacific. They traveled up the Roanoke River and crossed first the Blue Ridge and then the eastern continental divide. Failing in their objective to reach the ocean, they nevertheless returned convinced that they had seen tidewater on what was in fact the New River. Their flair for the dramatic was less developed than Lederer's, but the sensitive Fallam caught the feeling of the heart of the "Apalataeans" in his phrase, "a curious prospect of hills like waves rais'd by a gentle breeze of Wind rising one after another."[2]

From the beginning of English settlement at Roanoke, there was a non-exploitative interest in the flora, fauna, fossils, and landscape features of the New World. This interest grew in part from the rapidly expanding information base of sixteenth- and seventeenth-century science to which the colonists themselves contributed. During the sixteenth century, returning ships brought the exotica of the new worlds to Europe. Plants, animals, and

2. Robert Fallam, an unpublished journal in Edmund Berkeley and Dorothy Smith Berkeley, *The Reverend John Clayton. A Parson with a Scientific Mind. His Scientific Writings and Other Related Papers* (Charlottesville: The University Press of Virginia, 1965), 74.

people, all were exhibited to the fascination of rich and poor alike. Botanical gardens, aviaries, and menageries were created ostensibly as exercises in Christian theology. Soon they became ends in themselves; ultimately, they were vehicles for the study of natural history. Once English colonies were well established, leisured aristocrats, churchmen, and tradesmen joined colonial entrepreneurs in collecting bird and animal skins and pressed plants. These were sent to England by colonists and travelers, men who were often paid, commissioned agents. The field collectors also sent seeds, cuttings, and living plants to landscape gardeners as well as to the more scientifically oriented naturalists and botanical gardeners. Throughout the seventeenth and eighteenth centuries, patrons encouraged collectors to provide ever rarer elements of the biota. Epitomized by Pennsylvania farmer John Bartram (1699–1777), these men often became better naturalists than their English correspondents. Some, including Mark Catesby and Bartram's son, William, became professional naturalists, as well as natural history writers, whose primary objective in travel was to study nature. Such was the value of their discoveries that they were able to fund their expeditions entirely through patronage.

Despite the extensive collecting, relatively little scientific work was done in the colonies before the middle of the eighteenth century. Although Hariot, the Rev. John Banister at Charles City, and the Rev. John Clayton at Jamestown had scientific training, they sent their collections back to England where they were studied and disseminated by the Royal Society. Oxford-trained John Clayton was a fellow of the society; his reports, made largely after his return to England, added a heretofore missing element of rigor to scientific observations from the New World. A generation later, a second, distantly related John Clayton of Gloucester County, Virginia, produced the first taxonomic work from America, *Flora Virginica*, which he and Johann Gronovius published at Leiden in 1739.

One imagines the eighteenth century as a time of great revolutions—the Enlightenment, the American and French Revolutions, the beginning of the Industrial Revolution. In fact, these great transitions were incremental, building step by step until a summit of observation was reached from which a new view of both past and future seemed clear. From the days of Rev. John Clayton and Mark Catesby to those of Thomas Jefferson, science as well as politics built a new edifice. In *Notes on the State of Virginia*, Jefferson combines these two disparate disciplines to declare America's scientific independence from Europe. The French naturalist Comte Georges Louis Leclerc de Buffon had asserted that New World animals are smaller and of fewer species than the Old World's. Jefferson's spirited rebuttal rests on close argument from data, some of which is Catesby's. But in his zeal to produce a really big American mammal, he resurrects the mammoth and commits himself to the doctrine of the immutability of species. Jefferson's use of Indian legend as a support is more comical than effective and demonstrates how willing Native Americans were to produce stories to please (or confound) their interlocutors. Published in 1787, *Notes* is Jefferson's most complete statement on politics, government, art, education, science, religion, and slavery. The chapter, "Productions Mineral, Vegetable and Animal," contains the first improvement on Catesby's bird list, a plant list based on the *Flora Virginica*, a significant discussion of the origin of marine fossils, and a good deal more. His apparent approval of the theory that shell fossils are crystalline productions caused him as much criticism among scientists as did his rejection of the Deluge among churchmen. From the chapters "Mountains" and "Cascades" come two famous landscape descriptions, one of the Potomac water gap through the Blue Ridge and the other of Natural Bridge, which Jefferson owned, near Roanoke. Jefferson's passionate evoking of the forces of nature at Harpers Ferry is unusual in the American writing of his time. However, it is unusual for its restraint rather than its grandiloquence, which was the preferred style for depicting scenery up to the time of John Muir and beyond.

Even more restrained and far more sophisticated in style was Jefferson's contemporary, J. Hector St. John de Crèvecoeur. De Crèvecoeur's writings may be the first examples of truly *American* literature. It is therefore doubly paradoxical that not only was he a Frenchman but also an Anglophile and a Tory. His *Letters from an American Farmer* (1787) includes both social criticism and nature essays that have more in common with Mark Twain and John Burroughs than with Jefferson and Ben Franklin. De Crèvecoeur might well be credited with independent invention of the personal nature essay, for *Letters* was published before the book usually regarded the genre's source, Gilbert White's *Natural History of Selborne* (1789). De Crèvecoeur's descriptions are vivid, personal, and seemingly accurate; yet his imaginative powers suggest fiction rather than essays, perhaps removing him from close kinship with the naturalists.

Picturesque America

The nineteenth century was a time of profound change for nature writing. The simultaneous appearance of literary and general-interest periodicals and a large audience ready for the diversion of reading them expanded the record of our changing landscape. While not the center of publishing, the Cen-

tral Atlantic was nonetheless the subject of a significant body of landscape appreciation and travel writing that the magazines and railroad travel made possible.

During the quarter century after de Crèvecoeur published *Letters from an American Farmer*, the Industrial Revolution transformed urban life in Europe and America. Many of the changes increased popular knowledge of nature and expanded the potential market for nature-associated literature: New technologies made printing cheaper; transport, travel, and communications became easier; and science advanced at an ever more rapid pace. As material prosperity increased, the romantic spirit, always the companion of appreciation of nature, arose in reaction, first in Germany and then in England. This was an ideal time for the birth of American literature, for heroic actions fit perfectly into the wild setting of the western frontier. First Washington Irving and then James Fenimore Cooper made successful marriages of European romantic themes to the American landscape.

Opposition to romanticism in literature appeared in America simultaneously with the poetry and novels of Sir Walter Scott, who, while being the inspiration for some of Irving's and Cooper's works, was despised by Irving's coauthor of the *Salmagundi* papers, James Kirke Paulding. Paulding's *Letters from the South* (1817) are witty, matter-of-fact descriptions of rural Virginia's people and countryside; they express the admiration of this New York Federalist for the realities of Jeffersonian democracy.

From the 1820s to the present day, the mainstay of nature literature has been the essays, sketches, and travelogues published by popular magazines. It was principally through them, as well as the lyceum lectures, that the transcendentalists promulgated their nature-based philosophy. Population growth, urbanization, and increased wealth and literacy created a large and receptive public that was able to take Emerson's advice and turn to nature. Many took up amateur nature studies, which were in their heyday from 1820 until 1890. For most, these activities were merely pastimes. Collecting and pressing plants; keeping aquariums; collecting birds' nests and eggs; collecting insects, ferns, seaweed, shells, and minerals—all these recreations were made intellectually attractive and morally defensible by the generally held belief that nature was an ethical guide.

As the nineteenth century progressed, literary interest in the eastern landscape grew. This was partly a consequence of these nature fads and partly an outgrowth of the success of American landscape painting and the painterly interpretation of common scenery advocated in England first by

William Gilpin and later by John Ruskin. Mostly, however, interest arose from the influence of the patriotic spirit in landscape appreciation first displayed in Jefferson's *Notes on the State of Virginia* and carried forward by nearly every American intellectual for the next century. Emerson's essays and the poetry of Henry Wadsworth Longfellow, John Greenleaf Whittier, and William Cullen Bryant inspired a more sophisticated public, a public that was sufficiently leisured not only to read but to travel. This was the first great era of public transportation—the heyday of the railroads as well as of nature appreciation.

Every nineteenth-century social commentator of note had an opinion about the railroads. They were celebrated as symbols of progress and castigated as examples of the degradation of people and the landscape by industrialism. Dostoyevsky pouted over them; Dickens complained; Daniel Webster was skeptical. But no matter what their opinion, everybody rode. In *Walden*, Henry Thoreau gave them their economic due and then, in an outburst of insight, exposed the environmental destruction caused by uncontrolled human industry. But Thoreau rode, too; he rode and wrote of what he saw, as did every person so inclined in every region of the country. Lacking Thoreau's insight, ironic humor, and style, and displaying an unbecoming chauvinism, many local writers championed their region's grandeur in overexcited prose. Nevertheless, they awakened Americans to natural wonders and beauties that were previously neglected. From the Dismal Swamp near the Carolina border to unexplored areas of the Alleghenies, the Central Atlantic yielded scenic treasures to the eager travel writers' pens. Newly discovered splendor like the limestone caverns of the Shenandoah Valley and newly appreciated landscapes like the Chickahominy River swamps competed for literary attention with rediscovered vistas like the Blue Ridge water gap at Harpers Ferry.

It is often, erroneously, said that the picturesque in American travel writing began with Thomas Star King's 1859 book, *The White Hills: Their Legends, Landscape, and Poetry*, an illustrated study of New Hampshire's White Mountains. Star King wandered the New England countryside selecting views for comment, shifting to poetry when overpowered by the scene. Under the influence of John Ruskin, he analyzed the landscape as one would a picture (hence the eighteenth-century term *picturesque*); but, American to the core, he slipped into patriotic ecstasy over the flora of Mount Washington. His style of landscape appreciation survived into the twentieth century in countless illustrated magazines and in Wallace Nutting's *America Beautiful* series of books.

Considerably less sophisticated than *The White Hills* is an earlier publication from the Central Atlantic, *The Blackwater Chronicle*, by Philip Pendleton Kennedy of Martinsburg, (now West) Virginia. In this rollicking story of a fishing expedition into the Canaan Valley backcountry, the principal actor is the wild and very much untamed land. Illustrations by Virginian David Strother pair with Kennedy's comic text to show that Americans can laugh at themselves while playing Daniel Boone. Comedy aside, Kennedy communicates the wilderness quality of the Allegheny Plateau, which is still felt by visitors to the West Virginia National Forests. Kennedy's exaggerated prose is not an isolated example of ineptitude; rather, it is the popular style of the time—a deliberate, common, and rather formal style which the versatile Strother—a writer as well as an artist—and many others used to tout their regions.

The whole phenomenon of the nineteenth-century landscape enthusiasm had a visual and literary summing up in *Picturesque America*, edited and published by William Cullen Bryant. Completely up-to-date in 1872, the first two volumes of *Picturesque America* contain accounts and steel engravings of Yosemite and the newly created Yellowstone National Park. Nine of the sixty-five chapters concern the Central Atlantic, more than any other region.

In *Picturesque America*, Bryant declares the independence of the American landscape as Jefferson had our fauna, waxing eloquent in its behalf:

> On our continent, and within the limits of our Republic, [art carries her conquest into new realms]—primitive forests, in which the huge trunks of a past generation of trees lie mouldering in the shade of their aged descendants; mountains and valleys, gorges and rivers, and tracts of sea-coast, which the foot of the artist has never trod; and glens murmuring with water-falls which his ear has never heard. Thousands of charming nooks are waiting to yield their beauty to the pencil of the first comer. On the two great oceans which border our league of States, and in the vast space between them, we find a variety of scenery which no other single country can boast of. . . . Among our White Mountains, our Catskills, our Alleghanies, our Rocky Mountains, and our Sierra Nevada, we have some of the wildest and most beautiful scenery in the world.[3]

At this time the country had been crossed by rail for only three years, and

3. William Cullen Bryant, *Picturesque America*, ed. William Cullen Bryant (New York: D. Appleton and Company, 1872), viii.

already Bryant's authors were instructing tourists on transcontinental travel to our most spectacular scenery. Yet for Bryant, Yellowstone, Yosemite, and the Canyon of the Colorado were no more artistically worthy than charming nooks and murmuring glens. Nor was wild nature to be more preferred, nor less, than the rural countryside or the cityscape. Ruskin's arcadian sensitivity was mingling with John Lederer's love of the wild, and these two cultural attitudes were spreading through a society rising up in wealth, literacy, and aspirations. At a time when cities were begrimed by large-scale industrialization and dehumanized by overcrowding, nature seemed to many a solace or an escape; and the desire to embrace it took three not-new, but rapidly growing forms: literature, conservation, and country life.

The Century of John Burroughs

Nature writing in America reached its apogee during the long lifetime of John Burroughs; no author better represents its subjects, style, and influences. Some of Burroughs's most significant work was done during his years in the Central Atlantic.

Nowadays we are predisposed to forget the extent of nature study in the nineteenth century and the fervor of popular and artistic involvement in the landscape. Our schools emphasize the enduring artifacts of intellectual history and the outstanding examples of literature; the social substrate out of which they arose is left obscure. In the resulting contextless isolation, great and significant writing in an unfamiliar style or of an unknown philosophy loses its accessibility. This educational inadequacy may explain why the eighteenth-century Enlightenment essayists and poets who celebrated nature have been neglected by modern students of nature writing. It also has hindered modern appreciation of the most prolific and best-loved nature writer of the nineteenth century, John Burroughs, whose reputation has declined as that of his contemporary, John Muir, has ascended. Muir is regarded as the father of the modern conservation movement, which he indeed helped to shape; and he is correctly recognized as a spokesman for a biocentric attitude. Unfortunately, Burroughs's limited conservation activity leads environmentalists to ignore the carefully formulated philosophy he developed in response to Walt Whitman's insights into art and to Charles Darwin's theory of natural selection.

Early on, Burroughs began to transcend his more scientifically inclined predecessors and contemporaries with what he thought to be a new approach to nature writing. He said that he wished to free the birds from science. That is, he wished to be true to fact but to transcend it. This he did; but he was continuing a well-developed theme in English prose and poetry that lay outside the technical confines of the nature essay. It is in this broader context that his writing is best understood.

The personal essay appeared in the sixteenth century, but not until Gilbert White's *Natural History of Selborne* (1789) did personal nature writing take on a form that critics accept as a separate genre. Looking back through English literature for models, we find an example so accessible that every literate person could have read it: Izaak Walton's *The Compleat Angler; or, The Contemplative Man's Recreation* (1653). Third in republication only to the Bible and the *Book of Common Prayer*—what overlooked influences this marvelous book must have had! Giving much more than a fishing lesson, Walton's gentle humor ranges over creation's wonders and humanity's infelicities. It begins with a debate between a hunter, a falconer, and an angler about which medium is superior: earth, air, or water; and it concludes with a homily on the Simple Life, which is similar in attitude to Thoreau's chapter "Economy" in *Walden*. Fragments—sometimes large fragments—of the text are personal responses to nature that foreshadow Victorian themes. They reveal a changing religious attitude toward nature—really a new natural attitude toward religion—which Walton, as much as Burroughs, typifies. Among Walton's many subjects, the falconer's birds signal the change:

The very birds of the air . . . are both so many, and so useful and pleasant to mankind, that I must not let them pass without some observations. They both feed and refresh him; feed him with their choice bodies, and refresh him with their Heavenly voices . . . those little nimble Musicians of the air, that warble forth their curious Ditties, with which Nature hath furnished them to the shame of Art.

At first the *Lark*, when she means to rejoyce, to chear her self and those that hear her, she then quits the earth, and sings as she ascends higher into the air, and having ended her Heavenly imployment, grows then mute and sad to think she must descend to the dull earth, which she would not touch, but for necessity. . . .

But the *Nightingale* (another of my Airy Creatures) breathes such sweet loud musick out of her little instrumental throat, that it might make mankind to think Miracles are not ceased. He that at midnight (when the very labourer sleeps securely) should hear (as I have very often) the clear airs, the sweet descants, the natural rising and falling, the doubling and redoubling of her voice, might well be lifted above earth, and say; "Lord, what Musick hast thou provided for the Saints in Heaven, when thou affordest bad men such musick on Earth!"[4]

These birds are nature's creatures, seen with eyes different from the colonizer, John Smith, or the naturalist, Thomas Jefferson. Placed on Earth for Heaven's glory and man's delight, they are the most congenial manifestation of the Christian God. Students of intellectual history would have us believe that Walton's uniquely western attitude was an outgrowth of two academic events: the first, the rediscovery of classical antiquity's natural philosophy and its extension in the Enlightenment science; the second, the attempt to prove the existence of God from the order seen in the natural world, which is called the "argument from design." Intellectual history may thus explain the philosophical equivalent of Walton's biocentric spirit: John Ray's straightforward assertion that "it is a generally received Opinion, that all this visible World was created for Man; that Man is the end of the Creation, as if there were no other end of any Creature, but some way or other to be serviceable to Man. This opinion is as old as Tully; . . . But though this be vulgarly receiv'd yet wise Men now-a-days think otherwise. Dr. More affirms, That Creatures are made to enjoy themselves, as well as to serve us; and that it's a gross Piece of Ignorance and Rusticity to think otherwise. . . . For my Part I cannot believe, that all the Things in the World were so made for Man, that they have no other use."[5]

The wellspring of the biocentric spirit is not the philosopher's work. It was nature herself as revealed to every Briton who hunted, fished, falconed or merely walked for recreation or even had the leisure to pause in his work to enjoy the sight of a passing swallow or the mists rising over the fields. Transcending classes, *love of nature* became, in Virginia Woolf's phrase, the English disease. Spread both by direct contact and by vectors like *The Compleat Angler*, Ray's *The Wisdom of God Manifested in the Works of Creation*, and Alexander Pope's satiric poetry, it breaks out in letters, journals,

4. Izaak Walton and Charles Cotton, *The Compleat Angler or the Contemplative Man's Recreation* (London: Richard Marriott, 1676; reprinted, Oxford: Oxford University Press, 1935), 26.

5. John Ray, *The Wisdom of God Manifested in the Works of Creation* (London: William Innys, 1717), 175–76.

poems, novels, travelogues, and newspaper reports well before the romantic movement and *The Natural History of Selborne*. It infected first the rich and country-bred and then attacked the lower classes as wealth and leisure spread. Despite purgatives offered by Thomas Hobbes and Samuel Johnson, by the nineteenth century, it was part of the cultural background of every urbanite who, appalled by dirt and poverty, sought refuge beyond the trolley line. Although distorted by the romantic's symbolic use and subordinated to the transcendentalist's zeal for self-fulfillment, love of nature had still been purified of superstition and folklore by two hundred years of natural science when it was freed from religion by Darwin. It remained only for John Burroughs to liberate love of nature from science to create a self-sufficient cultural attitude.

Burroughs began life on his parents' hardscrabble farm in the Catskills whose only natural crop was hay, as he euphemistically said. Like Thoreau, he was a childhood hunter and fisherman; and again like Thoreau, his interests in nature soon extended to all wild things. Although there was no nearby Emerson for a mentor, there was a unique teacher, James Oliver, whose example inspired the adolescent Burroughs to leave the farm and find a job teaching boys hardly younger than himself. Oliver also inspired Burroughs to write, and, at nineteen, his first published essay was not remarkable. During the next nine years, he alternately studied at provincial colleges, worked on his parents' farm, and taught. Reading widely in history and literature, he discovered first the nature essayist Wilson Flagg, next Emerson and Thoreau, and, finally, Walt Whitman. Caught up in Emerson's ideas and style, his writing and thinking advanced until, in 1860, his essay "Expressions" was mistaken by James Russell Lowell, the editor at the *Atlantic Monthly*, for a plagiarism of the Sage of Concord. Wishing to publish it, Lowell sent a copy to Emerson, who agreed that the style and point of view were his even though the authorship was not. That this anonymously published essay was (and remained) universally attributed to Emerson caused Burroughs to strike out on his own intellectually. He began writing about things he knew firsthand in a series of articles called "Back from the Country," which appeared in *Leader*, a small-circulation New York literary magazine. The rural scenes and experiences of his *rambles*, as he called his walks, became his stock in trade; soon he added ornithology to his interests and his writing. These subjects, and the personal style that Burroughs developed for them, attracted tens of millions of readers over the next fifty years. The love of nature flowed from his pen as it had from Izaak Walton's, and the public loved him for it. As he aged and as income from his writings rose, he was able to retire to the Catskills—to walk and write and to entertain, with equal ease, visiting admirers from grade-school children to the president of the United States. The picture of him, white-bearded in his seventies, seated by the hearth of his rustic cabin-sanctuary, calls up the terms of affectionate respect he earned from his readers: "Our Friend John Burroughs, the Sage of Slabsides." This valid but limited picture misses much about the man, about the breadth and depth of his intellect, and about the variety of his writing. In particular, it misses the philosophical edifice that he was building on the foundation of his apparently straightforward responses to nature. The seeming ease of his style belies both the labor of its creation and the avant-garde milieu of its development.

During the late 1850s, Burroughs introduced himself to New York City and its bohemian community. There, he met acquaintances and admirers of Walt Whitman. One was Henry Clapp, Burroughs's editor at the *Leader,* and later the first publisher of "Out of the Cradle Endlessly Rocking" and "O Captain! My Captain." Another, Elijah Allen, became Burroughs's close friend. Allen's move to Washington, D.C., at the end of 1862 coincided with Whitman's and induced Burroughs's. Suffering with an unsympathetic wife and an unremunerative teaching job, Burroughs decided to better his position by finding work in the wartime government. The change would also, at last, allow him to meet Whitman, about whom he was writing articles.

Whitman and Burroughs became close and lifelong friends; they seem to have had no literary differences. Burroughs soon transformed his enthusiasm for Whitman's poetry into his first book, *Notes on Walt Whitman as a Poet and Person* (1867). The father-son relationship that grew up between them allowed Whitman to help Burroughs with his writing without friction. Whitman's uniformly good advice to Burroughs concerning his nature writing not only demonstrates Whitman's literary insight and his understanding of Burroughs but also his disinterested wish to put him on his own path. Whitman believed that nature was most truly rendered into words by intuitive, poetic vision that captured both mystery and beauty. To this artistic approach, Burroughs added faithfulness to the facts of natural history. During their time in Washington, they took many rambles together, discussing nature, writing, and a myriad of other things. But Burroughs also often went alone, particularly to observe and collect birds, for scientific ornithology had become as great a passion for him as Whitman's poetry. Aided by Smithsonian scientists, Burroughs gained a specialist's knowledge which enabled him to combine truth to nature with personal, poetic response. This consciously-arrived-at art was intended to separate itself from what he saw to be the ethically based writing of Thoreau and the scientifically motivated Gilbert White. The first major essay to display these new precepts was the literary result of his Washington rambles, "Spring at the Capital," which became a chapter in Burroughs's first book of nature essays, *Wake-Robin*.

In these and in later works, Burroughs laid the foundation of his personal philosophical response to Darwin's *Origin of Species*, which, he thought, obviated the need for supernatural religion. Burroughs's dictum may be simply put: nature, and love of nature, is enough. This surprising and often overlooked innovation separates him from the transcendentalists, Thoreau, and Muir, who still required a god; and it anticipates and transcends Edward O. Wilson's *biophilia*, which requires a biological base. Again, for Burroughs, only love of nature is required. What an odd, illogical consequence to the theory of natural selection; and how wonderfully hopeful and uplifting the result! For here was a successor to the pantheism of the transcendentalists and an alternative to the racism and nationalism of the social Darwinists. Later in life, Burroughs formalized his attitudes and ideas in *Accepting the Universe* (1920), which is becoming a favorite with anthologists. His philosophy was never intended as a substitute for religion; for him, none was needed. For other less accepting natures, this philosophical minimalism offers little solace in life's misfortunes. The basic evolutionary forces and mechanisms—including competition, predation, pain, and death—are usually seen as evils that require at least a religious explanation if not a justification. Much of religion and art may be attempts to live with the inevitability of the dilemmas thus posed by nature. Direct literary confrontations with the dilemmas are, however, rare. In one of the most articulate and deeply felt responses to them, Annie Dillard, in *Pilgrim at Tinker Creek*, seeks religious solutions to these conundrums and in the end seems to find sanctuary from their terrors in the Virginia countryside.

For Whitman, Burroughs was an inexhaustible source of images from nature. The finest may be the hermit thrush in "When Lilacs Last in the Dooryard Bloom'd," Whitman's burial hymn for Lincoln. The haunting beauty of the thrush's song has enchanted every woodland wanderer who, at dusk, chances within its range. Burroughs's biographer, Edward J. Renehan Jr., tells of the writer's return from first hearing this lonely caroler. As Burroughs related his experience, Whitman, sensitive to the potential, made notes which he later molded into one of the poem's three central images. Recurring throughout the poem, the thrush and his song focus and assuage Whitman's grief. While nothing can substitute for reading the poem in its entirety, the stanza introducing the thrush yields a sense of Burroughs's experience and Whitman's sorrow:

> In the swamp, in secluded recesses,
> A shy and hidden bird is warbling a song.
> Solitary, the thrush,
> The hermit, withdrawn to himself, avoiding the settlements,
> Sings by himself a song,
>
> Song of the bleeding throat!
> Death's outlet song of life—(for well, dear brother, I know
> If thou wast not gifted to sing, thou would'st surely die.)[6]

Whitman's art derived much more than specific images from his friendship with Burroughs. After his Washington years, Whitman expanded his choice of subjects and varied his prose style with Burroughs's essays as his most obvious example. Perhaps Burroughs's success with the nature essay during the late 1860s and early 1870s led Whitman to record and publish in *Specimen Days* his own experiences in rural New Jersey where he recovered from his first stroke. Some of these brief, informal essays are, like Whitman's poetry, deeply personal, but others are natural history descriptions that could have been, but were not, written by Burroughs. It is mildly surprising that Whitman had not tried his hand at prose nature writing during his early days as a journalist, for long before *Leaves of Grass* was conceived, he had become familiar with the work of William Cullen Bryant, Emerson, and most of the other American nature poets and essayists of the day. There was little that Burroughs or anyone else could teach Whitman about feeling for nature. Like Burroughs, he had been raised on a farm and had close emotional contact with nature as a child. The Long Island beach of his youth is the setting of perhaps his finest poem, "Out of the Cradle Endlessly Rocking," which was written before he and Burroughs had met. Although the central event of this poem—the death of the female of a pair of mockingbirds—may be fancied rather than remembered, the setting was always fresh in his mind; the intensity of his feeling expressed by the male mockingbird's song is beyond anything Burroughs ever attempted.

6. Walt Whitman, *Leaves of Grass* (Philadelphia: David McKay, 1900), 367–68.

Science, Conservation, and the Audubon Movement

The relationships among science, conservation, sport hunting, and nature literature are complex. The presence of the federal government in the Central Atlantic made this region a focus of both science and conservation and so an ideal venue for examining the origins and literature of the Audubon movement.

In a way, Burroughs is as much the father of conservation as is John Muir. His writings greatly increased the public's appreciation of nature and its sympathy with nature's creatures, especially birds. Coming at a time when commerce and industry were exterminating wildlife and destroying the landscape, this sympathy among middle- and upper-class readers was easily transformed into social and political action by several agents. Significant among these was the Audubon movement, which brought together professional and amateur naturalists, nature lovers, and literary naturalists like John Burroughs. The movement both generated its own literature and participated in the already flourishing scientific and popular writing. Almost without exception, its major authors were in some way connected with the Central Atlantic or wrote about it.

Conservation in America is a complex and many-sided social phenomenon. One group of historians, led by Samuel P. Hays, emphasizes the role played by professional government scientists in establishing a federal policy of efficient and sustainable use of natural resources. The beginnings of this policy were occasioned by pressure from business and professional groups including the American Forestry Association and the American Association for the Advancement of Science. President Benjamin Harrison and his secretary of the interior, John Noble, were encouraged to create forest reserves to protect watersheds. Broadened under Presidents Cleveland and McKinley, the policy was extensively implemented during Theodore Roosevelt's administration by Chief Forester Gifford Pinchot and Reclamation Service head Frederick H. Newell. While the effects of federal conservation policy are usually associated with the West, they were no less significant in the East: The national forest system has revived the natural character of the Appalachians that was so admired by Robert Fallam on his first view in 1671. Three hundred years later, Maurice Brooks could write of that sea of wooded hills with equal enthusiasm for its returning wildness and once-again pristine beauty.

But, regardless of how much the resource conservation movement accomplished in the long term for the preservation of nature, it was others who initiated the creation of national, state, and private parks and wildlife refuges and who forced passage of the laws that protect wildlife. The roots of nature preservation lay in the nature fads, in sportsmen's clubs, in popular nature writing, and in amateur and professional science. The complex interactions of these distinct but related phenomena are revealed in the biographies of Elliott Coues, one of the Central Atlantic region's foremost scientists, and Florence Merriam Bailey, the leading female ornithologist of her time, an author of popular and scientific books about birds, and the founder of Audubon education programs for children and teachers.

Born in 1842 to a world largely unaware of the need for conservation of nature, Coues experienced firsthand the near-extinction of the bison, the coming extinction of the passenger pigeon, and the decimation of most wildlife populations by commercial hunting. As a field zoologist who collected throughout the country, his understanding of these depredations was unexcelled; yet, despite intimate knowledge, he played no direct role in conservation until, near the end of his life in 1897, he coauthored *Citizen Bird*, an illustrated children's book.

The Smithsonian Institution was the dominant factor in Coues's professional life. Its founding in 1846 began the Central Atlantic's change from a scientific backwater to a national center of research and—under congressional mandate and to the chagrin of its first director, the eminent physicist Joseph Henry—education. Despite his preference for experimental science and his consequent distaste for collections, Henry gave impetus to the Smithsonian's ornithological endeavors. He employed as assistant secretary the young Spencer Fullerton Baird, chairman of the Department of Natural History at Dickinson College. Baird knew all the important American naturalists of his day. He was a close friend of Audubon and a correspondent of Louis Agassiz, the great Swiss geologist at Harvard. Baird added his huge collection of plant and animal specimens to the Smithsonian's holdings. His enthusiasm for collection building had an enormous impact not only on taxonomic research but also on literature. For example, William Henry Hudson, the greatest nineteenth-century nature writer in England, acquired the knowledge and experiences that made his work unique during long years of collecting birds in Argentina, financed in large part by the Smithsonian. Baird's own technical writings had their impact. Published in 1858 as the ninth volume of the *Reports* of the Pacific Railroad survey, his

Birds was praised as the most influential of all works of American ornithology. Baird's personal influence was as significant as his writing; it affected Burroughs and countless others. Coues's parents had sought out Baird when they moved to Washington from New Hampshire, for both were amateur naturalists and nature writers. As a family friend, Baird drew the eleven-year-old Coues to study ornithology.

From the age of seventeen, Coues was a full-time professional zoologist, yet the straightforward record of his education and employment reveals neither his consuming passion for science nor his important contributions to it. He took his undergraduate degree at the Columbian College (now George Washington University) and his M.D. at its medical school, then called the National Medical College. The curricula were the then-customary required courses without natural history electives. Upon graduation, at the height of the Civil War, he became an army surgeon and spent the next two decades serving at posts from Arizona to Baltimore and from the Canadian border to the South Carolina swamps. In 1882, he left the Army and taught human anatomy at his alma mater. The outline of Coues's life approximates that of scores of other midcentury naturalists for whom specialized education was unavailable and who, lacking personal wealth, needed work which would take them to remote areas where they could collect the poorly explored American flora and fauna. Baird had an informal program of sponsorship for such young men. They were housed in a tower of the Smithsonian Castle and fed on his enthusiasm for natural history. When their skill and understanding had developed to the point that they could function as field collectors, Baird found them positions, often in the Army, in which they could effectively enrich the Smithsonian's holdings. Those of lesser scientific insight remained collectors only, perhaps publishing accounts of their experiences; others of greater intellect and ambition ranked among the foremost scientists of their day. Perhaps Baird's most successful protégés were Ferdinand Hayden, who became the leader of one of the four great western geological surveys and the first scientific explorer of Yellowstone National Park, and Elliott Coues, who was the greatest nineteenth-century American ornithologist after Baird himself.

In 1860, Baird sent Coues on his first field expedition in the footsteps of Audubon to the coast of Labrador. One result of this collecting trip was his first publication, "Notes on the Ornithology of Labrador." In the next year, Coues produced his first monograph, a study of sandpipers in which he described a species, new to science, which he named for Baird. Over the next four decades, Coues reported the results of his collecting in publication after publication. In many of his articles and monographs he also carried forward the taxonomic science of birds, mammals, and fishes. Most significant are his *Key to North American Birds* (1872, 1887, 1890, 1903, 1927), *Field Ornithology* (1874), *Birds of the Northwest* (1877), *Fur-Bearing Animals* (1877), *Monographs of North American Rodentia* (1877), *Birds of the Colorado Valley* (1878), and *Citizen Bird* with Mabel Osgood Wright (1897). Coues's *Key* was a manual of ornithology containing descriptions of anatomy and external characteristics as well as a discussion of classification and nomenclature. Its most striking innovation was the artificial key that permitted even beginning amateurs to identify specimens; this feature created a revolution in bird study comparable to the revolution in field identification caused by Roger Tory Peterson's field guide in 1934. Many outstanding amateur and professional naturalists credit the *Key* with a measure of their interest in birds. Theodore Roosevelt, who published both popular and technical natural history works, was so influenced that when he went to Harvard his goal was "to become a scientific man of the . . . Coues type."[7]

Coues varied his prose style from clear, straightforward exposition to flights of eloquence and, on not-infrequent occasions, sarcasm: Coues had an ego to match his matchless ornithological intellect. The second edition of *Avifauna Columbiana* (1883), which he wrote with his college classmate D. Webster Prentiss, is no mere bird list; it is a lively account of the natural environment of Washington complete with hunting guide, bird stories, and a less than complimentary commentary on the culinary expertise of his fellow citizens. The introduction to *Field Ornithology* is so spirited that one can imagine that its readers were, as they themselves admitted, inspired to go out and collect (that is, kill) birds.

Coues's scholarship set a standard that shames pedants and dilettantes. The product of phenomenal memory, great intellect, and utterly thorough research, it laid out the facts to an accompaniment of caustic wit that left no doubt about the inevitability of Coues's conclusions (right or wrong). His greatest academic achievement was the *Bibliography of* [American] *Ornithology*; published in four installments in 1879 and 1880, it contained more than sixteen thousand annotated titles. So great was the value of this work that thirty-eight British scientists signed a memorial to the U.S. government praising it; among the signatories were Charles Darwin and Alfred Russell Wallace. In the 1890s, Coues's interest shifted to historical research.

7. Theodore Roosevelt, *Theodore Roosevelt, an Autobiography* (New York: Charles Scribner's Sons, 1913), 23.

He began by editing the journals of Lewis and Clark; his was the first new edition since their original publication in 1814.

Coues was a fine popular nature writer. His sketches, essays, and reviews graced the pages of the *Nation*, the *Atlantic*, the *New York Sun, Science, Forest and Stream, American Sportsman*, and dozens of other newspapers and periodicals. In some of these writings, in his poetry, and in his exploration of the occult, he sought a mystic truth. What John Burroughs found in nature by transcending science was inadequate for Coues. Although the two men knew each other, discussed their views in an exchange of letters, and admired each other's work, Coues never seems to have grasped Burroughs's point that love of nature is enough. But Coues was willing to be taught intimate facts and responses to nature by Burroughs, as he eloquently declares in his reaction to *Wake-Robin*:

> Your book has been for me a green spot in the wilderness, where I have lingered with rare pleasure, enjoying birds as nowhere else excepting in the woods and fields—where you carry me straightway. . . .
>
> . . . [I] can bear witness to the minute fidelity of your portraiture. How many things you saw—how many more you *felt*. . . . You bring it all back to me—things which I felt at the time, but which passed like last night's dream, I find here fixed and crystallized clear. I have learned from you, too; the golden-crowned thrush never sang to me as he sang to you; when the grass-finch spoke to me, I did not understand. . . . I never read thrush-music aright before, nor had the least idea where the Canadian Warbler built its nest. . . .
>
> . . . Now you come to tell me things no longer strange or wonderful, indeed, but, like a friend, pointing out new beauties I missed before.[8]

Burroughs was quite willing to be taught ornithology by Coues and Baird; as we mentioned earlier, he studied at the Smithsonian during his Washington days. However, it is clear from Coues's letter that a skilled and patient observer could surpass most professional ornithologists in knowledge of the life histories of a particular bird species. At that time it may have been equally true that an informed and intelligent amateur might also surpass the professional in understanding principles. Tactfully, Burroughs never publicly confronted professionals with scientific critiques of their work, yet his privately expressed views often showed a justified impatience with their nomenclatural preoccupations. For example, he recognized the

8. Elliott Coues, a letter to John Burroughs quoted in Clara Barrus, *The Life and Letters of John Burroughs* (Boston: Houghton Mifflin, 1925), vol. 1, 151, 205.

geographic variations that led Coues to believe in the need of establishing a fixed subspecies designation for every specimen, but he rejected as unsound the universality of the subspecies concept. Thus, Burroughs seems to have understood Darwin's emphasis on the mutability of species while Coues missed the essential point.

Perhaps Coues's most important and lasting achievement was the founding of the American Ornithologists' Union in 1883. The AOU immediately pressed the federal government to create the Division of Economic Mammalogy and Ornithology in the Department of Agriculture. Destined to become first the U.S. Biological Survey and then, in 1939, combined with the Bureau of Fisheries to form the U.S. Fish and Wildlife Service, the division began by studying the distribution, migration, and economic impacts of birds. These studies involved countless amateur naturalists throughout the country and brought to Washington many of the finest scientists. The first was the division's head and Florence Merriam Bailey's older brother, C. Hart Merriam, called by his biographer "The Last of the Naturalists," a suggestive if inaccurate title. Vernon Bailey, who later married Florence, came from Minnesota to become the division's first field naturalist.

Merriam joined a growing community of federal scientists. Although federal spending on natural science began with the ill-fated collections of Lewis and Clark and continued with the early geological and western railroad surveys, it was not until the founding of the Department of Agriculture in 1862 that federal research and technical services were established in the nation's capital. From that time on, the Washington-based scientific bureaucracy expanded continuously: the Commission of Fish and Fisheries (1871), the Geological Survey (1879), the Division of Economic Mammalogy and Ornithology, the expansion of the Forest Service under Gifford Pinchot (1898–1909), the Reclamation Service (1902), and the Park Service (1916). Together with the Smithsonian, this scientific establishment has been the largest single source of the Central Atlantic's naturalist writers. In addition to Hart Merriam and Vernon Bailey, the Biological Survey employed James McAtee, author of the 1918 *Natural History of Washington*, and Rachel Carson who, as the Fish and Wildlife Service's chief editor, inaugurated its *Conservation in Action* series with a pamphlet on the Chincoteague National Wildlife Refuge. Biologist Paul Bartsch's career at the Smithsonian encompassed fifty years of Washington natural history from the time of Coues to that of Carson. These years saw the founding and flourishing of the Audubon movement, its recession during the 1930s and its reawakening in the 1940s and 1950s. Bartsch's longevity gave a unique historical perspective to the many articles that he contributed to the *Atlantic Naturalist*, the journal of the Audubon Society of the District of Columbia, now the Audubon Naturalist Society.

When Bartsch came to Washington in 1896, Florence Merriam was already a leading preservationist and a nationally known nature writer. Hunting was the ultimate cause of her activism; its commercial excesses made a conservation crusade necessary and its sporting side made it possible.

Sport hunting probably exceeded natural history in popularity as an outdoor recreation of middle- and upper-class men. Nearly all such men who spent any time in the country as children hunted. Thoreau hunted as a boy and recommended it in *Walden* as an introduction to nature study. Burroughs, Theodore Roosevelt, and Coues are typical of nineteenth-century naturalists and writers in that they continued their boyhood recreation into adult life. Most sport hunters in the eastern United States were members of private clubs that owned or leased land for their exclusive use. The first known club was in the Central Atlantic region, at the Gunpowder River's junction with the Chesapeake Bay; founded in 1832, it was a rather plush retreat for citizens of Baltimore. A club might be nothing more than an informal association of a few townsmen who paid a local farmer for the privilege of hunting on his land; or it might be an incorporated entity of formidable physical and social dimensions. The Jekyll Island Club, which purchased Jekyll Island, Georgia, in 1883, had as members J. P. Morgan, James J. Hill, William Rockefeller, George and Erwin Gould, Joseph Pulitzer, Vincent Astor, William Vanderbilt, and others equally rich. Regardless of size or affluence, the ubiquitous clubs were perfect grass-roots political organizations made up of precisely those who were accustomed to taking cooperative political action. And whenever game became scarce, that is what they did. Their influence in the environmental movement remains strong today, embodied in the National Wildlife Federation and the Izaac Walton League. However, their indirect effects on conservation were as great as the direct results of their campaigns to enact game protection measures and enforce the new laws.

The literature that sport hunting produced varies from instructional articles to some of the finest and most sensitive nature writing: Elliott Coues's guide to rail shooting in Washington's Anacostia River marshes illustrates the literary potential of even the simplest instructional situations. Hunter-turned-conservationist George Shiras continued his participation in the Revels Island Club after his conversion, but with a camera rather than a gun; his *National Geographic* articles from the early twentieth century tell of the positive effects of the game protection laws. The genre reached a peak of elegance in Aldo Leopold's "Smoky Gold" in *A Sand County Almanac* (1948), the book often viewed as the bible of the environmental movement.

From the mid–nineteenth century on, sporting journals of considerable literary merit brought hunting and fishing news and advice to hundreds of thousands of readers. Two leading journals, *Forest and Stream* and *American Sportsman*, extended their readership by including natural history articles, some written by Coues. In 1874, *Forest and Stream* was bought by one of its contributors: George Bird Grinnell, a most unusual man. Rare in this day of learned amateurs and self-taught professionals, he had received his Ph.D. at Yale in paleontology and avian osteology from the century's leading authority, Othniel C. Marsh. A big-game hunter, Grinnell was acutely aware of the need to control overhunting. As a cofounder of the Boone and Crockett Club, whose purpose was to preserve large game, he was instrumental in saving the American bison from extinction. In childhood, chance placed him in the day school taught by Audubon's widow, Lucy; so, of course, he was a bird and nature lover. Beginning with the first issue of *Forest and Stream* under his ownership, he preached wildlife conservation; commercial hunting in any form was not only bad game management, it was antisocial behavior. Grinnell was among the select few invited to join the AOU by its founding members; he was an initial member of its Committee on Bird Protection and led the campaign to implement its 1886 Model Law. In the same year, Grinnell began a campaign of his own in the pages of *Forest and Stream*. He called on the public to pledge its support for bird protection by joining an organization that he named the Audubon Society. Within a year there were 39,000 members receiving his publication, the *Audubon Magazine*. Having no plan for an organizational administration to cope with this success, Grinnell disbanded the society in 1888.

But the seeds had been sown. The AOU and *Forest and Stream* kept up the outcry against commercial hunting. For each year, millions of shorebirds, ducks, and geese were being harvested for local and urban sale to restaurants and the public. Millions of heath hens and quail and bobolinks, robins, and other of the larger songbirds met the same fate. And, in an expanding orgy of slaughter, millions of egrets, spoonbills, ibises, and terns were killed for their plumage for women's hats; many of the terns came from the Central Atlantic. As early as 1886, the Committee on Bird Protection saw the threat of the millinery use of birds; young Frank Chapman saw whole birds of more than forty species on hats on Fourteenth Street in New York. That "nature's most vital and potent expressions"[9] were sacrificed to women's vanity was an idea which was easy to understand and communicate and, in practice, to combat.

In 1896, the resurgent Audubon movement began in Massachusetts when Harriet Lawrence Hemenway organized the first state Audubon Society. Like the sister societies to follow, its founding members were prominent citizens—wealthy, well-connected women; ornithologists; sportsmen; and, of course, nature lovers. They had four weapons in their battle for bird protection: lobbying to pass protective legislation; employing wardens to enforce existing laws; education to discourage the wearing of feathers; and, perhaps most important, the education of children in the beauty and usefulness of birds. The close personal and professional connections of the Boston, New York, and Washington natural history and social communities brought rapid expansion of the Massachusetts model. The AOU and the several popular and scientific natural history journals spread the word, and within a year, nine new independent societies were crusading vigorously for bird protection. None was more successful than the Audubon Society of the District of Columbia.

Founded in 1897 by Mrs. John Dewhurst Patten, the society had a membership of unsurpassed distinction and energy. Surgeon General George M. Sternberg was its president. Among the active members were C. Hart Merriam and his assistant chief at the Biological Survey, Theodore Palmer, who was the national authority on protective legislation. Theodore Roosevelt was a participant throughout his life; during his presidency the society met occasionally at the White House. Most of the active members were women; under Patten's leadership they planned the society's programs and implemented them. Florence Merriam Bailey, already an accomplished naturalist and prominent nature writer, initiated the educational efforts. It is hard to overestimate their success. Quite possibly they reached every grade-schooler and teacher in the District of Columbia. Mrs. Bailey also worked with Lucy Warner Maynard to produce *Birds of Washington and Vicinity* (1898), to which she contributed the introduction; Theodore Roosevelt contributed his White House bird list to a later edition.

Inspired by Grinnell's *Forest and Stream* editorials, Florence had begun her career in bird protection in 1885 with an article titled, "An Appeal to

9. Frank Chapman, *Autobiography of a Bird-Lover* (New York: D. Appleton-Century Company, 1933), vii.

Women." After corresponding with Grinnell, she founded the Smith College Audubon Society while an undergraduate in 1887. Her first book, *Birds through an Opera Glass* (1890) was a more important contribution. Never before had a manual instructed beginning students *not to shoot birds!* Her writing style was so well suited to the taste of the times that she was compared to Thoreau and Burroughs.

In 1893, Florence joined fellow author Olive Thorne Miller on a trip to Utah, where her brother Hart was collecting; thus began her love affair with the American West which would result in half a dozen popular books and many popular and technical papers on birds, all accomplished without the aid of a shotgun. Her scientific studies culminated in 1902 in *Handbook of Birds of the Western United States*, which stayed in print through eleven editions. Her 1899 marriage to Vernon Bailey, field naturalist for the Biological Survey, created a productive scientific partnership.

Like Coues, Mrs. Bailey had been raised by parents who were nature lovers; however, in many ways she is Coues's obverse. Neither ambitious nor egocentric, she nevertheless overcame the prejudice that denied scientific careers to women and became the first female associate member of the AOU and its first woman fellow. She was an eminent scientist, yet her early technical ornithological training was limited to study using Coues's *Key*. Her early influences were not Baird and Coues but Emerson and Burroughs, whom she knew and whose doctrine that nature is enough satisfied her. Unlike Coues, she loved ornithology less than birds: She never shot one. Even more important than her scientific accomplishments are the educational programs she originated; the Audubon classes for children and teachers had an unparalleled success in spreading the love of nature through the middle and working classes at a time when the nature fads were on the wane.

The principal voice of the Audubon movement was *Bird-Lore*, created, owned, published, and edited by Frank Chapman, curator at the American Museum of Natural History in New York. "In Warbler Time," by John Burroughs, opened the first issue (February 1899). Bailey's essay on the chipping sparrow, which is included in this anthology, occupied the children's section. During the next several issues, a discussion developed concerning the appropriateness of the humanizing of animals in children's stories; later it became part of the famous "nature faker" controversy in which John Burroughs and Teddy Roosevelt attacked Jack London, Ernest Thompson Seton, and William J. Long. Burroughs and Roosevelt accused the three other authors of falsifying observations of nature and deliberately misinterpreting the psychological meaning of animal behavior. "Our Doorstep Sparrow" was then considered blameless of humanizing, yet it has an emotional flavor that, while suiting its turn-of-the-century audience, is not to today's taste. This difference in tastes leads some to see a great blank space in nature writing between Thoreau and Rachel Carson. Today, much of the writing from this period is viewed as ornate and sentimental. We should beware of faulting its deliberate style. The authors were generally not overwrought sentimentalists blindly expressing uncontrolled feelings; writers of Bailey's stature were sophisticated naturalists and publicizers with ethical and educational objectives. Their techniques served them well in their own day. At its best, their expression of sentiments was a stylistic device used to reach a readership readied to sympathize with animals first by the romantics and transcendentalists and then by Burroughs and his peers. Much of the so-called humanizing of nature seemed to be necessary at the time to communicate the biocentric spirit; some was a clear but fictionalized presentation of the fact, recognized by scientists from Darwin on, that animals share common biological heritages and so also share many common physiological and psychological processes and states. The scientific research and conservation ethics of Jane Goodall and other contemporaries show that this last sort of humanizing is not sentimental anthropomorphizing at all but a scientifically reasonable and morally justified expression of empathy with fellow creatures who are in many ways much like us. Although comparative zoology demonstrates the commonality of emotions in humans and other animals, it is in turn-of-the-century essays—like John Muir's story of the dog Stikeen—that the demonstration assumes an irrefutable form.

Country Life

Since there were cities, there have been people who have preferred to escape them to a more relaxed life. We know that wealthy Romans moved between urban amenities and agricultural leisure; that the alternation of court entertainments and the pleasures of the hunt occupied medieval aristocracy; and that modern-day robber barons imitated this round of seasonal diversions as part of the ostentatious flaunting of their wealth. Country life would not concern us here if all there were to it were the pig farms of the emperor Claudius and a rustic setting for rooms in Edith Wharton's *House of Mirth*. But at some forgotten time, wild nature was recognized as a pleasing component of the rural landscape. As we have seen, Izaak Walton found it so, as did Thomas Jefferson. Nature's presence in domestic architecture seems to have begun in 1715 when Alexander Pope designed the first informal garden. From that date on, the appreciation of wildness at the doorstep would grow until its culmination in the celebration of "gardens and grim ravines" by John Ruskin and the Pre-Raphaelite poets, painters, and photographers.

The natural side of country life affected American nature literature in two ways. First, the move to the country produced several of our authors and countless of their readers. And second, aspiration to country living and concern for agriculture as a way of life combined into a social movement; it had its own philosophy codified in the turn-of-the-century writings of Liberty Hyde Bailey, dean of agriculture at Cornell; its own political niche formalized by Theodore Roosevelt's Country Life Commission; and its own magazines and books. From the early nineteenth-century *Rural Magazine* to the contemporary *Country Life*, specialty periodicals have instructed and inspired each generation of residents and migrants from the city.

The increasing wealth of the nineteenth-century middle class enabled many people to escape the city to wild areas only a railroad commute away. For most, however, it was a long commute. Some, like Florence Merriam Bailey's parents, became rich enough in the city to retire to the country. Others, like Frank Chapman's father, who was a New York lawyer, chose the commute. Frank commuted, too, at least until the throng of later-comers caught up with him; his reaction to the march of the suburban side of country life is so poignant that we quote it at length:

> Our farm of forty acres extended eastward to within the corporate limits of the village of Englewood [New Jersey], through the orchards to sloping hay fields, and into boggy marshes traversed by spring-fed brooks and bordered by well-watered woods, some of it with heavy timber and dense undergrowth.
>
> Westward, in the valley now occupied by the West Shore Railroad, there were extensive forests penetrated only by wood roads, and a brook where trout could be found. Beyond, on the slopes reaching up to the crest of the hills overlooking the valley of the Hackensack, were fields partly grown with red cedar, bayberry and sweet gum. Southward lay the marshes of the Hackensack and its tributary, Overpeck Creek, the headwaters of the latter bringing tidal water to within two miles of my home.
>
> To the east, beyond the village of Englewood and the wooded slopes

to the south and north of it, rose the Palisades with, in minor details, the topography of a mountain. I have never seen, within the same limits, a more diversified country or a better one for birds. . . .

. . . Standing with me one June evening in the West Shore woods, listening to a chorus of Veerys and Wood Thrushes such as I have never heard elsewhere, John Burroughs said: "No wonder you love birds!"

I lived in the place of my birth until I reached middle age. . . . [M]y environment remained much the same until 1905. Then came the period of suburban developments which have mutilated vast areas but given fresh air and individuality to hundreds of thousands of city folk and new life to their children.

Sadly I saw the forests fall and the fields erupt flimsy cottages, but when the Phelps estate was placed upon the market I had not the heart to witness the rapid dismemberment of haunts on which I had held a "rambler's lease" so long that they seemed to be mine, and I moved to the now City of Englewood, never again to return to the still nearby haunts of my boyhood.

In Englewood, with singular short-sightedness, I thought I should find conditions so established that at once I would know the worst. But the exodus from the city continued to demand added living space and when a bridge across the Hudson was assured, the changes came so rapidly that each week-end found some cherished shrine invaded or destroyed and I acknowledged my defeat and took refuge in New York City. Here a widespreading view across Central Park so dominates my outlook that man and his transportation activities become merely an unseen compound noise to which, in time, one grows insensible, while in a protected nook in the Catskills and on an island in Gatun Lake [Panama], I find that association with nature which gives relaxation for body and mind and re-creation for the spirit.[10]

In the same year that Chapman moved to Englewood, Thomas Dixon published perhaps the most enthusiastic piece to come out of the whole country life genre, *The Life Worth Living*. The author of many popular novels, Dixon had acquired the wealth necessary to move to an estate in Gloucester County, Virginia, where he and his family lived an idyllic life farming, hunting, fishing, and enjoying nature on the Chesapeake Bay.

10. Ibid., 11–13.

The Environmental Awakening and the New Nature Writing

An environmental awakening occurred throughout the country after the Second World War. A new, holistic attitude transformed resource conservationists, nature preservationists, and nature lovers into political activists who sought to instill in the public's mind the doctrine of a sustainable way of life within the limits set by a healthy environment. A new ecologically motivated nature writing led this change and articulated the enlarged view of nature. Scientists and writers in the Central Atlantic region had a leading role.

Although its appearance after the Second World War seemed sudden at the time, the ecological perspective, like other new worldviews, had emerged slowly from the culture and science of past eras. The ideal of country living, the education programs of the conservation crusades, and the nature writings of John Burroughs's century had engendered appreciation of nature in a large public. During the quarter century after the First World War, the legacy of awareness of nature combined with a growing understanding of ecology to create the foundations of our present environmental movement and its associated literature. A broad approach to conservation had been first debated as public policy at Theodore Roosevelt's 1908 governors' conference. This idea was carried forward in the technical and popular writings of academic ecologists. The earliest example was Charles Van Hise's 1910 treatise, *The Conservation of Natural Resources in the United States*, which discussed every environmental issue then known—resource depletion, population, pollution, soil exhaustion, and even the greenhouse effect. The Great Depression refocused public and scientific attention on resource conservation problems, perhaps diverting interest from nature pure-and-simple to the plight of the land. Many books appeared which used ecology as a tool to understand the all-too-visible consequences of bad agricultural and forest management practices and to suggest solutions based on this new science. Notable among these were Paul Sears's *Deserts on the March*, which was written under the cloud of the 1935 dust storms, and *100,000,000 Guinea Pigs* (1933), by Arthur Kallett and F. J. Schlink, which exposed the hazards of arsenate pesticides as, thirty years later, *Silent Spring* would expose the consequences of chlorinated hydrocarbons. While none of these books is considered nature writing, the great nature writers whose works appeared during the 1940s and 1950s read them and learned their lessons. The need for jobs in the 1930s made the federal government willing to implement resource and wildlife conservation programs that had been heretofore too expensive for congressional taste.

The protection of avian predators was an early sign of the ecological influence. The story of the founding of the Hawk Mountain sanctuary in 1934 reveals the depth of popular misunderstanding of the role of predators in nature. That this sanctuary was established by a small group of dedicated activists outside the National Audubon Society shows the declining radicalism of the Audubon movement's leadership and the reserve with which a part of the scientific community had come to regard conservation. National organizations concentrated on national objectives, for they now viewed wildlife protection as a task primarily for the federal government.

During this time, nature writing declined in popularity, perhaps as a consequence of the distractions of the Great Depression and two world wars. The death of John Burroughs in 1920 marked the end of an era— never again would a nature essayist achieve his success. To honor Burroughs and to perpetuate the memory of his life and works, the John Burroughs Memorial Association maintains Burroughs's rustic study Slabsides as a historic site and annually awards the John Burroughs Medal for nature writing. The 1950 recipient was Roger Tory Peterson, who took the declining popularity to heart. In his acceptance address, he blamed the publishers, the public "who no longer take the time to read reflective things, and Hundreds of magazines,...radio, the movies—and now television." He lamented,

> It is probably impossible today to be a Burroughs, Muir, Thoreau, or Hudson. Most of us who write get our books published because we are already known for something else. I am sure I got *Birds over America* published because I was already known for my *Field Guides*. . . .
> Among the most successful nature writers of the last decade have been Edwin Way Teale and the Jaques. Every one of their books has been a success yet none has exceeded a sale of 15,000 copies. This seems to be about the limit. Yet twenty-five or thirty years ago Dallas Lore Sharpe's books often ran to 100,000. . . . I hope that the tendency towards mass production and the tendency of advertising to be interested only in reaching the greatest number, and therefore the lowest common denominator, will not result in a day when none of our more thoughtful writers can be heard, when publishers, harassed by rising costs, can no longer afford to publish what they have to say.[11]

11. Roger Tory Peterson, "The State of Nature Writing (Extracts of Remarks Made in Acceptance of John Burroughs Medal)," *Atlantic Naturalist* 6, no.1 (1950): 3–4.

However, Peterson had his foot firmly in his mouth, for, as he spoke, Rachel Carson was agonizing over the final touches to a book that would win a National Book Award as well as the Burroughs Medal and sell more than 250,000 copies in its first year in print. Proving that fine nature writing still could sell, *The Sea Around Us* sat atop the best-seller list for thirty-nine weeks, all the while garnering laudatory reviews. Although its approach is traditional scientific exposition, it communicates Carson's quiet feeling for nature as well as a wealth of information on marine biology. The day had passed when the learned amateur could outshine the professional as Burroughs had on occasion outshone Coues; twentieth-century scientific exposition required a technical sophistication that no amateur could easily attain. *The Sea Around Us* also demonstrates that a scientist can have a poetic vision and express that vision in prose outside the personal essay form. The public, it appears, was not entirely caught up in "radio, the movies and television"; its new educational level and taste readied it for Carson's detailed but subtly lyrical writing. The public was also ready for the new ecological approach to nature that was apparent in some passages in *The Sea Around Us*, for a broadened conservation ethic had evolved from the previously limited protectionist goals and from the ecological insights learned during the depression.

Aldo Leopold summarized these insights and ethical concerns in the phrase "something is not right in the Man-Land relationship." His *A Sand County Almanac* (1948) proposed a new, scientifically based worldview that he hoped would right the wrong relations. Founding his philosophy on ideas of duty and moral obligation as well as on utilitarian principles, he went beyond Van Hise and the depression-era ecologists by extending ethical considerations to the environment as a whole. Of unusual literary quality, the *Almanac*'s personal essays gave both emotional and practical realization to Leopold's philosophical dialectics. To nature writing, they added the new aspect of *ecological motivation*, which had its fullest impact in Rachel Carson's *Silent Spring*. Peterson's assessment of public attitudes had missed a fundamental change. Not only did *A Sand County Almanac* reach out to an enlarged audience for nature writing but two 1948 best-sellers found the general reading public eager to hear what the ecologists had to say. William Vogt's *Road to Survival* and Fairfield Osborn's *Our Plundered Planet* are prototypes of the hundreds of later environmental critiques of modern societies. Their success indicated that nature writing could appeal to people's environmental concerns as well as to their desire to be entertained. Rachel Carson had read Leopold, Vogt, and Osborn as well as the depression-era authors and, like most more-recent contemporary nature writers, agreed that it is essential to address the problems of population, pollution, and habitat loss that threaten the existence of both nature and human society. Carson's professional experience at the Fish and Wildlife Service provided a factual basis for the incidental critiques of human destructiveness mentioned in *The Sea Around Us*. When she turned her full attention to environmental problems in *Silent Spring*, her scientific rigor set a standard that dominates the last half of the twentieth century. As the title indicates, birds were a symbolic and a material focus of the environmental awakening that ensued. After *Silent Spring*, nature writers generally confronted the environmental issues that related to their main subject.

Perhaps Peterson's misjudgments of the public were occasioned by the unusual situation in Washington, D.C., for the Central Atlantic had had its own natural history renaissance before the publication of *A Sand County Almanac, Road to Survival*, and *Our Plundered Planet*. The Second World War and its aftermath brought many outstanding scientists, conservationists, and writers to work in the nation's capital. Newcomers Louis Halle, Charlton Ogburn, William Vogt, Howard Zahniser, and Peterson associated through the Audubon Naturalist Society with Florence Bailey, Paul Bartsch, Rachel Carson, William O. Douglas, and Shirley Briggs, who edited the society's publication *The Wood Thrush*, now the *Atlantic Naturalist*. Today, the 1940s and 1950s appear a golden age, for not since the days of Theodore Roosevelt and Hart Merriam had the society, or the country for that matter, known such a constellation of natural history notables. As before, they made significant contributions to conservation and to nature writing, but this time their efforts were largely individual rather than collective. No distinctive literary style or form emerged from this association. The only communal conservation effort of note was Justice Douglas's campaign to preserve the C & O Canal right-of-way as a park. Apart from the inchoate ecological perspective, the only obvious literary ties are those between Rachel Carson and the writers who had the good fortune to learn from her while she was chief editor of the Fish and Wildlife Service. The golden years faded with the deaths of Bailey and Bartsch, and later of Carson, Zahniser, and Douglas. Peterson, Halle, and Vogt moved on, leaving legends as well as a remarkable written record in the Audubon Naturalist Society's journal.

The boom in environmental lawmaking that swept through Democratic and Republican administrations from Kennedy to Carter was in part the outgrowth of the golden years: *Silent Spring* laid the popular foundations for the National Environmental Policy Act and the Environmental Protection Agency; Zahniser led the Wilderness Society's efforts that convinced Congress to pass the Wilderness Act; Vogt made international population problems part of the environmental agenda. The preservationist's spirit was abroad in these years and the nature writing of the period is as imbued with it as it is with ecological concern. Charlton Ogburn's *The Winter Beach* describes both the establishment of Assateague National Seashore in Maryland and the Committee to Preserve Assateague's efforts to protect the seashore from road building. Peter Mazzeo's herbarium researches led to the rediscovery of the rarest of North American trees: Virginia's round-leaf birch. Although his work was begun before the first of the endangered species acts, it exemplifies the increased concern for preservation among professionals that the acts embody. The *New Yorker's* publication of Eugene Kinkead's article about the rediscovery reflects the public's interest in endangered plants and animals, an interest that The Nature Conservancy transformed into a nationally successful program. The Virginia Coast Reserve, a Conservancy project, now protects nearly all the barrier islands from Assateague to Cape Charles; these were the sites of the bird slaughter that the horrified Frank Chapman described in "Cobb's Island." Within the sanctuary, Cobb Island bird populations have recovered; in "Barrier Island Birds," George Reiger describes the labors of the researchers that monitor the recovery. Despite the Coast Reserve's success, *Wanderer on My Native Shore,* from which "Barrier Island Birds" is taken, displays frustration with society's inability to coexist with nature except by isolating it.

The regional nature writing after the golden age was rich in subject matter, stylistic variation, and ideas. The two Pulitzer Prize winners, William Warner's *Beautiful Swimmers* and Annie Dillard's *Pilgrim at Tinker Creek,* though quite different from each other, separate themselves from their modern regional predecessors by their broader social and natural perspectives. Dillard's theme is the human need to answer the age-old questions: Who are we? What are we? Squarely and honestly facing the dilemmas implicit in the half-formed answers that science and religion provide, she finds comfort in what seems to be a bitter version of John Burroughs's *Accepting the Universe.* In *Bay Country* and *Turning the Tide,* Tom Horton blends *A Sand County Almanac's* holistic worldview with *Silent Spring's* mastery of detail. *Bay Country* recounts the natural and environmental history of the Chesapeake and its tributaries; *Turning the Tide* examines the progress and problems of the Chesapeake Bay Program, the cooperative regional effort to restore the bay to ecological health. "Phenomena," John Wiley's *Smithsonian* magazine column, charms us with warm and subtle humor while present-

ing an ecological point of view on current affairs that is both intensely personal and socially comprehensive.

Two of Wiley's articles conclude this anthology: "Make Room and They
Will Come" and "Leaving Earth to Save It"—fitting pieces with which to
end a historical collection, for the ecological vision that they contain is built
on the legacy of western attitudes toward nature. "Make Room and They
Will Come" illustrates how cities can invite wildlife to return to an urban
environment, thus perpetuating Alexander Pope's initiative to bring an aspect of wildness to our doorsteps. In "Leaving Earth to Save It," Wiley offers
a science-fiction scenario in which humans vacate the planet so that natural processes can reestablish the balances that we are now destroying. Environmentalists throughout the world share the hope that people can create
societies sustainable within limits imposed to maintain a healthy biosphere;
but Wiley moves beyond this necessary accommodation with nature, for he
is motivated by a uniquely American attitude that unites William Cullen
Bryant's love for landscape with Daniel Boone's passion for wilderness. He
explains that, "the strongest appeal [of a restored earth] is really the vision
I started with: Fish leaping in clear water, forests growing to the water's
edge, swamps and marshes pulsating with life. The way things were here
just five or six lifetimes ago."[12] Were we all to feel and to act on Wiley's com-
pelling need to save wild nature, we might discover that, in the doing, we
humans would be saving not only our physical environment but also our
psychological selves.

12. John Wiley, *Natural High* (Hanover: University Press of New England, 1993), 31.

Design for Nature Writing

Rachel Carson (1907–1964)

Beyond doubt, Rachel Carson is the most significant nature writer of
the twentieth century. Twice her books have changed America's attitudes.
In 1951, after a thirty-year recession in the popularity of nature writing,
The Sea Around Us reawakened the reading public's dormant interest in
the natural world. Then, in 1962, *Silent Spring* brought the nation to environmental consciousness and shocked us into action with its detailing of
the abuse of pesticides.

Rachel Carson spent most of her adult life in the Central Atlantic
region. A Johns Hopkins–trained marine biologist, she taught at the University of Maryland and then was employed by the U.S. Fish and Wildlife
Service in Washington, D.C., until 1952, when the popularity of her books
made it possible for her to devote all her time to writing. Her first book,
Under the Sea Wind (1941), was not an initial success, but *The Sea Around
Us* was an immediate best-seller and won the John Burroughs Medal as
well as a National Book Award.

As a leader in the Audubon Society of the District of Columbia, she
associated with Roger Tory Peterson, Louis Halle, Charlton Ogburn,
and the many other naturalist-authors whom the Second World War
had gathered in Washington.

Carson's brief acceptance address on receiving the Burroughs Medal
is a splendid hortatory piece. Tactfully but forcefully she urges her fellow
nature writers to reach out to popular audiences; offering wonder and humility as answers to humanity's destructive tendencies, she reveals her mo-
tivations, which define her as an ecologically inspired literary naturalist.

From *Atlantic Naturalist* 7, no. 5 (1952)

IN PRESENTING ME with the John Burroughs Medal you have welcomed
me into an illustrious company, and you have given *The Sea Around Us* one
of its most cherished honors. Any writer in the field of the natural sciences
should feel a certain awe and even a sense of unreality in being linked during his or her own lifetime with the immortals in the field of nature writing.
The tradition of John Burroughs, which you seek to keep alive through

these awards, is a long and honorable one. It is a tradition that had its beginnings in even earlier writings. On the other side of the Atlantic it flowered most fully in the works of Richard Jefferies and W. H. Hudson; and in this country the pen of Thoreau—as that of John Burroughs himself—most truly represented the contemplative observer of the world about us. These four, I think, were the great masters. To those of us who have come later, there can scarcely be any greater honor than to be compared to one of them.

Yet if we are true to the spirit of John Burroughs, or of Jefferies or Hudson or Thoreau, we are not imitators of them but—as they themselves were—we are pioneers in new areas of thought and knowledge. If we are true to them, we are the creators of a new type of literature as representative of our own day as was their own.

I myself am convinced that there has never been a greater need than there is today for the reporter and interpreter of the natural world. Mankind has gone very far into an artificial world of his own creation. He has sought to insulate himself, in his cities of steel and concrete, from the realities of earth and water and the growing seed. Intoxicated with a sense of his own power, he seems to be going farther and farther into more experiments for the destruction of himself and his world.

There is certainly no single remedy for this condition and I am offering no panacea. But it seems reasonable to believe—and I do believe—that the more clearly we can focus our attention on the wonders and realities of the universe about us the less taste we shall have for the destruction of our race. Wonder and humility are wholesome emotions, and they do not exist side by side with a lust for destruction.

All of us here tonight are united by the strong bond of a common interest. In one way or another all of us have been touched by an awareness of the world of nature. No one present needs to be "sold" on this subject. But I should like to talk briefly about the non-naturalists and our attitude toward them—that large segment of the public that does not belong to the John Burroughs Association or to Audubon Societies and that really has very little knowledge of natural science. I am convinced that we have been far too ready to assume that these people are indifferent to the world we know to be full of wonder. If they are indifferent it is only because they have not been properly introduced to it—and perhaps that is in some measure our fault.

Since I am speaking of the John Burroughs Medal and what it means, perhaps I should confine my illustration to nature writing. I feel that we have too often written only for each other. We have assumed that what we had to say would interest only other naturalists. We have too often seemed to consider ourselves the last representatives of a dying tradition, writing for steadily dwindling audiences.

It is difficult to say these things without seeming to refer too directly to *The Sea Around Us*. Yet I feel they ought to be said, for in justice not only to ourselves but to the public we ought to develop a more confident and assured attitude toward the role and the value of nature literature. I am certain that what happened to *The Sea Around Us* could happen to many another book in the field of the natural sciences—and that it should happen.

Perhaps writers and publishers and magazine editors have all been at fault in taking, too often, a deprecating attitude which assumes in advance that a nature book will not have a wide audience, that it cannot possibly be a "commercial success."

This attitude is not only psychologically unsound; it is a mistaken and illfounded one. The public is trying to show us how mistaken it is, if we will only listen. It proves our mistake when it fills Audubon Screen Tour showings with overflow audiences. It proves it when it buys Roger Peterson's bird guides by the many scores of thousands and goes afield with guide and binoculars. And if I may use a personal illustration, the letters that have come to me in the past nine months have taught me never again to underestimate the capacity of the general public to absorb the facts of science.

If these letters mean anything it is this: that there is an immense and unsatisfied thirst for understanding of the world about us, and every drop of information, every bit of fact that serves to free the reader's mind to roam the great spaces of the universe, is seized upon with almost pathetic eagerness.

I have learned from these letters, too, if I did not fully realize it before, that those who hunger for knowledge of their world are as varied as the passengers in a subway. The mail the other day brought letters from a Catholic sister in a Tennessee school, a farmer in Saskatchewan, a British scientist, and a housewife. There have been hairdressers and fishermen and musicians and classical scholars and scientists. So many say, in one phrasing or another: "We have been troubled about the world, and had almost lost faith in man; it helps to think about the long history of the earth, and of how life came to be. When we think in terms of millions of years, we are not so impatient that our problems be solved tomorrow."

These are the people who want to know about the world that is our chosen one. If we have ever regarded our interest in natural history as an escape from the realities of our modern world, let us now reverse this attitude. For the mysteries of living things, and the birth and death of continents and seas, are among the great realities.

The John Burroughs Medal is the only literary award that recognizes achievement in nature writing. In so doing, it may well be a force working toward a better civilization, by focusing attention on the wonders of a world known to so few, although it lies about us every day.

A Map of Virginia

Captain John Smith (1580–1631)

The stories told of John Smith's life would make Sinbad the Sailor blush; the strangest thing about them is that, except for the romantic involvement with Pocahontas, they are all true. It was not unusual for a young, landless man of the English rural middle class to be a soldier of fortune in the European and Turkish wars and a privateer, as Smith had been. But Smith's physical skills and leadership abilities brought him success where the common fate was death or maiming or, at best, quiet retirement in England. While leading Hungarian troops against the Turks, he fought three single combats, bloody triumphs with the sword that saved his troops many casualties. Once, while sailing from the New World to England, his lone vessel was captured by a French fleet. His mastery of men and ships so impressed his captors that he became their battle commander, at least when they engaged the Spanish; tactfully, he remained below decks when English vessels were the prey.

Yet, more marvelous than Smith's adventures are his contributions to the colonization of English North America. He accurately mapped the Chesapeake Bay and the New England coast in a day when there was no good way to measure longitude. In his post-Jamestown writings, he developed a unique, practical plan for organizing and governing a settlement and extracting commercial products. That the Puritans knew his ideas and had his maps may have helped their colony succeed where the previous three New England attempts had failed. These tools certainly aided the more commercially motivated and mentally flexible settlers in Maine: Henry Jocelyn [*sic*] took his advice, traded in lumber and fish, and so was able to prosper and support his brother, John Josselyn [*sic*], the first natural history writer of New England.

A Map of Virginia was the first of Smith's books that he published himself. In it, he gives an accurate picture of the region's natural environment and its prospects for colonial enterprises. Unlike many later writers, his goal was to prepare the settlers for what they would find and to correct the rumors of certain death on the one hand and of unimaginable wealth on the other.

From *A Map of Virginia. With a Description of the Countrey, the Commodities, People, Government and Religion* (Oxford: J. Barnes, 1612)

VIRGINIA is a Country in America that lyeth betweene the degrees of 34 and 44 of the north latitude. The bounds thereof on the East side are the great Ocean. On the South lyeth Florida: on the North nova Francia. As for the West thereof, the limits are unknowne. Of all this country wee purpose not to speake, but only of that part which was planted by the English men in the yeare of our Lord, 1606. And this is under the degrees 37. 38. and 39. The temperature of this countrie doth agree well with English constitutions being once seasoned to the country. Which appeared by this, that though by many occasions our people fell sicke; yet did they recover by very small meanes and continued in health, though there were other great causes, not only to have made them sicke, but even to end their daies. . . .

The sommer is hot as in Spaine; the winter colde as in Fraunce or England. The heat of sommer is in June, Julie, and August, but commonly the coole Breeses asswage the vehemencie of the heat. The chiefe of winter is halfe December, January, February, and halfe March. The colde is extreame sharpe, but here the proverbe is true that no extreame long continueth.

In the yeare 1607 was an extraordinary frost in most of Europe, and this frost was founde as extreame in Virginia. But the next yeare for 8. or 10. daies of ill weather, other 14 daies would be as Sommer.

The windes here are variable, but the like thunder and lightning to purifie the aire, I have seldome either seene or heard in Europe. From the Southwest came the greatest gustes with thunder and heat. The Northwest winde is commonly coole and bringeth faire weather with it. From the North is the greatest cold, and from the East and South-East as from the Bermudas, fogs and raines.

Some times there are great droughts other times much raine, yet great necessity of neither, by reason we see not but that all the variety of needfull fruits in Europe may be there in great plenty by the industry of men, as appeareth by those we there planted.

There is but one entraunce by sea into this country and that is at the mouth of a very goodly Bay the widenesse whereof is near 18. or 20. miles. The cape on the Southside is called Cape Henry in honour of our most noble Prince. The shew of the land there is a white hilly sand like unto the Downes, and along the shores great plentie of Pines and Firres.

The north Cape is called Cape Charles in honour of the worthy Duke of Yorke. Within is a country that may have the prerogative over the most pleasant places of Europe, Asia, Africa, or America, for large and pleasant navigable rivers, heaven and earth never agreed better to frame a place for mans habitation being of our constitutions, were it fully manured and inhabited by industrious people. here are mountaines, hils, plaines, valleyes, rivers and brookes, all running most pleasantly into a faire Bay compassed but for the mouth with fruitfull and delightsome land. In the Bay and rivers are many Isles both great and small, some woody, some plaine, most of them low and not inhabited. This Bay lieth North and South in which the water floweth neare 200 miles and hath a channell for 140 miles, of depth betwixt 7 and 15 fadome, holding in breadth for the most part 10 or 14 miles. From the head of the Bay at the north, the land is mountanous, and so in a manner from thence by a Southwest line; So that the more Southward, the farther off from the Bay are those mounetaines. From which fall certaine brookes which after come to five principall navigable rivers. These run from the Northwest into the Southeast, and so into the west side of the Bay, where the fall of every River is within 20 or 15 miles one of an other.

The mountaines are of diverse natures for at the head of the Bay the rockes are of a composition like milnstones. Some of marble, etc. And many peeces of christall we found as throwne downe by water from the mountaines. For in winter these mountaines are covered with much snow, and when it dissolveth the waters fall with such violence, that it causeth great inundations in the narrow valleyes which yet is scarce perceived being once in the rivers. These waters wash from the rocks such glistering tinctures that the ground in some places seemeth as guilded, where both the rocks and the earth are so splendent to behold, that better judgements then ours might have beene perswaded, they contained more then probabilities. The vesture of the earth in most places doeth manifestly prove the nature of the soile to be lusty and very rich. The colour of the earth we found in diverse places, resembleth *bole Armoniac, terra sigillata* and *lemnia,* Fullers earth marle and divers other such appearances. But generally for the most part the earth is a black sandy mould, in some places a fat slimy clay, in other places a very barren gravell. But the best ground is knowne by the vesture it beareth, as by the greatnesse of trees or abundance of weedes, etc.

The country is not mountanous nor yet low but such pleasant plaine hils and fertle valleyes, one prettily crossing an other, and watered so conveniently with their sweete brookes and christall springs, as if art it selfe had devised them. By the rivers are many plaine marishes containing some

20 some 100 some 200 Acres, some more, some lesse. Other plaines there are fewe, but only where the Savages inhabit: but all overgrowne with trees and weedes being a plaine wildernes as God first made it.

On the west side of the Bay, wee said were 5. faire and delightfull navigable rivers, of which wee will nowe proceed to report. The first of those rivers and the next to the mouth of the Bay hath his course from the West and by North. The name of this river they call Powhatan according to the name of a principall country that lieth upon it. The mouth of this river [the James] is neere three miles in breadth, yet doe the shoules force the Channell so neere the land that a Sacre will overshoot it at point blanck. This river is navigable 100 miles. . . . In the farthest place that was diligently observed, are falles, rockes, showles, etc. which makes it past navigation any higher. Thence in the running downeward, the river is enriched with many goodly brookes, which are maintained by an infinit number of smal rundles and pleasant springs that disperse themselves for best service, as doe the vaines of a mans body. From the South there fals into this river: First the pleasant river of Apamatuck: next more to the East are the two rivers of Quiyoughcohanocke. A little farther is a Bay wherein falleth 3 or 4 prettie brookes and creekes that halfe intrench the Inhabitants of Warraskoyac then the river of Nandsamund, and lastly the brooke of Chisapeack. From the North side is the river of Chickahamania, the backe river of James Towne; another by the Cedar Isle, where we lived 10 weekes upon oisters, then a convenient harbour for fisher boats or smal boats at Kecoughtan, that so conveniently turneth it selfe into Bayes and Creeks that make that place very pleasant to inhabit, their cornefields being girded therein in a manner as Peninsulaes. The most of these rivers are inhabited by severall nations, or rather families, of the name of the rivers. They have also in every of those places some Governour, as their king, which they call *Werowances*. In a Peninsula on the North side of this river are the English planted in a place by them called James Towne, in honour of the Kings most excellent Majestie, upon which side are also many places under the Werowances. . . .

In somer no place affordeth more plentie of Sturgeon, nor in winter more abundance of fowle, especially in the time of frost. There was once taken 52 Sturgeons at a draught, at another draught 68. From the later end of May till the end of June are taken few, but yong Sturgeons of 2 foot or a yard long. From thence till the midst of September, them of 2 or three yards long and fewe others. And in 4 or 5 houres with one nette were ordinarily taken 7 or 8: often more, seldome lesse. In the small rivers all the yeare there is good plentie of small fish, so that with hookes those that would take paines had sufficient. . . .

Of such things which are naturall in Virginia and how they use them.

Virginia doth afford many excellent vegitables and living Creatures, yet grasse there is little or none, but what groweth in lowe Marishes: for all the Countrey is overgrowne with trees, whose droppings continually turneth their grasse to weedes, by reason of the rancknesse of the ground which would soone be amended by good husbandry. The wood that is most common is Oke and Walnut, many of their Okes are so tall and straight, that they will beare two foote and a halfe square of good timber for 20 yards long; Of this wood there is 2 or 3 severall kinds. The Acornes of one kind, whose barke is more white, then the other, is somewhat sweetish, which being boyled halfe a day in severall waters, at last afford a sweete oyle, which they keep in goards to annoint their heads and joints. The fruit they eate made in bread or otherwise. There is also some Elme, some black walnut tree, and some Ash: of Ash and Elme they make sope Ashes. If the trees be very great, the ashes will be good, and melt to hard lumps, but if they be small, it will be but powder, and not so good as the other. Of walnuts there is 2 or 3 kindes; there is a kinde of wood we called Cypres, because both the wood, the fruit, and leafe did most resemble it, and of those trees there are some neere 3 fadome about at the root very straight, and 50, 60, or 80 foot without a braunch. By the dwelling of the Savages are some great Mulbery trees, and in some parts of the Countrey, they are found growing naturally in prettie groves. There was an assay made to make silke, and surely the wormes prospered excellent well, till the master workeman fell sicke. During which time they were eaten with rats.

In some parts were found some Chesnuts whose wild fruit equalize the best in France, Spaine, Germany, or Italy, to their tasts that had tasted them all. Plumbs there are of 3 sorts. The red and white are like our hedge plumbs, but the other which they call *Putchamins* [persimmons], grow as high as a Palmeta: the fruit is like a medler; it is first greene then yellow, and red when it is ripe; if it be not ripe it will drawe a mans mouth awrie, with much torment, but when it is ripe, it is as delicious as an Apricock.

They have Cherries and those are much like a Damsen, but for their tastes and colour we called them Cherries. we see some few Crabs, but very small and bitter. Of vines great abundance in many parts that climbe the toppes of the highest trees in some places, but these beare but few grapes. But by the rivers and Savage habitations where they are not overshadowed from the sunne, they are covered with fruit, though never pruined nor manured. Of those hedge grapes wee made neere 20 gallons of wine, which was neare as good as your French Brittish wine, but certainely they would prove good were they well manured. There is another sort of grape neere as great as a Cherry, this they call *Messaminnes*, they bee fatte, and the juyce thicke. Neither doth the tast so well please when they are made in wine. They have a small fruit growing on little trees, husked like a Chesnut, but the fruit most like a very small acorne. This they call *Chechinquamins* which they esteeme a great daintie. They have a berry much like our gooseberry, in greatnesse, colour, and tast; those they call *Rawcomenes*, and doe eat them raw or boyled. Of these naturall fruits they live a great part of the yeare, which they use in this manner, The walnuts, Chesnuts, Acornes, and *Chechinquamens* are dryed to keepe. When they need them they breake them betweene two stones, yet some part of the walnut shels will cleave to the fruit. Then doe they dry them againe upon a mat over a hurdle. After they put it into a morter of wood, and beat it very small: that done they mix it with water, that the shels may sinke to the bottome. This water will be coloured as milke, which they cal *Pawcohiscora*, and keepe it for their use. The fruit like medlers they call *Putchamins*, they cast uppon hurdles on a mat and preserve them as Pruines. Of their Chesnuts and *Chechinquamens* boyled 4 houres, they make both broath and bread for their chiefe men, or at their greatest feasts. Besides those fruit trees, there is a white populer, and another tree like unto it, that yeeldeth a very cleere and an odoriferous Gumme like Turpentine, which some called Balsom. There are also Cedars and Saxafras trees. They also yeeld gummes in a small proportion of themselves. Wee tryed conclusions to extract it out of the wood, but nature afforded more then our arts. . . .

During Somer there are either strawberries which ripen in April; or mulberries which ripen in May and June. Raspises hurtes [raspberries huckleberries]; or a fruit that the Inhabitants call *Maracocks*, which is a pleasant wholsome fruit much like a lemond. Many hearbes in the spring time there are commonly dispersed throughout the woods, good for brothes and sallets, as Violets, Purslin, Sorrell, etc. Besides many we used whose names we know not.

The chiefe roote they have for foode is called *Tockawhoughe* [tuckahoe], It groweth like a flagge in low muddy freshes. In one day a Savage will gather sufficient for a weeke. These rootes are much of the greatnes and taste of Potatoes. They use to cover a great many of them with oke leaves and ferne, and then cover all with earth in the manner of a colepit; over it, on each side, they continue a great fire 24 houres before they dare eat it. Raw it is no better than poison, and being roasted, except it be tender and the heat abated, or sliced and dried in the sun, mixed with sorrell and meale or such like, it will prickle and torment the throat extreamely, and yet in sommer they use this ordinarily for bread. . . .

In the low Marishes growe plots of Onyons containing an acre of ground or more in many places; but they are small not past the bignesse of the Toppe of ones Thumbe.

Of beastes the chiefe are Deare, nothing differing from ours. In the deserts towards the heads of the rivers, ther are many, but amongst the rivers few. There is a beast they call *Aroughcun* [raccoon], much like a badger, but useth to live on trees as Squirrels doe. Their Squirrels some are neare as greate as our smallest sort of wilde rabbits, some blackish or blacke and white, but the most are gray.

A small beast they have, they call *Assapanick* but we call them flying squirrels, because spreading their legs, and so stretching the largenesse of their skins that they have bin seene to fly 30 or 40 yards. An Opassom hath a head like a Swine, and a taile like a Rat, and is of the bignes of a Cat. Under her belly shee hath a bagge, wherein shee lodgeth, carrieth, and suckleth her young. *Mussascus*, is a beast of the forme and nature of our water Rats, but many of them smell exceeding strongly of muske. Their Hares no bigger then our Conies, and few of them to be found.

Their Beares are very little in comparison of those of Muscovia and Tartaria. The Beaver is as bigge as an ordinary water dogge, but his legges exceeding short. His fore feete like a dogs, his hinder feet like a Swans. His taile somewhat like the forme of a Racket bare without haire, which to eate the Savages esteeme a great delicate. They have many Otters which as the Beavers they take with snares, and esteeme the skinnes great ornaments, and of all those beasts they use to feede when they catch them.

There is also a beast they call *Vetchunquoyes* in the forme of a wilde Cat. Their Foxes are like our silver haired Conies of a small proportion, and not smelling like those in England. Their Dogges of that country are like their Wolves, and cannot barke but howle, and their wolves not much bigger then our English Foxes. Martins, Powlecats, weessels and Minkes we know they have, because we have seen many of their skinnes, though very seldome any of them alive. But one thing is strange that we could never perceive their vermine destroy our hennes, Egges nor Chickens nor do any hurt, nor their flyes nor serpents anie waie pernitious, where in the South parts of America they are alwaies dangerous and often deadly.

Of birds the Eagle is the greatest devourer. Hawkes there be of diverse sorts, as our Falconers called them, Sparowhawkes, Lanarets, Goshawkes,

Falcons and Osperayes, but they all pray most upon fish. Partridges there are little bigger then our Quailes, wilde Turkies are as bigge as our tame. There are woosels or blackbirds with red shoulders, thrushes and diverse sorts of small birds, some red, some blew, scarce so bigge as a wrenne, but few in Sommer. In winter there are great plenty of Swans, Craynes, gray and white with blacke wings, Herons, Geese, Brants, Ducke, Wigeon, Dotterell, Oxeies, Parrats and Pigeons. Of all those sorts great abundance, and some other strange kinds to us unknowne by name. But in sommer not any or a very few to be seene.

Of fish we were best acquainted with Sturgeon, Grampus, Porpus, Seales, Stingraies, whose tailes are very dangerous. Brettes, mullets, white Salmonds, Trowts, Soles, Plaice, Herrings, Conyfish, Rockfish, Eeles, Lampreyes, Catfish, Shades, Pearch of 3 sorts, Crabs, Shrimps, Crevises [crayfish], Oysters, Cocles and Muscles. But the most strange fish is a smal one so like the picture of St. George his Dragon, as possible can be, except his legs and wings, and the Todefish which will swell till it be like to brust, when it commeth into the aire.

Concerning the entrailes of the earth little can be saide for certainty. There wanted good Refiners, for these that tooke upon them to have skill this way, tooke up the washings from the mountaines and some moskered shining stones and spangles which the waters brought down, flattering themselves in their own vaine conceits to have bin supposed what they were not, by the meanes of that ore, if it proved as their arts and judgements expected. Only this is certaine, that many regions lying in the same latitude, afford mines very rich of diverse natures. The crust also of these rockes would easily perswade a man to beleeve there are other mines then yron and steele, if there were but meanes and men of experience that knew the mine from spare.

The First Bison! The Last Bison!

Sir Samuel Argall (?–1626)
William Temple Hornaday (1854–1937)

Pioneer conservationist William Temple Hornaday was the first superintendent of the National Zoological Park in Washington, D.C., and later, the first director of the Bronx Zoo. His battle for preservation of wildlife began when he realized that the American bison was near extinction. More than any other man, he may be credited with establishing the Montana and Dakota preserves that saved the remnant herds. His 1889 National Museum publication *The Extermination of the American Bison* was both a scholarly treatise and a conservation polemic. In the brief excerpt below, Hornaday establishes the extent of the bison's former range in eastern North America in order to demonstrate the magnitude of the slaughter. In so doing, he has given us an account of the first and last bison seen in the area of Washington, D.C.

Samuel Argall, whose letter records the sighting of the bison, was an English sea captain whose well-provisioned fishing barque arrived fortuitously on Chesapeake Bay in 1609 and resupplied the starving Jamestown colonists. On his second trip to the New World in 1612, he transported Governor de la Warr to the colony. He visited the head of navigation on the Potomac to obtain corn from the Indians. Argall later became deputy governor of the colony.

From "The Extermination of the American Bison," *Report of the US National Museum 1886–87* (Washington, D.C.: GPO, 1889)

THE EARLIEST DISCOVERY of the bison in Eastern North America, or indeed anywhere north of Coronado's route, was made somewhere near Washington, District of Columbia, in 1612, by an English navigator named Samuell Argoll [sic],[*] and narrated as follows:

"As soon as I had unladen this corne, I set my men to the felling of Timber, for the building of a Frigat, which I had left half finished at Point Com-

[*]*Purchas: His Pilgrimes.* (1625). Vol. IV, p. 1765."A Letter of Sir Samuel Argoll [sic] touching his Voyage to Virginia, and actions there. Written to Master Nicholas Hawes, June, 1613."

"... great store of Cattle as big as Kine." A Bison, from *A New Voyage to Carolina*

fort, the 19. of March: and returned myself with the ship into Pembrook [Potomac] River, and so discovered to the head of it, which is about 65. leagues into the Land, and navigable for any ship. And then marching into the Countrie, I found great store of Cattle as big as Kine, of which the Indians that were my guides killed a couple, which we found to be very good and wholesome meate, and are very easie to be killed, in regard they are heavy, slow, and not so wild as other beasts of the wildernesse."

It is to be regretted that the narrative of the explorer affords no clew to the precise locality of this interesting discovery, but since it is doubtful that the mariner journeyed very far on foot from the head of navigation of the Potomac, it seems highly probable that the first American bison seen by Europeans, other than the Spaniards, was found within 15 miles, or even less, of the capital of the United States, and possibly within the District of Columbia itself.

The First Expedition to the Blue Ridge Mountains

John Lederer (1644?–?)

Little is known of the early life and background of Johann (John) Lederer. Perhaps he was a native of Hamburg, Germany, for he studied at the Hamburg Academic Gymnasium. However and why ever he came to the New World, he was commissioned in 1669 by Virginia Governor William Berkeley to explore westward from the colony's outposts along the fall line that separates the tidewater coastal plain from the piedmont plateau. The report of his three journeys reveals Lederer to be an experienced woodsman who had substantial knowledge of the Indians and their languages and a friendly contempt for more settled men. The frontiersman's yarns with which Lederer seasoned his journal display an appreciation of wilderness which Americans came to love under the tutelage of Daniel Boone and James Fenimore Cooper's Leatherstocking.

After leaving Virginia in 1671, Lederer moved to Maryland, where he was befriended by William Talbot, the secretary of the province. On returning to England, Talbot published Lederer's journals. Some commentators think that Talbot anticipated that Lederer's maps and itineraries would help locate an overland passage to the Pacific Ocean, which had been the ultimate object of Lederer's adventures. This was not unreasonable at that time, for no one had any idea how wide the continent was in the latitudes of the English settlements. Without an accurate chronometer, no measure of longitude was possible, and all geographical evidence favored a relatively short crossing: Central America was narrow and Mexico had been routinely traversed, ocean to ocean, for a century and a half. Indians reported as tidal ebb and flow what must have been the rise and fall of transmontane rivers with rain. Sir Frances Drake's ninety-year-old claim to the Pacific coast north of Spanish exploration motivated the Atlantic colonists, who hoped for riches from expansion to the west. The expectation of an easy passage up an eastern river and down a western one was only refuted when Lewis and Clark found the Missouri-Columbia connection impractical.

From *The Discoveries of John Lederer, In three several Marches from Virginia To the West of Carolina, And other parts of the Continent* (London: Samuel Heyrick, 1672)

The First Expedition, From the head of Pemaeoncock, alias York-River (due West) to the top of the Apalataean Mountains.

Upon the ninth of March, 1669, (with three Indians whose names were Magtakunh, Hopottoguoh and Naunnugh) I went out at the falls of Pemaeoncock, alias York-River in Virginia, from an Indian village called Shickehamany, and lay that night in the woods, encountring nothing remarkable, but a rattle-snake of extraordinary length and tickness, for I judged it two yards and a half or better from head to tail, and as big about as a mans arm: by the distention of her belly, we believed her full with young; but having killed and opened her, found there a small squirrel whole; which caused in me a double wonder: first, how a reptile should catch so nimble a creature as a squirrel; and having caught it, how he could swallow it entire. The Indians in resolving my doubts, plunged me into a greater astonishment, when they told me that it was usual in these serpents, when they lie basking in the sun, to fetch down these squirrels from the tops of the trees, by fixing their eye steadfastly upon them; the horrour of which strikes such an affrightment into the little beast, that he has no power to hinder himself from tumbling down into the jaws of his enemy, who takes in all his sustenance without chewing, his teeth serving him onely to offend withal. But I rather believe what I have heard from others, that these serpents climb the trees, and surprise their prey in the nest.

The next day falling into marish grounds between the Pemaeoncock and the head of the River Matapeneugh, the heaviness of the way obliged me to cross Pemaeoncock, where its North and South branch (called Ackmick) joyn in one. In the peninsula made by these two branches, a great Indian king called Tottopottoma was heretofore slain in battle, fighting for the Christians against the Mahocks and Nahyssans, from whence it retains his name to this day. Travelling thorow the woods, a doe seized by a wild cat crossed our way; the miserable creature being even spent and breathless with the burden and cruelty of her rider, who having fastened on her shoulder, left not sucking out her bloud until she sunk under him: which one of the Indians perceiving, let fly a lucky arrow, which piercing him thorow the belly, made him quit his prey already slain, and turn with a terrible grimas at us; but his strength and spirits failing him, we escaped his revenge, which had certainly ensued, were not his wound mortal. This creature is something bigger than our English fox, of a reddish grey colour, and in figure

"... the miserable creature being spent and breathless with the burden and cruelty of her rider." A Wildcat and Stag, from *A New Voyage to Carolina*

every way agreeing with an ordinary cat; fierce, ravenous and cunning: for finding the deer (upon which they delight most to prey) too swift for them, they watch upon branches of trees, and as they walk or feed under, jump down upon them. The fur of the wilde cat, though not very fine, is yet esteemed for its virtue in taking away cold aches and pains, being worn next to the body; their flesh, though rank as a dogs, is eaten by the Indians.

The eleventh and twelfth, I found the ways very uneven and cumbred with bushes.

The thirteenth, I reached the first spring of Pemaeoncock, having crossed the river four times that day, by reason of its many windings; but the water was so shallow, that it hardly wet my horses patterns. Here a little under the surface of the earth, I found flat pieces of petrified matter, of one side solid stone, but on the other side isinglas, which I easily peeled off in flakes about four inches square: several of these pieces, with a transparent stone like crystal that cut glass, and a white marchasite that I purchased of the Indians, I presented to Sir William Berkley, Governour of Virginia.

The fourteenth of March, from the top of an eminent hill, I first descried that Apalataean mountains, bearing due west to the place I stood upon: their distance from me was so great, that I could hardly discern whether they were mountains or clouds, until my Indian fellow travellers prostrating themselves in adoration, howled out after a barbarous manner, *Okee paeze* i. e. God is nigh.

The fifteenth of March, not far from this hill, passing over the South-branch of Rappahanock-river, I was almost swallowed in a quicksand. Great herds of red and fallow deer I daily saw feeding; and on the hill-sides, bears crashing mast like swine. Small leopards I have seen in the woods, but never any lions, though their skins are much worn by the Indians. The wolves in these parts are so ravenous, that I often in the night feared my horse would be devoured by them, they would gather up and howl so close round about him, though tethr'd to the same tree at whose foot I my self and the Indians lay: but the fires which we made, I suppose, scared them from worrying us all. Beaver and otter I met with at every river that I passed; and the woods are full of grey foxes.

Thus I travelled all the sixteenth; and on the seventeenth of March I reached the Apalataei. The air here is very thick and chill; and the waters issuing from the mountain-sides, of a blue colour, and allumish taste.

The eighteenth of March, after I had in vain assayed to ride up, I alighted, and left my horse with one of the Indians, whilst with the other two I climbed up the rocks, which were so incumbred with bushes and brambles, that the ascent proved very difficult: besides the first precipice was so steep, that if I lookt down, I was immediately taken with a swimming in my head; though afterwards the way was more easie. The height of this mountain was very extraordinary: for notwithstanding I set out with the first appearance of light, it was late in the evening before I gained the top, from whence the next morning I had a beautiful prospect of the Atlantick Ocean washing the Virginian-shore; but to the north and west, my sight was suddenly bounded by mountains higher than that I stood upon. Here did I wander in snow, for the most part, till the four and twentieth day of March, hoping to find some passage through the mountains; but the coldness of the air and earth together, seizing my hands and feet with numbness, put me to a *ne plus ultra*; and therefore having found my Indian at the foot of the mountain with my horse, I returned back the same way that I went.

The Natural History of
the New World—Three Views

Mark Catesby (1682–1749)

William Byrd II (1674–1744)

John Lawson (16??–1711)

The botanical gardens of Essex, England, are an ideal environment in which to discover the fascinations of natural history; there, in childhood, Mark Catesby had the tutelage of great English naturalists like Nicolas Jekyll and John Ray, "the father of English botany." It is no wonder that he became a professional—a collector of plants and animals, an artist and illustrator, and a biological theoretician of note.

At his emigrant sister's invitation, Catesby began his American experience in Virginia in 1712, returning to England after seven years. His excellence as a plant collector brought him the patronage of Sir Hans Sloane, president of the Royal Academy; with Sloane's encouragement, he commenced an exploration whose results he published as *The Natural History of Carolina, Florida and the Bahama Islands.* This work includes his observations on Virginia. Catesby illustrated his rather brief text with 220 plates of birds, amphibians, reptiles, fishes, insects, mammals, and plants, the finest examples of their kind until Alexander Wilson's *American Ornithology* (1808). However, not all these pictures are Catesby's own work: Through his connection with Hans Sloane, he had access to John White's sketches from the Roanoke colony. He appropriated several of these without acknowledgment. He also borrowed some few parts of his written descriptions. Yet, Catesby was an original scientific observer; for example, his Bahama studies convinced him that birds migrate rather than hibernate as was then commonly believed.

Catesby's source was his immediate predecessor in the region, John Lawson, a collector for the bishop of London's botanical garden. Lawson traveled to North Carolina in 1700; he became a surveyor, explorer, landholder, founder of towns, and natural historian. He was killed by Indians in 1711, just two years after the appearance of the first of many editions of his *A New Voyage to Carolina*, which contains an eighty-page chapter on natural history.

Much more comprehensive and orderly than Thomas Hariot's *A briefe and true report of the new found land of Virginia* (1588), but not as substantial as John Josselyn's New England natural history writings, *A New Voyage* suffers from casual observation, secondhand information, and folktales uncritically reported as fact, faults which Catesby avoided. Nevertheless, *A New Voyage* was plagiarized no less than three times, not counting Catesby's quite limited borrowing. The most interesting of these thefts is William Byrd II's *Natural History of Virginia, or The Newly Discovered Eden*. Published in German in Switzerland by S. Jenner in 1737, this document was intended to attract Swiss settlers to land that Byrd, a second-generation American, was selling near Roanoke, Virginia. Substantial editing by Byrd added advice on farming and a critique of Virginia's dependence on tobacco culture. Other changes reflect Byrd's superior knowledge of natural history—he was educated at the Middle Temple, London, and was a fellow of the Royal Society. His ironic sense of humor is revealed in his subtitle; "Eden" does not refer to a biblical pleasure garden but to the man from whom he acquired the land: North Carolina governor Eden. Unfortunately, Byrd's personal style is lost in the translation into German, for his other published writings are witty, colorful accounts of colonial life. The bracketed interpolations in William Byrd's writing were made by the translators of the German text.

[Topography]

From Mark Catesby, *The Natural History of Carolina, Florida and the Bahama Islands* (London: 1731–1743)

Mark Catesby

In the year 1714 I traveled from the lower part of St. James's river in Virginia to that part of the Appalachian mountains where the sources of that river rise, from which to the head of the Savannah river, is about four degrees distance in latitude. . . .

At sixty miles from the mountains, the river, which fifty miles below was a mile wide, is here contracted to an eighth part, and very shallow, being fordable in many places, and so full of rocks, that by stepping from one to another it was everywhere passable. Here we killed plenty of a particular kind of wild geese; they were very fat by feeding on fresh water snails, which were in great plenty, sticking to the tops and sides of the rocks. The low lands joining to the rivers were vastly rich, shaded with trees that naturally dislike a barren soil, such as black walnut, plane, and oaks of vast stature. This low land stretched along the river many miles, extending back half a mile more or less, and was bounded by a ridge of steep and very lofty rocks, on the top of which we climbed, and could discern some of the nearer mountains, and beheld most delightful prospects, but the country being an entire forest, the meanders of the rivers, with other beauties, were much obscured by the trees. On the back of this ridge of rocks the land was high, rising in broken hills, alternately good and bad. Some miles further the banks of the river on both sides were formed of high perpendicular rocks, with many lesser ones scattered all over the river, between which innumerable torrents of water were continually rushing.

At the distance of twelve miles from the mountains we left the river, and directed our course to the nearest of them. But first we viewed the river, and crossed it several times, admiring its beauties, as well as those of the circumjacent parts. Ascending the higher grounds we had a large prospect of the mountains, as well as of the river below us, which here divided into narrow rocky channels, and formed many little islands.

So soon as we had left the river, the land grew very rugged and hilly, increasing gradually in height all the way. Arriving at the foot of the first steep hill we pursued a bear, but he climbing the rocks with much more agility than we, he took his leave. Proceeding further up, we found by many beaten tracts, and dung of bears, that the mountains were much frequented by them, for the sake of chesnuts, with which at this time these mountains amounted.

The rocks of these mountains seem to engross one half of the surface; they are most of a light gray color; some are of a coarse grained alabaster, others of a metallic luster, some pieces were in form of slate and brittle, others in lumps and hard; some appeared with spangles, others thick, sprinkled with innumerable small shining specks like silver, which frequently appeared in stratums at the roots of trees when blown down.

These different spars appeared most on the highest and steepest parts of the hills, where was little grass and fewest trees, but the greatest part of the soil between the rocks is generally of a dark-colored sandy mold, and shallow, yet fertile, and productive of good corn, which encourages the Tallipooses, a clan of the Cherokee nation of Indians, to settle amongst them, in the latitude of 34, and are the only Indian nation that has a constant residence upon any part of this whole range of mountains.

Certain places in Virginia, towards the heads of rivers, are very much impregnated with a nitrous salt, which attracts for many miles round numerous herds of cattle, for the sake of licking the earth, which at one place is so wore away into a cave, that a church, which stands near it, has attained the indecent name of Licking hole Church.

Of the Water

The larger rivers in Carolina and Virginia have their sources in the Appalachian mountains, generally springing from rocks, and forming cascades and waterfalls in various manners, which being collected in their course, and uniting into single streams, cause abundance of narrow rapid torrents, which falling into the lower grounds, fill innumerable brooks and rivulets, all which contribute to form and supply the large rivers.

All those rivers which have their sources in the mountains, have cataracts about one-third of the distance from the mountains to the sea. These cataracts consist of infinite numbers of various sized rocks, scattered promiscuously in all parts of the river, so close to one another, and in many places so high, that violent torrents and lofty cascades are continually flowing from between and over them. The extent of these cataracts (or falls, as they are commonly called) is usually four or five miles; nor are the rivers destitute of rocks all the way between them and the mountains; but between these falls and the sea, the rivers are open, and void of rocks, and consequently are navigable so far, and no further, which necessitates the Indians in their passage from the mountains, to drag their canoes some miles by land, till they get below the cataracts, from which they have an open passage down to the sea, except that the rivers in some places are encumbered by trees carried down and lodged by violent torrents from the mountains.

The coasts of Florida, including Carolina and Virginia, with the sounds, inlets, and lower parts of the rivers, have a muddy and soft bottom.

At low water there appears in the rivers and creeks immense beds of oysters, covering the muddy banks many miles together; in some great rivers extending thirty or forty miles from the sea, they do not lie separate, but are closely joined to one another, and appear as a solid rock a foot and a half or two feet in depth, with their edges upwards.

The rivers springing from the mountains are liable to great inundations, occasioned not only from the numerous channels feeding them from the mountains, but the height and steepness of their banks, and obstructions of the rocks.

When great rains fall on the mountains, these rapid torrents are very sudden and violent; an instance of which may give a general idea of them, and their ill consequences.

In September 1722, at Fort Moore, a little fortress on the Savannah river, about midway between the sea and mountains, the waters rose twenty-nine feet in less than forty hours. This proceeded only from what rain fell on the mountains, they at the fort having had none in that space of time.

It came rushing down the river so suddenly, and with that impetuosity that it not only destroyed all their grain, but swept away and drowned the cattle belonging to the garrison. Islands were formed, and others joined to the land. And in some places the course of the river was turned. A large and fertile tract of low land, lying on the south side of the river, opposite to the fort, which was a former settlement of the Savannah Indians, was covered with sand three feet in depth, and made unfit for cultivation. This sterile land was not carried from the higher grounds, but was washed from the steep banks of the river. Panthers, bears and deer were drowned, and found lodged on the limbs of trees. The smaller animals suffered also in this calamity; even reptiles and insects were dislodged from their holes, and violently hurried away, and mixing with harder substances were beat in pieces, and their fragments (after the waters fell) were seen in many places to cover the ground.

There is no part of the globe where the signs of a deluge more evidently appears than in many parts of the northern continent of America; which, though I could illustrate in many instances, let this one suffice. Mr. Woodward, at his plantation in Virginia, above an hundred miles from the sea, towards the sources of Rappahannock river, in digging a well about seventy feet deep, to find a spring, discovered at that depth a bed of the Glossopetrae, one of which was sent me.

All parts of Virginia, at the distance of sixty miles, or more, abound in fossil shells of various kinds, which in stratums lie imbedded a great depth in the earth, in the banks of rivers and other places, among which are frequently found the vertebras, and other bones of sea animals. At a place in Carolina called Stono, was dug out of the earth three or four teeth of a large animal, which, by the concurring opinion of all the Negroes, native Africans, that saw them, were the grinders of an elephant; and in my opinion they could be no other; I having seen some of the like that are brought from Africa.

From William Byrd II, *The Natural History of Virginia, or the Newly Discovered Eden* (Richmond: Dietz Press, 1940; translation from the German *Neu-gefundenes Eden,* published by S. Jenner, 1737)

William Byrd

Air and Weather in Virginia

ONE CAN TRUTHFULLY SAY, that no better or healthier air can be found in the whole wide world, especially towards the mountainous regions [than in that province. There] it is so pure and fine that it cheers up and strengthens the animal spirits, [and] contrarily chases away all sadness; consequently no people of melancholic temperament and few of phlegmatic temperament can be found. Whenever such people come there, they very soon change their nature, as one can sufficiently see in the case of many foreigners, who daily arrive there. One can find in this beautiful and fruitful land all the delightful enjoyments which a rational being can ever desire. Indeed what am I saying! One enjoys, along with the most delicate pleasure, the refreshing and kindly influence of an ever shining and warming sun, from the rays of which he can cover and refresh himself nearly all year long under the agreeable shade of the trees and pleasing woods which are almost always green. [Here] all our senses can revel in the contemplation and observation of a beautiful and charitable nature. There is almost no day in the year that one cannot see the great luminary which warms everything and produces vegetation because one has no fog in that land [and] also one knows no hail nor hoar-frost. The rains do not last long but rather pass by soon. They recur frequently, however, and put in their appearance mostly during the night [and] last usually no longer than until morning. [This] cools the heat in summer very much as [do] the heavy dews, which fall in summer in this country every night when it does not rain. To sum up, this excellent land is so mild and so healthful, that one hears of very nearly no diseases. Indeed many of the European [diseases] disappear immediately, as soon as one gets there (for example the gout, scurvy, and some other diseases with which the Europeans are tormented), and the people become alert and healthy in a very short time. Indeed, what is much more miraculous, the old people receive quite new strength, feel as if they were wholly born anew, that is, much stronger, much more light-footed, and in every way much more comfortable than before, which is not to be wondered at (if one wants to speak according to physics) since the Virginia air is much warmer, much more delicate, and much lighter than the northern European [air], in which we were born. In addition, the Virginia foods are of far more strength and effect than ours; from which [fact it] must necessarily follow, that our animal spirits, thus increased by this new addition, are made better, are strengthened, are indeed made much more spiritual. This is so true that all those who come into this blessed land feel [the effect] noticeably in their own bodies and spirits in a very short time.

Brief Remarks on How One May Clean and Clear the Land Very Easily and Conveniently

The Indians do this in a very brief and quite easy manner, namely they go, when the trees are full of sap, and skin about three or four feet of bark from the trunks, which causes them soon to dry up, so the foliage falls down. This no sooner happens than they begin at once to work the soil and to sow it with grain, or whatever they wish, which soon springs forth and produces manifold fruit. When the aforementioned trees have become quite withered by the removal of the bark, they then go and cut a broad strip from the nearest green trees, which are standing there, [to a point] as far as they wish to clear, in order to prevent the whole forest from burning. They then set fire to the dry trees, which burn immediately. Thus in a short time a very large section of land can be cleared and made neatly available for planting, [a practice] which saves the planters very much trouble and expense. The English have up to now with little difference imitated the Indians in this. I think, however, that it always causes a damage to the good wood, or [that] one at least ought to put to some use the ashes [of the trees], because the soil is rich enough of itself without such fertilizer.

[The Plants and Animals]

From John Lawson, *A New Voyage to Carolina* (London: 1709)

John Lawson

THE *Buffelo* is a wild Beast of *America*, which has a Bunch on his Back, as the Cattle of St. *Laurence* are said to have. He seldom appears amongst the *English* inhabitants, his chief Haunt being in the Land of *Messiasippi*, which is, for the most part, a plain Country; yet I have known some kill'd on the

Hilly Part of *Cape-Fair*-River, they passing the Ledges of vast Mountains from the said *Messiasippi*, before they can come near us. I have eaten of their Meat, but do not think it so good as our Beef; yet the younger Calves are cry'd up for excellent Food, as very likely they may be. It is conjectured, that these Buffelos, mixt in Breed with our tame Cattle, would much better the Breed for Largeness and Milk, which seems very probable. Of the wild Bull's Skin, Buff is made. The *Indians* cut the Skins into Quarters for the Ease of their Transportation, and make Beds to lie on. They spin the Hair into Garters, Girdles, Sashes, and the like, it being long and curled, and often a chestnut or red Colour. These Monsters are found to weigh (as I am informed by a Traveller of Credit) from 1600 to 2400 weight.

The Bears here are very common, though not so large as in *Groenland*, and the more Northern Countries of Russia. The Flesh of this Beast is very good, and nourishing, and not inferiour to the best Pork in Taste. It stands betwixt Beef and Pork, and the young Cubs are a Dish for the greatest *Epicure* living. I prefer their Flesh before any Beef, Veal, Pork or Mutton; and they look as well as they eat, their fat being as white as Snow, and the sweetest of any Creature's in the World. If a Man drink a Quart thereof melted, it never will rise in his Stomach. We prefer it above all things, to fry Fish and other things in. Those that are Strangers to it, may judge otherwise; But I who have eaten a great deal of Bears Flesh in my Life-time (since my being an Inhabitant in *America*) do think it equalizes, if not excels, any Meat I ever eat in *Europe*. The Bacon made thereof is extraordinary Meat; but it must be well saved, otherwise it will rust. This Creature feeds upon all sorts of wild Fruits. When Herrings run, which is in March, the Flesh of such of those Bears as eat thereof, is nought, all that Season, and eats filthily. Neither is it good, when he feeds on Gum-berries, as I intimated before. They are great Devourers of Acorns, and oftentimes meet the Swine in the Woods, which they kill and eat, especially when they are hungry, and can find no other Food. Now and then they get into the Fields of *Indian* Corn, or *Maiz*, where they make a sad Havock, spoiling ten times as much as they eat. The Potatos of this Country are so agreeable to them, that they never fail to sweep 'em all clean, if they chance to come in their way. They are seemingly a very clumsy Creature, yet are very nimble in running up Trees, and traversing every Limb thereof. When they come down, they run Tail foremost. At catching of Herrings, they are most expert Fishers. They sit by the Creeksides, (which are very narrow) where the Fish run in; and there they take them up, as fast as it's possible they can dip their Paws into the Water. There is one thing more to be consider'd of this Creature, which is, that no Man, either Christian or *Indian*, has ever kill'd a She-bear with Young.

It is supposed, that the She-Bears, after Conception, hide themselves in some secret and undiscoverable Place, till they bring forth their Young, which, in all Probability, cannot be long; otherwise, the *Indians*, who hunt the Woods like Dogs, would, at some time or other, have found them out. Bear-Hunting is a great Sport in *America*, both with the *English* and *Indians*. Some Years ago, there were killed five hundred Bears, in two Counties of *Virginia*, in one Winter; and but two She-Bears amongst them all, which were not with Young, as I told you of the rest. The *English* have a breed of Dogs fit for this sport, about the size of Farmers Curs, and, by Practice, come to know the Scent of a Bear, which as soon as they have found, they run him, by the Nose, till they come up with him, and then bark and snap at him, till he trees, when the Huntsman shoots him out of the Trees, there being, for the most part, two or three with Guns, lest the first should miss, or not quite kill him. Though they are not naturally voracious, yet they are very fierce when wounded. The Dogs often bring him to a Bay, when wounded, and then the Huntsmen make other Shots, perhaps with the Pistols that are stuck in their Girdles. If a Dog is apt to fasten, and run into a Bear, he is not good, for the best Dog in *Europe* is nothing in their Paws; but if ever they get him in their Clutches, they blow his Skin from his Flesh, like a Bladder, and often kill him; or if he recovers it, he is never good for any thing after. As the Paws of this Creature, are held for the best bit about him, so is the Head esteem'd the worst, and always thrown away, for what reason I know not. I believe, none ever made Trial thereof, to know how it eats. The Oil of the Bear is very Sovereign for Strains, Aches, and old Pains. The fine Fur at the bottom of the Belly, is used for making Hats, in some places. The Fur itself is fit for several Uses; as for making Muffs, facing Caps, *&c.* but the black Cub-skin is preferable to all sorts of that kind, for Muffs. Its Grain is like Hog-Skin. . . .

Our wild Pigeons, are like the Wood-Queese or Stock-Doves, only have a longer Tail. They leave us in the Summer. This sort of Pigeon (as I said before) is the most like our Stock-Doves, or Wood-Pigeons that we have in *England*; only these differ in their Tails, which are very long, much like a Parrakeeto's? You must understand, that these Birds do not breed amongst us, (who are settled at, and near the Mouths of the Rivers, as I have intimated to you before) but come down (especially in hard Winters) amongst the Inhabitants, in great Flocks, as they were seen to do in the Year 1707, which was the hardest Winter that ever was known, since *Carolina* has been seated by the Christians. And if that country had such hard Weather, what must be expected of the severe Winters in *Pensylvania, New-York*, and *New-England*, where Winters are ten times (if possible) colder than with us. Although the Flocks are, in such Extremities, very numerous; yet they are not to be mention'd in Comparison with the great and infinite Numbers of these Fowl, that are met withal about a hundred, or a hundred and fifty, Miles to the Westward of the Places where we at present live; and where these Pigeons come down, in quest of a small sort of Acorns, which in those Parts are plentifully found. They are the same we call Turky-Acorns, because the wild Turkies feed very much thereon; and for the same Reason, those Trees that bear them, are call'd Turky-Oaks. I saw such prodigious Flocks of these Pigeons, in *January* or *February*, 1701–2, (which were in the hilly Country, between the great Nation of the *Esaw Indians*, and the pleasant Stream of *Sapona*, which is the West-Branch of the *Clarendon*, or *Cape-Fair* River) that they had broke down the Limbs of a great many large Trees all over those Woods, whereon they chanced to sit and roost; especially the great Pines, which are a more brittle Wood, than our sorts of Oak are. These Pigeons, about Sun-Rise, when we were preparing to march on our Journey, would fly by us in such vast Flocks, that they would be near a Quarter of an Hour, before they were all pass'd by; and as soon as that Flock was gone, another would come; and so successively one after another, for great part of the Morning. It is observable, that wherever these Fowl come in such Numbers, as I saw them then, they clear all before them, scarce leaving one Acorn upon the Ground, which would, doubtless, be a great Prejudice to the Planters that should seat there, because their Swine would be thereby depriv'd of their Mast. When I saw such Flocks of the Pigeons I now speak of, none of our Company had any other sort of Shot, than that which is cast in Moulds, and was so very large, that we could not put above ten or a dozen of them into our largest Pieces; Wherefore, we made but an indifferent Hand of shooting them; although we commonly kill'd a Pigeon for every Shot. They were very fat, and as good Pigeons, as ever I eat. I enquired of the *Indians* that dwell'd in those parts, where it was that those Pigeons bred, and they pointed towards the vast Ridge of Mountains, and said, they bred there. Now, whether they make their Nests in the Holes in the Rocks of those Mountains, or build in Trees, I could not learn; but they seem to me to be a Wood-Pigeon, that build in Trees, because of their frequent sitting thereon, and their Roosting on Trees always at Night, under which their

Dung commonly lies half a Foot thick, and kills every thing that grows where it falls. . . .

Live-Oak chiefly grows on dry, sandy Knolls. This is an Ever-green, and the most durable Oak all *America* affords. The Shortness of this Wood's Bowl, or Trunk, makes it unfit for Plank to build Ships withal. There are some few Trees, that would allow a Stock of twelve Foot, but the Firmness and the great Weight thereof, frightens our Sawyers from the Fatigue that attends the cutting of this Timber. A Nail once driven therein, 'tis next to an Impossibility to draw it out. The Limbs thereof are so cur'd, that they serve for excellent Timbers, Knees, *& c.* for Vessels of any sort. The Acorns thereof are as sweet as Chesnuts, and the *Indians* draw an Oil from them, as sweet as that from the Olive, tho' of an Amber-Colour. With these Nuts, or Acorns, some have counterfeited the Cocoa, whereof they have made Chocolate, not to be distinguished by a good Palate. Window-Frames, Mallets, and Pins for Blocks, are made thereof, to an excellent Purpose. I knew two Trees of this Wood among the *Indians*, which were planted from the Acorn, and grew in the Freshes, and never saw any thing more beautiful of that kind. They are of an indifferent quick Growth; of which there are two sorts. The Acorns make very fine Pork.

From Mark Catesby, *The Natural History of Carolina, Florida and the Bahama Islands* (London: 1731–1743)

Mark Catesby

The Opossum

THE OPOSSUM is an animal peculiar to America, particularly all the northern continent abound with them as far north as New England, and as Merian has described them at Surinam, it is probable they inhabit as far to the south as they do to the north. This beast being of a distinct genus, has little resemblance to any other creature. It is about the size of a large rabbit, the body is long, having short legs, the feet are formed like those of a rat, as are also its ears, the snout is long, the teeth like those of a dog; its body is covered thinly with long bristly whitish hair, the tail is long, shaped like that of a rat, and void of hair. But what is most remarkable in this creature and differing from others, is its false belly, which is formed by a skin or membrane (enclosing its dugs) which it opens and closes at will. Though contrary to the Laws of Nature, nothing is more believed in America than that these creatures are bred at the teats of their dams. But as it is apparent from the disection of one of them by Dr. Tyson, that their structure is formed for generation like that of other animals, they must necessarily be bred and excluded the usual way of other quadrupeds; yet that which has given cause to the contrary opinion is very wonderful, for I have many times seen the young ones just born, fixed and hanging to the teats of their dams when they were not bigger than mice; in this state all their members were apparent, yet not so distinct and perfectly formed but that they looked more like a fetus than otherwise, and seemed inseparably fixed to the teats, from which no small force was required to pull their mouths, and then being held to the teat, would not fix to it again. By what method the dam after exclusion fixes them to her teats, is a secret yet unknown. . . .

Herrings

Herrings in March leave the salt waters, and run up the rivers and shallow streams of fresh water in such prodigious shoals, that people cast them on shore with shovels. A horse passing these waters, unavoidably tramples them under his feet; their plenty is of great benefit to the inhabitants of many parts of Virginia and Carolina.

But the most extraordinary inundation of fish happens annually a little within the northern cape of Chesapeake Bay in Virginia, where there are cast on shore usually in March, such incredible numbers of fish, that the shore is covered with them a considerable depth, and three miles in length along the shore. At these times the inhabitants from far within land, come down with their carts and carry away what they want of the fish; there remaining to rot on the shore many times more than sufficed them; from the putrefaction that this causes, the place has attained the name of Magotty Bay.

These fish are of various kinds and sizes, and are drove on shore by the pursuit of porpoises and other voracious fish, at the general time of spawning; amongst the fish that are thus drove on shore, is a small fish called a fat-back; it is thick and round, resembling a mullet, but smaller. It is an excellent sweet fish, and so excessive fat that butter is never used in frying, or any other preparation of them. At certain seasons and places there are infinite numbers of these fish caught, and are much esteemed by the inhabitants for their delicacy.

"Catesby illustrated his rather brief text with 220 plates of birds, amphibians, reptiles, fishes, insects, mammals, and plants." A Fish Hawk [Osprey], Mark Catesby, from *The Natural History of Carolina, Florida and the Bahama Islands*, 1747

All the sea and river fish that I observed in Carolina, differ from those in Europe of the same kind, except pikes, eels and herrings, though possibly there may be more that escaped my knowledge.

The Sturgeon

At the approach of the spring, sturgeons leave the deep recesses of the sea, and enter the rivers, ascending by slow degrees to the upper parts to cast their spawn; in May, June and July, the rivers abound with them, at which time it is surprising, though very common to see such large fish elated in the air, by their leaping some yards out of the water; this they do in an erect posture, and fall on their sides, which repeated percussions are loudly heard some miles distance in still evenings; it is also by this leaping action that many of them are taken, for as some particular parts of the rivers afford them most food, to those places they resort in greater plenty. Here the inhabitants (as the Indians taught them) place their canoes and boats, that when the sturgeon leap, these boats and canoes may receive them at their fall. It is dangerous passing over these leaping holes, as they are called, many a canoe, and small boat having been overset by the fall of a sturgeon into it.

At the latter end of August, great numbers of these sturgeons approach to the cataracts, and rocky places of the river, where the English and Indians go to strike them, which they do with a cane 14 feet in length, and pointed at the smaller end; with this the striker stands at the head of the canoe, another steering it. The striker when he discovers one lying at the bottom (which they generally do in six or eight feet depth) gently moves the pointed end of the cane to the fish, giving it a sudden thrust between the bony scales into its body, at which the fish scuds away with great swiftness, drawing the cane after it, the great end of which appearing on the surface of the water, directs the striker which way to pursue his chase. The fish being tired, slackens its pace, which gives the striker an opportunity of thrusting another cane into it, then it scuds away as before, but at length by loss of blood falters, and turning its belly upwards, submits to be taken into the canoe.

A she sturgeon contains about a bushel of spawn, and weighs usually three hundred, and some three hundred and fifty pounds, and are about nine feet long; the males are less.

Notes on the State of Virginia

Thomas Jefferson (1743–1826)

Notes on the State of Virginia is Jefferson's only book and the single most significant source of his reputation as an universal intellect. It combines a comprehensive, factual report on economics, government, geography, and natural history with Jefferson's views on every subject of interest to him. Begun in 1780 during his troubled governorship, it was a response to a questionnaire circulated by the secretary of the French legation at the Continental Congress in Philadelphia. The public turmoil caused by Benedict Arnold's invasion of Virginia and the private tragedy of his infant daughter's death distracted Jefferson from his literary task. Once he was out of office, however, it became his principal refuge.

In the first two of the four selections that follow, Jefferson describes his favorite Virginia landmarks: the Natural Bridge and the Blue Ridge water gap at Harpers Ferry. The third contains his rebuttal to the French naturalist Comte Georges Louis Leclerc de Buffon, who disparaged the New World fauna. In the fourth, Jefferson analyzes and rejects the various theories that sought to explain fossil shells. See the introduction to this anthology for comments on the place of *Notes* in both science and literature.

All four selections from *Notes on the State of Virginia* (London: John Stockdale, 1785; 1787)

Natural Bridge

THE *Natural bridge*, the most sublime of Nature's works. . . .is on the ascent of a hill, which seems to have been cloven through its length by some great convulsion. The fissure, just at the bridge, is, by some admeasurements, 270 feet deep, by others only 205. It is about 45 feet wide at the bottom, and 90 feet at the top; this of course determines the length of the bridge, and its height from the water. Its breadth in the middle, is about 60 feet, but more at the ends, and the thickness of the mass at the summit of the arch, about 40 feet. A part of this thickness is constituted by a coat of earth, which gives growth to many large trees. The residue, with the hill on

"... so beautiful an arch, so elevated, so light, and springing, as it were, up to heaven."
Natural Bridge, H. Fenn, steel engraving from *Picturesque America*, 1872

both sides, is one solid rock of limestone. The arch approaches the Semi-elliptical form; but the larger axis of the ellipsis, which would be the cord of the arch, is many times longer than the semi-axis which gives it's height. Though the sides of this bridge are provided in some parts with a parapet of fixed rocks, yet few men have resolution to walk to them and look over into the abyss. You involuntarily fall on your hands and feet, creep to the parapet and peep over it. Looking down from this height about a minute, gave me a violent head ach. This painful sensation is relieved by a short, but pleasing view of the Blue ridge along the fissure downwards, and upwards by that of the Short hills, which, with the Purgatory mountain is a divergence from the North ridge; and, descending then to the valley below, the sensation becomes delightful in the extreme. It is impossible for the emotions, arising from the sublime, to be felt beyond what they are here: so beautiful an arch, so elevated, so light, and springing, as it were, up to heaven, the rapture of the Spectator is really indiscribable! The fissure continues deep and narrow and, following the margin of the stream upwards about three eights of a mile you arrive at a limestone cavern, less remarkable, however, for height and extent than those before described. It's entrance into the hill is but a few feet above the bed of the stream. This bridge is in the county of Rockbridge, to which it has given name, and affords a public and commodious passage over a valley, which cannot be crossed elsewhere for a considerable distance. The stream passing under it is called Cedar creek. It is a water of James river, and sufficient in the driest seasons to turn a grist-mill, though its fountain is not more than two miles above.

Mountains

. . . It is worthy notice, that our mountains are not solitary and scattered confusedly over the face of the country; but that they commence at about 150 miles from the sea-coast, are disposed in ridges one behind another, running nearly parallel with the sea-coast, though rather approaching it as they advance north-east-wardly. To the south-west, as the tract of country between the sea-coast and the Mississipi becomes narrower, the mountains converge into a single ridge, which, as it approaches the Gulph of Mexico, subsides into plain country, and gives rise to some of the waters of that Gulph, and particularly to a river called the Apalachicola, probably from the Apalachies, an Indian nation formerly residing on it. Hence the mountains giving rise to that river, and seen from its various parts, were called the Apalachian mountains, being in fact the end or termination only of the great ridges passing through the continent. European geographers however extended the name northwardly as far as the mountains extended; some giving it, after their separation into different ridges, to the Blue ridge, others to the North mountain, others to the Alleghaney, others to the Laurel ridge, as may be seen in their different maps. But the fact I believe is, that none of these ridges were ever known by that name to the inhabitants, either native or emigrant, but as they saw them so called in European maps. In the same direction generally are the veins of lime-stone, coal and other minerals hitherto discovered: and so range the falls of our great rivers. But the courses of the great rivers are at right angles with these. James and Patowmac penetrate through all the ridges of mountains eastward of the Alleghaney; that is broken by no watercourse. It is in fact the spine of the country between the Atlantic on one side, and the Missisipi and St. Laurence on the other. The passage of the Patowmac through the Blue ridge is perhaps one of the most stupendous scenes in nature. You stand on a very high point of land. On your right comes up the Shenandoah, having ranged along the foot of the mountain an hundred miles to seek a vent. On your left approaches the Patowmac, in quest of a passage also. In the moment of their junction they rush together against the mountain, rend it asunder, and pass off to the sea. The first glance of this scene hurries our senses into the opinion, that this earth has been created in time, that the mountains were formed first, that the rivers began to flow afterwards, that in this place particularly they have been dammed up by the Blue ridge of mountains, and have formed an ocean which filled the whole valley; that continuing to rise they have at length broken over at this spot, and have torn the mountain down from its summit to its base. The piles of rock on each hand, but particularly on the Shenandoah, the evident marks of their disrupture and avulsion from their beds by the most powerful agents of nature, corroborate the impression. But the distant finishing which nature has given to the picture is of a very different character. It is a true contrast to the fore-ground. It is as placid and delightful, as that is wild and tremendous. For the mountain being cloven asunder, she presents to your eye, through the cleft, a small catch of smooth blue horizon, at an infinite distance in the plain country, inviting you, as it were, from the riot and tumult roaring around, to pass through the breach and participate of the calm below. Here the eye ultimately composes itself; and that way too the road happens actually to lead. You cross the Patowmac above the junction, pass along its side through the base of the mountain for three miles, its terrible precipices hanging in fragments over you, and within about 20 miles reach Frederic town and the fine country around that. This scene is worth a voyage across the Atlantic. Yet here, as in the neighbourhood of the natural bridge, are people who have passed their lives within half a dozen miles, and have never been to survey these monuments of a war between rivers and mountains, which must have shaken the earth itself to its center.—The height of our mountains has not yet been estimated with any degree of exactness. The Alleghaney being the great ridge which divides the waters of the Atlantic from those of the Missisipi, its summit is doubtless more elevated above the ocean than that of any other mountain. But its relative height, compared with the base on which it stands, is not so great as that of some others, the country rising behind the successive ridges like the steps of stairs. The mountains of the Blue ridge, and of these the Peaks of Otter, are thought to be of a greater height, measured from their base, than any others in our country, and perhaps in North America. From data, which may found a tolerable conjecture, we suppose the highest peak to be about 4000 feet perpendicular, which is not a fifth part of the height of the mountains of South America, nor one third of the height which would be necessary in our latitude to preserve ice in the open air unmelted through the year. The ridge of mountains next beyond the Blue ridge, called by us the North mountain, is of the greatest extent; for which reason they were named by the Indians the Endless mountains.

[Animals]

Our quadrupeds have been mostly described by Linnaeus and Mons. de Buffon. Of these the Mammoth, or big buffalo, as called by the Indians, must certainly have been the largest. Their tradition is, that he was carnivorous, and still exists in the northern parts of America. A delegation of warriors from the Delaware tribe having visited the governor of Virginia, during the present revolution, on matters of business, after these had been discussed and settled in council, the governor asked them some questions relative to their country, and, among others, what they knew or had heard of the animal whose bones were found at the Saltlicks, on the Ohio. Their chief speaker immediately put himself into an attitude of oratory, and with a pomp suited to what he conceived the elevation of his subject, informed him that it was a tradition handed down from their fathers, "That in antient times a herd of these tremendous animals came to the Big-bone licks, and began an universal destruction of the bear, deer, elks, buffaloes, and other animals, which had been created for the use of the Indians: that the Great Man above, looking down and seeing this, was so enraged that he seized his lightning, descended on the earth, seated himself on a neighbouring mountain, on a rock, of which his seat and the print of his feet are still to be seen, and hurled his bolts among them till the whole were slaughtered, except the big bull, who presenting his forehead to the shafts, shook them off as they fell; but missing one at length, it wounded him in the side; whereon, springing round, he bounded over the Ohio, over the Wabash, the Illinois, and finally over the great lakes, where he is living at this day." It is well known that on the Ohio, and in many parts of America further north, tusks, grinders, and skeletons of unparalleled magnitude, are found in great numbers, some lying on the surface of the earth, and some a little below it. A Mr. Stanley, taken prisoner by the Indians near the mouth of the Tanissee, relates, that, after being transferred through several tribes, from one to another, he was at length carried over the mountains west of the Missouri to a river which runs westwardly; that these bones abounded there; and that the natives described to him the animal to which they belonged as still existing in the northern parts of their country; from which description he judged it to be an elephant. Bones of the same kind have been lately found, some feet below the surface of the earth, in salines opened on the North Holston, a branch of the Tanissee, about the latitude of 36⅞°. North. From the accounts published in Europe, I suppose it to be decided, that these are of the same kind with those found in Siberia. Instances are mentioned of like animal remains found in the more southern climates of both hemispheres; but they are either so loosely mentioned as to leave a doubt of the fact, so inaccurately described as not to authorize the classing them with the great northern bones, or so rare as to found a suspicion that they have been carried thither as curiosities from more northern regions. So that on the whole there seem to be no certain vestiges of the existence of this animal further south than the salines last mentioned. It is remarkable that the tusks and skeletons have been ascribed by the naturalists of Europe to the elephant, while the grinders have been given to the hippopotamus, or riverhorse. Yet it is acknowledged, that the tusks and skeletons are much larger than those of the elephant, and the grinders many times greater than those of the hippopotamus, and essentially different in form. Wherever these grinders are found, there also we find the tusks and skeleton; but no skeleton of the hippopotamus nor grinders of the elephant. It will not be said that the hippopotamus and elephant came always to the same spot, the former to deposit his grinders, and the latter his tusks and skeleton. For what became of the parts not deposited there? We must agree then that these remains belong to each other, that they are of one and the same animal. . . .

The opinion advanced by the Count de Buffon, is 1. That the animals common both to the old and new world, are smaller in the latter. 2. That those peculiar to the new, are on a smaller scale. 3. That those which have been domesticated in both, have degenerated in America: and 4. That on the whole it exhibits fewer species. And the reason he thinks is, that the heats of America are less; that more waters are spread over its surface by nature, and fewer of these drained off by the hand of man. In other words, that *heat* is friendly, and *moisture* adverse to the production and developement of large quadrupeds. I will not meet this hypothesis on its first doubtful ground, whether the climate of America be comparatively more humid? Because we are not furnished with observations sufficient to decide this question. And though, till it be decided, we are as free to deny, as others are to affirm the fact, yet for a moment let it be supposed. The hypothesis, after this supposition, proceeds to another; that *moisture* is unfriendly to animal growth. The truth of this is inscrutable to us by reasonings a priori. Nature has hidden from us her modus agendi. Our only appeal on such questions is to experience; and I think that experience is against the supposition. . . .

Mons. de Buffon himself informs us that the roe, the beaver, the otter, and shrew mouse, though of the same species, are larger in America than Europe. This should therefore have corrected the generality of his expressions XVIII. 145. and elsewhere, that the animals common to the two countries are considerably less in America than in Europe, "and that without any exception." He tells us too that on examining a bear from America, he remarked no difference "in the *shape* of this American bear compared with that of Europe." But adds from Bartram's journal, that an American bear weighed 400 lb. English, equal to 367 lb. French: whereas we find the European bear examined by Mons. D'Aubenton weighed but 141 lb. French. Kalm tells us that the Moose, of America, is as high as a tall horse; and Catesby, that it is about the bigness of a middle sized ox. I have seen a skeleton 7 feet high, and from good information believe they are often considerably higher. The Elk of Europe is not two-thirds of his height. The wesel is larger in America than in Europe, as may be seen by comparing its dimensions as reported by Mons. D'Aubenton and Kalm. The latter tells us, that the lynx, badger, red fox, and flying squirrel, are the *same* in America as in Europe. . . . The white bear of America is as large as that of Europe. . . . The bones of the Mammoth which have been found in America, are as large as those found in the old world. It may be asked, why I insert the Mammoth, as if it still existed? I ask in return, why I should omit it, as if it did not exist? Such is the œconomy of nature, that no instance can be produced of her having permitted any one race of her animals to become extinct; of her having formed any link in her great work so weak as to be broken. To add to this, the traditionary testimony of the Indians, that this animal still exists in the northern and western parts of America, would be adding the light of a taper to that of the meridian sun. Those parts still remain in their aboriginal state, unexplored and undisturbed by us, or by others for us. He may as well exist there now, as he did formerly where we find his bones. If he be a carnivorous animal, as some Anatomists have conjectured, and the Indians affirm, his early retirement may be accounted for from the general destruction of the wild game by the Indians, which commences in the first instant of their connection with us, for the purpose of purchasing matchcoats, hatchets, and fire locks, with their skins. . . .

[Fossil Shells]

Near the eastern foot of the North mountain are immense bodies of *Schist*, containing impressions of shells in a variety of forms. I have received petrified shells of very different kinds from the first sources of the Kentucky, which bear no resemblance to any I have ever seen on the tide-waters. It is said that shells are found in the Andes, in South-America, fifteen thousand feet above the level of the ocean. This is considered by many, both of the learned and the unlearned, as a proof of an universal deluge. To the many considerations opposing this opinion, the following may be added. The atmosphere, and all its contents, whether of water, air, or other matters, gravitate to the earth; that is to say, they have weight. Experience tells us, that the weight of all these together never exceeds that of a column of mercury of 31 inches height, which is equal to one of rainwater of 35 feet high. If the whole contents of the atmosphere then were water, instead of what they are, it would cover the globe but 35 feet deep; but as these waters, as they fell, would run into the seas, the superficial measure of which is to that of the dry parts of the globe as two to one, the seas would be raised only 52 žfeet above their present level, and of course would overflow the lands to that height only. In Virginia this would be a very small proportion even of the champaign country, the banks of our tide-waters being frequently, if not generally, of a greater height. Deluges beyond this extent then, as for instance, to the North mountain or to Kentucky, seem out of the laws of nature. But within it they may have taken place to a greater or less degree, in proportion to the combination of natural causes which may be supposed to have produced them. History renders probable some instances of a partial deluge in the country lying round the Mediterranean sea. It has been often supposed, and is not unlikely, that that sea was once a lake. While such, let us admit an extraordinary collection of the waters of the atmosphere from the other parts of the globe to have been discharged over that and the countries whose waters run into it. Or without supposing it a lake, admit such an extraordinary collection of the waters of the atmosphere, and an influx of waters from the Atlantic ocean, forced by long continued Western winds. That lake, or that sea, may thus have been so raised as to overflow the low lands adjacent to it, as those of Egypt and Armenia, which, according to a tradition of the Egyptians and Hebrews, were overflowed about 2300 years before the Christian æra; those of Attica, said to have been overflowed in the time of Ogyges, about 500 years later; and those of Thessaly, in the time of Deucalion, still 300 years posterior. But such deluges as these will not account for the shells found in the higher lands. A second opinion has been entertained, which is, that, in times anterior to the records either of history or tradition, the bed of the ocean, the principal residence of the shelled tribe, has, by some great convulsion of nature, been heaved to the heights at which we now find shells and other remains of marine animals. The favourers of this opinion do well to suppose the great events on which it rests to have taken place beyond all the æras of history; for within these, certainly none such are to be found: and we may venture to say further, that no fact has taken place, either in our own days, or in the thousands of years recorded in history, which proves the existence of any natural agents, within or without the bowels of the earth, of force sufficient to heave, to the height of 15,000 feet, such masses as the Andes. The difference between the power necessary to produce such an effect, and that which shuffled together the different parts of Calabria in our days, is so immense, that, from the existence of the latter we are not authorised to infer that of the former.

M. de Voltaire has suggested a third solution of this difficulty. He cites an instance in Touraine, where, in the space of 80 years, a particular spot of earth had been twice metamorphosed into soft stone, which had become hard when employed in building. In this stone shells of various kinds were produced, discoverable at first only with the microscope, but afterwards growing with the stone. From this fact, I suppose, he would have us infer, that, besides the usual process for generating shells by the elaboration of earth and water in animal vessels, nature may have provided an equivalent operation, by passing the same materials through the pores of calcareous earths and stones: as we see calcareous dropstones generating every day by the percolation of water through lime-stone, and new marble forming in the quarries from which the old has been taken out; and it might be asked, whether it is more difficult for nature to shoot the calcareous juice into the form of a shell, than other juices into the forms of chrystals, plants, animals, according to the construction of the vessels through which they pass? There is a wonder somewhere. Is it greatest on this branch of the dilemma; on that which supposes the existence of a power, of which we have no evidence in any other case; or on the first, which requires us to believe the creation of a body of water, and its subsequent annihilation? The establishment of the instance, cited by M. de Voltaire, of the growth of shells unattached to animal bodies, would have been that of his theory. But he has not established it. He has not even left it on ground so respectable as to have rendered it an object of enquiry to the literati of his own country. Abandoning this fact, therefore, the three hypotheses are equally unsatisfactory; and we must be contented to acknowledge, that this great phænomenon is as yet unsolved. Ignorance is preferable to error; and he is less remote from the truth who believes nothing, than he who believes what is wrong.

Ant-hill Town

J. Hector St. John de Crèvecoeur (1735–1813)

French immigrant J. Hector St. John de Crèvecoeur's *Letters from an American Farmer* (1787) is often viewed as the first great work of American literature. This collection of personal essays about his adopted country was written at his home in Orange County, New York, during the early years of the Revolution. "Ant-hill Town," the only piece set in the Central Atlantic, is one of several essays that were omitted from *Letters* and discovered and published in 1925 under the title *Sketches of Eighteenth-Century America*. Several of the *Letters* and *Sketches* are largely or entirely nature essays, but most are slices of American life worthy of Mark Twain. De Crèvecoeur, like Thoreau, sought every opportunity to use nature for ethical teaching: "Ant-hill Town" displays his skill at weaving moral challenges and social criticism into Arcadian idylls. His approach to nature writing is the now completely familiar personal style associated with John Burroughs and later authors.

From *Sketches of Eighteenth-Century America* (New Haven: Yale University Press, 1925)

I am now sitting under one of the most enchanting groves of Virginia; 'tis the work of art, but executed with so much simplicity as greatly to resemble that of Nature. 'Tis an octagon frame round which vines and honeysuckles have been planted. They have grown with such luxuriancy; their limbs and foliage are so interwoven as to refuse all admittance to the rays of the sun, yet leave a free passage to the air. Round this verdant temple, at an equal distance, stands a double row of the mellifluous locusts, the umbrageous catalpas, and the soft magnolias. Alternately planted, they expand their friendly limbs all round and repel the scorching rays of the sun. 'Tis a grove of Tempé; 'tis a Druidical temple, in point of gloom, shade, and solitude.

From this predilected spot, which is my daily resort, an avenue leads to the house, a second to a private garden, and a third to a bath; while the front expands towards an extensive lawn, a very rare thing here, and opens the view to a variety of luxuriant fields of tobacco, corn, etc., reaching to the very shores of that noble river which is the boundary of this province. By extending beyond the Potomac, the country rises into a most delightful perspective, composed of plantations, buildings intermixed with copses of trees, peach orchards, etc. There is still something wanting: the pride and principal ornaments of more moist, more northern climates. Here they want the verdant lawns of England, of Ireland, and Normandy; all their art cannot produce that which Nature and the soil seem to refuse. To the south, you have an imperfect view of that great and capacious bay where all the great rivers of this province disembogue themselves. The great number of small gulfs, of bays, islands, and shoals formed by the confluence of so many streams affords food and asylum to an amazing number of ducks, of geese, swans, etc. This is the place where the sport they afford presents itself to all those who care not what fatigues they undergo provided that pleasure is annexed to it.

This rural scene where I am now, this sylvan bower, appears to me so much the more enchanting on account of the cool, the calm, the placid retreat it affords because I contrast it with the scorching fury of their sun, which is now ripening with its fullest energy their extensive harvests. Here it is that I forget the toils of my late journey; the fatigues it occasioned seem now but a moderate purchase for the ease I feel. I am in that state which conveys the most harmless and indefinable happiness. . . . Harvest and the joys it spreads are themes which ought to inspire me with the rural song. Unfortunately it is not very applicable to this country where the grain is gathered by slaves and where their daily toils absorb the very idea of joys.

What revolutions do we experience in great as well as in small concerns! Life is but a checkered surface, every step of which is perpetually diversified. 'Tis not two months ago that in the province of Massachusetts I thought myself happy to sit by the comfortable fireside of ———; and I thought his warm room, his clean hearth afforded the greatest felicity and amply supplied the place of their then heatless sun. 'Tis not two months since his potent Madeira, his enlivening pipe afforded me a fund of cheerfulness that now would be improper. There, reading their provincial newspapers, I beheld with pleasure a fictitious renovation of the spring in the growth of the evergreen which overran his mantle-piece. Now, on the contrary, I stand surrounded with these southern blasts, big with igneous particles and ready to inflame one of the most irascible of matters. We had, three days ago, a most solemn trial, one of the most awful thunder-storms ever remembered.

But, however agreeable this part of America is in consequence of the hospitality of its inhabitants, the temperate zones of Europe are much superior to it. There it is that mankind enjoy a gentleness of seasons which is much more favourable to the increase of mankind and to the preservation of their health. There, husbandry may be displayed in all its perfection and beauty; here, one sees and feels nothing but extremes. But exclusive of those primary advantages to be enjoyed, nowhere but in the country is there a great variety of other pleasing sensations which never entered into the head of an inhabitant of cities. I don't mean those belonging to the well-pursued plan of an extensive rural economy, which govern and pursue the useful labours of a large landed estate; much less do I mean those fantastic ones often transplanted from the bosom of cities. No, those I mean are those which indeed I have often felt. They, properly speaking, afford no vulgar enjoyment; 'tis a multitude of pleasing sensations from whence one may collect instruction, morality, rectitude of judgement, motives of gratitude.

Here, they have no towns of any note, and I am glad of it. How I hate to dwell in these accumulated and crowded cities! They are but the confined theatre of cupidity; they exhibit nothing but the action and reaction of a variety of passions, which, being confined within narrower channels, impel one another with the greatest vigour. The same passions are more rare in the country; and, from their greater extent and expansion, they are but necessary gales. I always delighted to live in the country. Have you never felt at the returning of spring a glow of general pleasure, an indiscernible something that pervades our whole frame, an inward involuntary admiration of everything which surrounds us? 'Tis then the beauties of Nature, everywhere spread, seem to swell every sentiment as she swells every juice. She dissolves herself in universal love and seems to lead us to the same sentiments. Did you ever, unmoved, pass by a large orchard in full bloom without feeling an uncommon ravishment, not only arising from the exquisite perfumes surrounding you on all sides, but from the very splendour of the scene? Who can at this time of the year observe the ushering in of buds, the unfolding of leaves, the appearance of flowers, the whole progress of vegetation, and remain insensible? The well-known industry of bees, that excellent government which pervades their habitations, that never-ceasing industry by which they are actuated, though sung by so many poets and long since become the subject of so many allusions, metaphors, and the theme of so many orators—yet 'tis a subject ever new. Set yourself down under some trees in their neighborhood; see them arriving with the spoils from the fields; observe the digested dews, the concocted ethereal particles of flowers and blossoms converted by them into honey. When these industrious citizens are all out, open one of their hives and see the wonderful instinct which leads them by the most invariable rules to project and to execute with so much regularity that variety of cells calculated to contain their honey, their coarser food, as well as the eggs from whence new swarms are to arise.

Have not the regular arrival and departure of certain birds ever set you a-thinking whence they came? Have you never reflected on the sublimity of the knowledge they possess in order to overcome so many difficulties, to steer so invariable a course to other more favourable regions unseen by men, either in their flight or return? When in the spring you happen to revisit some trees of your own planting, have you never felt something of the paternal affection, of that peculiar satisfaction which attends viewing the works of our hands? Have you never enjoyed as you ought the transcendent pleasure attending that magnificent scene—unheeded, alas, by most men—because it is often repeated? Have you never worshipped the Master of Nature in the most August of all temples, in that extensive one of His own framing where He no doubt presides as the great invisible Pontiff but where He permits His awful representative to become visible in order to bless mankind with light and life? Have you never observed the sun rising on a calm morning? What majesty pervades, then, all Nature when the variegated aspect of the heavens, when those mixed tinges of emerging light and vanishing shades, united with that diffusive [emanation] issuing from the fecundated earth, exhibit the most August spectacle which this transitory life affords!

How often have I viewed with admiration that sublime gradation of objects reaching and filling the whole extent of my perception: from the refulgent luminary to the fainting moon, to the dimmed stars, down to the vocal choir, even to the polygonal cobweb, perpendicularly hung or horizontally suspended—all bespangled with dewdrops refulgent as the diamond, waving to the raptured eyes! 'Tis not that I would mean to recommend to you the worship of fire in this solar appearance. I am far from believing with the disciples of Zoroaster, that the sun is the true Shekinah of the divine presence, the grand tabernacle, the Keblah where He alone resides. No, but relegated as we are at such a distance from the great Author of all, is not it a consolation to view scenes of this nature, by which we are elevated and permitted in thought to approach nearer to His throne? 'Tis in the country alone that you can follow this rotation of objects which feeds contemplation, which delights, improves, and often assuages the pains of an afflicted mind. Even the approach of a thunder-storm, though so dreaded by the generality of mankind—how solemn, how awful, what reverence does it not inspire us with! Nature seems angry. Yes, but it is for our good, and she wisely draws from that strife of elements the salubrity of the air we breathe.

As soon as the sea breeze came, I took a walk towards the shores of the river. As I was searching for the most convenient spot to descend to the shores, I perceived a large flat stone lying on the ground. As they are very scarce in this part of the country, I stopped to view it and to consider whether it had not been left there on some peculiar account. On looking at it more attentively, I perceived the marks of ancient sea-shells encrusted on its surface. How could this stone have received these marine impressions? How could it be brought here where stones are so scarce? Hoping to find some of these shell fragments better preserved on the opposite side, I lifted it up with some difficulty, when to my great surprise and amusement I found that it served as a roof to a subterranean structure of a very singular appearance. It covered the upper walks of a town seemingly composed of arches, of vaults, of a multitude of passages intermixed throughout the whole. From these obscure mansions there were a number of apertures leading to the excavated surface which was covered by the stone. It was cut into a great number of streets, sometimes contiguous and parallel to each other, sometimes receding in various directions. These streets were divided from each other by little banks of earth of a different thickness, as is the case in winter-time in the streets of Quebec. The whole surface was about thirty-five inches long and about twenty-three broad. It contained seventy-one streets and had fourteen subterraneous openings. The first idea it conveyed was that of a labyrinth; but on following with attention any one of the streets, the intricacy vanished.

In order to have a fuller view of this scene of mysterious ingenuity, I removed the stone with the utmost care. On the south-east and north-west sides, I perceived two considerable breaches full three inches wide gradually sloping from the surface of the ground to the subterranean avenues. These were, I suppose, the two great communications to fetch their foods and to carry off their unnecessary materials.

Here lived thousands of ants of the pismire class. But no pen can delineate the seeming confusion and affright which my bold intrusion caused among them; it was a whole republic thrown into the most imminent danger. The never-failing impulse of instinct immediately led them to provide for the preservation of their young. They appeared to be as big as small grains of wheat and seemed to have been brought up from the lower habitations in order to receive more immediately the prolific effects of the sun's heat and to swell their limbs into life and action. These embryos appeared to be in a different degree of animal advancement. Some seemed quite torpid and lifeless; others showed marks of feeling and pains on being suddenly seized, though by maternal claws. No sooner was the first effect of their panic over than they hurried away their young out of my sight; but as they were more numerous than the parents, more assistance immediately came from below, or else the same individuals returned to the pious office. In about five minutes, not the least vestiges were left of that numerous society, and no one could have believed that it had been replenished with so many inhabitants. In this great national dismay, no one quitted the mansion or attempted to make his escape although they knew not what sort of enemy I was. The whole community, bound by the ties of the firmest confederacy, unanimously went down, trusting, perhaps, to their works of defence or to my inability to pursue them where all appeared so dark and so intricate.

What a situation for this Virginia republic when the refulgent sun at once pervaded every corner of their habitation, where his rays had never reached before! We may, then, pronounce that what the stone covered were their paths of life and health, the cradles of their rising generations. Their other and invisible recesses must have far exceeded this little insignificant surface; for, no doubt, it must have afforded them convenient rooms for their winter-stores, receptacles for their daily food, besides capacious lodgings for so many thousand inhabitants.

Should I turn up and destroy so fair a monument of industry? Should I overwhelm in death and desolation so many harmless animals? No, I could not permit myself to satisfy so impious a curiosity at the expense of so much evil and to pollute my hands by the commission of so atrocious a deed; on the contrary, I replaced the stone.

A few days afterwards, I paid them a second visit, when I observed a great number of ants decorated with wings. But this gaudy attire did not appear to add any celerity to their flight; they never expanded them. Like the preposterous dress of some ladies it served only to render them more conspicuous than the rest. Upon a closer inspection, they appeared more inactive and wholly deprived of that quickness of motion for which the unwinged sort are so remarkable. Perhaps they were the matrons of the republic, never departing from that formal gravity appointed to the rank by Nature; perhaps they were young damsels embarrassed by the rule of modesty and decorum; perhaps they were young ones just hatched, not having as yet ventured to traverse the air in order to harden their limbs in the aspect of the sun. How sorry that I never have read Buffon! I could have explained myself technically, whereas I am now speaking to you in the language of a schoolboy who possesses as yet nothing of knowledge besides curiosity.

Within a few rods and nearer to the river were erected eleven great conical buildings three feet high and two and a half broad at the bottom. They were perforated with an immense number of holes. The whole appeared to be built of slight materials; yet, by means of sticks and straws, the ends of which only were visible, they had given it a great degree of stability. The inhabitants of this second colony appeared to be of a much larger size, much stronger, and more capable of lifting heavy burthens. What surprised me was that although so near this subterranean settlement, yet there appeared no kind of communication between them. Weak and defenceless as the first were, a perfect peace and tranquility prevailed, a most marvellous thing considering the superiority which the one had over the other species. This harmony must have arisen from their feeding on different things. In this case, there could be no room either for contention or competition, no cause that could influence their little passions and produce those sanguinary commotions so frequent among mankind. The circumjacent ground which surrounded these eleven pyramids was perfectly cleaned; neither bush, shrub, nor herbage, or any foliage whatever grew nigh that might conceal or harbour any enemy. They had made considerable paths to the waterside, as well as to different fields in which they invariably travelled; but I never followed them in any of their excursions.

The same Pythagorean disposition which prevented me from turning up the bowels of the first republic in order to satisfy a vain curiosity made me refrain from tumbling down one of these cones which might have showed me the structure within. Whether these serve them only as summer habitations and are but a collection of materials excavated from below, I dare not ascertain. Such as it presented itself to my view, it seems to answer all their purposes and to preserve them from the inclemency of the air, wind, and rain. What other casual accidents may happen is no doubt quickly repaired by the mutual assistance of so many alert and vigorous insects.

Annalostan Island *and*
The Great Falls of the Potomac

David Ballie Warden (1772–1845)

Like many other Irish patriots, David Ballie Warden was exiled by British justice. After becoming an American citizen, Warden served this country as a diplomat in Paris, where he eventually took up permanent residence. While living in Washington, he collected both documents of American history and native plants and animals. His natural history collections were contributed to French museums; his collections of books were purchased for Harvard and the State Library of New York. Although he published two monumental histories of America—one in English and one in French—his most significant contribution to historiography was his bibliography of American history.

During his Washington years, Warden produced the first comprehensive report on the city and its environs: *A Chorographical and Statistical Description of the District of Columbia*. This imposing title belies the amusing mix of personal anecdotes, landscape appreciation, natural history, and cultural information that makes up most of the *Description*'s text. And, of course, there are several tables of statistical facts and lists of plants and animals that are firsts for the District.

The following excerpts give benchmark information on two landmarks on the Potomac River: Annalostan Island (now renamed for Theodore Roosevelt) and the Great Falls.

Both selections from *A Chorographical and Statistical Description of the District of Columbia* (Paris: 1816)

Annalostan Island

ANNALOSTAN ISLAND, the seat of General Mason, is situated in the river Potomac, opposite Georgetown, and contains nearly seventy acres. A flat boat, of a rude construction, awkwardly impelled by an oar, placed near each extremity, affords a safe conveyance between the island and the main land, a distance of about two hundred yards. . . . On one side, the island is now connected with the main land by an artificial mound, or causeway, which was raised at the expense of the government, for the purpose of stopping the current on this side of the island, and thereby increasing the depth of the water in the Georgetown Channel. This current, in 1784, was considerably deepened by the passage of an immense quantity of ice, that forced itself down after a sudden thaw, and carried with it large masses of the muddy bottom. The Georgetown Channel has been but little deepened by the erection of this causeway. . . .

Annalostan Island is evidently of modern formation. In searching for water, a mass of trees was discovered at the depth of fifteen feet. General Mason instructed a workman (Bryan Duffy) to cut through them. After having removed several of large dimensions, he threw aside his axe, swearing by J——s "that he now met huge ones with their tops upwards." In other places, water was found at the depth of twenty-five or thirty feet. The highest eminence, on which the house stands, is fifty feet above the level of the river. The common tide rises to the height of three feet. I can never forget how delighted I was with my first visit to this island. The amiable ladies whom I had the pleasure to accompany, left their carriage at Georgetown, and we walked to the mansion-house under a delicious shade. The blossoms of the cherry, apple, and peach trees, of the hawthorn and aromatic shrubs, filled the air with their fragrance. We found Mrs. M. at home, in the midst of her family, composed of nine children. . . .

Their house, of a simple and neat form, is situated near that side of the island which commands a view of the Potomac, the President's House, Capitol, and other buildings. The garden, the sides of which are washed by the waters of the river, is ornamented with a variety of trees and shrubs, and, in the midst, there is a lawn covered with a beautiful verdure. . . .The summer-house is shaded by oak and linden-trees, the coolness and tranquility of which invite to contemplation. The refreshing breezes of the Potomac, and the gentle murmuring of its waters against the rocks, the warbling of birds, and the mournful aspect of weeping-willows, inspire a thousand various sensations. What a delicious shade—

"Ducere solicitae jucunda oblivia vitae."

The view from this spot is delightful. It embraces the picturesque banks of the Potomac, a portion of the city, and an expanse of water, of which the bridge terminates the view. Numerous vessels ply backwards and forwards to animate the scene. Directing the eye over a corner of the garden, we perceive the sails only, as if by enchantment, gliding through the trees. A few feet below the summer-house the rocks afford seats, where those who are fond of fishing may indulge in this amusement. . . .

This island has a great variety of trees and shrubs, owing to the seeds brought by the stream from mountainous regions—different species of oak, walnut, mulberry, poplar, locust, ash, willow, the papaw and spindle tree, or burning-bush.

At the summer-house there is a white walnut of about a foot in diameter, perforated by a grape vine of three inches in circumference, which has been squeezed to death by the growth of the tree.

Near the causey there is a species of eglantine, thirty feet in length, and three inches in diameter, which is supported by a neighbouring friendly tree.

The poison-oak, or poison-vine, grows here, and entwines itself among trees, but is easily distinguished by the mossy appearance of its stem. Its touch creates an irruption over the body, which is usually accompanied with fever; and this disease is said to renew itself yearly about the time of the first attack. The poison-ash, or fringe-tree, grows at the extremity of the island, near the causey. A foreign plant of this species was sent to General Mason as a curiosity, and it was recognised by a farmer, unacquainted with botany, to be the same as that which inhabits the American woods.

The Virginia jessamine grows in all parts of the island, entwining itself among trees and bushes. It flowers in June. The flowers, during sun-shine, are infested with red ants.

Several species of asclepias grow here. That with purple flowers, which blows in July, contains in its seed capsules, a kind of silk, which, mixed with cotton, forms a very durable thread.

The asclepias with orange flowers is here called pleurisy-root, a name derived from this malady, for which it is supposed to be a sovereign remedy. A decoction of the root is a powerful sudorific, and is employed by the blacks as a cure for all diseases.

The crimson flowers of the American redbud, or Judas-tree, appear early in spring, and have a fine effect.

The sassafras-tree thrives well here: its leaves are the first which change their colour in autumn. Mrs. M. informed me, that an infusion of them affords a beverage of a pleasant aromatic taste, which might be employed as a substitute for tea. . . .

This island is the resort of various reptiles. We found the nest of the terrapin, or fresh-water turtle, in the garden, at the distance of about thirty feet from the water, containing nineteen eggs, laid close to each other, and the interstices filled with earth. The greater circumference of the egg was four inches and a half; the lesser, three. The nest, or hole, was of an oval form, and four inches in depth. The eggs of this species are deposited from the first of June to the middle of July. Before the turtle commences the formation of the hole for her eggs, she urines on the spot, then scrapes out a little earth, again urines, and thus continues until the operation is finished. I saw another nest, from which the turtle was taken at the moment when she had placed herself in an almost erect position to deposit her eggs, which she always performs during the day, and, it is said, never returns to the spot. The young ones are hatched by the heat of the sun, and are supposed to remain in the nest till spring. Several persons, whom I consulted on this subject, assured me, that they have turned them up with the plough at this season. The turtle, when shaken before she lays her eggs, makes a hollow noise, as if she contained water. One in this state weighed six pounds, which, it appears, is the common size. The species known by the name of the terrapin is very shy, and ceases to walk as soon as it sees a person approach near it. When endeavouring to escape, it runs nearly as fast as a duck. The blacks make soup and eat the eggs of this species, of which they are very fond.

The snapping turtle is also seen in the waters of this river, some of which weigh from forty to fifty pounds, and lay forty or fifty eggs. General Mason, some years ago, caught one of a huge size, which he threw into his canoe, and it attacked him so furiously therein, that he was obliged to leap into the water. The reptile followed, and thus made its escape. Its bite is severe and dangerous.

Two species of fresh-water tortoise inhabit the island; namely, the painted tortoise, *emys picta* or *testudo picta*, and the streaked tortoise, *emys virgulata*. . . .

The head of the painted turtle manifested symptoms of life two hours after decapitation. Three cherry stones were found in the stomach. It is said that small snails are its daily food. This species is not eaten. The musk-rat inhabits the banks of this island. The surface being now cleared, there is no place for its habitation, which was formerly constructed of vegetable substances, in the midst of the reeds of a marsh, and was generally five or six feet in height, and as many in breadth. The family reposed in a dry and neat apartment above the surface of the water, into which they descended when attacked, and retreated by a subterraneous passage to a neighbouring stream. If the family were numerous, there were three such passages; if otherwise, one or two only. A method of taking them, practised by the savages, was to discover and intercept this communication, by means of knots of twisted grass. The animal then returned to the water under its abode, where, forced to seek air, it shewed its head, and was struck dead with a stick or club. The musk-rat abounds in the swamp adjoining the Potomac Bridge, and is killed by the blacks in a curious manner. A square board, bearing a considerable weight of stones or mud, is placed in an inclined position, and is supported by three sticks in a particular manner. Parsnips are put underneath, of which the rats are very fond; while devouring them, they necessarily move one of these sticks, by which the board suddenly falls, and crushes them to death. The skin sells at twenty-five cents.

The deer, wild turkey, canvas-back duck, and wild goose, which inhabited this place about fifty years ago, have all disappeared. This species of duck, so delicious to the taste, was then sold for sixpence.

The following method was formerly employed to kill the wild goose. This bird, shy and cunning, feeds in the midst of a plain or open field, and forms a regular line, at the extremity of which is placed a centinel, to give warning in case of danger, which, if remote, is indicated by a certain position of the head, and if imminent, by a certain cry. The sportsman, by means of a docile horse, which concealed him from the view, approached slowly, until he brought them within the reach of his gun.

By an act of 1730, the shooting of deer was prohibited from the first of January to the first of August. The penalty was four hundred pounds of tobacco. By other acts of 1728, any master, mistress, owner of a family, or single taxable person, was obliged to produce yearly, to the justice of the county, three squirrel-scalps, or crows' heads. The penalty in this case was three pounds of tobacco. A premium of two pounds was given for every scalp more than three. The reward for a wolf's head was two hundred pounds.

Annalostan Island abounds with birds of various kinds. The cat-bird is almost tame. When its nest is in danger, it makes a loud noise, and seems as if it would tear the face of the person who approaches it. We saw in the garden a partridge nest, containing nineteen eggs. The humming-bird frequents this place. When caught, it feigns death, like the opossum, and, by this means, escapes from the hand. We saw one thus escape from the pretty hand of Mrs. B——e.

The mocking-bird does not frequent this island, though it is seen on the adjacent borders of the river. Perhaps it has been expelled by the crow black-bird, its natural enemy, which swarms in this place. It is a pity that so enchanting a spot is deprived of the notes of this inimitable songster.

"The wild and romantic scenery of the Great Falls . . . is scarcely to be equalled." Great Falls, Potomac River, W. Sheppard, steel engraving from *Picturesque America*, 1872

[The Great Falls of the Potomac]

The distance from Washington to the falls of the Potomac on the Virginia side is about twenty miles. By the bridge, above Georgetown, near the Little-Falls, it was five miles shorter; but, some years ago, this bridge was destroyed, by the pressure of accumulated ice and water after a sudden thaw, and has not been since repaired. The wild and romantic scenery of the *Great Falls,* which are seen most to advantage from the Virginia side, is scarcely to be equalled. There is a stupendous projecting rock covered with cedar, where one may sit and gaze at the waters dashing with impetuosity over the rugged surface. At the close of winter, vast masses of ice, rolling over the rocks with hideous crash, present a scene truly sublime. To those whose curiosity leads them to visit this terrific sport of nature, it may be useful to mention, that at a small distance, M. de Caraman, and the writer of this account, found a hospitable cabin that afforded oats to their horses, and eggs, milk, and ham for themselves. Several delicious springs issue from a neighbouring hill, which commands an enchanting prospect. The trees which abound here most are willow, birch, cedar, and oaks, of different species. The yellow jessamine is of a prodigious size. The prickly pear grows on the banks of the canal. White hore-hound and sweet-fennel, of which there is great plenty, are employed by the inhabitants for medicinal drinks. The odour of aromatic plants seems to be much stronger here than in the Low-Lands. Of wild cherries and strawberries there is great redundance. The banks of the river are infested by different species of snakes, particularly the black, rattle, and copper-head snake.

Views of the Blue Ridge and the Shenandoah Valley

James Kirke Paulding (1778–1860)

James Kirke Paulding was an unabashed lover of every region of his country. A New Yorker by birth and upbringing, he was nonetheless Jeffersonian in outlook. An antiromantic, he wrote essays, poems, history, and novels that satirized European society and literary styles and promoted pride in America's institutions and landscape. Together with Washington Irving, his relation by marriage, he produced *Sal-magundi* in 1807 and 1808. His other best-known works are *The Diverting History of John Bull and Brother Jonathan* (1812), a comic and anti-English history of America, and *Westward Ho!* (1832), a novel of the Kentucky frontier.

In 1816, Paulding toured Virginia; the next year, he published his experiences in a two-volume book entitled *Letters from the South*. Brief descriptions of nature and landscape complement his friendly comments on Virginia's people and transmontane agricultural establishment. Paulding's direct style and his honest emotional responses to nature separate him from the more effusive and the more sentimental American followers of Sir Walter Scott, whose work Paulding parodied, and from the English romantic poets who sought symbolic meaning or transcendent experience in nature.

From *Letters from the South* (New York: 1817)

Letter IX

Dear Frank,

The first view we got of the mountains was from a hill a few miles from Louisa courthouse. You know I was raised, as they say in Virginia, among the mountains of the North, and I never see one that it does not conjure up a hundred pleasing associations. . . . It was . . . evening when we first caught a view of the distant undulating mountain, whose fading blue outline could hardly be distinguished from the blue sky with which it almost seemed to mingle. Between us and the mountain was spread a wide landscape,—shade softening into shade, with such imperceptible gradations, as blended the whole an indescribable harmony. Over all was spread that rich purple hue, which painters have often attempted to imitate in vain. All that they have been able to do is, to put us in mind of it, and leave the rest to imagination—This is a good hint to me, and so I will say no more at present about the mountain. . . .

Letter X

Dear Frank,

. . . We rose in the morning, bright and early, to descend the mountain, "all in the merry month" of June, the sweetest month of all the year, notwithstanding what our poets sing about May. This may be a very pleasant month in Italy or Greece, but commend me to something a little warmer than our May, which deals too much in north-east storms, to be quite to my taste. Were I a first-rate poet, that is to say, a lord or a Scotsman, I would certainly pluck the crown of flowers from the head of May, to place it on the sunny brow of June, there to bloom in the midst of genial gales and fostering sunbeams.

In descending the mountain, we had a view, which, not being common even here, and entirely unknown among you, citizens, deserves at least an attempt to sketch it. We saw what seemed a vast and interminable waste of waters, spreading far and wide, and covering the whole face of the lower world. The vapours of the night had settled in the wide valley, at the foot of the hill, and enveloped it in one unbroken sheet of mist, that in the grey obscurity of the morning, looked like a boundless ocean. But as the sun rose, a gentle breeze sprung up, and the vapours began to be in motion. As they lifted themselves lazily from the ground, and rolled in closer masses toward the mountains, the face of nature gradually disclosed itself in all its varied and enchanting beauty. The imaginary sea became a fertile valley, extending up and down, as far as the eye could reach. In the midst of green foliage of oaks and solemn pines, were seen rich cultivated lands, and comfortable farm-houses, surrounded by ruddy fields of clover, speckled with groups of cattle grazing in its luxuriant pasture, or reposing quietly among its blossoms. Still, as the mists passed silently away, new objects disclosed themselves, with a sweet delay, that enhanced their beauty. Here was seen a little town, and near it a field, animated with sturdy labourers. In one place two little rivers, after winding and coquetting through the meadows, some-times approaching, sometimes receding, sometimes hid, and sometimes seen, joining their currents, and finally disappeared in the distant woods, beyond which a high peaked cliff, towering above the ascending vapours, glittered in the beams of the morning sun, like a giant capt with helmet of burnished gold. It seemed as if a new and blooming world was gradually emerging from chaos, and assuming the most beautiful arrangement, under the hand of some invisible agent cradled in the mists of the morning.

It seldom falls to the lot of the city mortals to see such a scene—and it is seldom, I am told, that it fall to the lot of a traveler to behold it more than once. The impression it made I have since recalled with new delight. I hope to retain the remembrance for a long time, and when at last it fades away in the succession of new scenes, new objects, new enjoyments, and new suf-ferings, I shall think I have lost a cherished relic of past times.

The Blackwater Chronicle

Philip Pendleton Kennedy (1808–1864)

By the middle of the nineteenth century, settlement was filling in the gaps left by the westward movement of the Manifest Destiny years. The approaches to the mountain valleys and remote plateau lands in the Appalachians had become accessible by good roads and even rail. Sportsmen seeking virgin hunting grounds and fishing streams hired local guides for backcountry expeditions that reenacted on a smaller, less risky scale the explorations of colonial times.

The fishing party assembled by Martinsburg, (now West) Virginia, lawyer Philip Kennedy produced two books: Kennedy's *The Blackwater Chronicle* and *A Visit to the Virginian Canaan* by David Strother, alias Porte Crayon. Strother made a second trip to the Canaan Valley, West Virginia, and the nearby falls of the Blackwater River; his journals were published in *Harper's* and later as a book. Both Kennedy's *Chronicle* and Strother's reprint were national and international successes, putting this high and heavily forested region on the tourist's map.

From *The Blackwater Chronicle: A Narrative of an Expedition into the Land of Canaan in Randolph County, Virginia* (New York: Redfield, 1853)

IF THE READER will take down the map of Virginia, and look at Randolph county, he will find that the Blackwater is a stream that makes down from the north into the Cheat river, some few miles below the point where that river is formed by the junction of the Dry fork, the Laurel fork, and the Glade fork—the Shavers, or Great fork, falling in some miles below: all rising and running along the western side of the Backbone of the Alleganies.

The country embraced by these head-waters of the Cheat river is called "The Canaan"—a wilderness of broken and rugged mountains—its streams falling through deep clefts, or leaping down in great cataracts, into the Cheat, that sweeps the base of the Backbone.

It is to the Blackwater, one among the largest of these streams of the Canaan, that we purpose to take the reader. If, therefore, his fancy urges him to the venture, let him come with us. All he has to do is to set himself down in his easy-chair, and lend us his ears. By the magic of this scroll we shall take him.

This Blackwater (it should be called Amberwater), and north source of the Cheat, rises high up on the western slope of the Backbone, directly across from the Fairfax stone—where the head-spring of the Potomac has its source on this the eastern side of the mountain; and it is supposed that these head-waters of the two rivers are not more than some half a mile (or mile at most) apart. The Backbone, following a general course from north to south, here turns at almost a right-angle, and takes across to the eastward some fifteen miles, when it regains its former southerly direction, thus forming a zigzag in its course. At the point where it first makes the bend to the east, a large spur—apparently the Backbone itself—keeps straight to the south, and butts down on the Cheat, at the distance of some ten or twelve miles. Between this large spur and the point where the Backbone bends to the south again, is contained the cove of mountains which is called the Canaan. This region of country is in the very highest range of the Alleganies, lying in the main some three thousand feet above the level of the sea.

Until a few years past, the whole of the district embraced by the head-waters of the Potomac and the Cheat was as remote and inaccessible as any part of the long range of the Alleganies. But some few years ago, the state of Virginia constructed a graded road from Winchester to Parkersburg, which passes over the Backbone through the Potomac limits; and consequently this portion of the district has become opened out somewhat to the knowledge of the world, and has since been settled to a considerable extent. The Baltimore and Ohio railroad also passes near here—at a distance from the head-waters of the Potomac varying from ten to twenty miles. The railroad will bring all this region within a day's travel of the seaboard; and as the country lies about the head of the Maryland glades—in themselves a source of attraction—and contains within its range many tracts of land of great fertility and beauty, it is not irrational to suppose that it will be cleared out and settled with rapidity.

As it is, there is a good settlement around here already—the result, in the main, of the construction of the Northwestern road. Long, however, before this road was made, there was a Mr. Smith who pitched his tent in these wilds some fifty years or more ago, I am informed, and cleared out and improved a handsome estate for himself, lying along the Maryland shore of the Potomac, and containing some fifteen hundred acres of fine land of varied hill and dale. The Smiths are now gone, and the estate has passed into other hands. In the older times a tavern was kept here, for the accommodation of the few people who crossed these mountains. But when the north-western road came by, the marvels of a good highway were made manifest in the increased travel, that soon became too great for the capabilities of the once-unfriended inn. About this period, a gentleman from the city of Washington, journeying this way to escape the heats of the seaboard, was so taken with the pleasant temperature of the air and the wild beauty of the mountains, that he bought the place—impelled somewhat thereto, no doubt, by the trout in the streams and the deer in the forests. Under his rule a new house was erected, large enough to hold a goodly company. This is the house—fair enough to look upon in its outside array, and comfortable enough within—that now stands imposing, not far away from the old one, on the brow of a lofty hill overlooking the Potomac. "Winston" the place is called—so called because the eighty-seventh milestone from Winchester is won when you reach its door. Edward Towers keeps it—or did, when the Blackwater expedition won the stone. Here, for some years past, many of our citizens, of both Virginia and Maryland, have been in the habit of resorting in the summer and fall months, to fish for trout, hunt the deer, shoot pheasants, wild turkeys, woodcock in their season, and enjoy the invigorating atmosphere of a country whose level is so high above the sea.

The ride to this place over the Northwestern road is exquisitely delightful, and withal as easy as a ride can well be. You travel over a graded slate road—the perfection of a summer highway—engineered skilfully, and at but a low grade, through the gorges and defiles of these fine mountains, and, when crossing any of them, seeming to have been carried over purposely at those points where the scenery is of the grandest or most beautiful character. Take it altogether, for the excellence of the road, and the varied combinations of scenery that are ever presenting themselves to view, there is no route across the mountains anywhere that excels it. With a pair of good horses in a light carriage, you can speed along all the way as if you were taking an evening drive about your home, even though your home be where the roads are the best in the land. And then, what exhilaration of spirit is felt by you as you roll smoothly along at the rate of some ten miles an hour, your horses scarcely stretching a trace—seeming merely to keep out of the way of the wheels!—on one side of you a deep gorge, a thousand feet down, dark with hemlocks and firs, where a mountain-stream breaks its way to the sea; above you, high-towering peaks and overhanging cliffs, where the oak or stately fir has cast anchor, and held on for ages in defiance of all the storms of the Alleganies; while before you, afar off, glittering in the sunshine, are seen in glimpses the green fields and meadows of some fair, luxuriant valley; and the whole horizon bounded by lofty mountains that seem to defy all approach, but which you at length wind your way through by some concealed cleft, the bed of a stream, with scarcely any more of obstruction than a bowling-green would present to your glowing wheels.

There are but few things more agreeably exciting to the spirits than a rapid drive through the country on a good road. There are some who will not assent to this proposition; but they are not to be deferred to in these matters of *fastness*, and do not understand the philosophy of the human soul. "The power of agitation upon the spirits," says Dr. Johnson, "is well known. Every man has felt his heart lightened by a rapid drive or a gallop on a swift horse.". . .

It was toward the first of June last past, that a number of gentlemen, residing near each other, in a pleasant part of that rich valley vaunted to the world as *the garden of Virginia*, and called by the people of the mountain-ranges back of it *the land of Egypt*, from the quantity of grain which it produces, determined to make a pleasure expedition into the Allegany country, having it chiefly in view to harry its streams for trout. Accordingly, on one fine morning—it was on the last day of the universally-lauded month of May—we gathered together, prepared as best we knew how for the expedition. . . .

We drove to Winchester, a town when George II. was king here in Virginia: not one of your recent cities, grown up to a hundred thousand people within the memory of men alive, but an old, time-honored town, of some five thousand souls, with remembrances about it; familiar to the footsteps of Thomas, the sixth Lord Fairfax, when he lived at Greenway court (some ten miles off), and held power as lieutenant of the county of Frederick, hunted the boar, wrote for "The Spectator," and set twenty covers daily at his table: famous, too, in our provincial history, as the military headquarters of Washington during the war of '65 against the French for the possession of the western country. Here, to this old border stronghold of the Dominion, where the dismantled ramparts of Fort Loudon still look down upon the town, we drove over night, a matter of some twenty miles, ready to make a more sustained movement the next morning on Winston—some eighty-seven miles distant, as already stated, on the Northwestern road.

The expedition travelled in three light carriages, such as are commonly called *wagons*, all tight and sound, freshly washed, oiled, and rubbed, and glittering in the sun "like images:" each wagon drawn by a vigorous trotter in fine condition, and able on a good road easily to make such time as would have satisfied Dr. Johnson, even though his philosophy of happiness should have required a greater speed than ten miles an hour. We were five in all: the sixth didn't go, that gentleman having failed us by the way, owing to some anxieties he entertained about trusting himself so high up on the continent. But no matter; we were yet five. There was—

Mr. Peter Botecote, generally called Butcut by his familiars—sometimes But;

Mr. Guy Philips, the Master of the priory of St. Philips: hence familiarly the master, sometimes the Prior, and occasionally "the county Guy;"

Triptolemus Todd, Esq., our Murad the Unlucky, and sometimes Trip;

Doctor Adolphus Blandy, physician to the expedition: Galen he was called for short;

And the Signor Andante Strozzi, our artist, also amateur musician. . . .

After an early breakfast at about sunrise, we left the hotel in Winchester on the morning of the 1st of June; and taking out the Northwestern road, we went on our way rejoicing. Passing through the North mountain, five miles out, where it breaks down almost on a level with the valley we had just left, we entered fairly into the mountain region—whence it is nothing but chain after chain, until you cross over the broad belt to the great, spreading, western, shining plain, watered by the Mississippi and its tributaries.

For several hours we travelled along without stint or stay, filled with the bliss of this first morning of June. Our horses tread the ground lightly, vigorous and nimble-footed, no touch of weariness yet upon them; and our swift wheels turn with scarce-perceptible sound—a mere low hum along the slaty road. Delicious is the summer's day, delicious to both soul and sense! No poet's dream of June was ever so enchanting. It has rained over night, and fresh and fragrant everywhere is the morning. The forest-leaves are all washed clean as the waters of heaven can make them, and the grasses are more delicately green in their renewal. The rain-drops, not yet dried up, sparkle all over the forest, in the glittering sunshine, like beads of pearl. All nature, animate and inanimate—on four legs, two, or none—feels the heavenly influence of the hour. The woods are vocal with the rapturous voice of birds. The wild-flowers—the wild-rose and the wood-violet, the gorgeous laurel, and the sweet elder-bloom—in all their freshened glory, give their delicate perfumes to the liberal air, and their hues of heaven to the enraptured sight. The streams, sometimes crossing our path, and sometimes flowing on by our side—seeming to go with us whichever way we go—flowing on adown the dell or by the rifted rock, and all embowered with shrubs and tangled vines: these sing their sweet songs tuneful to the ear, until at length, ecstasy—born of the murmuring waters, the balm of the air, the glory of the wild-flowers, the warble of the birds, and the smooth velocity of your rheda—enters into the heart, and pervades your countenance with a radiance that is almost divine.

Thus full of all joy that is born of summer and the mountains, we speed on our way—to happiness and to Winston! . . .

[A]fter some two hours' travel, through the green valleys and over other mountains, we at length came in sight of the little town of Romney, beautifully situated upon a sloping plateau of land that lies back of the high banks and bluffs of the South Branch; the river here flowing along in all its winding lines of beauty—on through rich bottoms and bold over-hanging mountains, to its junction with the Potomac.

Somewhere about four o'clock—after descending a long and beautiful sweep of road, grand enough in all its features to be the avenue to some lordly city—we drove up to the door of the village inn (the old Virginia designation is ordinary), situated pleasantly on the main street of Romney, and kept by Mr. Armstrong, formerly a member of Congress from this district, but who has for some years past chosen the better part—shaken the dust of the capitol from his feet, and commanded the respect and good will of all considerate people who travel this way, by the manner in which he discharges his present representative duty to the public. In this comfortable inn, we took our ease for the rest of the day, having accomplished just forty-four miles over those mountains, since first we drew rein in the morning. . . .

What time the skylark plumed his wing, the expedition awoke from its slumbers, and betimes arose; what time the sun peeped into the casements of the village hostel, it sat triumphant over a routed breakfast-table, and, like Alexander, sighed that it had no more to conquer. In this condition, he of Macedon took to drink—but we to our wagons, with a good-by to pleasant Romney.

The morning was delightfully bracing. Whether it was the mountain-air, or the mountain-oats, that inspired them, our horses carried themselves as proud as reindeers, and went down the main street of Romney with a free swing, fully up to the requirements of the Dr. Johnson philosophy in this matter. As we crossed the high plain to the bluffs of the river, the scenery of the South-Branch valley was just developing into expression—the mountain in bold masses, the winding river with its mists, the rich bottoms striped with cornfields, the long range of brown cliffs in the distance, and in the foreground the high plain on which sat the picturesque town: all in striking contrasts of light and shade; the dark shadows of the mountains, and the golden mists of the river; the spangled dewdrops on the meadows, and the funeral drapery of the pine-forests; Apollo, from his chariot of the sun, elimning some new glory of the picture, as he drove on up the steeps of the skies.

This glimpse of the sunrise-picture was all we saw, for it is but a mile from the town to the bluffs of the river, and these we have already gained. We now descended from the table-land, and crossed the South Branch by a good bridge. With the river on one side and the overhanging mountain on the other, we drove on for a mile or so; when we turned off, and passed through the mountain on almost a dead-level road, winding along the side of a stream that here makes its way through a deep cleft to the river. For some fifteen miles the road is a beautiful one—smooth, and of easy grade in its gradual rise toward the Alleganies; now hugging the hills, now following the bends of the streams, now through valleys spotted with farm-houses and green with luxuriant grass. At length we came to the Knobley, which we ascended, passing through a hamlet scattered carelessly along the cultivated slopes of the mountain. This mountain presents a very remarkable outline, being a succession of high knobs or peaks with intervening low depressions, giving it the appearance of an indented castle-wall. Through one of these depressions we crossed, and descended by easy traverses to the other side. For a mile or so we wound our way through the defiles of a broken range of hills, and emerged at length into a narrow and beautifully-picturesque valley—the Allegany piled up in grand masses on one side, and the road running for some miles along the banks of a clear, rapid stream, known hereabouts as New creek—just such a stream, so wild and cool, as the imagination would fill with trout a foot and a quarter long, and some four inches deep behind the shoulders.

By the side of the sparkling creek, with (no doubt) trout to be had for the casting of a fly, or the impaling of a worm, we found a large and comfortable brick house, where a Mr. Reese keeps an inn highly spoken of in these parts for its excellent accommodations. At the base of the Allegany stands invitingly the mountain-embowered inn. In front of this is the clear, cool, wild, dancing stream; and up beyond this again, rises with bold ascent, almost at right-angles to the water, a richly-wooded spur of the Allegany, colored with all-blended hues of green, from the pale tea-color of the mountain-ash, to the dark, grand, gloom green, almost invisible green, of the clustered fir-trees and hemlocks—these the nobler pines that more particularly distinguish the forests of the Allegany ranges.

From Reese's house, at the base, it is seven miles to the top of the Allegany—something of an Olympus to the warts behind us. Mindful of our horses, we gird up our loins for the encounter, and take to the heaven-kissing hill afoot. Half-way up there is a fountain of pure spring-water caught in a rude trough by the roadside; and men and horses gather around, and revel in the mountain hippocrene. The lookout from here is already grand. Far and wide you behold the land we have travelled. On we go again, up and up, still up; and the air you breathe is freer, and the scene wilder and yet more widely revealed at every turn of the road, rounding each rocky promontory that juts the mountain-side.

In something more than two hours we reached the toll-gate, situated near the summit of the ridge, and commanding a prospect of all the land lying abroad to the eastward. This is one of the grandest and most diversified mountain-scenes in the whole range of our country: mountains piled on mountains everywhere, of every variety of size and shape, with all their valleys, glens, gorges, dells, and narrow defiles—all yet varied by the changing light and shade that falls upon them from the heavens—as the heavens are ablaze with sunshine, or swept by passing summer-clouds. . . .

The sun by this time is riding nearly midway in the skies, and we hasten on to the summit of the mountain, seven miles up from its base. We have climbed "the mighty Helvelyn;" and, what is more, we have said our say in doing it, to the honor and glory of the land, and the confounding of its enemies, their aiders and abettors. Here you gaze over the plateau of the wide Allegany ranges—some twenty miles across by the road; and far in the distance you behold the Backbone—the Taurus of the belt—down whose rugged sides the waters flow east and west into the far seas.

Some four or five miles on our way, more or less descending, on the side of a long hill that slopes down to Stony river, we stopped for the middle of the day at a large stone inn, kept open to the world by William Poole. . . .

In due course of time we once more encountered the road; and after a drive of some twelve miles, over the undulating tops of this wide belt of mountains, down their gorges, through the passes, by farms lately cleared and green with wild timothy, bluegrass, and white clover—the natural growth of these fine grazing regions—we at length crossed the Potomac, and winding up a long, fair sweep of hill, slackened rein before the gates of Winston.

It was somewhere about five o'clock when we won the stone, having driven some forty-three miles since we left the pleasant town of Romney in the early morning: forty-three miles of such delightful travel as can hardly be found elsewhere within our borders.

We hailed our resting-place with divers and manifold exclamations of surprise and delight, which brought the alert Towers to the hostel-gates, in a very broad-brimmed straw hat, stuck all over with fishing hooks and lines. The castle of Winston stands, like the castle of Richmond, "fair on the hill;" and although it did not greet our eyes with the feudal grandeur of Norham—with warders on the turrets, donjon-keep, loophole grates where captives weep, and the banner of St. George flapping idly in the breeze, as that famous hold met the gaze of Marmion and his train as they came "pricking o'er the hill," yet it looked cheerful and pleasant enough—had an air of something even like elegance as the western sun shed its splendor upon it. The porches with which it was arrayed imparted a look as of something "bedecked, ornate, and gay," like Delilah, Samson's wife, "this way sailing." Above all, it filled the mind perforce with comfortable thoughts of the mountain-breeze, as it spread itself out on the brow of a commanding hill—a grand hill, that stretches down for half a mile in bold, lawn-like sweeps, to the Potomac: the river here flowing along in all wild beauty, some twelve or fifteen miles below where it emerges, a wimpling rill, from the slopes of the Backbone. . . .

The head-fountain of the Potomac rises high on the eastern side of the dividing Allegany ridge, not far below the cone of the mountain, and near the boundary stone planted by Lord Fairfax to mark the farthest limit of that princely territory—embracing all the country lying between the waters of the Potomac and Rappahannock rivers—which he inherited as a grant from the British crown. The Potomac is formed, in its very beginnings, by the union of several smaller springs with this head-spring, as they descend the steeps of the mountain. The little rivulet, pursuing its course along the base of the Backbone, is gradually augmented by the springs that flow down in every direction through the ravines around, until it attains a breadth of some thirty feet at the small falls, about five miles below its source. Below the falls there are some eight or ten streams making into it: the Big Laurel, Little Laurel, Sand run, and Shields's run, on the Maryland side; the Horseshoe, Buffalo run, the Dog's Hind-Leg, and some others, on the Virginia shore. This accession of little streams swells it into quite a sizeable mountain river by the time it reaches opposite to Winston. It is here some sixty feet wide—a clear, fresh, wild stream, reflecting every pebble that lies in its bed—shaded by stately forests, and fringed with vines and flowers. Of course, it is filled with trout; and although it is a good deal fished by those who frequent here in the summer, yet it still continues to yield up its treasure in sufficient abundance for the constant supply of the table at Winston.

For two days we made unceasing war throughout this Potomac region, as far up as the falls. The first day we brought in over two hundred fish, some of them of fine size. The second day we took more, having invaded some of the larger tributary streams mentioned above. So it will be seen we had trout in abundance.

When the third day came round, there was a general desire expressed, when we assembled at the breakfast-table, to foray in some new country. We had invaded the Potomac in all reason—having in these two days pretty well gone over the ground hereabouts. The mind of desultory man is still as studious of change, and pleased with novelty, under our republican order of things, as it has been heretofore under the older polities of the world. Indeed, it is a characteristic of our American Saxon, exceeding that of all others of the Saxon, or any other combination. . . . But where to go?—that is the question. Mexico has been taken—and where shall we find a Cuba? Some proposed an incursion into the Glades, over about Snow creek, said to be unfrequented ground: one was for the Evergreen-glades, another for the Oak-glades; some for the lower Potomac—but there were rattlesnakes down the river, it was said, and that was a damper. In this variety of opinion, the indolent policy prevailed: and it was determined to pass the day *sub tegmine*—rambling over the hills, and in the enjoyment of an easy, lounging time of it about the porches of the inn.

Sitting on the long porch that fronts the river, enjoying the cool breeze that seems always to fan these hill-tops, some mention, among our other talk, happened to be made of "THE CANAAN," or wilderness-country, over on the head-waters of the Cheat. It so happened that one of our party had been told, many years ago, that this land of Canaan was as perfect a wilderness as our continent contained, although it was not many miles away from the Glades on one side, and the long settled parts of Hardy and Randolph counties on the other; a country where the wild beasts of the forest yet roamed as unmolested as they did when the Indians held possession of our borders; a howling wilderness of some twenty or thirty miles' compass, begirt on all sides by civilization, yet unexplored. This statement was brought to mind by the casual mention of the country as we sat talking upon the porch; and it led to much inquiry in regard to the wilderness. Our landlord, as soon as the subject was broached, entered largely into it, and dilated upon the wonders of the Canaan in very glowing terms. It was only a few years ago, he told us, that elk had been killed upon its boundaries, not far from the settlements, at a place called the Elk-lick. He said there were deer in great herds—so wild, that they were almost tame. "And, gentlemen," he continued, with great animation, "if you can only reach the falls of the Blackwater, you can take more trout in an hour than you ever took before in all your lives."

"Ugh—uh!" exclaimed Triptolemus, with his usual chuckle.

"You don't tell me so!" said Peter, with open eyes and mouth.

"If you say so," resumed Mr. Towers, "we'll go into the country—Andrew can take care of the house—and we'll have such fishing as was never heard of. But understand now, gentlemen, you've go to do a little of the roughest and hardest sort of walking and climbing. Then there's the laurel you must go through. And you mustn't mind sleeping on hemlock, and in the rain too—it's always raining over on the Bone."

This was only applying additional stimulus to the desire that had already taken possession of us, and at all risks we determined to go on the morrow, provided we could secure the aid of two well-known hunters of this region to lead us on our way. Accordingly, we despatched a messenger to the house of Joe Powell, who lived on the borders of the Winston property, with a request that he would get John Conway, another hunter, living some miles farther off, and come down in the evening to see us. These men came over during the day, and it was all arranged before they left us, that we would set off in the morning early for the Blackwater.

Everything being put in train for the expedition, we gathered together on the long porch toward nightfall, and passed the time in much further discourse upon the Canaan—commenting variously on the information we had gathered from Powell and Conway, who had been out as far as the smaller falls of the Blackwater, hunting deer in the winter-season, but had never been at the great falls of the stream—the existence of which they only inferred from the roar of water that filled the forest, when they were out there. . . .

It was somewhere about four o'clock next morning when we began to give out in sleeping; and so, lightly and airily, with gentle breathings, whisperingly, we now soon finished off the last delicate touches and roundings of our dreams about bears, and panthers, and rattlesnakes, and lost babes in the woods (meaning thereby ourselves), &c., &c., just as the early cock uplifted his clear clarion, and roused his dame Pertelotte and all the attendant damsels of the roost from their slumbers. . . .

It was in this order that we began our march: Three of us were on horseback, with wallets hung across our saddles, containing the provant for the expedition—which provision consisted of six large loaves of bread; some pounds of ground coffee; sugar; about ten pounds of middling of bacon, to fry our trout with; a boiled ham; salt, pepper—and that's about all. Cigars and tobacco to smoke, each adventurer carried about his own person, together with a flask of spirits to cure himself in case he was bitten by a rattlesnake, or peradventure to prepare his system beforehand against any deleterious effects from the bite—a somewhat unnecessary precaution, indeed, since we were all pretty well convinced there were no snakes in the Canaan.

Three of us were afoot—two of our original party and Powell, one of the hunters—he equipped, among other things, with his rifle; Conway, the other hunter, we were to pick up on the way.

We were to ride and walk alternately—ride and tie—until we reached the end of the settlements, which was as far as we could take the horses.

Pursuing the Northwestern road some three miles, we reached the top of the Backbone ridge. Here, turning at right-angles to the left, we followed a mountain-road along the top of the ridge for some miles, which at length took its course along the eastern side of the mountain, gradually growing into a mere single horse-track, until we reached Conway's house, the last settlement in this direction. Here we picked up Conway, with his rifle and frying-pan; and after a walk of some six miles or more through a most noble forest of sugar-trees, the beech, maple, wild cherry, balsam-firs, and hemlocks, and over tracts of land wonderfully fertile, judging by the great size of the trees, and the growth of the wild timothy upon one or two slight clearings we passed through, we at length descended into a beautiful little glade—more properly a dale in the mountains—some three hundred yards wide and two or three miles long, where we were to turn out our horses to pasture until our return.

This dale is girt round upon its edges by a broad belt of the *Rhododendron*—commonly called the *big laurel* out here—which makes the dale a safe enclosure for keeping our horses; for it is impossible that a horse can make his way through it, so thick and lapped together everywhere are its branches. We had to enter it by a path cut out for the purpose. When within, we barricaded the entrance by piling up some young trees and brushwood (which was equivalent to putting up the bars in a fenced field), and rode on down the middle of the wild meadow, through green grass, knee-high, and waving gently in the summer wind, until we reached a small stream, whose banks were overgrown with osiers and other delicate shrubs.

This was the infant Potomac, destined before it reached the sea to expand into that mighty river on whose broad bosom whole navies may ride in safety or "flame in battle;" and also famous all over Christendom for that it holds fast-founded by its shores the capital of the star-emblazoned republic. Here we halted and dismounted—took off saddles and bridles—turned our horses loose—and prepared ourselves to enter the untrodden wild that rose up before us, dark with the glimmer and the gloom of the immemorial woods! . . .

Powell is in the lead followed by Conway, and we all start with a shout upon our walk—jumping the baby Potomac with a bound, and falling into a line of single file—winding through the long grass by a track made by the deer coming down into the dale to drink. The Signor waved his frying-pan aloft, and shouted out gayly the burden of some old hurrah song. The Master doubled up his hand and blew upon it for a buglet. Peter capered along nimbly, in dancing measure, like a fairy on the green—big wallet and all. Trip threw out his game leg, sweeping it against the tall grass, as a mower sweeps his scythe. And the Doctor took his last lingering look of Rinaldo— waved his lily hand and sighed adieu—

—"Adieu, for evermore, my love,
And adieu, for evermore!"

The horses snorted and plunged around us, with their tails flung over their backs, and hovered along our line, until we came to the belt of laurel that girts the edge of the meadow, when they wheeled, and left us to our fate—and we them to theirs. In a few moments we were breaking our way through the thick tangled branches of the laurel, and in mud and water half up to our knees. But we fought the way gallantly, and, gaining the firm ground, began the ascent of the mountain by a winding deer-track—the same we had followed through the dale. . . .

It was hard work in good earnest. But we went on up the rugged steep, scrambling our way as best we could, now through the thick underwood, now in among great masses of rock, and over fallen trees so decomposed that they would not bear your weight, until we reached what seemed to be the top of the mountain. . . .

The wilderness was growing wilder. We had, some time since, lost all trace of anything like even a deer-path. Still, pleasantly, and in fine spirits, we pursued our way. Now we had to climb some steep hill-side, clinging to the undergrowth to pull ourselves up, and now we would come up against a barrier of fallen trees—some of them six feet high as they lay along the ground, and coated with moss half a foot thick—some so decomposed that they recreated themselves in the young hemlocks and firs that grew up out of them—some more recently fallen, with great mounds of earth and stone heaved up with their roots; these mounds sometimes covered over by other trees thrown across them, and thus affording shelter to the wild animals from the snows and storms of winter. Over all these we would climb and roll ourselves across; and sometimes, such obstruction did they present to our course, we would be obliged to make a detour round for the length of a quarter of a mile may be, and find ourselves only advanced a hundred paces on the straight line of our route. It was thus we went along—up-hill and down—now along the side of a rib of the mountain—now over its cone, and now along it—down through deep ravines and up out of them, and scarcely able at any time to see further ahead than some twenty yards, so thick were the leaves about us; and not often able to catch a glimpse of the sun, so dense was the mass of foliage *umbrellaed* out everywhere above us. Still there was a great wild delight in it all; and by this time we had become somewhat inured to the work; we were beginning to improve in condition, and we felt our sinews and muscles coming into better play every step we took.

After awhile, thus pursuing our steady advance, we came to a small rivulet, trickling its way down a shallow ravine, and evidently making its course to the west. This was a little rill that sent forth its mite, high up in these loftiest regions, to form the waters of the Cheat river; the Cheat falling into the Monongahela—the Monongahela into the Ohio—the Ohio into the Mississippi—and so to the great Atlantic reservoir. It was clear, now, that we were on the other side of the Backbone. . . .

The hunters discoursing their lore of the forest, we came down to the edge of some swampy ground, and found ourselves in front of a wide stretch of laurel, tangled and thick everywhere around. To cross it—as it was clear it could not be avoided in any way—the hunters looked about for the best place to go in. At length, finding a spot that bid the fairest, they made their way into the brake, and desperately after them we all followed, as best we could. Such pulling and tugging—such twisting, plunging, breaking, crashing, and tearing—

"I never remember ever to have heard"—

or seen. Here was one held fast by his wallet, and twisting about like an eel to get himself loose; there another who had got upon a huge fallen tree— thus avoiding the laurel by walking along its surface as far as it reached

"Such pulling and tugging—such twisting, plunging, breaking, crashing, and tearing—
'I never remember ever to have heard'—or seen." Passing the Laurels, Porte Crayon
(D. H. Strother), from *Blackwater Chronicle*, 1853

through the swamp; but it was so decomposed, that presently he sank into it up to his arms—and he was stuck. Here another who had reached a stream, walking in it as far as in its windings it kept a course that corresponded with our direction. There one grown entirely desperate, and endeavoring to break his way through by main strength. The hunters took it more knowingly, and would search about for the thinnest places—sometimes going back upon their tracks when they would get into a very thick part of the brake, and trying it another way.

To tell how at last we all did get out, overtaxes any powers of description that I possess. . . .

[C]ommenting on the passage of the laurel, we moved on; and after a while, descending a long hillside, we came to the head of a glade, through which a stream of some size ran—its waters of a light-chocolate hue. We were very much jaded by this time; and so we threw ourselves down upon the soft, beautiful grass, knee-high everywhere around, and for half an hour enjoyed such grateful rest as seldom comes to the sons and daughters of men who stay in civilized regions; it recompensed even the laurel, so exquisite was the rest, and so gorgeous the bower where we took it! . . .

While yet the sun in his westward journey had but about an hour to go, before he left the Canaan to darkness and the expedition—not to mention the bears and owls, &c., about—a snake stole into our bower, and disturbed the heavenly repose of the glade. A very harmless, inoffensive little grass-snake—polished and slippery, disturbed by the rolling about of some one of the party, wound itself along swiftly over one of the extended arms of Doctor Blandy, as he lay sprawled out upon his back—gazing up into the heavens, and dreaming dreams of the balmy summer's eve. Galen sprang to his feet, and jumped some ten paces off into the meadow. Whereupon we all did the same. It was a rattlesnake at least to our startled imagination!—until we saw, to our shame, that it was not. Being on our feet, however, the word was given to take up the line of march again—and off we went: the guides being of opinion, that by crossing the ridge before us, we would come upon the Blackwater by night.

We made our way out of the glade, encountering but a small strip of laurel; and once more filed into the dense wild forest. As we advanced we grew more and more silent. We were evidently beginning to flag in spirit. It was our first day, and we were not yet inured to the toil. Every now and then some startled deer would give a little life to the party—but it would not last, and we trudged along almost noiseless over the mossy ground. Instead of the country's giving indication of our being near a stream such as the Blackwater, it was growing more hilly and broken ever since we left the glade. The shades of evening too, were fast closing in upon us. Something was wrong—we ought certainly to have reached the Blackwater before this. The hunters were evidently in doubt about their course, and they now held frequent consultations with each other. They had told us before we set off from the dale of the Potomac, that they would certainly take us to our destination by night, and they were anxious to accomplish their purpose; they feared their skill as guides would be called in question if they failed in what they had been so certain of accomplishing. It was now near sundown, and we were hemmed in, on all sides, by mountains. The impression that we were really lost was uppermost in the minds of all of us; and presently we held a general council—the result of which was, that if we did not come to some indication of the Blackwater, when we crossed the next ridge, we would encamp for the night.

Crossing over this ridge, everything looked as before. It was all the same rugged, dense, dark, deep, grand gloom of mountainous forest that we had left behind us—no appearance of laurel—the sure harbinger of water; no such sloping down of the hills anywhere, as looked like the descent into a valley, such as a stream of any size would find its way through; and above all, listen as intently as we might, no sound of a waterfall (such as we were assured would greet our ears from the river we sought) was mingled with the song of the evening wind. Therefore there was but one voice in the general assembly of the expedition—and that was to halt for the night, and take counsel of to-morrow's sun as to our direction. Finding a little tricking rill in the bed of a rugged ravine close at hand, we resolved upon taking up our abode by its waters for the night. Accordingly the most appropriate spot we could find was selected; and throwing down our burdens in a pile, we commenced the construction of a camp, with a great deal of busy bustle. As the reader unacquainted with the ways of a wilderness life, may take some interest in knowing how this was done, we will enter, for his benefit, into the particulars.

In the first place, then, the hunters set to work and gathered together a number of dried logs and limbs of trees, that they found scattered about the forest, making a pile some ten or twelve feet long, and three or four feet high. They then picked out the driest bark and branches of pine they could find, and laid them about through the pile. Next they raised some fire by striking sparks from the flints of their rifles into tow, and carefully applying this to the pine bark and other combustible wood they had gathered; it was not long before we had our wood-pile in a blaze—which was soon increased into a spreading and swelling flame, by the young hemlocks and fir trees that we were busily engaged for some time in cutting down and throwing upon the pile.

While a part of the force were engaged in this work, others were busy in arranging the camp. The ground was cleared away in front of the fire, and this place was covered over with the softest branches of hemlock that we could gather—two of the party being out cutting for the purpose. A large log was brought and laid along the back of the camp, and this was covered over to the height of two or three feet with hemlock and fir branches, serving as a sort of wall to protect us from any intrusion from that side, of beasts, or what not, that might be disposed to invade us during the night. The camp was so arranged, that when we slept, our heads would be against this barrier, and our feet to the fire. The sides also were filled up between the trees with branches. When it was all completed, we had a tenement—a lodge in the wilderness—the ground floor of which was hemlock branches a foot deep, three sides, also, hemlock and fir, and the fourth side a woodpile, twelve feet long, four feet high, and all afire. And the roof above us:—

"'Tis the blue vault of heaven, with its crescent so pale,
And all its bright spangles—quoth Allen-a-Dale!"

and where will you find a grander in a king's palace.

Our rifles, bags of provisions, coffee-pot, tin-cups, and frying-pan—all we had, were safely deposited in one corner of the lodge. The wallets were unrolled, and the blankets, great coats, &c., &c.—including the knives and pistols, were thrown out for use. Having cut down as many small trees as would serve to keep the fire going for the night, we now assembled in the camp, and commenced preparations for supper, for which we were by this time about as ravenous as the beasts of a menagerie about feeding time. The bread, biscuits, and cold ham, were brought forth. The sugar was untied. Conway sat about preparing the coffee: Powell started the frying-pan on the hot embers, and soon had it hissing and crackling with the slices of fat middling of bacon with which he filled it; until at length the more delicate aroma of the hemlock was lost to our noses, in the ascendancy of the bacon-side.

Those of us who were not engaged in these enticing preparations, were lying about on the hemlock, enjoying ourselves in the abandonment of forest undress—that is, in our stocking feet, with ungirded vest, unsuspendered; and spread out around, in all the various attitudes that it was possible for a set of tired men to stretch themselves in. At length the supper was announced as ready—and then it was devoured. To say that it was merely eaten up, would be a preposterous defamation of any ideas of eating, such as the word generally conveys in civilized life. In an exceeding short space of time, of all the liberal preparation, there were, at all events, no visible evidences remaining—except the table-service—the tin and the iron. . . .

[T]he supper was gone—juggled, or jugged away; and the animals to all appearances appeased. We now gathered into the inner penetralia of our hold; and stowed ourselves away in every violation of the rules of ceremony known to any of the nations of Christendom, or of the heathen—smoking cigars or pipes—telling stories, and singing songs, of love, war, romance, the chase, intermixed with our national anthems, and local ballads, pathetic or humorous, now in the harmony of Germany or of Italy, of France or old romantic Spain, and now to the strains of some low, dulcet, African refrain. Thus were passed the first watches of the night, until, at length, tired na-ture yielded to the omnipotence of sleep; and, hushed by the night winds murmuring among the immemorial trees, while the blazing pile at our feet illumined the forest around and above us with its silver and golden flame, imparting a magic sheen to the leaves and branches of the woods, until it all seemed the lighted tracery of some vast Gothic minster of the wild; and with nothing above us but the vault of heaven, studded with its glittering stars (which we couldn't see)—and nothing beneath us but the spicy smelling hemlock—and nothing over us but a blanket—we fell asleep, as sweetly and confidingly here in the wild, as children beneath the roof-tree of some guardian home. . . .

Presently the sun reddened the eastern sky, and the hunters getting the direction they proposed to try their fortune in, we set off through the yet dank and dewy forest. Our way was broken and rugged, up and down, through ravines that were deep chasms, and over great fallen trees covered with moss and wet as a sponge. Deer we saw frequently browsing about, and out here where perhaps they had never seen a human being before, they would lift up their heads and for a while gaze at us as if in wonder at what it all meant. Once or twice it was proposed to shoot one of them, but this was cried down as an act of wantonness, since we were already burdened with as much as we could carry; and, uncertain as to our being at all in the right di-rection, we were somewhat anxious and desirous to hasten on our way, while yet fresh from the night's rest.

There was one part of the wilderness which we traversed this morning, where we came frequently upon the traces of bear. Sometimes we would come upon the trunk of a dead tree, some hundred feet long, and five or six feet in diameter, scattered and raked about in all directions by the bears to get at the worms to eat. Sometimes we would find a cluster of trees, with the bark worn smooth, which the hunters told us was a certain indication that a family of these animals had been here raised, and were no doubt now in some hollow tree or fastness not far off.

Thus we walked along for several hours, probably at no greater rate than a mile an hour, and in some evident disheartenment—for we were not at all so light of spirit as we might have been, and would, had we felt more certain of our course. Every now and then when we stopped to rest, the conversation would take a debating turn, the subject discussed being generally the points of the compass; one asserting that here was the north, and another that it was in the very opposite direction. Peter's mind was always opposed to the hunters'; if they pointed this way for north, he was sure to point in the opposite, and maintain his point of the compass with much vehement speech; for he was by this time fully assured that the hunters had no knowledge of the country—in fact knew nothing of wood-craft at all. These debates were generally wound up by some very direct remark of Triptolemus's, proclaiming it as his opinion, that the hunters didn't know any more than he did, where we were—when some one of the more discreet members of the party would have to intimate to Powell and Conway, that Trip didn't mean as much as he said, for fear they might possibly lose their good temper, and leave the whole expedition in the lurch, by deserting us upon the first favorable opportunity: in which event it is altogether likely we would have remained out in the Canaan long enough to have resolved ourselves into our original wild elements, or to have become a pile of bones. But Powell and Conway were good-tempered men, and set down to the proper account all our insinuations against their knowledge; and generally retired to a little distance, and held some rational parley with each other upon the matter in doubt. . . .

We pursued our march along the cone of the ridge we were on for something better than a mile, when, coming to a halt, we distinctly heard a waterfall below us. There was no doubt about it now: and we descended the mountain-side with a shout. We met the laurel about half-way down the mountain—and breaking into it, after the necessary fighting, we filed down, one by one, along a great fir-tree that had, happily for us, fallen there some ten or twenty years before, and stepped out into the Blackwater, on a broad surface of rock—the very top itself of the falls we were seeking. In a few minutes we fixed up our fishing-lines, and, dotted along the edge of the fall which was about ten feet high, middle of the day as it was when the fish generally cease to bite, we took from the pool below some sixty trout, as fast as we could bait our hooks for them. Satisfied with this taste of the stream, and assured of our hopes of trout innumerable, we descended the falls, and looked about for a suitable spot to construct a camp, and prepare our dinner—for which, by this time, we were in no little need, having eaten nothing since the early twilight.

In the meantime, Mr. Butcut and Conway—fishing down the middle of the stream, and having caught some thirty or forty more trout as they came along—arrived at the falls, and thus the party were once more together— boastful over all our toil and suffering, and in high and happy spirits at the successful achievement of the enterprise out.

In the course of an hour a camp was constructed by the banks of the stream, about a hundred yards below the falls. A great blazing fire, such as we had the night before, was soon under way; and lazily stretched about on the hemlock, or out upon the large, moss-covered rocks that bordered the stream—now frying and eating a pan of trout at returning intervals, as a not quite sated appetite prompted, or taking a little sleep, as nature in- clined—we passed the hours until about four o'clock, when it was deemed advisable to sally forth for the purpose of laying in provision for our supper and the next morning's breakfast.

Leaving some of the party to perfect the works at the camp, and make everything as comfortable as possible for the night, we divided the rest into two bands, and set out—one up the stream, the other down—to make a somewhat extensive foray upon the trout.

We will not give a minute account of the evening's fishing. We will state generally that the inroad was very successful; that we took the trout as fast as we could bait for them; that in a walk of about a mile up the stream, and two miles down, and back, we at length arrived in camp with about as many fish as we could well carry—and were back all of us about an hour before dark, and all rather indifferent about taking any more trout that evening.

Immediately in front of the camp, and about a step out in the stream, is a large rock, in shape a parallelogram, of some five feet by ten, rising above the water about three feet, and of almost an entirely flat surface, except where at one end it is scooped into a slight hollow, that will hold some two or three buckets of water. This rock we have appropriated as our kitchen; and upon it we have counted out some five hundred trout, varying in size from six to ten inches—some of them, the black trout, with deep red spots—and some salmon-colored, with lighter red spots—all of them very beautiful, though not, of course, of the largest size of the fish; for we have yet to go down below the great falls of the Blackwater to get at them. . . .

Our Blackwater villa is placed in the most picturesque position imaginable—almost immediately upon the banks of the most lovely of all amber streams. It is protected on one side by masses of gray sandstone rock, dashed with spots of a darker and lighter hue of gray, and occasionally a tinge of red—these rocks coated over in places with moss of various mingled colors—gray, blue, green, yellow, and purple, and soft and glossy as the richest velvet. A noble overshadowing fir-tree rises up from one corner of the villa, some hundred and fifty feet, to the skies. The laurel grows thick and matted back of it, in impenetrable masses; and the glory of its flower, now just swelling into bloom, gives an air of elegance—even of splendor, to the embowered dwelling. In front, the pure cool stream leaps over the falls like a river of calf's-foot jelly with a spray of whipped syllabub on top of it, and tumbles wildly down through its rocky and obstructed bed, filling your imagination with the poetry of unpolluted mountain waters—running pure to your ideal, as the kingdom of heaven.

The valley of the Blackwater is not more than a hundred yards wide, here where we have made our home; and embowered on all sides, by mountains of noble forms and various, it wears an air of entire seclusion from the world we have deserted. No intruding footsteps of man, we instinctively feel, will here disturb our chosen, perfect solitude. All customs, manners, modes of life, that we have heretofore known, are felt to be the remembrance of an almost forgotten dream. The earth is entirely new to our senses; and it is all our own—an entire and absolutely perfect fee-simple estate of inheritance in land and water, the deed recorded in the most secret recesses of our own breasts. Therefore we feel an unbounded liberty of thought, speech, and action, and this is manifest in all we say and do; and hence the reader will easily understand how it is, that there is such entire freedom of remark among us, one to another; how it is that we lay about on the hemlock, now that night has set in upon us, in such careless luxuriance of attitude; how that the Prior is now stretched out with his feet to the fire, and one of the hunters squatted down confidingly between them; how the Signor goes on all fours over our bodies, in getting to a snug place in a corner of the camp, whither his fancy now urges him; how that Mr. Butcut is flat upon his back in the middle of the softest hemlock, his face direct to the heavens, and his body spread out as usual in his favorite position of a supple-jack distorted to the utmost; how Triptolemus's lame leg is thrown over one of old Conway's shoulders, with a view to the convenient drying of a wet stocking before the fire; how it is that Adolphus, with a blanket sweeping his shoulders, half sits, half reclines in among the roots of the great fir-tree, wishing he could smoke a mild Havana like the rest of us—but compensating his soul for his inability, by indulging in visions of trout swimming about in all beautiful imaginary waters—the daydream haunting the lights and shadows of his face like an angel of Paradise.

Lying about thus in all unrestrained felicity, we told stories, and discoursed much learning of the fisherman and the hunter, ancient and modern; every now and then interweaving some very entertaining and free—sometimes very slashing comment upon one another; all of which we regret it is out of the question for us to impart to the reader, because of its too great freedom, even for this outspoken age. Herein, therefore, that we may not fall below the dignity of history—having pitched our chronicle up to the very highest standard—we must exercise a becoming self-denial, hard as it is to refrain.

The moon has now risen, and although a few light fleecy clouds are gathering about here and there above us, yet the goddess of the night shines down as silvery soft upon the Canaan, as she did of old upon the garden of Verona, where Lorenzo and Jessica vied with each other in chanting her worship in such beautiful strains. . . .

The moon and the soft south wind held us now completely enthralled in their divine ravishment; and in this mood we grew musical—the Signor Andante at length tuning his voice to the beautiful serenade of Henry Neele: perhaps the most exquisite song that has yet been composed by any of our countrymen. It was thus Andante's voice, murmured a music sweeter than the Blackwater in our ears:—. . . .

The last notes of the serenade died away upon the air; and not a sound disturbed the repose of the wilderness, save the murmur of the waters, and the whisperings of the trees. Each one of us, according to his gifts, was enjoying a little world of romance of his own—his soul lapped up in the creations of his gently-inspired brain—thinking not at all of the external world, but only of the ideal, conjured up by his teeming, beguiling fancy; when all at once a sudden blow sprung up fitfully out of the stillness of the air, and threw the whole forest in commotion. The fire at our feet shot up a startling blaze, in among the branches of the piled-up fir and hemlock hitherto untouched, and the crackling flames, with their myriad spangles, rose high aloft in spiral curls, almost up to the overhanging branches of the forest. Startled out of all the glory of our visioned romance, we arose and looked out upon the night. Clouds were gathering like mustering bands everywhere in the heavens, and fast concentrating their forces. The stars disappeared by squadrons from the just now blue and shining vault of heaven; and the fair goddess of the night, queen of the glittering realm—pale Dian, veiled her mild glories altogether from our eyes. The southwest—harbinger of summer storms, is a swift and impetuous power in the air, and wonderfully does he bestir himself sometimes. So it was with him to-night; for he sprang up suddenly upon us, without any warning, and vented himself, for some cause or other to us unknown, in outbursts of gusty bluster and passion, that made us think of a whole deluge of waters descending upon our devoted camp, drowning out our fires and drenching our very beds. But for the present there was more of bravado than performance in his high mightiness; and the storm blast blew by. Still darkness was everywhere over the face of the earth, and the forest sent forth a low wail, and the waters murmured a sullen and monotonous song—falling upon the ear more like a heavy sea breaking lazily upon a flat shore, than the light, airy, wild, sportive, notes of the playful, impetuous, young streams of the mountains.

Each man now wrapped himself around more closely in his blanket. No word was spoken, but filled with the gloom of the night, we thought wistfully of our pleasant homes—dry and snug, and of household security and comfort—books, lights, music, fruits, flowers, jocund children—that is those who had them—the sly flirtation by the light of the chandelier—

"And mama, too, blind to discover
The small white hand in mine"—

—all that makes civilization tolerable; and we out here, in the wilds of the Canaan, far away from the knowledge of men—to say nothing of women— perhaps lost—and to all reasonable certainty a night of wind and rain before us—bears, panthers, wolves, owls, around us, and may be not so far off as we might desire! The melancholy soughing of the pines, too, above all the voices of the Canaan, had entered into our hearts, and awakened our superstition, and no diversion of thought could dispossess our souls of its influence. The Master, indeed, seemed rather to encourage it; for presently from out a dark corner, where half in the glimmer of the fire and half in the gloom of the hemlock he lay propped away in a very Ossianly state of mind, in a low, wild voice, all in harmony with the soughing sound of the firs and the sullen murmur of the waters, he broke in upon the gloom of the camp, crooning the beautiful ballad of Rossmore. . . .

"Hush your horrible croaking!" said Adolphus, when the Master's voice had come to a stand-still. "Shut up, or I'll leave the room! Isn't it all miserable enough already, but you must be keeping us from going to sleep with ballads about dying men, and such unearthly things?"...

About this time some drops of rain fell down heavily upon the leaves of the forest—premonitory of what was in store for us; and in five minutes more, we, our camp, and everything around, were drenched. As it seemed to be a rather settled, steady pouring down of the clouds, without any wind or noise of any sort about it—and as there was no help for it, the hunters secured the fire as well as they could (covering it over partially with some pieces of hemlock-bark); when, rooting ourselves about among each other like a litter of pigs in a barnyard, we soon fell asleep, in defiance of the pitiless elements. . . .

Undisturbed by any of the wild beasts, we slept through the rain until broad daylight, when we crawled out of our litter, and started the nearly-extinguished fire. The rain had ceased to fall sometime in the night; but the mist covered the mountains and enveloped the river; the forest was everywhere dripping wet, and for a while it was rather cheerless as we sat drooping before the slow fire. Soon, however, the flames took hold of the wood, and, as the blaze spread, our spirits revived.

The worst possible thing for a man to do, under any circumstances, is to sit down and droop: the very best, all the philosophers agree, is to go to work. So we picked up the hatchets and axe, and soon had a wagon-load of young hemlocks and firs upon the fire, making a flame that dried the atmosphere all around our villa. In doing this, it was discovered that we were as supple of joint and limb as if we had slept in moonshine; and when Triptolemus looked for his cold (which he had brought with him into the country), and couldn't find it—and Mr. Butcut felt himself lighter and freer in body than he had done since he started—it would have puzzled any one, coming fresh among us, to believe that we had slept out all night in the open air, in a drenching rain.

After breakfast, however, going beyond the encampment, and seeing everything still wet and uncomfortable, the hearts of some of the party began to fail them—and it was proposed that we should strike our camp for home. . . .

Although we were all perfectly unharmed by the exposure of the last night, yet the recollection of it affected the mind unpleasantly, and suggested visions of the comfort of Towers's hostel, which made against any very strong wish to remain out another night—such night in our Blackwater villa. But the secret of this desire to leave was attributable to the fact that the sun had not yet risen high enough to clear the hilltops, and disperse the mists and fogs of the morning, which after such a night of rain, had enveloped everywhere the beautiful world around. Let but the sun shine awhile, and the glory of the rhododendron—the beauty of light and shade—the splendor of the living green of the wild—the sheen and the sparkle of the waters—the summer-morning breeze—the song of the birds—all the glories of the month of June in the mountains—all these must enter into the heart, and bring gladness to despair itself. . . . [T]he two hunters, it was very evident, were keen-set for the exploration of the falls. No one up here knew anything about these falls, other than the conjecture of their existence: at any rate, there was no known man who had seen them. The pride of discovery, therefore, operated on the hunters. . . . [T]he sun began to shine out about this time, breaking through the mists of the valley; and it was agreed that the exploring party should go out, while the others would amuse themselves fishing or shooting in the neighborhood of the camp, and, if they tired of that, occupy themselves in ornamenting our villa, and in improving its sleeping apartment with a roof—so that, in case we abode here another night, we might be able to sleep without being drenched with the rain. . . .

[W]e pursued our way down the stream—now up to our knees in the water—now stooping under some great tree that had fallen across the stream—again along the banks, as they presented a better footway—now through the little meadows of luxuriant grass that skirted the shores of the stream—over islands of great rocks—breaking into the laurel to get round some hanging cliffs—sometimes stepping on a slippery stone, and going down soused all over in the water—until at length, some two miles below our camp, we came to the second falls. These are twelve feet high—a clear pitch, and in the shape of a horseshoe. The pool below them looked deep and dark, spotted with flakes of white foam and bubbles, and no doubt contained some large-sized trout. We did not stop, however, to test it, but proceeded on our course.

The sun by this time had risen high above the mountains, and was shining down upon the Canaan with all his refulgence. The river was ever turning in its course, and every few moments some new charm of scenery was given to our view. The atmosphere was soft and pleasantly warm, and the breeze gently fanned the trees. The wilderness was rich everywhere with hues of all dyes, and the banks of the river gleamed for miles with the flowers of the rhododendron. A scene of more enchantment it would be difficult to imagine. The forest with its hues of all shades of green—the river of delicate amber, filled with flakes of snow-white foam—and the splendor of

the rhododendron everywhere in your eye. Picture all this in the mind—
then remember that you were far beyond the limits of the world you had
known—and say, was it of heaven, or was it of earth! . . .

While we have stopped to dilate a little on the heavenly delights of the
Canaan, the exploring expedition did not stop, but wound its way down the
bed of the stream; and presently turning a rocky promontory that jutted
the mountain side, the Blackwater, some hundred yards ahead, seemed to
have disappeared entirely from the face of the earth, leaving nothing visible
down the chasm through which it vanished, but the tops of fir-trees and
hemlocks—and there stood on the perilous edge of a foaming precipice,
on a broad rock high above the flood, the Signor Andante (who had gone a-
head), demeaning himself like one who had lost his senses, his arms
stretched out wide before him, and at the top of his voice (which couldn't
be heard for the roar and tumult around him), pouring forth certain extravagant and very excited utterances; all that could be made out of which,
as the rest drew close to his side, was something or other about

—"The cataract of Lodore
Pealing its orisons,"

and other fragments of sublime madness about cataracts and waterfalls, to
be found at large in the writings of the higher bards.

Not stopping at all to benefit by the poetic and otherwise inspired out-
pouring of the wild and apparently maddened artist, thus venting himself
to the admiring rocks and mountains and tumbling waters around, the expedition stepped out upon the furthest verge and very pinnacle of the
foaming battlements, and gazed upon the sight, so wondrous and so wild,
thus presented to their astonished eyes.

No wonder that the Signor demeaned himself with so wild a joy: for

"All of wonderful and wild,
Had rapture for the artist child;"

and perhaps in all this broad land of ours, whose wonders are not yet half
revealed, no scene more beautifully grand ever broke on the eye of poet or
painter, historian or forester. The Blackwater here evidently breaks its way
sheer down through one of the ribs of the backbone of the Alleganies. The
chasm through which the river forces itself thus headlong tumultuous
down, is just wide enough to contain the actual breadth of the stream. On
either side, the mountains rise up, almost a perpendicular ascent, to the
height of some six hundred feet. They are covered down their sides, to the

very edge of the river, with the noblest of firs and hemlocks, and as far as the eye can see, with the laurel in all its most luxuriant growth—befitting undergrowth to such noble growth of forest, where every here and there some more towering and vast Balsam fir, shows his grand head, like

"Caractacus in act to rally his host."

From the brink of the falls, where we now stand, it is a clear pitch of some forty feet. Below, the water is received in a large bowl of some fifteen or twenty feet in depth, and some sixty or eighty feet across. Beyond this, the stream runs narrow for a short distance, bound in by huge masses of rock—some of them cubes of twenty feet—then pitches down another fall of some thirty feet of shelving descent—then on down among other great rocks, laying about in every variety of shape and size—all the time falling by leaps of more or less descent, until it comes to something like its usual level of running before it begins the pitch down the mountain. This level of the stream, however, is but

"The torrent's smoothness ere it dash below;"

for it leads you to a second large fall, a clear pitch again of some forty feet. From the top of this you look down some two hundred feet more of such shelving falls and leaping descent, as we have described above, until you come again to another short level of the stream. This, in its turn, is the approach to another large fall. Here the river makes a clear leap again of about some thirty feet, into another deep basin; and looking on below you, you see some two hundred feet or more of like shelving falls and rapid rush-down of the stream, as followed upon the other large falls. Getting down below all these, the river having now tumbled headlong down some six hundred feet, more or less, in somewhere about a mile, it makes a bend in its course, along the base of the mountain to the left, and mingles its amber waters with the darker flow of the Cheat: the Cheat some three times the size of the Blackwater; and roaring down between mountains (twelve or fifteen hundred feet sheer up above us), through, not a valley, but a rocky and savage chasm, scarcely wide enough to hold the river. . . .

We now prepared ourselves for the trout. It was by this time, near the middle of the day, too late, as we supposed, for any very good fishing; for the large fish generally by this time lie about in the bed of the streams, and are indifferent to the lure of the bait. Notwithstanding this, we had scarcely thrown our lines into the deep water before us, before our bait was seized. The Master drew up the first fish. He had thrown in just at the edge of the foam and spray of the fall, and a quick, bold pull swept his line through the foam. On the instant, with a switch of his rod sidewise, then throwing it up aloft, he *landed*, between his thighs (for it was water all around him) a fine vigorous trout, breaking off about two feet of the switch-end of his maple rod. This trout was a foot long, and some three inches deep behind the shoulders. Presently Powell drew out another of about the same size. Then the artist brought out a fine one from the bowl. And Conway, who by this time had picked up the best stick he could find, and tied a short bit of sea-weed to it—squatting down on his haunches, on a mossy rock, and looking the picture of some old sleepy satyr of the woods, pulled out his large fish without a word to anybody. It was great work; and the excitement intense. In the course of a quarter of an hour we had caught, among all of us, some twenty fine fish—some of them thirteen inches long—and this with no other bait than the common red worm. Indeed, if to take a quantity of trout be your only object, so full is the stream of them, and so ravenous are they, that with any sort of a line, and anything of a hook—a pin-hook if you can get no other—you may take as many as you can carry. But our tackle was good, and with the exception of a regular rod (which it would have been troublesome to have brought along upon so difficult an enterprise) we were reasonably well provided for the sport. If the reader will bear it in mind, that the Blackwater never in all probability had a line thrown in it before, he need wonder at nothing we can tell him about the quantity of trout it contains, or the greediness with which they bite at any sort of bait.

As our purpose to-day was rather to explore the falls than fish, we drew up our lines and proceeded down the torrent. By dint of much scrambling, and crawling, climbing, leaping, hanging, and every other sort of means you can think of, of getting yourself along—sometimes swept down by the strength of the current, and lodged in some side eddy or pool—driving out the trout, and getting up and shaking yourself, with some two or three craw-fish, about the size of your hand, sticking to your clothes—we made our way down below the second of the large falls. Here we fished again for a while, and caught some fifty more trout; some of us baiting our hooks with the gullets of the fish, cut out for that purpose; and some with the red fins, which we would cut off and use, by way of substitute for the fly, and which was found to answer the purpose as well as anything else.

Satisfied with the trial of the stream here, we drew up, and proceeded down our rugged way. Presently, missing the artist, who had gone ahead of us, we were under some apprehension that he had fallen down some of the rocks, and ended his mortal career, here and elsewhere—especially, when, after repeated calls, we could hear no answer from him. Moving down the stream, therefore, somewhat rapidly, we came upon a wide rock, over which the water lay about in pools; and where we saw scattered about, high and dry, a goodly number of large trout, dying and dead. Below this rock the Signor had let himself down some ten feet; and standing on a flat ledge, enveloped in spray from the water flowing down on either side of him, he was intently engaged in hauling out from a pool before him, the fine trout we saw around about as fast as he could bait his hook. He told us he had been here only some fifteen minutes; and when he ascended, without a dry shred upon him, from the watery grotto wherein he had enshrined himself, he gathered up some sixteen fish of the largest size we had taken that day.

Leaving our rods at this point, we went on as rapidly as we could make our way, down the falls, and finished our exploration to the mouth of the Blackwater. Here, sitting down to rest, we summed up our review of the falls—in which we settled down to the estimate above given, that the leap-down of the Blackwater must be some six hundred feet, in somewhere about a mile. The reader will understand that this estimate is made, not by guesswork, but upon some certain data; for we measured all the larger falls. It will be perceived, however, that we can not be far wrong in our computation, when we make the statement, that from the top of each of the larger falls, you see, at the distance of a few hundred yards down before you, the tops of fir-trees (their bodies not visible) peering up like bushes; and when you get down to them, you find they are great trees of some hundred feet or more in height. Standing upon the top of the first large fall, you look down upon some hundred and fifty feet or more, of the leap-down of the river—going down, then, to this point, you make a turn for some distance, and presently come upon the next large fall—from the top of which you look down upon about the same descent—and so on to the third. But enough. Let us now go back.

About half way up the falls a thunder-storm passed over us; and the reverberation down the chasm was exceedingly grand. Stopping under a hanging rock that afforded us shelter from the storm, we saw in the wet sand the footprints of otter, and other evidences of their inhabiting the stream. Presently there came a volleyed discharge of the heaven's cannon; and as the roar muttered itself away throughout the refts of the mountains, the sun broke out, and we proceeded on our way up the steep ascent—a rainbow over-arching the waterfalls, and the spray everywhere golden with sunbeams. At length, reaching the top of the grand chasm, and standing again on the brink of the impending rocks where we first hailed so rapturously, the leap-down of the river—we took a last look of the wild scene and went on our way to the camp.

Somewhere about five o'clock in the evening we came in, and depositing our spoils of the stream—about a hundred and fifty fine trout; we eat and recounted our adventures alternately, until we and our audience grew tired and fell asleep. . . .

Morning has dawned again upon the camp, and with it we arose to prepare for our homeward march. We took our last bath in the Blackwater, and at breakfast eat up all that remained of our provisions. . . .

With our wallets strapped on our shoulders, and all equipped for the march, we waited the rising of the sun, to marshal us the way we should go; for having no compass along, the god of day was our only guide, preserver, and friend. Presently, the sun arose, "blushing discontented" at the clouds around, and Powell, with his rifle in one hand and the frying-pan in the other, started up from his seat, followed first by Conway, then by all of us— and thus we broke our way into the laurel, making straight up the mountain, that rose high above us, dark and dense with all the green leaves of summer. . . .

Crossing the Cumberland Mountains

John Muir (1838–1914)

Published two years after his death, *A Thousand-Mile Walk to the Gulf* was John Muir's first book. It is the earliest portion of his diaries that has been published as a narrative. On this 1867 trek from Louisville, Kentucky, to the Florida Gulf Coast, Muir crossed the Appalachian Mountains near the Tennessee-North Carolina-Georgia border. His reaction to the mountains and their people is a mix of enthusiastic landscape description and caustic social anecdote that shows him, frankly, not at his best—intolerant of human weakness and exaggerating his pseudoreligious praise of nature. Yet, it is well worth reading because it contains Muir's first response to mountains of any kind and is a true record of the poverty of the mountain people.

The editors have not erred in including this piece whose milieu lies about one hundred miles south of the Central Atlantic proper, for the social and topographic conditions were and are much the same from central West Virginia to Georgia down the Appalachians. Although Muir correctly named the mountains through which he passed, they are now called the Unicois and the Snowbirds.

From *A Thousand-Mile Walk to the Gulf* (Boston: Houghton Mifflin, 1916)

I HAD long been looking from the wild woods and gardens of the Northern States to those of the warm South, and at last, all drawbacks overcome, I set forth on the first day of September, 1867, joyful and free, on a thousand-mile walk to the Gulf of Mexico. . . . Crossing the Ohio at Louisville . . . , I steered through the big city by compass without speaking a word to any one. Beyond the city I found a road running southward, and after passing a scatterment of suburban cabins and cottages I reached the green woods and spread out my pocket map to rough-hew a plan for my journey.

My plan was simply to push on in a general southward direction by the wildest, leafiest, and least trodden way I could find, promising the greatest extent of virgin forest. Folding my map, I shouldered my little bag and plant press and strode away among the old Kentucky oaks, rejoicing in splendid visions of pines and palms and tropic flowers in glorious array, not, however, without a few cold shadows of loneliness, although the great oaks seemed to spread their arms in welcome. . . .

September 17. . . .This is the most primitive country I have seen, primitive in everything. The remotest hidden parts of Wisconsin are far in advance of the mountain regions of Tennessee and North Carolina. But my host speaks of the "old-fashioned unenlightened times," like a philosopher in the best light of civilization. "I believe in Providence," said he. "Our fathers came into these valleys, got the richest of them, and skimmed off the cream of the soil. The worn-out ground won't yield no roastin' ears now. But the Lord foresaw this state of affairs, and prepared something else for us. And what is it? Why, He meant us to bust open these copper mines and gold mines, so that we may have money to buy the corn that we cannot raise." A most profound observation.

September 18. Up the mountain on the state line. The scenery is far grander than any I ever before beheld. The view extends from the Cumberland Mountains on the north far into Georgia and North Carolina to the south, an area of about five thousand square miles. Such an ocean of wooded, waving, swelling mountain beauty and grandeur is not to be described. Countless forest-clad hills, side by side in rows and groups, seemed to be enjoying the rich sunshine and remaining motionless only because they were so eagerly absorbing it. All were united by curves and slopes of inimitable softness and beauty. Oh, these forest gardens of our Father! What perfection, what divinity, in their architecture! What simplicity and mysterious complexity of detail! Who shall read the teaching of these sylvan pages, the glad brotherhood of rills that sing in the valleys, and all the happy creatures that dwell in them under the tender keeping of a Father's care?

September 19. Received another solemn warning of dangers on my way through the mountains. Was told by my worthy entertainer of a wondrous gap in the mountains which he advised me to see. "It is called Track Gap," said he, "from the great number of tracks in the rocks—bird tracks, bar tracks, hoss tracks, men tracks, all in the solid rock as if it had been mud." Bidding farewell to my worthy mountaineer and all his comfortable wonders, I pursued my way to the South.

As I was leaving, he repeated the warnings of danger ahead, saying that there were a good many people living like wild beasts on whatever they could steal, and that murders were sometimes committed for four or five dollars, and even less. While stopping with him I noticed that a man came regularly after dark to the house for his supper. He was armed with a gun, a pistol, and a long knife. My host told me that this man was at feud with one of his neighbors, and that they were prepared to shoot one another at sight. That neither of them could do any regular work or sleep in the same place two nights in succession. That they visited houses only for food, and as soon as the one that I saw had got his supper he went out and slept in the woods, without of course making a fire. His enemy did the same.

My entertainer told me that he was trying to make peace between these two men, because they both were good men, and if they would agree to stop their quarrel, they could then both go to work. Most of the food in this house was coffee without sugar, corn bread, and sometimes bacon. But the coffee was the greatest luxury which these people knew. The only way of obtaining it was by selling skins, or, in particular, "sang," that is ginseng, which found a market in far-off China.

My path all to-day led me along the leafy banks of the Hiwassee, a most impressive mountain river. Its channel is very rough, as it crosses the edges of upturned rock strata, some of them standing at right angles, or glancing off obliquely to right and left. Thus a multitude of short, resounding cataracts are produced, and the river is restrained from the headlong speed due to its volume and the inclination of its bed.

All the larger streams of uncultivated countries are mysteriously charming and beautiful, whether flowing in mountains or through swamps and plains. Their channels are interestingly sculptured, far more so than the grandest architectural works of man. The finest of the forests are usually found along their banks, and in the multitude of falls and rapids the wilderness finds a voice. Such a river is the Hiwassee, with its surface broken to a thousand sparkling gems, and its forest walls vine-draped and flowery as Eden. And how fine the songs it sings!

Spring at the Capital

John Burroughs (1837–1920)

It was in his Washington, D.C., years that John Burroughs, the most popular of all the nineteenth-century nature writers, found his literary voice. Here, he refined his subject matter and wrote his first book, *Notes on Walt Whitman as Poet and Person*. Here, under the guidance of Smithsonian scientists, he gained the technical knowledge that made his writing true to fact.

"Spring at the Capital" relates Burroughs's rambles through countryside now within the city of Washington, often in the company of Whitman, who had become his friend and teacher. First published in 1868, this essay later became a chapter in *Wake-Robin*, his first book of nature writing. The narrow valleys of Rock Creek and its tributaries enchanted Burroughs, as they have Washington residents since the city was founded. Eighty years later, Louis Halle recorded his pleasure there in *Spring in Washington*. He, like Burroughs and the present editors, thrilled to hear the veery's song in what seemed a wilderness, now less than one city block from rush-hour traffic.

The introduction to this anthology comments extensively on Burroughs's art and life.

From *Wake-Robin* (New York: Hurd and Houghton, 1871)

Spring at the Capital
With an Eye to the Birds

I CAME TO Washington to live in the fall of 1863, and, with the exception of a month each summer spent in the interior of New York, have lived here ever since.

I saw my first novelty in Natural History the day after my arrival. As I was walking near some woods north of the city, a grasshopper of prodigious size flew up from the ground and alighted in a tree. As I pursued him, he proved to be nearly as wild and as fleet of wing as a bird. I thought I had reached the capital of grasshopperdom, and that this was perhaps one of the chiefs or leaders, or perhaps the great High Cock O'lorum himself, taking an airing in the fields. I have never yet been able to settle the question, as every fall I start up a few of these gigantic specimens, which perch on the trees. They are about three inches long, of a gray striped or spotted color, and have quite a reptile look.

The greatest novelty I found, however, was the superb autumn weather, the bright, strong, electric days, lasting well into November, and the general mildness of the entire winter. Though the mercury occasionally sinks to zero, yet the earth is never so seared and blighted by the cold but that in some sheltered nook or corner signs of vegetable life still remain, which on a little encouragement even asserts itself. I have found wild flowers here every month in the year; violets in December, a single houstonia in January (the little lump of earth upon which it stood was frozen hard), and a tiny, weed-like plant, with a flower almost microscopic in its smallness, growing along graveled walks and in old plowed fields in February. The liverwort sometimes comes out as early as the first week in March, and the little frogs begin to pipe doubtfully about the same time. Apricot-trees are usually in bloom on All-Fool's Day and the apple-trees on May Day. By August, mother hen will lead forth her third brood, and I had a March pullet that came off with a family of her own in September. Our calendar is made for this climate. March is a spring month. One is quite sure to see some marked and striking change during the first eight or ten days. This season (1868) is a backward one, and the memorable change did not come till the 10th.

Then the sun rose up from a bed of vapors, and seemed fairly to dissolve with tenderness and warmth. For an hour or two the air was perfectly motionless, and full of low, humming, awakening sounds. The naked trees had a rapt, expectant look. From some unreclaimed common near by came the first strain of the song sparrow; so homely, because so old and familiar, yet so inexpressibly pleasing. Presently a full chorus of voices arose, tender, musical, half suppressed, but full of genuine hilarity and joy. The bluebird warbled, the robin called, the snowbird chattered, the meadowlark uttered her strong but tender note. Over a deserted field a turkey buzzard hovered low, and alighted on a stake in the fence, standing a moment with outstretched, vibrating wings till he was sure of his hold. A soft, warm, brooding day. Roads becoming dry in many places, and looking so good after the mud and the snow. I walk up beyond the boundary and over Meridian Hill. To move along the drying road and feel the delicious warmth is enough. The cattle low long and loud, and look wistfully into the distance. I sympathize with them. Never a spring comes but I have an almost irresistible desire to depart. Some nomadic or migrating instinct or reminiscence stirs within me. I ache to be off.

As I pass along, the high-hole calls in the distance precisely as I have heard him in the North. After a pause he repeats his summons. What can be more welcome to the ear than these early first sounds! They have such a margin of silence!

One need but pass the boundary of Washington city to be fairly in the country, and ten minutes' walk in the country brings one to real primitive woods. The town has not yet overflowed its limits like the great Northern commercial capitals, and Nature, wild and unkempt, comes up to its very threshold, and even in many places crosses it.

The woods, which I soon reach, are stark and still. The signs of returning life are so faint as to be almost imperceptible, but there is a fresh, earthy smell in the air, as if something had stirred here under the leaves. The crows caw above the wood, or walk about the brown fields. I look at the gray, silent trees long and long, but they show no sign. The catkins of some alders by a little pool have just swelled perceptibly; and, brushing away the dry leaves and debris on a sunny slope, I discover the liverwort just pushing up a fuzzy, tender sprout. But the waters have brought forth. The little frogs are musical. From every marsh and pool goes up their shrill but pleasing chorus. Peering into one of their haunts, a little body of semi-stagnant water, I discover masses of frogs' spawn covering the bottom. I take up great chunks of the cold, quivering jelly in my hands. In some places there are gallons of it. A youth who accompanies me wonders if it would not be good cooked, or if it could not be used as a substitute for eggs. It is a perfect jelly, of a slightly milky tinge, thickly imbedded with black spots about the size of a small bird's eye. When just deposited it is perfectly transparent. These hatch in eight or ten days, gradually absorb their gelatinous surroundings, and the tiny tadpoles issue forth.

In the city, even before the shop-windows have caught the inspiration, spring is heralded by the silver poplars which line all the streets and avenues. After a few mild, sunshiny March days, you suddenly perceive a change has come over the trees. Their tops have a less naked look. If the weather continues warm, a single day will work wonders. Presently each tree will be one vast plume of gray, downy tassels, while not the least speck of green foliage is visible. The first week in April these long mimic caterpillars lie all about the streets and fill the gutters.

The approach of spring is also indicated by the crows and buzzards, which rapidly multiply in the environs of the city, and grow bold and demonstrative. The crows are abundant here all winter, but are not very noticeable except as they pass high in air to and from their winter quarters in the Virginia woods. Early in the morning, as soon as it is light enough to discern them, there they are, streaming eastward across the sky, now in loose, scattered flocks, now in thick, dense masses, then singly and in pairs or triplets, but all setting in one direction, probably to the waters of eastern Maryland. Toward night they begin to return, flying in the same manner, and directing their course to the wooded heights on the Potomac, west of the city. In spring these diurnal mass movements cease; the clan breaks up, the rookery is abandoned, and the birds scatter broadcast over the land. This seems to be the course everywhere pursued. One would think that, when food was scarcest, the policy of separating into small bands or pairs, and dispersing over a wide country, would prevail, as a few might subsist where a larger number would starve. The truth is, however, that, in winter, food can be had only in certain clearly defined districts and tracts, as along rivers and the shores of bays and lakes.

A few miles north of Newburgh, on the Hudson, the crows go into winter quarters in the same manner, flying south in the morning and returning again at night, sometimes hugging the hills so close during a strong wind as to expose themselves to the clubs and stones of schoolboys ambushed behind trees and fences. The belated ones, that come laboring along just at dusk, are often so overcome by the long journey and the strong current that they seem almost on the point of sinking down whenever the wind or a rise in the ground calls upon them for an extra effort.

The turkey buzzards are noticeable about Washington as soon as the season begins to open, sailing leisurely along two or three hundred feet overhead, or sweeping low over some common or open space where, perchance, a dead puppy or pig or fowl has been thrown. Half a dozen will sometimes alight about some such object out on the commons, and, with their broad dusky wings lifted up to their full extent, threaten and chase each other, while perhaps one or two are feeding. Their wings are very large and flexible, and the slightest motion of them, while the bird stands upon the ground, suffices to lift its feet clear. Their movements when in air are very majestic and beautiful to the eye, being in every respect identical with those of our common hen or red-tailed hawk. They sail along in the same calm, effortless, interminable manner, and sweep around in the same ample spirals. The shape of their wings and tail, indeed their entire effect against the sky, except in size and color, is very nearly the same as that of the hawk mentioned. A dozen at a time may often be seen high in air, amusing themselves by sailing serenely round and round in the same circle.

They are less active and vigilant than the hawk; never poise themselves on the wing, never dive and gambol in the air, and never swoop down upon their prey; unlike the hawks also, they appear to have no enemies. The crow fights the hawk, and the kingbird and crow blackbird fight the crow; but neither takes any notice of the buzzard. He excites the enmity of none, for the reason that he molests none. The crow has an old grudge against the hawk, because the hawk robs the crow's nest and carries off his young; the kingbird's quarrel with the crow is upon the same grounds. But the buzzard never attacks live game, or feeds upon new flesh when old can be had.

In May, like the crows, they nearly all disappear very suddenly, probably to their breeding-haunts near the seashore. Do the males separate from the females at this time, and go by themselves? At any rate, in July I discovered that a large number of buzzards roosted in some woods near Rock Creek, about a mile from the city limits; and, as they do not nest anywhere in this vicinity, I thought they might be males. I happened to be detained late in the woods, watching the nest of a flying squirrel, when the buzzards, just after sundown, began to come by ones and twos and alight in the trees near me. Presently they came in greater numbers, but from the same direction, flapping low over the woods, and taking up their position in the middle branches. On alighting, each one would blow very audibly through his nose, just as a cow does when she lies down; this is the only sound I have ever heard the buzzard make. They would then stretch themselves, after the manner of turkeys, and walk along the limbs. Sometimes a decayed branch would break under the weight of two or three, when, with a great flapping, they would take up new positions. They continued to come till it was quite dark, and all the trees about me were full. I began to feel a little nervous, but kept my place. After it was entirely dark and all was still, I gathered a large pile of dry leaves and kindled it with a match, to see what they would think of a fire. Not a sound was heard till the pile of leaves was in full blaze, when instantaneously every buzzard started. I thought the treetops were coming down upon me, so great was the uproar. But the woods were soon cleared, and the loathsome pack disappeared in the night.

About the 1st of June I saw numbers of buzzards sailing around over the great Falls of the Potomac.

A glimpse of the birds usually found here in the latter part of winter may be had in the following extract, which I take from my diary under date of February 4th:—

"Made a long excursion through the woods and over the hills. Went directly north from the Capitol for about three miles. The ground bare and the day cold and sharp. In the suburbs, among the scattered Irish and negro shanties, came suddenly upon a flock of birds, feeding about like our northern snow buntings. Every now and then they uttered a piping, disconsolate note, as if they had a very sorry time of it. They proved to be shore larks, the first I had ever seen. They had the walk characteristic of all larks; were a little larger than the sparrow; had a black spot on the breast, with much white on the under parts of their bodies. As I approached them the nearer ones paused, and, half squatting, eyed me suspiciously. Presently, at a movement of my arm, away they went, flying exactly like the snow bunting, and showing nearly as much white." (I have since discovered that the shore lark is a regular visitant here in February and March, when large quantities of them are shot or trapped, and exposed for sale in the market. During a heavy snow I have seen numbers of them feeding upon the seeds of various weedy growths in a large market-garden well into town.) "Pressing on, the walk became exhilarating. Followed a little brook, the eastern branch of the Tiber, lined with bushes and a rank growth of green-brier. Sparrows started out here and there, and flew across the little bends and points. Among some pines just beyond the boundary, saw a number of American goldfinches, in their gray winter dress, pecking the pine cones. A golden-crowned kinglet was there also, a little tuft of gray feathers, hopping about as restless as a spirit. Had the old pine-trees food delicate enough for him also? Farther on, in some low open woods, saw many sparrows,—the fox, white-throated, white-crowned, the Canada, the song, the swamp,—all herding together along the warm and sheltered borders. To my surprise, saw a chewink also, and the yellow-rumped warbler. The purple finch was there likewise, and the Carolina wren and brown creeper. In the higher, colder woods not a bird was to be seen. Returning, near sunset, across the eastern slope of a hill which overlooked the city, was delighted to see a number of grass finches or vesper sparrows,—birds which will be forever associated in my mind with my father's sheep pastures. They ran before me, now flitting a pace or two, now skulking in the low stubble, just as I had observed them when a boy."

A month later, March 4th, is this note:—

"After the second memorable inauguration of President Lincoln, took my first trip of the season. The afternoon was very clear and warm,—real vernal sunshine at last, though the wind roared like a lion over the woods. It seemed novel enough to find within two miles of the White House a simple woodsman chopping away as if no President was being inaugurated! Some puppies, snugly nestled in the cavity of an old hollow tree, he said, belonged to a wild dog. I imagine I saw the 'wild dog,' on the other side of Rock Creek, in a great state of grief and trepidation, running up and down, crying and yelping, and looking wistfully over the swollen flood, which the poor thing had not the courage to brave. This day, for the first time, I heard the song of the Canada sparrow, a soft, sweet note, almost running into a warble. Saw a small, black, velvety butterfly with a yellow border to its wings. Under a warm bank found two flowers of the houstonia in bloom. Saw frogs' spawn near Piny Branch, and heard the hyla."

Among the first birds that make their appearance in Washington is the crow blackbird [grackle]. He may come any time after the 1st of March. The birds congregate in large flocks, and frequent groves and parks, alternately swarming in the treetops and filling the air with their sharp jangle, and alighting on the ground in quest of food, their polished coats glistening in the sun from very blackness as they walk about. There is evidently some music in the soul of this bird at this season, though he makes a sad failure in getting it out. His voice always sounds as if he were laboring under a severe attack of influenza, though a large flock of them, heard at a distance on a bright afternoon of early spring, produce an effect not unpleasing. The air is filled with crackling, splintering, spurting, semi-musical sounds, which are like pepper and salt to the ear.

All parks and public grounds about the city are full of blackbirds. They are especially plentiful in the trees about the White House, breeding there and waging war on all other birds. The occupants of one of the offices in the west wing of the Treasury one day had their attention attracted by some object striking violently against one of the window-panes. Looking up, they beheld a crow blackbird pausing in midair, a few feet from the window. On the broad stone window-sill lay the quivering form of a purple finch. The little tragedy was easily read. The blackbird had pursued the finch with such murderous violence that the latter, in its desperate efforts to escape, had sought refuge in the Treasury. The force of the concussion against the heavy plate-glass of the window had killed the poor thing instantly. The pursuer, no doubt astonished at the sudden and novel termination of the career of its victim, hovered a moment, as if to be sure of what had happened, and made off.

(It is not unusual for birds, when thus threatened with destruction by their natural enemy, to become so terrified as to seek safety in the presence of man. I was once startled, while living in a country village, to behold, on entering my room at noon, one October day, a quail sitting upon my bed. The affrighted and bewildered bird instantly started for the open window, into which it had no doubt been driven by a hawk.)

The crow blackbird has all the natural cunning of his prototype, the crow. In one of the inner courts of the Treasury building there is a fountain with several trees growing near. By midsummer the blackbirds become so bold as to venture within this court. Various fragments of food, tossed from the surrounding windows, reward their temerity. When a crust of dry bread defies their beaks, they have been seen to drop it into the water, and, when it has become soaked sufficiently, to take it out again.

They build a nest of coarse sticks and mud, the whole burden of the enterprise seeming to devolve upon the female. For several successive mornings, just after sunrise, I used to notice a pair of them flying to and fro in the air above me as I hoed in the garden, directing their course, on the one hand, to a marshy piece of ground about half a mile distant, and disappearing, on their return, among the trees about the Capitol. Returning, the female always had her beak loaded with building material, while the male, carrying nothing, seemed to act as her escort, flying a little above and in advance of her, and uttering now and then his husky, discordant note. As I tossed a lump of earth up at them, the frightened mother bird dropped her mortar, and the pair scurried away, much put out. Later they avenged themselves by pilfering my cherries.

The most mischievous enemies of the cherries, however, here as at the North, are the cedar waxwings, or "cherry-birds." How quickly they spy out the tree! Long before the cherry begins to turn, they are around, alert and cautious. In small flocks they circle about, high in air, uttering their fine note, or plunge quickly into the tops of remote trees. Day by day they approach nearer and nearer, reconnoitring the premises, and watching the growing fruit. Hardly have the green lobes turned a red cheek to the sun before their beaks have scarred it. At first they approach the tree stealthily, on the side turned from the house, diving quickly into the branches in ones and twos, while the main flock is ambushed in some shade tree not far off. They are most apt to commit their depredations very early in the morning and on cloudy, rainy days. As the cherries grow sweeter the birds grow bolder, till, from throwing tufts of grass, one has to throw stones in good earnest, or lose all his fruit. In June they disappear, following the cherries to the north, where by July they are nesting in the orchards and cedar groves.

Among the permanent summer residents here (one might say city residents, as they seem more abundant in town than out), the yellow warbler or summer yellowbird is conspicuous. He comes about the middle of April, and seems particularly attached to the silver poplars. In every street, and all day long, one may hear his thin, sharp warble. When nesting, the female comes about the yard, pecking at the clothes-line, and gathering up bits of thread to weave into her nest.

Swallows appear in Washington from the first to the middle of April. They come twittering along in the way so familiar to every New England boy. The barn swallow is heard first, followed in a day or two by the squeaking of the cliff swallow. The chimney swallows, or swifts, are not far behind, and remain here, in large numbers, the whole season. The purple martins appear in April, as they pass north, and again in July and August on their return, accompanied by their young.

The national capital is situated in such a vast spread of wild, wooded, or semi-cultivated country, and is in itself so open and spacious, with its parks and large government reservations, that an unusual number of birds find their way into it in the course of the season. Rare warblers, as the black-poll, the yellow red-poll, and the bay-breasted, pausing in May on their northward journey, pursue their insect game in the very heart of the town.

I have heard the veery thrush in the trees near the White House; and one rainy April morning, about six o'clock, he came and blew his soft, mellow flute in a pear-tree in my garden. The tones had all the sweetness and wildness they have when heard in June in our deep northern forests. A day or two afterward, in the same tree, I heard for the first time the song of the ruby-crowned wren, or kinglet,—the same liquid bubble and cadence which characterize the wren-songs generally, but much finer and more delicate than the song of any other variety known to me; beginning in a fine, round, needle-like note, and rising into a full, sustained warble,—a strain, on the whole, remarkably exquisite and pleasing, the singer being all the while as busy as a bee, catching some kind of insects. It is certainly one of our most beautiful bird-songs, and Audubon's enthusiasm concerning its song, as he heard it in the wilds of Labrador, is not a bit extravagant. The song of the kinglet is the only characteristic that allies it to the wrens.

The Capitol grounds, with their fine large trees of many varieties, draw many kinds of birds. In the rear of the building the extensive grounds are peculiarly attractive, being a gentle slope, warm and protected, and quite thickly wooded. Here in early spring I go to hear the robins, catbirds, blackbirds, wrens, etc. In March the white-throated and white-crowned sparrows may be seen, hopping about on the flower-beds or peering slyly from the evergreens. The robin hops about freely upon the grass, notwithstanding the keeper's large-lettered warning, and at intervals, and especially at sunset, carols from the treetops his loud, hearty strain.

The kingbird and orchard starling [red-winged blackbird] remain the whole season, and breed in the treetops. The rich, copious song of the starling may be heard there all the forenoon. The song of some birds is like scarlet,—strong, intense, emphatic. This is the character of the orchard starlings, also of the tanagers and the various grosbeaks. On the other hand, the songs of other birds, as of certain of the thrushes, suggest the serene blue of the upper sky.

In February one may hear, in the Smithsonian grounds, the song of the fox sparrow. It is a strong, richly modulated whistle,—the finest sparrow note I have ever heard.

A curious and charming sound may be heard here in May. You are walking forth in the soft morning air, when suddenly there comes a burst of bobolink melody from some mysterious source. A score of throats pour out one brief, hilarious, tuneful jubilee and are suddenly silent. There is a strange remoteness and fascination about it. Presently you discover its source skyward, and a quick eye will detect the gay band pushing northward. They seem to scent the fragrant meadows afar off, and shout forth snatches of their songs in anticipation.

The bobolink does not breed in the District, but usually pauses in his journey and feeds during the day in the grass-lands north of the city. When the season is backward, they tarry a week or ten days, singing freely and appearing quite at home. In large flocks they search over every inch of ground, and at intervals hover on the wing or alight in the treetops, all pouring forth their gladness at once, and filling the air with a multitudinous musical clamor.

They continue to pass, traveling by night and feeding by day, till after the middle of May, when they cease. In September, with numbers greatly increased, they are on their way back. I am first advised of their return by hearing their calls at night as they fly over the city. On certain nights the sound becomes quite noticeable. I have awakened in the middle of the night, and, through the open window, as I lay in bed, heard their faint notes. The warblers begin to return about the same time, and are clearly distinguished by their timid *yeaps*. On dark, cloudy nights the birds seem confused by the lights of the city, and apparently wander about above it.

In the spring the same curious incident is repeated, though but few voices can be identified. I make out the snowbird, the bobolink, the war-blers, and on two nights during the early part of May I heard very clearly the call of the sandpipers.

Instead of the bobolink, one encounters here, in the June meadows, the black-throated bunting [dickcissel], a bird closely related to the sparrows and a very persistent if not a very musical songster. He perches upon the fences and upon the trees by the roadside, and, spreading his tail, gives forth his harsh strain, which may be roughly worded thus: *fscp fscp, fee fee fee.* Like all sounds associated with early summer, it soon has a charm to the ear quite independent of its intrinsic merits.

Outside of the city limits, the great point of interest to the rambler and lover of nature is the Rock Creek region. Rock Creek is a large, rough, rapid stream, which has its source in the interior of Maryland, and flows into the Potomac between Washington and Georgetown. Its course, for five or six miles out of Washington, is marked by great diversity of scenery. Flowing in a deep valley, which now and then becomes a wild gorge with overhanging rocks and high precipitous headlands, for the most part wooded; here reposing in long, dark reaches, there sweeping and hurrying around a sud-den bend or over a rocky bed; receiving at short intervals small runs and spring rivulets, which open up vistas and outlooks to the right and left, of the most charming description,—Rock Creek has an abundance of all the elements that make up not only pleasing but wild and rugged scenery. There is, perhaps, not another city in the Union that has on its very thresh-old so much natural beauty and grandeur, such as men seek for in remote forests and mountains. A few touches of art would convert this whole re-gion, extending from Georgetown to what is known as Crystal Springs, not more than two miles from the present State Department, into a park un-equaled by anything in the world. There are passages between these two points as wild and savage, and apparently as remote from civilization, as anything one meets with in the mountain sources of the Hudson or the Delaware.

One of the tributaries to Rock Creek within this limit is called Piny Branch. It is a small, noisy brook, flowing through a valley of great natural beauty and picturesqueness, shaded nearly all the way by woods of oak, chestnut, and beech, and abounding in dark recesses and hidden retreats.

I must not forget to mention the many springs with which this whole region is supplied, each the centre of some wild nook, perhaps the head of a little valley one or two hundred yards long, through which one catches a glimpse, or hears the voice, of the main creek rushing along below.

My walks tend in this direction more frequently than in any other. Here the boys go, too, troops of them, of a Sunday, to bathe and prowl around, and indulge the semi-barbarous instincts that still lurk within them. Life, in all its forms, is most abundant near water. The rank vegetation nurtures the insects, and the insects draw the birds. The first week in March, on some southern slope where the sunshine lies warm and long, I usually find the hepatica in bloom, though with scarcely an inch of stalk. In the spring runs, the skunk cabbage pushes its pike up through the mould, the flower appearing first, as if Nature had made a mistake.

It is not till about the 1st of April that many wild flowers may be looked for. By this time the hepatica, anemone, saxifrage, arbutus, houstonia, and bloodroot may be counted on. A week later, the claytonia or spring beauty, water-cress, violets, a low buttercup, vetch, corydalis, and potentilla appear. These comprise most of the April flowers, and may be found in great profusion in the Rock Creek and Piny Branch region.

In each little valley or spring run, some one species predominates. I know invariably where to look for the first liverwort, and where the largest and finest may be found. On a dry, gravelly, half-wooded hill-slope the bird's-foot violet grows in great abundance, and is sparse in neighboring districts. This flower, which I never saw in the North, is the most beautiful and showy of all the violets, and calls forth rapturous applause from all persons who visit the woods. It grows in little groups and clusters, and bears a close resemblance to the pansies of the gardens. Its two purple, velvety petals seem to fall over tiny shoulders like a rich cape.

On the same slope, and on no other, I go about the 1st of May for lupine, or sun-dial, which makes the ground look blue from a little distance; on the other or northern side of the slope, the arbutus, during the first half of April, perfumes the wildwood air. A few paces farther on, in the bottom of a little spring run, the mandrake shades the ground with its miniature umbrellas. It begins to push its green finger-points up through the ground by the 1st of April, but is not in bloom till the 1st of May. It has a single white, wax-like flower, with a sweet, sickish odor, growing immediately beneath its broad leafy top. By the same run grow water-cresses and two kinds of anemones,—the Pennsylvania and the grove anemone. The bloodroot is very common at the foot of almost every warm slope in the Rock Creek woods, and, where the wind has tucked it up well with the coverlid of dry leaves, makes its appearance almost as soon as the liverwort. It is singular how little warmth is necessary to encourage these earlier flowers to put forth. It would seem as if some influence must come on in advance under-

ground and get things ready, so that, when the outside temperature is pro-
pitious, they at once venture out. I have found the bloodroot when it was
still freezing two or three nights in the week, and have known at least three
varieties of early flowers to be buried in eight inches of snow.

Another abundant flower in the Rock Creek region is the spring beauty.
Like most others, it grows in streaks. A few paces from where your attention
is monopolized by violets or arbutus, it is arrested by the claytonia, growing
in such profusion that it is impossible to set the foot down without crush-
ing the flowers. Only the forenoon walker sees them in all their beauty, as
later in the day their eyes are closed, and their pretty heads drooped in
slumber. In only one locality do I find the lady's-slipper,—a yellow variety.
The flowers that overleap all bounds in this section are the houstonias. By
the 1st of April they are very noticeable in warm, damp places along the
borders of the woods and in half-cleared fields, but by May these localities
are clouded with them. They become visible from the highway across wide
fields, and look like little puffs of smoke clinging close to the ground.

On the 1st of May I go to the Rock Creek or Piny Branch region to hear
the wood thrush. I always find him by this date leisurely chanting his lofty
strain; other thrushes are seen now also, or even earlier, as Wilson's, the
olive-backed, the hermit,—the two latter silent, but the former musical.

Occasionally in the earlier part of May I find the woods literally swarming with warblers, exploring every branch and leaf, from the tallest tulip to
the lowest spice-bush, so urgent is the demand for food during their long
northern journeys. At night they are up and away. Some varieties, as the
blue yellow-back [northern parula], the chestnut-sided, and the Blackburnian, during their brief stay, sing nearly as freely as in their breeding-
haunts. For two or three years I have chanced to meet little companies of
the bay-breasted warbler, searching for food in an oak wood on an elevated
piece of ground. They kept well up among the branches, were rather slow in
their movements, and evidently disposed to tarry but a short time.

The summer residents here, belonging to this class of birds, are few. I
have observed the black and white creeping warbler, the Kentucky warbler,
the worm-eating warbler, the redstart, and the gnatcatcher, breeding near
Rock Creek.

Of these the Kentucky warbler is by far the most interesting, though
quite rare. I meet with him in low, damp places in the woods, usually on
the steep sides of some little run. I hear at intervals a clear, strong, bell-like
whistle or warble, and presently catch a glimpse of the bird as he jumps up
from the ground to take an insect or worm from the under side of a leaf.

This is his characteristic movement. He belongs to the class of ground warblers, and his range is very low, indeed lower than that of any other species with which I am acquainted. He is on the ground nearly all the time, moving rapidly along, taking spiders and bugs, overturning leaves, peeping under sticks and into crevices, and every now and then leaping up eight or ten inches to take his game from beneath some overhanging leaf or branch. Thus each species has its range more or less marked. Draw a line three feet from the ground, and you mark the usual limit of the Kentucky warbler's quest for food. Six or eight feet higher bounds the usual range of such birds as the worm-eating warbler, the mourning ground warbler, the Maryland yellow-throat. The lower branches of the higher growths and the higher branches of the lower growths are plainly preferred by the blackthroated blue-backed warbler, in those localities where he is found. The thrushes feed mostly on and near the ground, while some of the vireos and the true flycatchers explore the highest branches. But the warblers, as a rule, are all partial to thick, rank undergrowths.

The Kentucky warbler is a large bird for the genus and quite notable in appearance. His back is clear olive-green, his throat and breast bright yellow. A still more prominent feature is a black streak on the side of the face, extending down the neck.

Another familiar bird here, which I never met with in the North, is the gnatcatcher, called by Audubon the blue-gray flycatching warbler. In form and manner it seems almost a duplicate of the catbird on a small scale. It mews like a young kitten, erects its tail, flirts, droops its wings, goes through a variety of motions when disturbed by your presence, and in many ways recalls its dusky prototype. Its color above is a light gray-blue, gradually fading till it becomes white on the breast and belly. It is a very small bird, and has a long, facile, slender tail. Its song is a lisping, chattering, incoherent warble, now faintly reminding one of the goldfinch, now of a miniature catbird, then of a tiny yellow-hammer, having much variety, but no unity and little cadence.

Another bird which has interested me here is the Louisiana waterthrush, called also large-billed water-thrush, and water-wagtail. It is one of a trio of birds which has confused the ornithologists much. The other two species are the well-known golden-crowned thrush [ovenbird] or woodwagtail, and the northern, or small, water-thrush.

The present species, though not abundant, is frequently met with along Rock Creek. It is a very quick, vivacious bird, and belongs to the class of ecstatic singers. I have seen a pair of these thrushes, on a bright May day, flying to and fro between two spring runs, alighting at intermediate points, the male breaking out into one of the most exuberant, unpremeditated strains I ever heard. Its song is a sudden burst, beginning with three or four clear round notes much resembling certain tones of the clarinet, and terminating in a rapid, intricate warble.

This bird resembles a thrush only in its color, which is olive-brown above and grayish white beneath, with speckled throat and breast. Its habits, manners, and voice suggest those of the lark.

I seldom go the Rock Creek route without being amused and sometimes annoyed by the yellow-breasted chat. This bird also has something of the manners and build of the catbird, yet he is truly an original. The catbird is mild and feminine compared with this rollicking polyglot. His voice is very loud and strong and quite uncanny. No sooner have you penetrated his retreat, which is usually a thick undergrowth in low, wet localities, near the woods or in old fields, than he begins his serenade, which for the variety, grotesqueness, and uncouthness of the notes is not unlike a country *skimmerton*. If one passes directly along, the bird may scarcely break the silence. But pause a while, or loiter quietly about, and your presence stimulates him to do his best. He peeps quizzically at you from beneath the branches, and gives a sharp feline mew. In a moment more he says very distinctly, *who, who*. Then in rapid succession follow notes the most discordant that ever broke the sylvan silence. Now he barks like a puppy, then quacks like a duck, then rattles like a kingfisher, then squalls like a fox, then caws like a crow, then mews like a cat. Now he calls as if to be heard a long way off, then changes his key, as if addressing the spectator. Though very shy, and carefully keeping himself screened when you show any disposition to get a better view, he will presently, if you remain quiet, ascend a twig, or hop out on a branch in plain sight, lop his tail, droop his wings, cock his head, and become very melodramatic. In less than half a minute he darts into the bushes again, and again tunes up, no Frenchman rolling his *r*'s so fluently. *C-r-r-r-r-r,—whrr,—that's it,—chee,—quack, cluck,—yit-yit-yit,—now hit it,—tr-r-r-r,—when,—caw, caw,—cut, cut,—tea-boy,—who, who,—mew, mew,*—and so on till you are tired of listening. Observing one very closely one day, I discovered that he was limited to six notes or changes, which he went through in regular order, scarcely varying a note in a dozen repetitions. Sometimes, when a considerable distance off, he will fly down to have a nearer view of you. And such a curious, expressive flight,—legs extended, head lowered, wings rapidly vibrating, the whole action piquant and droll!

The chat is an elegant bird, both in form and color. Its plumage is remarkably firm and compact. Color above, light olive-green; beneath, bright yellow; beak, black and strong.

The cardinal grosbeak, or Virginia redbird, is quite common in the same localities, though more inclined to seek the woods. It is much sought after by bird-fanciers, and by boy gunners, and consequently is very shy. This bird suggests a British redcoat; his heavy, pointed beak, his high cockade, the black stripe down his face, the expression of weight and massiveness about his head and neck, and his erect attitude, give him a decided, soldier-like appearance; and there is something of the tone of the fife in his song or whistle, while his ordinary note, when disturbed, is like the clink of a sabre. Yesterday, as I sat indolently swinging in the loop of a grapevine, beneath a thick canopy of green branches, in a secluded nook by a spring run, one of these birds came pursuing some kind of insect, but a few feet above me. He hopped about, now and then uttering his sharp note, till, some moth or beetle trying to escape, he broke down through the cover almost where I sat. The effect was like a firebrand coming down through the branches. Instantly catching sight of me, he darted away much alarmed. The female is tinged with brown, and shows but little red except when she takes flight.

By far the most abundant species of woodpecker about Washington is the red-headed. It is more common than the robin. Not in the deep woods, but among the scattered dilapidated oaks and groves, on the hills and in the fields, I hear almost every day his uncanny note, *ktr-r-r, ktr-r-r*, like that of some larger tree-toad, proceeding from an oak grove just beyond the boundary. He is a strong-scented fellow, and very tough. Yet how beautiful, as he flits about the open woods, connecting the trees by a gentle arc of crimson and white! This is another bird with a military look. His deliberate, dignified ways, and his bright uniform of red, white, and steel-blue, bespeak him an officer of rank.

Another favorite beat of mine is northeast of the city. Looking from the Capitol in this direction, scarcely more than a mile distant, you see a broad green hill-slope, falling very gently, and spreading into a large expanse of meadow-land. The summit, if so gentle a swell of greensward may be said to have a summit, is covered with a grove of large oaks; and, sweeping back out of sight like a mantle, the front line of a thick forest bounds the sides. This emerald landscape is seen from a number of points in the city. Looking along New York Avenue from Northern Liberty Market, the eye glances, as it were, from the red clay of the street, and alights upon this fresh scene in the distance. It is a standing invitation to the citizen to come forth and be refreshed. As I turn from some hot, hard street, how inviting it looks! I bathe my eyes in it as in a fountain. Sometimes troops of cattle are seen grazing upon it. In June the gathering of the hay may be witnessed. When the ground is covered with snow, numerous stacks, or clusters of stacks, are still left for the eye to contemplate.

The woods which clothe the east side of this hill, and sweep away to the east, are among the most charming to be found in the District. The main growth is oak and chestnut, with a thin sprinkling of laurel, azalea, and dogwood. It is the only locality in which I have found the dogtooth violet in bloom, and the best place I know of to gather arbutus. On one slope the ground is covered with moss, through which the arbutus trails its glories.

Emerging from these woods toward the city, one sees the white dome of the Capitol soaring over the green swell of earth immediately in front, and lifting its four thousand tons of iron gracefully and lightly into the air. Of all the sights in Washington, that which will survive longest in my memory is the vision of the great dome thus rising cloud-like above the hills.

1868

The White House by Moonlight, Birds Migrating at Midnight, *and* By Broad Potomac's Shore

Walt Whitman (1819–1892)

Walt Whitman's Civil War years in Washington produced *Memoranda During the War* and several of his best-known poems. Some of these, like "When Lilacs Last in the Dooryard Bloom'd," contain extended symbolic images from nature. *Specimen Days* includes several short prose natural history sketches written during this period and many written during his long New Jersey recuperation from his 1873 stroke. Both Whitman's prose and poetry were influenced by his friend John Burroughs. In the introduction, we describe Burroughs's contribution to Whitman's nature symbolism and his example as a nature essayist. The following three selections illustrate Whitman's mastery of the uses of nature in literary art. In "The White House by Moonlight," winter trees and moonlight create an emotional mood; "Birds Migrating at Midnight" is Whitman's nature observation (at Burroughs's best); "By Broad Potomac's Shore" revisits, in seeming old age, nature's balm for the pain caused by awareness of death that Whitman treated brilliantly from the point of view of youth in "Out of the Cradle Endlessly Rocking."

From *Specimen Days* (Philadelphia: D. McKay, 1882)

The White House by Moonlight

February 24th [1863].—A spell of fine soft weather. I wander about a good deal, sometimes at night under the moon. To-night took a long look at the President's house. The white portico—the palace-like, tall, round columns, spotless as snow—the walls also—the tender and soft moonlight, flooding the pale marble, and making peculiar faint languishing shades, not shadows—everywhere a soft transparent hazy, thin, blue moon-lace, hanging in the air—the brilliant and extra-plentiful clusters of gas, on and around the facade, columns, portico, &c.—everything so white, so marbly pure and dazzling, yet soft—the White House of future poems, and of dreams and dramas, there in the soft and copious moon—the gorgeous front, in the trees, under the lustrous flooding moon, full of reality, full of illusion—the forms of the trees, leafless, silent, in trunk and myriad-angles of branches, under the stars and the sky—the White House of the land, and of beauty and night—sentries at the gates, and by the portico, silent, pacing in blue overcoats—stopping you not at all, but eyeing you with sharp eyes, whichever way you move.

From *Specimen Days* (Philadelphia: D. McKay, 1882)

Birds Migrating at Midnight

Did you ever chance to hear the midnight flight of birds passing through the air and darkness overhead, in countless armies, changing their early or late summer habitat? It is something not to be forgotten. A friend called me up just after 12 last night to mark the peculiar noise of unusually immense flocks migrating north (rather late this year). In the silence, shadow, and delicious odor of the hour (the natural perfume belonging to the night alone), I thought it rare music. You could *hear* the characteristic motion— once or twice "the rush of mighty wings," but oftener a velvety rustle, long drawn out—sometimes quite near—with continual calls and chirps, and some song notes. It all lasted from 12 till after 3. Once in a while the species was plainly distinguishable; I could make out the bobolink, tanager, Wilson's thrush, white-crowned sparrow, and occasionally from high in the air came the note of the plover.

From *Leaves of Grass* (Philadelphia: D. McKay, 1900)

By Broad Potomac's Shore

1
By broad Potomac's shore—again, old tongue!
(Still uttering—still ejaculating—canst never cease this babble?)
Again, old heart so gay—again to you, your sense, the full flush
    spring returning;
Again the freshness and the odors—again Virginia's summer sky,
    pellucid blue and silver,

Again the forenoon purple of the hills,
Again the deathless grass, so noiseless, soft and green,
Again the blood-red roses blooming.

2

Perfume this book of mine, O blood-red roses!
Lave subtly with your waters every line, Potomac!
Give me of you, O spring, before I close, to put between its pages!
O forenoon purple of the hills, before I close, of you!
O smiling earth—O summer sun, give me of you!
O deathless grass, of you!

Pine Woods

Wilson Flagg (1805–1884)

Although he is not well known today, Wilson Flagg was a popular and influential writer from the time of his first article in the *Atlantic* in 1858. It is said that his *Studies in the Field and Forest* sparked John Burroughs's interest in birds. Flagg's one trip outside his native New England was to the coastal South, where he caught the essence of the pine woods as only a lover of trees and their associated flowers can. In a later selection, the great twentieth-century Harvard botanist M. L. Fernald describes the biological richness of Virginia's Zuni pine barrens, which perfectly fit the aesthetic feeling captured by Flagg.

From *The Woods and By-Ways of New England* (Boston: J. R. Osgood, 1872)

I HAVE OFTEN THOUGHT of the pleasure I should feel on entering a forest of tree-ferns, and observing their elegant fronds spread out above my head, displaying a form of vegetation never witnessed except in a tropical country. Yet I doubt whether an assemblage of tree-ferns, a grove of magnolias, or an island of palms could equal a forest of pines in the expression of grandeur and solemnity. A pine wood expresses characters entirely unique, and affects us with sensations which nothing else in nature seems capable of inspiring. Whether this arises from the contrast between the light outside and the darkness within,—a certain harmonious blending of cheerfulness and gloom,—or from the novelty of the whole scene, there comes up from every deep recess and shadowy arbor, every dripping dell, every mossy fountain, and every open glen throughout the wood, an indescribable charm. Notwithstanding the darkness of its interior, and the sombre character of its dense masses of evergreen foliage, as seen from without,—and whence the name of *black timber*, which has been applied to it,—yet the shade and shelter it affords, and the sentiment of grandeur it inspires, cause it to be allied with the most profound and agreeable sensations.

In a pine wood Nature presents one of her most remarkable features; and there is so much that is healthful and delightful in its emanations, and in the atmosphere that is diffused around it, that she has not denied its ben-

efits to any clime. Pines are found in every latitude save the equatorial region, where the broad-leaved palms supply the same enduring shade. Even
there pines are distributed over mountains at a height corresponding with
the northern temperate zone. Nature has spread these trees widely over the
earth, that the inhabitants of the sunny South and the inhospitable North
may equally derive benefit from their protection and their products. There
is not a region this side of the equator, where a man may not kneel down
under the fragrant shade of a pine wood, and thank the Author of nature
for this beneficent gift. . . .

The pine barrens of the Southern States are celebrated as health retreats
for the inhabitants of the seaports, whither they resort in summer to escape
the prevailing fevers. They are generally of a mixed character, consisting of
the Northern pitch-pine, the long-leafed pine, and a few other species, intermixed with the Southern cypress, occasional red maples, and a few other
deciduous trees. Pines, however, constitute the dominant growth; but the
trees are, for the most part, widely separated, so that the surface is green
with herbs and grasses, and often covered with flowers. The thinness of
these woods may be attributed to the practice, for two centuries past, of
tapping the trees for turpentine, causing their gradual decay. Their tall
forms and branchless trunks show that they obtained their principal growth
in a dense wood.

The first visit I made to the pine barrens was after a long ride by railroad
through the plains of North Carolina. It was night; and I often looked from
the car windows into the darkness, made still more affecting by the sight of
the tall pines that raised their heads almost into the clouds, like monsters
watching the progress of our journey. The prospect was rendered almost
invisible by the darkness that gave prominence to the dusky forms of the
trees as they were pictured against the half-luminous sky. At length the day
began to break, and the morning beams revealed to my sight an immense
wilderness of giant spectres. The cars made a pause at this hour, allowing
the passengers to step outside; and while absorbed in the contemplations
of this desolate region, suddenly the loud and mellow tones of the mocking-bird came to my ears, and, as if by enchantment, reversed the character
of my thoughts. The desert, no longer a solitude, inspired me with emotions of unspeakable delight. Morning never seemed so lovely as when the
rising sun, with his golden beams and lengthened shadows, was greeted by
this warbling salutation, as from some messenger of light who seemed to
announce that Nature over all scenes has extended her beneficence, and to
all regions of the earth dispenses her favors and her smiles.

At the end of my journey I took a stroll into the wood. It was in the month of June, when vegetation was in its prime, before it was seared by the summer drought. Many beautiful shrubs were conspicuous with their flowers, though the wood contained but a small proportion of shrubby undergrowth. During my botanical rambles in this wood I was struck with the multitude of flowers in its shady arbors, seeming the more numerous to me as I had previously confined my observations to Northern woods. The phlox grew here in all its native delicacy, where it had never known the fostering hand of man. Crimson rhexias—called by the inhabitants deer-weed—were distributed among the grassy knolls, like clusters of picotees. Variegated passion-flowers were conspicuous on the bare white sand that checkered the green surface, displaying their emblematic forms on their low repent vines, and reminding the wanderer in these solitudes of that faith which was founded on humility and crowned with martyrdom. Here too the spiderwort of our gardens, in a meeker form of beauty and a paler radiance, luxuriated under the protection of the wood. I observed also the predominance of luxuriant vines, indicating our near approach to the tropics, rearing themselves upon the tall and naked shafts of the trees, some, like the bignonia, in a full blaze of crimson, others, like the climbing fern, draping the trees in perennial verdure.

Picturesque America:
The Chickahominy
and Weyer's Cave

G. W. Bagby

Sallie A. Brock

Travel writing in the age of railroad tourism is best exemplified by *Picturesque America*, William Cullen Bryant's illustrated anthology celebrating the scenic aspects of both countryside and city. Selecting local writers to tout their regions, Bryant (1794–1878) produced coffee-table books which are both a source of pleasure and an artifact of cultural history in which we discover how the Central Atlantic viewed itself and nature after the Civil War.

The two selections concern completely different natural phenomena: a tidal, fresh-water tributary of the James River and one of the many remarkable limestone caverns in the Shenandoah Valley. Newspaperman G. W. Bagby interprets the Chickahominy River as a beautiful southern wetland rich in biological diversity. Sallie Brock introduces us not only to the wonders of underground geology but also to the frivolous fancies of human imagination when given the opportunity to name formations in a commercially developed cave.

Both selections from *Picturesque America*, ed. William Cullen Bryant (New York: D. Appleton and Company, 1872)

G. W. Bagby

Scenes in Virginia: The Chickahominy

W E APPEND to our series of Virginia scenes a view . . . of the Chickahominy. This now historic stream was hardly known outside the limits of the State previous to the war; and yet there is much that is interesting about it, not only to the lover of the picturesque, but to the observer and student of Nature. The stream is a tributary to the James. Its volume is inconsiderable until it nears Richmond, and it is navigable for some twenty-five or thirty miles only from its junction.

"The cypress here protrudes its curious roots, and the funereal moss trails from the trees." The Chickahominy, W. Wellstood, steel engraving from *Picturesque America*, 1872

To the physical geographer the Chickahominy is interesting, from the fact that it is the northernmost locality that retains features, in its flora, which are common on the rivers of the Carolinas and the States farther south, in company with the growth of the colder climates. The cypress here protrudes its curious roots, and the funereal moss trails from the trees. The beech sends its horizontal branches over the darksome waters; the maples, so brilliant in their autumn foliage; and the gum-tree, more gorgeous still at the same season, with its rich variations from vermilion to royal purple— here keep company with the Southern interlopers. Vines encumber the trees, and harassing bamboo-thickets bar the way on the higher banks. The columnar gum-trees, in most cases, rise from an intertwined assembly of arched and knotted roots, especially where they are liable to be washed by the overflow of the stream. These arched bases have sometimes a clear distance from the earth of three and four feet, and constitute a unique feature in the forest. Immense masses of *debris* washed down by the freshets lodge against the standing timber, and the stream is bridged in hundreds of places by the trees which have lost their equilibrium from being undermined. The river contiguous to Richmond is invariably spoken of as the Chickahominy Swamp; and here, in effect, it is a swamp. The main stream, with its coffee-colored water, is well defined, but in many places, for a quarter of a mile on both sides of it, the ground is a slimy ooze, affording a very unstable footing. Where this ooze exists, it is covered with a dense growth of water-plants, generally of the peculiar whitish green found in plants little exposed to the light of the sun.

The Chickahominy is the chosen abode of all the known varieties of "varmints" of that region. The raccoon can here ply his trade of fisherman for the cat-fish and pike, or raid upon sleeping creepers or young wood-ducks. The "possum" has store of gum-berries, with the same variety in meat-diet which his conocturnal fancies; otters are still to be found; muskrats innumerable, and snakes—some of the aquatic species beautifully colored—in proportion. The wood-duck, of splendid plumage, flits like a prismatic ray over the brown water, and, though web-footed, builds his nests in the towering trees. In fine, the Chickahominy cannot fail to attract the artist and naturalist; it always would have done this, but now the added interest of historical association brings hundreds to visit its banks; and the stream which, heretofore, had but scanty mention in the common-school geography will find a place in man's record beside the Rubicon and the Tweed.

Sallie A. Brock

Weyer's Cave, Virginia

WEYER'S CAVE, which has been not inappropriately termed the Antiparos of Virginia, is situated in the northwestern part of Augusta County, about seventeen miles north of Staunton, and a few miles west of the Blue-Ridge Mountains. It is located in a large hill, or rather a spur of a range of small mountains, branching out southwesterly from this spine of the Atlantic watershed, and for many miles overhanging its uppermost tributaries.

This cavern derives its name from one Bernard Weyer, a dweller in the neighborhood, who discovered it while hunting an opossum, ferreting out the little animal to its retreat within the mouth. It is approached from the rustic inn, half a mile distant, by a broad carriage-road to the foot of the hill, and thence by a zigzag, precipitous foot-path to the opening near the crest of the summit.

The entrance, when discovered, was scarcely large enough for Mr. Weyer to enter on his hands and knees; and his astonishment and terror may be imagined when on and on he groped in the darkness, without finding the cunning little quadruped which had secured such commodious and gorgeous quarters. Since then the entrance has been enlarged, so as to be about seven feet in height, and is covered over by a rustic shed, to which is affixed a strong wooden gate, secured by a heavy lock.

A chill creeps over one upon entering, and he feels an intensity of awe as he looks forward, beyond the dim, flickering lights in the sconces, to the profound darkness which spreads its impenetrable gloom in the distance. But the guide is master of his business; he is cheerful, facetious, loquacious; and, winding a yarn of some adventurous explorer before his visitor (perhaps some illustrious personage—the Duke of Buckingham, who sadly offended a liege lord of America; Frederika Bremer, who, in her geological researches here, was taken by a neighboring husbandman to be an escaped unfortunate from the Staunton Lunatic Asylum), or cracking some wily joke, leads on until dusky, indefinable figures loom up in the midnight, when by a skilful shifting of his lights are discovered all around grim, grotesque stalagmites, and opening out is a long gallery, at the nether end of which a single mute, stark-white figure gives to this apartment its significant title, the Ghost-Chamber.

From this the Hall of Statuary is entered, when imagination readily conjures up the galleries of the Vatican by moonlight, or rather by torchlight.

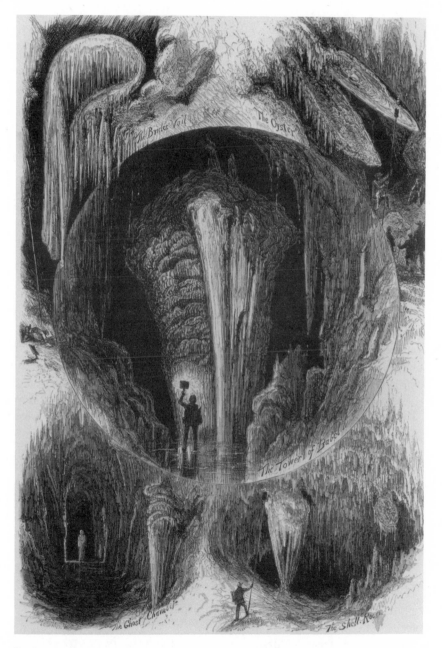

"And, on and on, one is conducted, through narrow passages and more commodious arches; up and down precipices; among tumbling heaps of pilasters, columns, and friezes." Scenes in Weyer's Cave, H. Fenn, steel engraving from *Picturesque America*, 1872

Above, in the ceiling, is a circular opening, about fifteen feet in diameter, fringed around with white, sparkling stalactites. Through this opening is seen the interior of a dome many feet higher, draped and columned as by the deft hand of some fantastic architect. Upon one side of this hall is the similitude of an altar, with curtains and candlesticks on the top; and, on the other, fancy brings out a cathedral-organ, with its rows of pipes and pendent cornices.

A few paces forward, and down a rude flight of some twenty steps, we reach the Cataract, seemingly a water-fall petrified in its leap, affording one of the finest spectacles in the cave. The sullen stillness of this hushed Niagara is very impressive, and instinctively leads the imagination to the roaring and rushing green waters of the true cataract after which it is named.

A little farther on is the Senate-Chamber, with the speaker's chair at one end, in front of which are rude representations of the desks of the honorable members; and above, at one side, is an unmistakable gallery, fenced around by a fanciful balustrade, over which seemingly peer the heads of waiting visitors.

Next in order comes the Cathedral, from the centre of which hangs the fancied resemblance to a chandelier; and beyond it rises the pulpit, an elevated circular desk, covered with the most graceful folds of white drapery. On the opposite side is a baldachin fringed with glittering crystals, the whole ceiling being hung with stalactites, dropping in long points and broad, wavy sheets, some of milky whiteness, others of a muddy red bordered with white, or with the darker cornelian shades of the Piedmont brown. This apartment has also been vulgarly termed the Tan-Yard, the broad sheets of yellow spar suggesting a striking resemblance to hides hung to dry. These stone draperies are translucent, faintly emitting the rays of light when a candle is held behind them; and also sonorous, yielding soft musical tones, like the gently-touched keys of an organ, on being struck, while all the notes of the gamut may be produced by skilful blows, the side-walls responding to blows of the hand or foot with the echoing notes of "deep-toned bells."

In this vicinity a huge pyramidal heap of cornelian-tinted stalagmite, veined and spotted with white, as is the Swiss stone, sustains on one side a tall, slender, towering column, which has received the name of Cleopatra's Needle; and on the right a more massive and taller shaft, bearing the appellation of Anthony's Pillar, rears its pointed head until it touches the sparkling stalactites that stud the dark ceiling; and all around are formations more or less resembling objects in Nature, or as wild and weird as the most imaginative brain could conjure out for fiction.

From this section of the cavern, a natural stairway, with natural supports on the left hand, is descended, called Jacob's Ladder; and, beyond, a square rock covered with a white incrustation, resembling a table-cloth, is called Jacob's Tea-Table; and near by is an ominous-looking cavity, bearing the name of Jacob's Ice-House, or the Bottomless Pit. Whether bottomless or not, has never yet been fully ascertained; but, it is certain, a torch dropped in seems to twinkle away into infinite nothingness, and a stone let fall returns no sound to the waiting listener.

In this part of Weyer's Cave is what, for want of a more appropriate term, must be called the Geyser, an immense stalagmitic accretion, with streaks and sparkles of white, lighting the waves of the cumuli as the play of sunlight the turbulent volumes of one of Nature's boiling springs.

Farther on is Washington's Hall, otherwise called the Gnome-King's Palace, rising into a vaulted roof, upward of *ninety feet* in height and *two hundred and fifty* in length. An intelligent traveller, who once visited Weyer's Cave at an annual illumination, has thus finely described this magnificent apartment:

"There is a fine sheet of rock-work running up the centre of this room, and giving it the aspect of two separate and noble galleries, till you look above, where you observe the partition rises only about twenty feet toward the roof, and leaves the fine arch expanding over your head. There is a beautiful concretion here, standing out in the room, which certainly has the form and drapery of a gigantic statue. It bears the name of the nation's hero; and the whole place is filled with these projections—appearances which excite the imagination by suggesting resemblances and leaving them unfinished. The general effect, too, was perhaps indescribable. The fine perspective of this room, four times the length of an ordinary church; the numerous tapers, when near you so encumbered by deep shadows as to give only a dim, religious light, and, when at a distance, appearing in their various attitudes like twinkling stars on a deep-dark heaven; the amazing vaulted roof spread over you, with its carved and knotted surface, to which the streaming lights below in vain endeavored to convey their radiance; together with the impression that you had made so deep an entrance, and were so entirely cut off from the living world and ordinary things—produce an effect which, perhaps, the mind can conceive but once, and will retain forever."

It is a trick of the guide to extinguish the tapers when in this hall, and leave the visitors for a few moments to experience the Cimmerian darkness—darkness which can almost be felt—the utter abstraction of what gives life and beauty to the outer world.

Near this apartment is Lady Washington's Bedchamber, on one side of which is a rude resemblance to a couch, with a milk-white canopy, richly fluted around; while on the other side of the beautiful little room is a toilet-table, with snowy drapery, over-hung by an imaginary mirror, and scattered over with the usual paraphernalia of a lady's dressing room.

In this vicinity is the Bridal Veil, a splendid sheet of white, glittering, translucent spar, which seems thrown over a hat, or, as has been suggested by others, the shelving back of an immense Spanish comb, and hangs in full, classic folds or heavy volutes almost to the clay-red flooring of the little chamber.

And, on and on, one is conducted, through narrow passages and more commodious arches; up and down precipices; among tumbling heaps of pilasters, columns, and friezes, divided by strata at regular or irregular intervals, and pillared with the skill of the architect and mathematician, like the ruins of some vast Old-World temple; before the Diamond Mountain, flashing with its buried gems, and stalked over by the gigantic and ghostly Crane, which looks inquiringly toward the Rising Moon that throws its silvery light out in the voiceless midnight; and on and on, until we arrive at the end of the cavern, and are refreshed by a glass of as sparkling water as ever gushed from upperworld fountain and made merry music in the glad sunlight.

This subterranean spring is perfectly incrusted with stalactites and stalagmites; and an earthen jar kept in this part of the grotto, where the water is constantly dripping from the ceiling, is incrusted with younger but similar concretions.

The egress is somewhat varied from the ingress; and, in returning, the visitor is conducted to the Tower of Babel, or Magic Tower, a huge, columnar accretion, rising to the height of thirty feet or more, irregularly divided by strata at distances of ten or twelve inches, and fluted around by pillars an inch or more in diameter.

The Tower of Babel is perhaps the most regular and symmetrical formation in all this wonderful grotto, and most readily suggests the title it bears. It occupies the centre of an apartment filled with indefinable figures, which may suggest statues, ghosts, goblins, or whatever will best please the fancy.

Near this is the Oyster-Shell, consisting of two huge, shelving pieces of spar, of a peculiar grayish white, and absurdly resembling the late home of a defunct monster bivalve. And Nature, to vindicate her providence, in close proximity to this fanciful concretion, has placed Solomon's Meat-House, from the fretted and groined roof of which is suspended a Leg of Mutton—a single instance of the old king's gastronomic propensities. In prudent nearness to the Meat-House is Solomon's Temple, or, as it is better known, the Shell-Room. In the centre of this apartment rises a massive column of dazzling white, as rich with grooves and flutings as if chiselled out to fill an artistic design; and this reaches the ceiling, which is thickly studded with sparkling stalactites, reflecting, as the tapers are held underneath them, the hue and lustre of every gem that holds light imprisoned. The Shell-Room, from the radish-like shape of the stalactites that hang from the ceiling, has also been called the Radish-Room; while almost every intelligent visitor finds some suggestive title to this magnificent hall.

And this, with the 'Possum-up-the-Gum-Tree—doubtless, Weyer's opossum, upon the final capture of which tradition is silent—completes a list of the most noticeable of the many noticeable freaks in which Nature indulges in these subterranean retreats.

Out of the usual route of exploration, but to be visited by special request, is a most beautiful pond, over which is the shelving sheet of spar from which the specimens usually sold are obtained. As a visit to this lake is very fatiguing and somewhat dangerous, it is not generally attempted, but well repays all fatigue or danger incurred.

A few moments after leaving the Shell-Room, the visitor grows sensible that the dim candles emit a dimmer light; if in summer, a warmer, and, if in winter, a colder, atmosphere greets one; and, climbing a slight ascent, he is once more in the face of day, and listening to other sounds than that of the human voice alone.

"Weyer's Cave," says the writer quoted, "is, in my judgment, one of the great natural wonders of the New World, and, for its eminence in its own class, deserves to be ranked with the Natural Bridge and Niagara, while it is far less known than either. Its dimensions, by the most direct course, are more than sixteen hundred feet, and, by the more winding paths, twice that length; and its objects are remarkable for their variety, formation, and beauty. In both respects, it will, I think, compare without injury to itself with the celebrated grotto of Antiparos."

Within a few hundred yards of Weyer's Cave is Madison's Cave, described by Mr. Jefferson; but it is less interesting than the former. Indeed, it is supposed that the entire mountain is a cavern, and, it is hoped, in time will be fully explored.

Where Now Will You Look for Birds?
and *Avifauna Columbiana*

Elliott Coues (1842–1899)

Recognized as one of the greatest ornithologists of the nineteenth century, Washington resident Elliott Coues earned his livelihood first as an army surgeon and then as professor of anatomy at the National Medical College (now the George Washington University Medical School). Coues was a life-long protégé and associate of Spencer Baird at the Smithsonian Institution. Professionally, Coues dominated systematics research in the 1870s and 1880s; he was one of the three founders of the American Ornithologists' Union. His technical publications influenced literary naturalists like John Burroughs, conservationists like Theodore Roosevelt, and younger scientists like Frank Chapman, later curator of birds at the American Museum of Natural History. His popular articles were published in many well-known magazines, including the *Atlantic*. Coues's unusual life story is detailed in the introduction to this anthology.

Coues's lively prose style enriched his technical writing with the same exuberant enthusiasm and sardonic wit that brought him success in the popular press. What a delight it must have been to the student of ornithology to find in his instruction manual passages like the following selection "Where Now Will You Look for Birds?"

Today's field guides are intended to permit the hobbyist to identify a bird on sight. And so they are books of schematic pictures accompanied by the briefest possible texts. In the nineteenth century, one class of books satisfied professionals and amateurs; texts were more expansive and pictures were drawn as much for beauty as for information. But texts then were often as dull as they are today. Coues's bird descriptions are notable exceptions: In the selection describing the Bobolink, Coues mixes information with nostalgia and humor in the easy manner that made him one of the most entertaining conversationalists of his day.

From *Field Ornithology, Comprising a Manual of Instruction for Procuring, Preparing and Preserving Birds, and a Check List of North American Birds* (Salem, Mass.: Naturalists' Agency, 1874)

Where Now Will You Look for Birds?

Birds may be sought anywhere, at any time; they should be sought everywhere, at all times. Some come about your doorstep to tell their stories unasked. Others spring up before you as you stroll in the field, like the flowers that enticed the feet of Proserpine. Birds flit by as you measure the tired roadside, lending a tithe of their life to quicken your dusty steps. They disport overhead at hide-and-seek with the foliage as you loiter in the shade of the forest, and their music now answers the sigh of the tree-tops, now ripples an echo to the voice of the brook. But you will not always so pluck a thornless rose. Birds hedge themselves about with a bristling girdle of brier and bramble you cannot break; they build their tiny castles in the air surrounded by impassible moats, and the drawbridges are never down. They crown the mountain-top you may lose your breath to climb; they sprinkle the desert where your parched lips may find no cooling draught; they fleck the snow-wreath when the nipping blast may make you turn your back; they breathe unharmed the pestilent vapors of the swamps that mean disease, if not death, for you; they outride the storm at sea that sends strong men to their last account. Where now will you look for birds?

From *Avifauna Columbiana* (Washington, D.C.: GPO, 1883)

Eastern Branch (Anacostia River) Region

Above the Baltimore and Potomac Railroad Bridge, . . . [the Anacostia River] becomes of more interest to the ornithologist. The "flats" of the stream become sufficiently shallow to meet the conditions necessary for the growth of the wild rice, and for three miles above the railroad bridge the channel winds tortuously between extensive marshes composed of wild rice (*Zizania aquatica*), saw-grass (*Polygonum arifolium* and *Polygonum sagitatum*), wanquapins (*Nelumbium luteum*), lily-pads (*Nuphar advena*), and several species of marsh grasses. . . .

   In these marshes the Long-billed Marsh Wren (*Telmatodytes palustris*) breeds abundantly. . . . At Beaver Dam is situated a good wild-rice marsh, known as McCormick's Marsh, while between this and Piney Run Gut the marsh is grown up with buttonwoods and alders, making good cover and feeding ground for Woodcock and King Rail. . . .

During the fall migrations these marshes afford refuge and food for innumerable hosts of Rail, Reed-birds [bobolinks], and Red-winged Blackbirds, which attract scores of "gunners," so that during the early days of September this locality reminds one of the firing of a skirmish line preceding a great battle. The crack of fowling-pieces is incessant from early morning to twilight. All classes in society are represented, from the gentleman sportsman with his pusher and favorite breech-loader, hunting Rail, to the ragged contraband with the cheap, old-fashioned, single-barreled muzzle-loader, or old style army musket, "wading" the marshes from knee to waist deep, to whom all flesh is game, who takes in principally Blackbirds and Reed-birds, and is particularly happy when he can surprise an unsophisticated Rail on the side of a "gut." The professional or market gunner is also well represented, and during the early days of the season reaps a good harvest. It is a common thing on the first day of the season for one gunner to secure from twelve to twenty dozen Carolina Rail [sora] and as many Reed-birds. These birds are protected by law until September 1.

It is rather a comical sight to witness the gathering of the clans at Benning's Bridge on the 1st day of September, preparatory to the slaughter of the innocents. As the light begins to appear in the east a motley line of sportsmen may be seen sitting upon the rail of the bridge waiting for sufficient light to see to shoot, dressed in all manner of costumes, and armed with all sorts of blunderbusses; some who have had the means and forethought to engage a skiff and pusher are off in style with the tide, others go in couples in skiffs and push each other, while the rabble, who constitute the great majority, take to the marshes and wade.

Rail Shooting on the Anacostia River Marshes

Rail shooting in the fall of the year affords sport to many who are fond of the gun, although to the true sportsman it is rather tame amusement. The flight of the bird is so sluggish that it requires but indifferent marksmanship to bring it down, as a rule; still, sometimes, when the birds are wild, before they become heavy with fat, it is not such an easy matter to bring them to bag. In the talk among Rail shooters it is the regular thing to ask, "Have you missed a bird to-day?" And it is looked upon as somewhat of a disgrace if the reply is in the affirmative. Nevertheless, we ven-

Rail shooting on the Anacostia Marshes
Washing on. D.C.   (page 13)

"Entering the Marsh both must stand, the sportsman in front, his left foot forward and right behind the seat, steadying himself as best he can." Rail Shooting on the Anacostia Marshes, H. Elliott, from *Avifauna Columbiana*, 1882

ture the assertion that few ever go on the marsh for a day's Rail shooting without missing not one only but several birds in the course of the day. Then, too, finding the bird after it is shot is not a simple matter, and very many are thus lost after being undoubtedly killed. The reeds of the wild rice grow to a height of from 4 to 6 feet, and though usually broken down sufficiently to give a clear view, they present so uniform an appearance that when a bird drops it disappears in the foliage, and if the eye be taken off the spot without "marking," the chances are greatly against its being found. "Marking" and gathering in the birds belong to the duties of the pusher, and that he should do these things well is fully as necessary to a successful day as that he should be able to propel the boat, or that the sportsman should be a good shot.

The mode of "marking" a shot bird is to fix in the mind something about the place where it falls which differs from its surroundings—a very tall reed, a broken stem, a wanquapin leaf, etc.—anything, however slight (and it is wonderful how slight a mark will suffice for an experienced pusher), that will serve to identify the place. The importance of this appears still greater when it is remembered that the pusher must always wait after a shot for the sportsman to reload, and frequently it will happen that before he reaches the spot where the first bird fell, six or eight more birds will be flushed and killed, each of which must be marked in like manner. It is not an uncommon thing to have as many as ten or a dozen birds down in the reeds and water before one has been picked up.

If any interested reader wishes to get a good day's Rail shooting in the District of Columbia, let him make his arrangements to try it upon the 1st day...the law protecting the birds expires; up to this time they have not been disturbed, and are consequently very abundant upon the open marshes. Wait for one week and it will be as difficult to secure one dozen birds as it is on September 1 to bag ten dozen. The boat and pusher must be engaged a week or two before the appointed time. . . . The boat which is used in Rail shooting is of peculiar construction, and especially adapted to forcing a way through the tangled reeds. In local vernacular it is a "skiff," and is a ticklish-looking affair for two men to navigate in *standing up.* And indeed it is a ticklish affair, as the greenhorn will be likely to learn in his first attempt at Rail shooting. The craft is usually about 16 feet long by 3 feet wide across the widest part, above. It is pointed at both ends, each end being covered over for about 2 feet. At the stern this affords a seat to the paddler, while at the bow it forms a locker for the reception of the game. The one seat is about the junction of the anterior and middle third of the length. The hull is constructed of three planks, one for the bottom and one each for the sides. The side planks are cut upon a pattern, so that when put together the bottom curves upwards towards each end very much after the manner of the ocean fisherman's dory. The advantage of this shape becomes immediately apparent when upon the marsh; the skiff is thus enabled to ride over the reeds and grass instead of plunging into the tangled masses. . . .

These skiffs, although very "precarious" to the uninitiated, are quite seaworthy in the hands of a skillful boatman, and are used also on the river for duck-shooting.

In getting into one of these little crafts for the first time the sensation is one of insecurity, and the feeling is well expressed by the phrase in common use, that "You must part your hair in the middle" to avoid an upset.

The sportsman gets in first and sits upon the middle seat, with his guns and ammunition in front of him. He should have two guns and not less than 300 loaded shells; two guns, to change when one becomes too hot to handle. Shells should be loaded with 2 drachms of powder and three-quarters of an ounce of No. 10 shot. Some use 2ž drachms of powder and one ounce No. 10 shot.

Having taken his position, the pusher shoves off and paddles over the channel to the marsh opposite. Entering the marsh both must stand, the sportsman in front, his left foot forward and right foot behind the seat, steadying himself as best he can. He soon becomes accustomed to the motion of the boat, which, if the pusher be a good one, is moderately steady, being propelled along at the rate of about 2 miles an hour. If propelled too slowly, the birds will run out of the way without flushing, and if too fast, they will dive and wait for the boat to pass. The pusher propels the skiff by means of a pole 16 feet in length, with a crotch at the distal end to prevent it from sinking in the mud.

By skillful use the boat is kept moving almost at a uniform rate, except where very thick masses of tangled reed are met, when all the strength and skill is taxed in getting through, and the sportsman must take care that he is not by a sudden lurch precipitated overboard.

On the marsh the little craft is much steadier than in open water, because supported by the undergrowth, and a tumble overboard results only in a disagreeable wetting, the water being but 2 or 3 feet deep.

The time of day for entering the marsh varies with the tide. The water is usually deep enough one hour and a half before the flood tide, and the shooting continues one and a half hours after, making about three hours' shooting for an average tide. The highest tides occur when the wind has been from the east or southeast for twenty-four hours and when the moon is in conjunction with the sun.

When the birds have not been much disturbed they will be found feeding all over the marsh; and as the centers are more easily accessible to the boat these are first gone over, and as many birds secured as possible. This drives them to such shelter as they can find in thick patches of tall reeds and tangled saw-grass and wanquapins usually found along the edges of the river and of the guts. These covers must then be beaten as the tide begins to fall. The boat is run along the edges and the reeds beaten with a pole, by which means many birds are frightened into taking flight and secured.

So they go, gliding through the marsh, and the birds begin to rise. Now both the pusher and shooter have all they can attend to. Birds rise in front, to the right, to the left, behind; the greenhorn becomes excited, confused; doesn't know which to shoot at; fires almost at random; misses oftener than he hits; swears at his gun, at his shells, at the unfortunate pusher, at everything but himself, who alone is at fault, and not unlikely tumbles overboard. If he is of the right mettle, however, he soon settles down to work, deliberately picks his bird each time, and then there is but little more missing.

Sometimes birds will get up behind him and out of the range of his vision. The pusher cries "Mark," when he wheels and fires. Nor has the pusher a sinecure; he advances, stops for loading, goes forward, backwards, zigzagging, retrieving the game; and so it continues until the retreating tide forces the skiff from the marsh.

Rail shooting is often termed "tame sport," and so it is as far as mere skill in shooting is concerned when compared with Quail shooting. But, after all, it is certainly exciting and enjoyable especially to the city sportsman, to whom an all-day tramp after Quail is very likely to prove exhausting or even painful.

Here there is no fatigue, no long tramp in the hot sun, only the labor of standing and balancing one's self in the quivering canoe, twisting to the right or left or backward to get a shot, while the position of the legs must remain unchanged; one experiences the excitement of constant shooting; birds are almost always on the wing; and, withal, the shooting lasts but three hours, not long enough for one to become satiated.

Since the great increase in the size of these marshes, the Rail shooting is much better than it was twenty years ago.

The Carolina Rails when feeding upon the wild rice become very fat and acquire a delicious flavor, for which they are much prized by epicures. Their flesh is soft, however, and they readily become tainted if the day is hot.

A Tidal Wave of Birds

We should not close this slight sketch without special reference to the phenomenal season of 1882, in which the ordinary course of migratory events was interrupted in an unprecedented manner. We had, in fact, a "tidal wave" of birds during the second and third weeks in May. It stormed for ten days, up to about the middle of the month, and before the cold rain ceased there was such a gathering of birds in the city as had never been witnessed by the "oldest inhabitant." Many thousands of birds filled the streets and parks; so great was the number and so brilliant the assemblage that the newspapers took it up and published their notes and queries. To account for the unwonted apparition, some one started the story that a vessel, just arrived at a wharf in Georgetown from the West Indies, had brought a cargo of tropical birds which had in some manner escaped! And no wonder, when the city was swarming with Scarlet Tanagers, Golden Orioles, Rose-breasted Grosbeaks, Redstarts, Summer and other Warblers, all as strange to the average Washingtonian as the most brilliant exotic birds could be. Yet these lovely creatures are with us always for those who can see and feel.

In the back yard of a private residence—a space 20 by 40 feet, containing one peach tree and some grape vine—we counted six species at once; a Baltimore Oriole, a Canada Flycatcher [Canada warbler], a Redstart, a Summer Yellow-bird [yellow warbler], a Black-Throated Blue Warbler, and a Chestnut-sided Warbler. In the parks it was common to see a flock of six or eight Scarlet Tanagers in one tree. There were flocks of Rose-breasted Grosbeaks in the Smithsonian Grounds; these birds were shot by boys near the city, one little fellow killing six. The most remarkable sight we witnessed ourselves was a great troop of a hundred or more Orchard Orioles in the Smithsonian Grounds, rambling with a few Baltimores over the new-mown grass like a flock of Blackbirds, while at the same moment, on turning the head, the black, white, and rose-color of the beautiful Grosbeak was seen contrasted with the green over head; Summer Warblers, Black-and-yellow Warblers, and Chestnut-sided Warblers were skipping together through the tender foliage; Hermit Thrushes were hiding in the evergreen shrubbery, and the ubiquitous Sparrows were chaffering and dickering on every hand.

The rare birds were in due proportion more numerous than ever before. We have knowledge of nine Cape May Warblers taken this season. The Golden-winged, Blue-winged Yellow, and Nashville Warblers were all not uncommon. Several specimens of the Connecticut Warbler, never seen here before in the spring, and the rare Mourning Warbler, seldom known to have been captured in the District, were also taken.

The weather was unquestionably the cause of this apparition. Considering the country at large, it held the birds back; they could not make their usual headway against so protracted a storm; and even after it ceased here, there was a cold wave north of us which retarded their advance. It also seemed to have deflected the ordinary line of migration from the highway of the Appalachian chain to the lower-lying land between these mountains and the sea-coast. In a word, a broad stream of birds flowing northward was contracted between comparatively narrow banks and then obstructed in its course, the District happening to fall just in the main channel. This seems sufficient to account for the phenomenon. As to the multitudes of birds in the city itself—for we cannot imagine the whole country round about to have been equally overcharged—we must suppose them to have been driven in by cold and hunger. They acted for the most part as though chilled and starved, showing no more fear of man than the Sparrows themselves, and some that were shot being found greatly emaciated.

Evidence of the correctness of this view of the case will be found by consulting the weather charts for the period in mention. Paragraphs in relation to the weather as affecting birds appeared in various northern journals, though nothing like the "tidal wave" we witnessed here seems to have been elsewhere noted. . . .

The Bobolink

Family ICTERIDAE: Blackbirds, &c
107. (140.) *Dolichonyx oryzivorus Linn.*) *Sw.* Bobolink (in the spring); Reedbird (in the fall).

A spring and autumn migrant, abundant. In the former season, the flocks on their way northward throw themselves into the fields and meadows, making their "mad music" and attracting general attention by their turbulency from the 1st to the 15th of May. They could always be depended upon, early in May, in the fields along Fourteenth street beyond N; and, though these are now built up, College Hill still receives the guests at the same season as formerly. In the spring of 1882, estopped like the rest of the migrants from passing northward, they "banked up" in the city parks, particularly the grounds about the White House; and very likely some of the cranks and quidnuncs which abound at the National Capital drew political augury from the unwonted babel of song. At this season the tawny females are inconspicuous, but the black-and-buff males have for the most part nearly finished their vernal tailoring, which they accomplish by dyeing their old suits without losing a feather. The familiar "clink" of the Reed-bird begins to be heard over the tracts of wild oats along the river banks about the 20th of August, and from that time until October the restaurants are all supplied with "Reed-birds"—luscious morsels when genuine; but a great many Blackbirds and English Sparrows are devoured by accomplished gourmands, who nevertheless do not know the difference when the bill of fare is printed correctly and the charges are sufficiently exorbitant.

Season of "Eclipse" in Zoo Duck Pond *and* Our Doorstep Sparrow

Florence A. Merriam Bailey (1863–1948)

Florence Merriam was raised to love nature by scientifically sophisticated parents in rural upstate New York. Sufficiently moneyed to be obliged neither to marry nor to work, she did both in her own good time. She made a home with Vernon Bailey in Washington that became a mecca for established scientists and aspiring students. Vernon's job as field naturalist at the Biological Survey took them all over the western United States, giving Florence the opportunity to study birds comprehensively. Her writing began during college with bird protection articles. Then came *Birding through an Opera Glass,* which was the first book to teach beginning birdwatchers how to study birds without killing them. The success of her many popular books and articles can be attributed both to her knowledge of natural history and to her skill as a writer; in her day, her style was compared to Thoreau's. She was the first woman associate and then the first woman fellow of the American Ornithologists' Union. Her technical papers, the *Handbook of Birds of the Western United States,* and *Birds of New Mexico* met the highest scientific standards. A conservationist and Auduboner throughout her life, she initiated Audubon classes for children and classes for teachers in the District of Columbia public schools. "Season of 'Eclipse'" illustrates Bailey's knowledge of bird life histories and her careful but very readable style of writing for a popular audience. The introduction to this anthology contains more details of Bailey's life; it also discusses the purposes of the humanizing of nature that was common in late-nineteenth-century writing and of which "Our Doorstep Sparrow," is a very restrained example. One of Bailey's many articles for children, it appeared in the first issue of *Bird-Lore*, the voice of the Audubon societies.

From *Washington Star*, August 4, 1926

Season of "Eclipse" in Zoo Duck Pond

Visitors to the duck pond—pointed to by the sign, "North American waterfowl"—at the west end of the bridge near the Harvard street Zoo gate—may well ask: "What's the matter with the ducks? Where have all the handsome drake mallards, shovelers and wood ducks gone, and what are those strange spotted looking ducks?"

The answer is a simple one, but it opens a fascinating chapter in the book of nature—a chapter on nature's protecting care of her wild children. The ducks are going into what is called eclipse plumage.

With the sun and moon, eclipse is merely a casual matter of the movements of the heavenly bodies. With the ducks, it is a matter of life or death, of protection from enemies during the most dangerous period in the lives of the brilliantly colored drakes.

Other birds molt their wing quills a few at a time so that it doesn't interfere with their flight, but the ducks lose all their wing quills at once and can't fly until they have grown out again.

During this period when the conspicuous plumage of the flightless birds would make them the easy prey of their enemies, they go into eclipse, lose their usual striking colors and markings, and assume an inconspicuous or eclipse plumage. At the same time they generally retreat to reedy marshes or other protected quiet waters where, unable to fly, they can swim to safe cover.

Meanwhile, their dull-colored mates, left alone to raise the broods, in some cases almost from the shell, do not become flightless until their young are at least partly able to care for themselves—another important provision of nature.

In the Zoo, where there is little need for protection from enemies, so firmly has the habit become established through ages of evolution that the protectively colored plumage is still assumed by the drakes for their flightless period.

It is assumed irregularly, however. Now, while some of the green-winged teal, pintails, scaups, widgeons, bald-pates, redheads and canvasbacks are almost or wholly unchanged, you may look the pond over for a mallard, a shoveler or a wood duck in the handsome familiar plumage and encounter all sorts of motley wear.

Most of the mallards, when found, partly by the help of their narrow, greenish yellow bills, have lost almost all the rich green of the head, the maroon of the breast and the characteristic curled-up tail feathers, being a thickly marked brown, very good for purposes of disguise. Some still have the curled-up tail feathers, greatly to the relief of a confused observer who said that was what she always told them by. One that was seen sunning himself on an island, with wing outstretched, still had the white-bordered bright purple patch or speculum, but that will probably soon be gone, for a time at least.

The shovelers, in which the eclipse was first noted in dark blotches on the white breast, now have little but the spatulate bill to relate them to their former selves.

The wood duck, whose coat of many colors is one of the wonders of the bird world, is now one of the plainest of birds, with only his red eyes, a touch of red on the bill, part of his former crest and a few white throat marks to name him.

Enough of the canvasbacks still have the wide white canvas body band for contrast with those of their kind which have lost it, but in most of them both the canvas and the reddish head are dulling, and in a number the curious spotty eclipse seems complete. In this case the bill identifies them—a long, almost straight line continuous with that from the top of the forehead—suggesting the line of the nose of a Greek profile—in marked contrast to the short bill starting from the middle of the forehead in the puffy-headed redhead, a close relative in the diving sea duck tribe.

Many of the pintails have lost, or are losing the long white finger mark seen when they stretch their long necks above the wheat in the Dakotas, and some of the little green-winged teal are losing the pretty brown of their heads, as are the baldpates and widgeons the white streak up the forehead.

In looking across the pond at the flaglike tails sticking up above the water while their surface-feeding river owners are standing on their heads feeding below—kicking their webbed feet comically so that they shall not lose their balance—you are struck by the absence of black patches and striking markings which at other times of the year enable birds of a feather to keep together even when their bodies are under water; but now, what's in a name?

No time should be lost in going to the duck pond if you would watch the progress of this marvelous eclipse. It is already too late to see the transformation of the earliest molters, some of which, notably the mallard, wood duck, gadwell, baldpate and pintail, have previously been observed by Mr. Hollister, the superintendent of the Zoo, going into eclipse during the last week of June.

But individuals vary so greatly in the date of molt that the last of the remarkable series of changes may still be seen in some, and there is yet time to watch the whole surprising process in others. But from now on, without a knowledge of what has gone before, it will be increasingly difficult to tell who's who in the duck pond.

The completed total eclipse lasts only three or four weeks and, while the mallards get back into full dress in October, by another complicated series of changes, most northern ducks hold off until November, and in some cases, as with the shoveler, blue-winged teal and ruddy, the return to full breeding plumage is not until Spring.

In the duck pond, with its 200 ducks, geese and swans of 35 different kinds, we have for the student a laboratory close at hand for the discovery of new material not only on eclipse plumage, but on courtship display and other phases of the life history of waterfowl that we would eagerly tramp their prairie breeding grounds over for a hint of; while for the casual Zoo visitor there is a continuing unrolling motion picture of intense human interest, exhibiting the martial and community life of these, our feathered brothers, taught by the wisdom of the ages to fulfill the purposes of nature.

From *Bird-Lore* 1 (1899)

Our Doorstep Sparrow

Don't think that I mean the House, or English Sparrow, for he is quite a different bird. Our little doorstep friend is the very smallest of all the brown Sparrows you know, and wears a reddish brown cap, and a gray vest so plain it hasn't a single button or stripe on it. He is a dear, plump little bird, who sits in the sun and throws up his head and chippers away so happily that people call him the Chipping Sparrow.

He comes to the doorstep and looks up at you as if he knew you wanted to feed him, and if you scatter crumbs on the piazza he will pick them up and hop about on the floor as if it were his piazza as well as yours.

One small Chippy, whom his friends called Dick, used to light on the finger of the kind man who fed him, and use his hand for dining-room, and sometimes when he had a very nice breakfast, he would hop up on a finger, perch, and sing a happy song!

Dick was so sure his friends were kind and good, that as soon as his little birds were out of the nest, he brought them to be fed too. They did not know what a nice dining-room a hand makes, so they wouldn't fly up to it, but when the gentleman held their bread and seeds close to the ground, they would come and help themselves.

Chippy's Nest

If you were a bird and were going to build a nest, where would you put it? At the end of a row of your brothers' nests, as the Eave Swallows do? Or would that be too much like living in a row of brick houses in the city? Chipping Sparrows don't like to live too close to their next door neighbors. They don't mind if a Robin is in the same tree, on another bough, but they want their own branch all to themselves.

And they want it to be a branch, too. Other birds may build their nests on the ground, or burrow in the ground, or dig holes in tree trunks, or even hang their nests down inside dark chimneys if they like, but Chippy doesn't think much of such places. He wants plenty of daylight and fresh air.

But even if you have made up your mind to build on a branch, think how many nice trees and bushes there are to choose from, and how hard it must be to decide on one. You'd have to think a long time and look in a great many places. You see you want the safest, best spot in all the world in which to hide away your pretty eggs, and the precious birdies that will hatch out of them. They must be tucked well out of sight, for weasels and cats, and many other giants like eggs and nestlings for breakfast.

If you could find a kind family fond of birds, don't you think it would be a good thing to build near them? Perhaps they would drive away the cats and help protect your brood. Then on hot summer days maybe some little girl would think to put out a pan of water for a drink and a cool bath. Some people, like Dick's friends, are so thoughtful they throw out crumbs to save a tired mother bird the trouble of having to hunt for every morsel she gets to give her brood. Just think what work it is to find worms enough for four children who want food from daylight to dark!

The vines of a piazza make a safe, good place for a nest if you are sure the people haven't a cat, and love birds. I once saw a Chippy's nest in the vines of a dear old lady's house, and when she would come out to see how the eggs were getting on she would talk so kindly to the old birds it was very pleasant to live there. In such a place your children are protected, they have a roof over their little heads so the rains won't beat down on them, and the vines shade them nicely from the hot sun.

When you are building your house everything you want to use will be close by. On the lawn you will find the soft grasses you want for the out-side, and in the barnyard you can get the long horse hairs that all Chipping Sparrows think they must have for a dry, cool nest-lining. Hair-birds, you know Chippies are called, they use so much hair. The question is how can they ever find it unless they do live near a barn? You go to look for it, some-day, out on a country road or in a pasture. It takes sharp eyes and a great deal of patience, I guess you'll find then. But if you live on the piazza of a house, with a barn in the back yard, you can find so many nice long hairs that you can sometimes make your whole nest of them. I have seen a Chip-py's nest that hadn't another thing in it—that was just a coil of black horse hair.

After you have built your nest and are looking for food for your young it is most convenient to be near a house. The worms you want for your nestlings are in the garden, and the seeds you like for a lunch for yourself are on the weeds mixed up with the lawn grass. You needn't mind taking them, either, for the people you live with will be only too glad to get rid of them, because their flowers are killed by the worms, and their lawns look badly when weeds grow in the grass, so you will only be helping the kind friends who have already helped you. Don't you think that will be nice?

Chippy's Family

Did you ever look into a Chippy's nest? The eggs are a pretty blue and have black dots on the larger end.

When the little birds first come out of the shell their eyes are shut tight, like those of little kittens when they are first born.

If you are very gentle you can stroke the backs of the little ones as they sit waiting for the old birds to feed them.

I remember one plum tree nest on a branch so low that a little girl could look into it. One day when the mother bird was brooding the eggs the little girl crept close up to the tree, so close she could look into Mother Chippy's eyes, and the trustful bird never stirred, but just sat and looked back at her. "Isn't she tame?" the child cried, she was so happy over it.

There was another Chippy's nest in an evergreen by the house, and when the old birds were hunting for worms we used to feed the nestlings bread crumbs. They didn't mind the bread not being worms so long as it was something to eat. It would have made you laugh to see how wide they opened their bills! It seemed as if the crumbs could drop clear down to their boots! Wouldn't you like to feed a little family like that sometime?

Cobb's Island

Frank M. Chapman (1864–1945)

Now a part of the Nature Conservancy's Virginia Coast Reserve,
Cobb Island has an unique place in the history of museology. From
its beaches, American Museum of Natural History curator Frank
Chapman created the first habitat group: His diorama of nesting skimmers was the first display combining a realistic, painted background
with mounted specimens in a foreground of natural objects.

Chapman's accomplishments far transcend this innovation. He
was among the founders of the turn-of-the-century Audubon movement and the owner, publisher, and editor of its organ, *Bird-Lore*.
A tireless advocate of bird protection, he came from New York to
Washington to deliver the first lecture, "Woman as Bird Enemy,"
at the inaugural meeting of the Audubon Society of the District of
Columbia. His many popular books and articles were potent instruments in educating the public to the significance and beauties of
birds. On his many scientific expeditions to both North and South
America, he discovered new species and extended our knowledge
of bird populations. His *Handbook of North American Birds* won the
John Burroughs Medal in 1929.

"Cobb's Island" is the first of five selections in this anthology that
chronicle the changes in bird hunting and protection on the coastal
barrier islands; the others are George Shiras's "Revels Island," Rachel
Carson's *Chincoteague: A National Wildlife Refuge*, Charlton Ogborn's
"Down the Coast to Assateague," and George Reiger's "Barrier Island
Birds."

From *Camps and Cruises of an Ornithologist* (New York: D. Appleton and Company,
1908)

THE ATLANTIC COAST, from New Jersey to North Carolina, is bordered by
an outlying chain of islets. Many of them are mere sand bars, more or less
grown with coarse grasses, and, on their western sides, fringed by marshes
which reach out into the bays separating them from the mainland.

Useless for agricultural purposes, these islands have a high commercial value only when they have become the sites of summer resorts; but when they have not suffered from an irruption of hotels and cottages they are, as a rule, tenanted only by an occasional fisherman or the crews of life-saving stations, whose presence does not materially alter their primeval conditions.

Lacking the natural foes of birds which exist on the mainland, these barren islets make ideal breeding-grounds for birds, which find on them the isolation their peculiar nesting habits require, while the surrounding waters furnish them an abundant supply of food.

In all this chain of bird homes, probably none has been better known to ornithologists than Cobb's Island, on the Virginia coast, north of Cape Charles. Seven miles long, it has been occupied by man only at the extreme southern end; a small sportsman's club-house and a life-saving station being now its only dwellings.

Twenty years ago, Willet, and Least Terns, in large numbers, and Royal Terns bred on Cobb's Island, but today the former is rare while the two latter are unknown, and there are left as breeding birds, Common, Forster's, and Gull-billed Terns, Laughing Gulls, Skimmers, Oyster-catchers, Wilson's Plovers, Clapper Rails and Seaside Finches. Willet have disappeared before spring shooting, in what was actually their nesting season. The Least Terns fell victims to the milliners, who greatly decreased the other species of Terns nesting on the island. The former captain of the life-saving station told me of 1,400 Least Terns being killed in one day; while the captain of the station and Mr. E.B. Cobb, owner of the island, informed me that when Terns were first killed for millinery purposes they, with another man, killed 2,800 birds in three days on and near Cobb's Island. The birds were packed in cracked ice and shipped to New York for skinning; ten cents being paid for each one.

In July, 1902 (23–25), I visited Cobb's Island to secure data, photographs and specimens with which to represent its summer bird-life in a Habitat Group. At the same time, it was proposed to study the Black Skimmer. Marvellously graceful in the air, the Skimmer is so conspicuously ugly when at rest, that not even the milliners consider it available for alleged hat decoration; consequently it was spared while its more beautiful neighbors, the Terns, were slaughtered, and it is numerous in favorable localities on the coast from Virginia to Texas.

But in spite of the Skimmer's abundance, its conservatism in the matter of habitat removes it from the field of observation of most ornithologists, and, at the time of which I write, accounts of its habits could be found only in the works of Wilson and Audubon. Neither of these remarkably keen and sympathetic students of bird-life appears, however, to have had an extended experience with the Skimmer during the nesting season. Both state, for instance, that it lays only three eggs; whereas the full complement is four; and, Wilson writes that the "female sits on them only during the night and in wet and stormy weather." As I desired especially to secure photographs of the sitting bird, this question of the day or night incubation was of importance. I made inquiry, therefore, of ornithologists who had been among Skimmers, but not one had ever seen a Skimmer on its nest. Hence the life history of the Skimmer appeared to be an unusually attractive subject for investigation. Unique in structure, he was known to be correspondingly unique in feeding habit; while there was something pleasantly mysterious in the birds' supposed habit of coming home only after dark.

Skimmers arrive on the Virginia coast early in May, and begin to lay about June 15; but their nests are so persistently robbed by fishermen that few young are hatched before July 20. The latter part of this month or early August is, therefore, the best season in which to study the domestic economy of the Skimmer household.

It is a memorable moment in the life of the naturalist when the animal of books or museums, or even zoological gardens, is first seen by him, a wild, free creature in its haunts; and when the animal is as singularly formed as the Skimmer, one's desire is intensified by a curiosity to see it use its peculiar and characteristic organs. Imagine, then, the joy of an ornithologist who, for the first time, finds himself in a breeding colony of thousands of Skimmers, where the air is filled with a yelping mob of birds whose eggs and young are so numerous on the broad shell-strewn beach, that one cannot walk without danger of stepping on them.

It was not difficult to find a spot in which to begin a study of the birds. Some minutes before reaching the boundary of the territory they inhabited, a band of birds arose in the air and, with more or less extended front, flew toward me only to swing to one side, wheel and fly back again; all uttering a trumpet-like note which is effectively emphasized by violent bill action, the bright red and black mandibles opening widely with each note. When the nests were reached, the uproar increased and with it the excitement and boldness of the particular birds near whose eggs or nests I chanced to be standing. Starting a hundred or more feet away, one after the other charged toward me with such speed and apparent fearlessness, that one could well be pardoned an involuntary dodge ere the birds, when only a few feet away, swerved and passed over one's head.

The nests are hollows in the sand, often only a few feet apart and with absolutely no lining, the Skimmer's bill being evidently not adapted to

gathering nesting material or constructing a nest. The four creamy white
eggs are conspicuously marked with black, and are by no means difficult
to see; but the downy young so closely harmonize with their surroundings
in color, that they are far less easy to discover than the young of any beach-
nesting bird with which I am familiar. Their partial invisibility, it should be
observed, is not due to their resemblance in form to their surroundings, or
to the necessity of distinguishing them from pebbles or shells, as is often
the case with young Terns. It is purely a matter of color and disposition of
color which makes them fade into the bare sand about them. Like most
young birds, they instinctively know that safety lies only in unquestioning
obedience to the parental command, which warns them of threatening danger, and bids them squat close to the sand with neck stretched out and eyes
half closed. I could scarcely believe, for a moment, that the first one seen
in this attitude was a living bird, but behold! when I stooped to pick him up,
at the touch of my finger tips, he evaded my grasp and scudded over the
beach so fast I scarce could catch him.

It was easier to discover the nests of the Skimmers than a vantage point
from which one might study the habits of their owners. As yet I had not
learned whether they incubated by day or night, and this could be done
only by concealing myself and waiting until peace and quiet in Skimmer-
land came, with the assurance that their enemy had departed. The blind
was therefore erected in a depression on a sand dune within one hundred
and fifty feet of twenty or more nests. The whole affair was then covered
with beach grass, and into it I crept.

For a time, the birds threatened this unfamiliar object, darting at it with
loud screams; but within one hour and a half, it ceased to annoy them and,
to my great satisfaction, bird after bird returned to its nest, some alighting
directly on the little hollow in the sand, others dropping near-by and with
waddling step, walking to the nest and settling themselves on their eggs or
newly hatched young with a low, brooding, *churring* note reserved for this
occasion, and evidently indicative of extreme contentment. This answered
the question of day or night incubation; but it would be well to illustrate
this fact in the bird's history, and cameras bound about with grasses were
placed near several nests, a thread run from them to the blind, and numerous pictures were thus made of the Skimmer at home.

I passed two days in my blind, enjoying to the full the isolation of the
Skimmer's retreat, and the privilege of seeing, unseen, a wild creature in its
haunts. Within this short time, some additions were made to our knowledge of the Skimmer's habits. Thus I learned that the hollow where the eggs

are laid is not a chance depression, but is made by the bird—the female, so far as was observed—which, squatting close, turns round and round, actually boring out a shallow cavity in the easily yielding sand.

Apparently only the female incubates, but the much larger male often comes and stands by her side while she sits on the eggs, a pleasant picture in bird life suggestive of domestic harmony. In all the pictures made of the sitting bird from the front, one or two of the eggs can be seen through the breast feathers, as though the bird had a larger "clutch" than she could cover. The period of incubation I had no means of determining, but certain it is that once the chick announces his coming by a chicken-like *peep*, the transformation of a pipped egg into a bright-eyed downy Skimmer, endowed with all the instincts of its kind, is a matter of only two and one-half or three hours.

As soon as the nestling emerges from the egg, the shell is taken by the parent, and, so far as was observed, carried out of sight; a singular custom, common to most birds. The habit is doubtless of importance to a tree-nesting bird, where the egg-shell below might advertise the young bird above; but why, with a beach-nesting species an egg-shell should be considered more conspicuous than an egg it is hard to say; but there can be no doubt that once it has released its contents, it must be disposed of as quickly as possible.

The chicks seem to appear on successive days, and to leave the nest when a day or two old. They are fed on small fish and doubtless other forms of aquatic life, which, at first, may be partially digested by the parent bird. Whether or not each parent finds its own chicks when the beach becomes alive with hungry youngsters, cannot be confirmed definitely, though there is evidence to show not only that the old birds recognize their offspring, but that the latter know their parents.

So singular in form is the bill of the adult Skimmer, that Buffon described it as an "awkward and defective instrument"; a somewhat surprising conclusion to proceed from so learned a naturalist, and one which Wilson pronounced an "impiety." With the lower mandible averaging half an inch longer than the upper, and with both so thin and flexible that they can be bent as readily as a table knife, one might be pardoned for believing the Skimmer's bill a deformity; but the belief is quickly dispelled when once the bird is seen feeding. Flying low, with bill opened wide, the lower mandible cuts the water like a knife edge, as the birds actually skim the surface for fish and small forms of aquatic life.

In the newly hatched bird, it is of exceeding interest to observe that the mandibles are of virtually equal length, and the lower mandible does not become pronouncedly longer than the upper until the bird takes wing. This may be considered as evidence that this highly specialized character has been developed late in the history of the species; or the development of the bill may be a correlation in growth which defers the perfection of an organ until it can be successfully employed. Certainly without the power of flight, a Skimmer could not "skim." Until, therefore, the bird can fly, it supplements the supply of food brought by the parents by picking up a living along the beach.

Skimmers were frequently seen feeding during the day, particularly along the meeting line of sand and sea, where they gleaned from the burden of the waves; but it was at dusk that they became really active. Then they followed the course of the streams winding through the marsh, now skimming for a short distance, again rising slightly and uttering a sharp *yap, yap,* like a pack of hounds on the trail.

The Life Worth Living

Thomas Dixon (1864–1946)

There is no better exemplar of country life as a genre of nature literature than Thomas Dixon's *The Life Worth Living*. A refugee "from the horrors of [New York] city living," Dixon brought his family to Gloucester County, Virginia, where they enjoyed every rural recreation from gardening to week-long, yacht-borne waterfowl hunts on the Chesapeake Bay. Unlike many nineteenth-century occupational vagabonds, Dixon was a success at everything he tried. A politician, Baptist minister, lawyer, and lyceum lecturer, he is best remembered as an author. He wrote many best-selling novels about his native South Land, including *The Clansman*; D. W. Griffith's genius and Dixon's photoplay transformed this story into *Birth of a Nation*, one of the most influential films of all time.

From *The Life Worth Living* (New York: Doubleday, Page, and Company, 1905)

Dreams and Disillusion

WHETHER LIFE is really worth living depends largely on where you try to live it.

The one great passion of my life was the dream of a beautiful home. This home-dream crept slowly into the soul long before the face of a woman came to smile at all other hopes and fears. It required no pleading to make her feel its beauty. She, too, had seen it in a vision long ago. Then tiny baby feet came trooping into a cottage before the money was in the bank to build this dream.

Another passion of my boyhood was the hope of life in a great city. From the distance of the farm this vision was radiant with the splendours of wealth and power. I dreamed of its boulevards, its parks, its palatial homes, and its gleaming lights. The lambent flame of its distant life filled the horizon with the glory of an endless sunrise.

So in the natural course of events New York swept us into its seething tide.

We struggled bravely to save both these dreams. First we rented a modest little slit-in-a-wall fourteen feet wide, far uptown, for which we paid one thousand dollars to the landlord annually, and five hundred, more or less, to the elevated road for the right to be jabbed in the ribs while we held to a strap to get there.

Then we tried a nice "airy apartment" downtown. It had six "rooms." One opened on the street, four looked down into a dark well, and the kitchen opened on an iron grillwork that gave it the appearance of a jail. The children were omnipotent and omnipresent. By the record in the family Bible we had only three. But they managed to get into every room in that flat at the same minute, and their name was legion.

We tried boarding with a nice old lady who had an eye that could chill the most turbulent child into silence. Our little girl took pneumonia, and we had two doctors and two trained nurses in that boarding house for six weeks.

Then the suburban home. We bought a vacant lot, with a waterfront of sixty feet, at Bensonhurst, and built on it. When finished it cost sixteen thousand dollars, and it took most of the time of one man to keep the tin cans, driftwood, dead cats and dogs off that sixty feet of waterfront.

The first time I tried to go home on Sunday, I got jammed in a cheerful crowd that started to Coney Island by way of Bensonhurst, gave it up after two hours, and didn't go home till morning. The first big snowstorm that came in the winter buried the trolley lines, and I didn't see my wife and children for two days. As the telephone wires were down I could only hope for the best. I sold the place to a bigger fool, after a patient search of four weeks for him. The ease with which I got out of that house, with only the loss of the carpets and window shades, I shall always regard as a mark of the special favour of God.

I bought a five-acre place on Staten Island on the top of the highest hill. It had a grand view of the sea, Sandy Hook and the shipping. The mosquitoes were so thick, so enormous, and so venomous, that they could attack and kill a horse if left to their mercy. Their fang was so poisonous that when they bit one of our boys his little legs and arms would swell as though a snake had struck him; and at the end of the summer he drooped into a deadly malarial fever from which we barely saved him alive, but with both legs paralyzed for life. With the shadow of this sorrow darkening the world, we sold the place to the first bidder, and tearfully returned to the city.

By this time we were convinced that the only way to really live in New York was to buy a decent home near Central Park, whatever the cost, and settle for life. We found it after a search of two months. It was located on West Ninety-fourth Street, within the block facing the park.

We had a delightful time spending a thousand dollars decorating it to our own taste. It was a neat brownstone front, nineteen feet wide, in a solid block of similar houses. It had a high stoop, iron bars on the basement windows through which we looked from the dining table, and a kitchen behind this dining-room opening into the paved cat-yard 19 x 20. The floor above contained a narrow hall, parlour and library. The next story had two bedrooms and a bathroom, and the top floor had two "large" rooms and two small ones inside. The wood was hard, the mantels and chandeliers pretty, the fireplaces poetic looking, with iron logs to imitate wood, and it cost us twenty-five thousand dollars.

The taxes, insurance and repairs still held a fixed charge on the place of about $350 annually. A house in New York is the easiest thing a tax-gatherer has to manage. Only one man in ten ever dares to own one. The others keep moving.

Within six months this dream had faded.

Our home was just a nineteen-foot slit in a block of scorched mud with a brownstone veneer in front. Our children were penned in its narrow prison walls through the long winters, and forbidden to walk on the grass in the cold, dreary spring. The doctor came to see us every week.

The disillusioning was complete. We had stayed in New York eleven years, moved twelve times, worn out three sets of household goods, and aided in the revival of the carpet trade, before we found out what ailed us.

At last we knew that the stamping-ground of the great herd might be a good place for trade, but that God never meant for man to build a home and rear children in it.

And then the longing for the country life in which we had both been reared came over us with resistless power. The smell of green fields and wild flowers, the breath of the open sea, the music of beautiful waters, the quiet of woodland roads, the kindly eyes of animals we had known, the memory of sun and moon and star long lost in the glare of electric lights, began to call. We sat down in our little narrow parlour, with its cast-iron firelogs and porcelain taper chandeliers, and cried over it all.

In Old Tidewater Virginia

We moved to Tidewater Virginia, the home of Captain John Smith, the oldest settlement in America and yet the most primitive, the most beautiful and least known spot in our continent—a bit of wild nature slumbering beside the pathway of the rushing life of the Atlantic seaboard.

Here we realized the first dream of life, a stately Colonial home two hundred years old, called Elmington Manor, situated on the shores of the Chesapeake Bay. Its ivory pillars flash their welcome from both sides of the house through the shadows of huge trees that shade its wide lawn.

The farm has five hundred acres, three hundred and fifty under cultivation and one hundred and fifty in woods. We keep eleven horses, six cows, a dozen sheep, four bird-dogs, chickens, ducks and turkeys. We have a two-acre garden with greenhouse for winter vegetables, an acre of strawberries, an acre of raspberries and dewberries and two acres in grapes; an old orchard and a young one with all the fruits of the temperate climate; and a mile water front with full riparian rights.

The Old Dominion steamer has an artistic little pier on the upper end of the lawn, which gives us daily mail and traffic with Old Point and Norfolk and the outside world. There are no railroads in the three counties of Gloucester, Matthews and Middlesex. We live in Gloucester, and around us on the beautiful landlocked arm of the Chesapeake called North River we see from our porch fourteen water-front homes. These three counties are intersected by a network of tide rivers and creeks, like the veins of a leaf, making it a veritable rural Venice.

Back two miles in the high hills rise cool streams of fresh water to turn our millwheels and pour their new life into the sea, giving us the finest oysters in the world. We have twenty-five acres of these oyster grounds in front of our home.

The fields are full of quail. They nest in the garden and orchard and sometimes mix with the chickens; while in unbroken reaches of three thousand acres of forests roam flocks of wild turkeys whose ancestors furnished food and sport for Powhatan, Pocahontas and Captain Smith.

The waters are full of fish, and our baby boy can catch enough for dinner within a hundred yards of the house any day from the first of May till the first of November. In the winter the wild ducks, geese and brant give the sport of kings.

We keep a pen full of diamond-back terrapin as we keep a pen of pigs, and fatten them on crabs. Crabs and clams are so plentiful that they are considered a very plebeian diet. We keep a naphtha launch, two small sailboats, three rowboats and a schooner yacht.

I had always desired a home that had some association with history and yet one on which I might stamp the imprint of my own mind. Elmington

Manor fulfilled both these desires. The house, when we bought the estate, was simply a square brick structure finished with Portland cement and painted brown. It is beautifully situated on a peninsula lawn of fifteen acres. From the land side the avenue drive stretches away from the gate through giant trees two miles to the hills and the country road. On the water side it looks majestically out to sea over a sunny stretch of greensward dotted with holly and flowering shrubs.

Its roots are deep set in Colonial history. Its broad acres were a Crown grant two hundred years ago. A short drive to the south is the village of Yorktown, the scene of the siege and surrender of Lord Cornwallis to Washington and our French allies. On this side the York River stands towering old Rosewell, the most palatial country establishment in America when built by the Pages. Near Rosewell is the ancient chimney of the Indian emperor, Powhatan. This chimney was built for Powhatan under the direction of Captain John Smith's colonists. Across the York but a few miles from us are old Williamsburg and Jamestown. . . .

Beside Beautiful Waters

It is the situation of a home that makes or mars it. Spend a million dollars on a palace, locate it poorly, and it is lost. You may build with all the art that genius and wealth can command, and if you build in an unhealthful climate or near a fish factory, art and wealth and genius have failed.

The one thing that makes New York impossible for a real home is the certainty that sooner or later a hotel, a flat, a store, a church, a factory, a stable or a saloon will be located near you. It is only a question of time when the palaces of millionaires are moved by these forces.

The thing which charmed me first with the spot in Tidewater Virginia which I selected, is the fact of its perfect healthfulness and security from nuisance.

The lawn is high ground rising abruptly from eight to ten feet from the water line, a stiff clay soil mixed with sand, with no marsh grass or mosquito pools. The grass of the lawn rolls sheer into the dead line of the salt tide. There are mosquitoes and malaria in Tidewater Virginia if you choose their location. The lawn of Elmington Manor is a beautiful little peninsula behind which stretches the estate of five hundred acres into the hills.

This little peninsula juts out into the waters of the river at the head of its navigable channel, just where the current makes a sharp bend to the right and two large creeks sweep inland to the left, giving views of the water from every window in the house and from every point at which a rustic seat may be placed on the lawn. The creek flows gracefully through the lawn and forms a landlocked harbor for our boats.

The water front commands an entrancing view. Straight before, two miles wide, stretches the North River southward until lost in the open sea of the Chesapeake Bay and Atlantic Ocean. The shores are marked with towering trees clustering around their old homesteads.

The things which fascinate me above all others are our trees.

The place was named "Elmington" from its giant elms. On the lawn now are three hundred and ninety trees, comprising thirty-seven varieties. About half of them are the evergreens, holly, pine, cedar and magnolia. Among them are water oaks four feet in diameter, lifting their immense limbs clothed in shimmering green far above the roof of the house.

There is no sameness anywhere. The lawn is level only on two sides. On the other sides are little hills and valleys and long open reaches of sunlit turf. A hundred cedars tower in line along the northern and western sides as guarding sentinels against the winds of winter. Two big magnolias, robed in everlasting green, stand beside the white pillars on the front porch and blossom all summer.

On the water side the hollies cast their dense shade in summer and lift triumphantly their bouquets of scarlet berry and green leaves through the fiercest storms of winter.

A mockingbird builds every summer in the flowering holly which we see on the water's edge from the dining-room window, while another nests in the rosebush nearby, and from every shrub and tree the chatter and song of an army of feathered musicians fill the air with melody.

We have nothing artificial, forced or cultivated—only the trees, hardy shrubs, grass and wild flowers.

Our friends from the barn with their babies often roam over the lawn, and their fellowship more than pays for any annoyances their presence may cause. They drink gracefully at our mermaid fountain and seem to think her bronze figure was cast and set there to give them water. And so it was.

In early spring the buttercups carpet every inch of earth in gorgeous yellow, while the jonquils lift their flame about the fountain's rim.

The buttercups stay a month, and then forget-me-nots, clover and daisies add their white and blue. We have a garden for the cultivated flowers. But I confess I've given my heart to the wild flowers of the lawn. They ask nothing and give everything.

The oaks and elms I love best of all the trees, especially the water oaks.

When tired of study, I stroll beneath their dark shadows, while their satin leaves flash above in the sun like so many swinging diamonds, lie down on the grass, and rest. Ah, such rest, with my beloved near!

The rush and roar and stupid din of the city I remember only as a fevered dream. I am akin to all life. The earth beneath is soft and tender as the touch of a mother, and these oaks that tower above me are my brothers. They have been tried as I have been tried. Their limbs have wrestled with the furies that rode on the wings of storms and have conquered. Their fibre is strong because they have suffered. The last storm twisted off the top of a mulberry and hurled it to the ground. But the oaks laughed for sheer joy in their strength when the wind was fiercest. I love them because they are strong. I hear them at night softly sighing when the wind is gentle. They are telling the others about them to be not afraid, for they have looked far out to sea and no storm is near.

Through the shadows of the trees the waters gleam.

How any man can build his home away from water so long as there is a water front left is something I cannot understand. The house is located just two hundred feet from the river's edge from one corner of the porch, and from the other corner the lawn stretches away into a reach of three hundred yards of open greensward before it merges into the tide.

This flashing glory of opal, emerald, and turquoise water, changing its tint with every passing cloud and breath of wind, reflecting every mood of sky and shore, with each white-winged sail that skims its surface—all now are of the rhythm of our very life. The storm, with its ten thousand whitecaps dancing and foaming and thundering on the shore, the mirrored pictures of the calm, the endless panorama of sun and moon and star are ours for the lifting of the eye.

And we got it all in exchange for a few feet of scorched mud, and a cement cat-yard 19 x 20.

The Music of the Seasons

Old Tidewater Virginia is the ideal spot in America for a home all the year round. Northern people have a very erroneous idea of the heat of its summers. I have spent summers at Gloucester, Massachusetts, on Long Island, and the Jersey coast; but there is no place on the Atlantic that compares in comfort to the shores of Old Virginia. The Gulf Stream, which almost touches the beaches here, maintains its temperature of 60 the year round. In winter it tempers the cold, and in summer it lowers the heat. We have the most even temperature to be found in the East.

We have long, beautiful springs. Winter never lingers in the lap of spring "until it creates talk." The earth seems alive with every species of early wild flowers.

The vegetable garden is a source of endless pleasure. We plant peas in January, and cabbage and lettuce grow all winter.

There is something about planting seeds, watching them sprout and grow, that links one with the creative process.

Production is communion with God, however stoutly the dogmatist may deny it.

I plant the seed in the soft warm earth and feel the glow of creative joy. I have joined with God in giving life, and when I reap my harvest, I join with him in taking it again.

There is not a month in the year that our garden will not grow the hardy vegetables, and from March to November it grows everything that flourishes this side the tropics. Celery will keep all winter bedded in the ground where it grows.

The spring calls the sportsman as loudly as the fall.

The fishing is fine, and the shore birds, curlew, snipe and plover, come in myriads in April and May and spend six weeks getting fat as they migrate northward. They have raised their young in the winter, far south, and spring is the proper season to kill them for food. They leave in the latter part of May and stop again as they return southward in July and August. They do not nest or stay permanently in our territory. Tidewater Virginia is simply their rich feeding ground.

In summer we have delightful breezes from every point of the compass. The long sweep inland of the Chesapeake Bay for 200 miles makes a hot land breeze impossible. The land breezes on the coast of New Jersey are insufferable to me. Here is water, water everywhere, and the land seems always the last significant feature of the picture Nature presents.

The fruits of the semi-tropical zone all grow luxuriantly. Gloucester county is famous for its fine watermelons and cantaloupes.

The drives in summer along the country roads are of surprising beauty. The wild grapevines festoon its dense woods and hang far out over the roadway. Even at noon the wide double-track highway is sheltered by these cooling shadows.

The summers offer the sportsman the same flight of migratory shore birds as spring, and adds to them some special varieties.

Autumn clothes field and forest with a new and peculiar glory. Here we have the long Indian Summer in September and October. Italy never saw such skies, and the glorious sunlight and peace that flood the earth in these days cannot be revealed by words. October is the only month when the windmill ever fails for two days to turn. Nature seems to hold her breath for sheer joy. Each day is a miracle of beauty—clear skies, warm genial sun, crisp pure air, with every tree that sheds its leaf robed in scarlet and purple flame.

It is hard to tell when our woods are most beautiful: in spring, with the dogwood blossoms so thick they look as if a snowstorm had covered their tender green, or in October, when the holly, as thick as the dogwood, lifts its great bouquets of glistening evergreen with scarlet berries amid the red and purple splendour of the oak and hickory, beech and maple, poplar and chestnut.

I confess a special love for our winters. Here the fire of the sun never dies. It warms and thrills even in February. The lawn is never quite bare. When the winds of November have swept clean the great limbs of oak and elm, the magnolia, cedar and holly smile still into the face of the sun. I love these big naked trees, too. To me their tall nymph-like limbs seem fashioned by some master artist of the nude against the azure background of the sky.

The roads in winter, that stretch through solemn aisles of towering pines, are as beautiful to me as the embowered drives of summer.

I love the ragged winter lines of the creek where the quail shelter in the tall grass at the water's edge ready to cross to the woods if hard pressed.

The cry of the wild duck and brant and the honk of the goose thrill the heart of the huntsman and call to the sport of kings.

There is not a day in the calendar from the first of January to the thirty-first of December that there is not good fishing or hunting, or both, in Tidewater Virginia.

On long winter nights we sit beside a roaring log fire, read and dream, listen to music, or chat with our kindly neighbours. Our neighbours are never in a hurry. They have more time than money, and spend it more freely. They really live, and we have fallen into their friendly ways. . . .

The Shouts of Children

I believe it is a crime to rear a child in New York city, or any great city. The man who is imprisoned in this living tomb by business, may plead a fair excuse, yet it is none the less a crime.

It is a physical and spiritual impossibility to rear a normal human being under the conditions which surround child-life in the modern city. His earth is merely a huge cobblestone with asphalt patches. There is no sun or moon or star. Day and night are one. The seasons disappear. Artificiality is the rule, and Nature becomes a synonyme for sin.

I shall never forget the sight of five hundred city waifs I ran into one hot July night as I was hurrying through the car shed of the Pennsylvania Railroad to catch the train for my home.

A philanthropist had given a mission society the money to send these five hundred poor children, who never saw a green field or sat beside beautiful waters, out into the country for two weeks. Poor little old wizen-faced men and women, they didn't know how to laugh or play! If they had been going to a funeral, they could not have been more serious. The word country had no meaning for them.

Who can measure the tragedy of these millions of tramping child feet crowding one another into the grave without one glimpse of this wonderful world through which they have passed?

I do not know of a single man of any force in modern civilization whose character was developed in a great city. President Roosevelt is the only man I can recall of any world prominence to-day who was born in a great city, and he became a man because he got out of it, and put himself in touch with Nature.

My children were prisoners in New York. In Old Virginia they find life and freedom. There the doctor came every week, here once a year is enough. We have no signs to "keep off the grass." The lawn is theirs, and on its open greensward or beneath its spreading elms and oaks every game that can tempt a child's heart they can play from year's end to year's end.

Here they learn to watch for the first signs of life in spring.

We have a boy whose eye discovers the first ripening strawberry, cherry, raspberry, melon and vegetable. Long before we think of looking, his keen little eyes have found them, and his swift bare feet come bounding to his mother as he holds the treasure aloft in triumph.

The whole round of country life is a thrilling daily drama for a child. When tired of play he explores the barn in search of hen's nests, and finds them in the most unheard of places, sometimes under the floor, sometimes in the hay rack far up near the ceiling. He has a duck house of his own at the barn, shuts his ducks up every night and keeps them there till eight or nine o'clock in the morning to be sure of their eggs. After Mrs. Duck has laid, he hustles them off to the creek to feed on bugs and worms and fiddlers and fish-eggs.

It is astonishing how many bird's nests that boy can find on the lawn and in the thick hedgerows around the garden and orchard. At first he would rob them all. But it was easy to teach him how much more fun he could get listening to the songs of mockingbirds, watching them sit and hatch, feed their babies and teach them to fly, than by breaking up their nests. Now he guards these nests with jealous care. The mockingbird, the wren, and song sparrow, the redbird and bluebird, catbird and thrush, hear his soft footfall without distress. His life has become larger and his heart bigger.

He watched a tiny sparrow build her nest in the grass this spring close beside the pathway to the Streamer's Pier. He saw the first egg and the last, and then the brooding mother, and then the little birds, with growing interest. He kept the dogs and the puppies away and guarded her with zealous care. Just as the bird babies were feathering and nearly ready to fly they made such a big houseful, some beast, a bird of prey, a rat or a crow perhaps, found them. As we went to the Pier at boat time they were all right, and the mother was chirping with pride in the tree above. When we returned, in half an hour, the nest was torn from its perch in the grass and every bird gone. The mother was crying as though her heart were broken. And then a boy's eyes grew dim. Who can weigh the value of such incidents in the shaping of a human soul? How many brass bands, monkeys and hand organs would it take to compensate for their loss?

When the children are tired of the land, the sea calls.

We have a beautifully curved sand beach on the lawn that invites for a bath, and rowboat and sailboat are always nodding their friendly challenge tethered to their pier. Somebody is always fishing in sight, and the crabs in the water's edge are a standing challenge. The horses and mules, colts and puppies, cows and calves are far more interesting to our children in their daily life than the wild animals of a circus. Daily life is a continuous performance in which the child is both audience and ringmaster. . . .

I believe in the gun for a normal boy. I teach my boy to shoot with me when he is so small he has to kneel and a number twelve gun kicks him flat on his back. It's funny to see a youngster pick himself up and declare he "didn't feel it at all!"

Narrow and poor is the child's life who never roamed the fields alone with his dog and a gun on his shoulder. He may make a man without it, but he will not have an equal chance with the boy whose heart has thrilled with the elemental joy that links him to the habits and instincts of four thousand years of human history. The first man was a hunter, a trapper and a fisherman. When man ceases to care for these things, or decries them, I fear he is either sick, a fool, or both.

It is not true that it makes him cruel or selfish. Upon the other hand, its effects are just the opposite. He draws close to Nature, learns her laws, and feels the sweep of her elemental life. He kills only what is fit to eat and needed for food. Every element of his character is strengthened by the care, skill, patience, judgment and zeal with which he follows game. Such boys rarely commit crime or display mental weakness. They make strong, clean, sane, wholesome men. . . .

Along Shining Shores

I hold that Old Tidewater Virginia is the most fascinating spot on our planet. I can prove it by the shorebirds, anyhow.

When the migrating snipe have raised their young in the far South, they come north to spend the summer. Far up in the sky, flying V-shaped, as the wild goose, the curlew leads the way in April. With his keen eye surveying from the heavens the glories of the world, he sweeps over the wild beauty of the tropics, calling now and then his silver trumpet-note of command to his flock.

But when he looks down from the clouds and sees the thousand rivers, creeks, channels and solemn marshes of Old Tidewater Virginia, his voice rings with joy, his wings droop with ecstasy, and the whole flock break their long silence with such a shout as the Greeks of old raised when, homeward bound, they first beheld the sea.

Gracefully they circle downward, chattering, calling, screaming their delight. They stop and spend six weeks. They know a good thing when they see it, and they see the world from pole to pole.

The curlew is to the shore what the ruffed grouse is to the woods, has about the same weight of body, and carries the same dark brown-and-black-spotted plumage, until sunburnt on his return in August. His bill is about four inches long, unless he is a sickle-bill, when it measures from five to nine inches. The jack-curlew is now the only variety seen in Virginia, though an occasional marlin or sickle-bill make the exception to the rule.

The jack-curlew is the wildest, shrewdest and most tantalizing bird with a snipe's bill that ever worried and fascinated a hunter. His eye is as keen as a wild duck's, and his ways past finding out. I have hunted them for ten years in Virginia, and many an evening have I gone home with but two or three birds for supper, while the sky above me rang with their shouts of derision.

I have watched them for days and weeks going in thousands to a certain spot on a marsh at a certain tide. I mark the spot and wait ten days for the tides to get back to the appointed hour. Then, all in readiness, I sneak away an hour ahead of my rival, whom I half suspect of knowing my secret.

Everything depends on the tides. By the calendar, the tide should make high water at sundown. If it does, and doesn't make too high or too low, and the birds don't find out I'm on the marsh by hearing the gun, or from the report of a scout—why, then, I'll get some of them. The hunting ground is nine miles wide and eighty miles long, and a curlew thinks nothing of a ten-mile flight.

Two hours before sundown, I reach the ground. I've marked the spot on a marsh a mile wide and seven miles long, surrounded by a stretch of mud-bars and channels at low tide, which melt into a beautiful silvery bay at high tide.

I go in my naphtha launch, following the winding channels, from twelve to fifteen miles, to get two miles as the crow flies. But I must get to the marsh, put out my decoys on the exact spot on that seven-mile stretch to which the birds are coming, and hide before the first bird appears, and this must be done before the tide rises. The curlew are now scattered over the vast reaches of this eighty-mile bay, eating bugs, worms and sand-fiddlers on the mud-bars and on the creek banks.

I leave the launch at the head of the channel and drag the hunting dink with guns and decoys over the mud-bar to the marsh.

I take an hour to locate the right spot. I'm dead sure of the place they went the last run of tides, but, if the conditions of weather differ, they may change their notion with the change of wind and stop a mile below or go a mile farther on, and to miss their track five hundred yards is to miss them five hundred miles. They will not listen to a call in their great flock flights on this run of tides.

At length I select the place in which to cast the fate of the day. I set the decoys in the short grass of a bald high place on the marsh, exactly where I believe they will assemble in grand conclave to sit out the high water. A hole is dug with a spade just deep enough to lie flat on one's back and hide below the surface of the ground, and tall green grass is cut and stuck carefully around the hole until it looks like a hundred other clumps of grass.

The calico birds begin to come in long before a curlew is seen or heard. I take a crack at them to get my hand in for Mr. Jack Curlew. The calico plover is a fine practice shot, for he is swift as lightning unless he sees fit to decoy perfectly.

At last the mud-flats are all covered and the hour has come for the flight to begin. I am on the lookout for a scout. The curlew send out a scout to survey the ground to which the great flocks are coming. If things look suspicious, he goes back and reports, and they change their flight ten or twenty miles in another direction.

No scout appears. I wait an hour and begin to grow uneasy. The tide is slow, a westerly wind has spoiled the flow, and not a curlew comes within five miles of me.

I try the next afternoon, and the wind jumps around to the east, the tide covers all creation and runs me out of my hole before I get a shot, even at a calico.

Again, not a curlew came to the marsh. They all went to the sand-dunes on Myrtle Island, fifteen miles below. I watched them for an hour. The heavens were streaked with them as far as the eye could reach—north, south, east and west. I ground my teeth and vowed vengeance. I have but one more day of this run of tides. If they don't come to the marsh the next night, they will not come till the tide gets around again in two weeks.

Again I've baled out my hole and rebuilt my grass blind, and, snugly resting on the rubber blanket, I gaze up at the southern sky, or away over the endless marsh and bay, and wait. My guide has gone a mile with the launch and hidden in the tall grass of the creek.

How still the world!

To the east, I see the dim white line of the ocean beaches, but the wind is from the south and I cannot hear the surf. North, south and west of me sweeps the dark green marsh, until it kisses the sky-line and fades into eternity. I begin to dream of great things. Nothing small disturbs my vision— not a house or man or woman is in sight.

I begin to feel pity for the feathered life I've come to take, when my eye rests on a mother fiddler in the mud beside me, peeping out of her hole to make sure no curlew is near before venturing out for food for her children. I clutch my gun and determine to take sides with the fiddlers.

"A curlew's a mean bird, anyhow," I muttered. "Confound 'em! let 'em come here and I'll burn 'em up! Besides, I've promised my wife enough birds for the table this week."

Suddenly the shrill call of a curlew scout rang over the marsh, and old Mrs. Fiddler cut a somersault to get into her cyclone cellar.

I slipped the safety-lock of my gun and tried to get under my hole in the ground.

I must either kill that scout or let him go back without seeing me. I tremble with excitement, afraid to answer his call lest I reveal my position. I know he has seen my decoys and determine to keep silent and still as death.

He came high, circled around me twice, and then came straight up behind, about a hundred yards in the air. Just over the decoys he poised, cocked his long-billed head to one side and peered down at me.

I knew he was coming no closer and it was a long chance shot, but I determined to make it before he could jump. Lying flat on my back, I snatched up my number ten and let him have a snap-shot.

He quivered a moment, and down he came, softly, without a struggle, and fell with his wings spread out three feet on the grass, so close to where I lay that I could reach him without rising.

I picked him up and found a tiny scarlet spot on his big fat brown breast. A single shot had taken effect.

He fell just at Mrs. Fiddler's door, and left a drop of blood in her front yard. When I lifted him, the fiddler emerged, with three trembling little fiddlers clinging to her skirts, smiled and thanked me. And then, seeing a baby snail toddling slowly along the road in front of her house, she ran out, grabbed him by the throat, broke his neck, tore him into bits with her big cruel claw, and handed the pieces to her hungry children.

"It's the way of life," I thought, grimly. "Life feeds on life; the man on fish and animal; the bird on the fiddler; the fiddler on the snail; the snail on the worm; the worm on the cabbage, and the cabbage on the vegetarian!"

And, when we get down to the last cell-life, no eye can tell the difference between the germ that will grow into a vegetarian and the one that will grow into a cabbage.

And yet the vegetarians put on holy airs, and say mean things about hunters and meat-eaters. I've often wondered what the cabbages, beets, turnips, peas and beans whisper to one another about these people in the still moonlit nights of the spring, when they are struggling to reproduce their kind. . . .

In the Haunts of Wild Fowl

We had dropped our anchor in the deep water at the head of a channel in one of the innumerable shallow bays of Tidewater Virginia. We were in the midst now of the haunts of almost every wild fowl that spreads his wings along the Atlantic Seaboard.

The prayer of the huntsman in search of ducks, geese and brant is for cold, stormy weather.

It is impossible to get many wild fowl in mild weather. They will not decoy, but will drift around the bay in great masses talking, laughing, screaming and joking at fool hunters they can see plainly squatting in blinds surrounded by wooden humbug birds. They never come closer than a mile in such weather, and what a man says on these days would not do to go in a Sunday School book.

But when a stiff breeze blows and the decoys begin to nod and bob in the water, with life in every movement, then we can fool Mr. Duck and Mr. Brant, stock our pantry for rainy days and make glad the heart of friends in town with the call of the expressman.

I never knew how much beautiful weather there was in winter until I began cruising for ducks and geese. I had an idea before that about half the days of our winter life are bleak and stormy. I have found by nine years' experience that on an average there are about four days in each winter month in which the weather is bad enough to make a good day for ducks. If we get more than four days of stormy weather in a month, fit for good shooting, it is a streak of extraordinary luck. And if one or two of those four grand storm days do not fall on Sundays, it is downright rabbit's foot luck.

At night in the snug crew's quarters forward, there is the hum of sportsman industry. The boys are loading shells with number two shot for brant.

The wind is howling a steady gale from the north and increasing the length of its gusts with steady persistence.

"Hear them shrouds talkin'?" cried George with a broad grin. "If this wind hangs on here till mornin' we'll burn them brant. Confound 'em, they're the most tantalizin' bird that ever pitched in this bay. I never killed a one of 'em the whole of last winter. There were no younguns among 'em. It's funny. Some years there's thousands of younguns. But last year I didn't hear the squawk of a dozen, and you can't kill an old brant. This year the bay's full of 'em and we'll burn 'em up to-morrow—see if we don't."

"I hope so" I replied. "They made me mad enough last winter's cruise, flying all over me, laughing and joking about us the whole month."

"Yes, and they kept it up till they left in the spring. Nobody killed any the whole season. But if we don't have brant for supper to-morrow night, I'll eat my old cap."

When George was willing to stake his old slouch cap with its long visor, that looked like a duck's bill, he was in dead earnest.

"If the wind will just hold on!" I exclaimed, with sad memories of high hopes many times shattered before.

"Don't worry. You'll git all you want to-morrow. It'll be a question whether we can git to the blind. Don't you hear them flaws gittin' longer and longer? That's been goin' on all day. It'll be as long goin' as it was comin' and it ain't got nigh the top yit."

Sure enough, the next morning, as we ate breakfast by lamplight at 5.30, the wind was howling and shrieking through the rigging like a thousand devils.

George looked grave. I asked what troubled his mind.

"I'm studyin' 'bout gittin' to that blind. We're goin' to the Boss blind and we'll have a tussle to make it with the wind on our quarter. We ought to 'a' gone to the wind'ard further before we anchored."

And we did have a tussle.

We took off half our decoys from the gunning dink and with two ten-foot oars began to shove our craft out over the foaming storm-tossed waters. It was all we could do to stand up against the wind; and with both oars fixed on the bottom, the strength of two men could barely move the fifteen-foot, light cedar boat. It took us an hour to push her three-quarters of a mile to the blind. It was freezing cold, but we were both wet with sweat when we got there.

The Boss blind is a famous one in this bay, that stands far out on the mud-flats near the edge of a ship channel. It was first stuck there by Uncle Nathan Cobb, the king of wild fowl hunters in Tidewater Virginia, nicknamed the "Old Boss" by his admirers.

This particular bay has 4,000 acres of mud-flats on which the wild celery grass grows, furnishing rich food for the birds. There are many blinds of cedar bushes stuck over its wide sweep, but the old Boss blind is yet the king of them all. It was placed there fifty years ago with consummate skill, in the track of the brant and ducks, and all the ingenuity of rival hunters has never been able to place a blind anywhere in that 4,000 acres to interfere with the flight of birds that pass it in stormy weather.

The tide was just right. It made high water at daylight. This gave us the whole of the ebb tide, the low water and the first movement of the flood tide for shooting. The tides are right for blind shooting on the two weeks of full and new moon, and wrong on the two quarters.

As the waters fall off the flats the birds come in to feed on the grass as soon as they can reach bottom with their bills, and, when hungry from a long run of high tides, they come out hours before they can reach bottom in search of shoal places.

We had just put out our decoys as the sun rose, and were pushing into the blind, when a broadbill swept in range before I had loaded a gun.

"They'll come to-day like chickens!" cried George.

"There's a blackduck in the decoys!" I whispered, as he handed me my number ten gun. I bagged him, and then for an hour we were kept busy with the broadbill and blackducks.

At last a flock of brant of about two hundred headed in straight for us. I seized my second gun, loaded with number two shot, and made ready. They were flying low in the teeth of the gale. Now I could see their long, black necks and snowy feathers around their legs, and they looked as big as geese. As they drew nearer, with every throat in full cry, the noise sounded like the roar of a fire sweeping a canebrake, exploding the joints of two hundred canes a second! I held my breath, and as they swept in range about thirty yards from the blind, I blazed away, *bang! bang!* I expected to see it rain brant. I hadn't touched a feather!

"Well, I'll be——!" exclaimed George.

I had the dry-grins, and looked down at my gun to see if it was really a gun, when I noticed my hands trembling like a leaf.

"Brant fever," was George's dry remark. "You must git over that, if we are to do our duty here to-day."

"I'll maul 'em next time," I promised.

In half an hour another bunch swung in and I brought down three with the first barrel and two with the second. Then for five hours we had the sport of which I had dreamed.

When the tide had ebbed off and left the flats dry, we counted our game, and we had 17 brant, 16 blackducks and 10 broadbill, a total of 43, as fat and toothsome birds as ever tickled the palate of man.

When the tide began to flow back in flood on the flats the wind had died down to a gentle breeze. We took up our decoys, stowed our birds under decks, set our little sail, and as the sun sank in a sea of scarlet glory swept slowly and contentedly back to the *Dixie*.

It was a red-letter day—one to tell young folks about in the far-away years when one becomes a grandpa and must ask his son for permission to venture out on a stormy day.

Outdoors and Indoors

Theodore Roosevelt (1858–1919)

Over his lifetime, Theodore Roosevelt probably spent more waking hours in pursuit of his natural history interests than in any other type of endeavor. His father had a more than casual interest in nature, and his uncle Robert, who lived next door, was the author of two scientific nature books, one on fish and the other on birds. Both men were friends of the Smithsonian's Spencer Baird and other leading scientists; they helped to found the American Museum of Natural History. At the age of nine, the precocious "Teedie" had amassed a personal museum collection of over one hundred items; within another year it had grown to over 250. In his early teens, Roosevelt's passion for collecting birds and other animals grew from a childhood fascination to the level of professional competence typical of many amateur nineteenth-century naturalists. Taxidermy lessons with the renowned John G. Bell brought his skills to the point at which the specimens that he gave to the Smithsonian Institution and the American Museum of Natural History remain useful today; one, an owl, is still on display in New York.

Roosevelt never outgrew his early interest in nature; he began college at Harvard with the object of "becoming a scientific man," and he published ornithological writings during his college years. The call of politics and an early marriage turned him from full-time scientific work, but he remained an active naturalist throughout his life, reviewing and writing both popular and scientific papers and books. After leaving the presidency, he returned to science, leading a Smithsonian collecting trip to Africa in 1909. Undoubtedly, his greatest achievement was the 1914 American Museum of Natural History expedition that mapped and studied fifteen hundred miles of the hitherto unexplored River of Doubt in the southwestern Amazonia.

Roosevelt's Washington years coincided with the birth of the Audubon movement, in which he played a part. He was an active member of both the New York and District of Columbia societies, and he encouraged their legislative programs first as governor of New York and later as president. His executive actions in establishing wildlife refuges are significant.

The following selection contrasts Roosevelt's family home on Long Island with his Albemarle County retreat near Charlottesville, Virginia, and describes his relationships with John Burroughs and John Muir.

From *Theodore Roosevelt: An Autobiography* (New York: Macmillan, 1913)

THERE ARE men who love out-of-doors who yet never open a book; and other men who love books but to whom the great book of nature is a sealed volume, and the lines written therein blurred and illegible. Nevertheless among those men whom I have known the love of books and the love of outdoors, in their highest expressions, have usually gone hand in hand. It is an affectation for the man who is praising outdoors to sneer at books. Usually the keenest appreciation of what is seen in nature is to be found in those who have also profited by the hoarded and recorded wisdom of their fellow-men. Love of outdoor life, love of simple and hardy pastimes, can be gratified by men and women who do not possess large means, and who work hard; and so can love of good books—not of good bindings and of first editions, excellent enough in their way but sheer luxuries—I mean love of reading books, owning them if possible of course, but, if that is not possible, getting them from a circulating library.

Sagamore Hill takes its name from the old Sagamore Mohannis, who, as chief of his little tribe, signed away his rights to the land two centuries and a half ago. The house stands right on the top of the hill, separated by fields and belts of woodland from all other houses, and looks out over the bay and the Sound. We see the sun go down beyond long reaches of land and of water. Many birds dwell in the trees round the house or in the pastures and the woods near by, and of course in winter gulls, loons and wild fowl frequent the waters of the bay and the Sound. We love all the seasons; the snows and bare woods of winter; the rush of growing things and the blossom-spray of spring; the yellow grain, the ripening fruits and tasseled corn, and the deep, leafy shades that are heralded by "the green dance of summer"; and the sharp fall winds that tear the brilliant banners with which the trees greet the dying year.

The Sound is always lovely. In the summer nights we watch it from the piazza, and see the lights of the tall Fall River boats as they steam steadily by. Now and then we spend a day on it, the two of us together in the light rowing skiff, or perhaps with one of the boys to pull an extra pair of oars; we land for lunch at noon under wind-beaten oaks on the edge of a low bluff, or among the wild plum bushes on a spit of white sand, while the sails of the coasting schooners gleam in the sunlight, and the tolling of the bell-buoy comes landward across the waters.

Long Island is not as rich in flowers as the valley of the Hudson. Yet there are many. Early in April there is one hillside near us which glows like a tender flame with the white of the bloodroot. About the same time we find the shy mayflower, the trailing arbutus; one member of the household always plucks a little bunch of mayflowers to send to a friend working in Panama, whose soul hungers for the Northern spring. Then there are shad-blow and delicate anemones, about the time of the cherry blossoms; the brief glory of the apple orchards follows; and then the thronging dogwoods fill the forests with their radiance; and so flowers follow flowers until the springtime splendor closes with the laurel and the evanescent, honey-sweet locust bloom. The late summer flowers follow, the flaunting lilies, and cardinal flowers, and marshmallows, and pale beach rosemary; and the golden-rod and the asters when the afternoons shorten and we again begin to think of fires in the wide fireplaces.

Most of the birds in our neighborhood are the ordinary home friends of the house and the barn, the wood lot and the pasture; but now and then the species make queer shifts. The cheery quail, alas! are rarely found near us now; and we no longer hear the whip-poor-wills at night. But some birds visit us now which formerly did not. When I was a boy neither the black-throated green warbler nor the purple finch nested around us, nor were bobolinks found in our fields. The black-throated green warbler is now one of our commonest summer warblers; there are plenty of purple finches; and, best of all, the bobolinks are far from infrequent. I had written about these new visitors to John Burroughs, and once when he came out to see me I was able to show them to him.

When I was President, we owned a little house in western Virginia; a delightful house, to us at least, although only a shell of rough boards. We used sometimes to go there in the fall, perhaps at Thanksgiving, and on these occasions we would have quail and rabbits of our own shooting, and once in a while a wild turkey. We also went there in the spring. Of course many of the birds were different from our Long Island friends. There were mocking-birds, the most attractive of all birds, and blue grosbeaks, and cardinals and summer redbirds [summer tanagers], instead of scarlet tanagers, and those wonderful singers the Bewick's wrens, and Carolina wrens. All these I was able to show John Burroughs when he came to visit us; although, by the way, he did not appreciate as much as we did one set of inmates of the cottage—the flying squirrels. We loved having the flying squirrels, father and mother and half-grown young, in their nest among the rafters; and at night we slept so soundly that we did not in the least mind the wild gambols of the little fellows through the rooms, even when, as sometimes happened, they would swoop down to the bed and scuttle across it.

One April I went to Yellowstone Park, when the snow was still very deep, and I took John Burroughs with me. I wished to show him the big game of the Park, the wild creatures that have become so astonishingly tame and tolerant of human presence. In the Yellowstone the animals seem always to behave as one wishes them to! It is always possible to see the sheep and deer and antelope, and also the great herds of elk, which are shyer than the smaller beasts. In April we found the elk weak after the short commons and hard living of winter. Once without much difficulty I regularly rounded up a big band of them, so that John Burroughs could look at them. I do not think, however, that he cared to see them as much as I did. The birds interested him more, especially a tiny owl the size of a robin which we saw perched on the top of a tree in mid-afternoon entirely uninfluenced by the sun and making a queer noise like a cork being pulled from a bottle. I was rather ashamed to find how much better his eyes were than mine in seeing the birds and grasping their differences. . . .

When I first visited California, it was my good fortune to see the "big trees," the Sequoias, and then to travel down into the Yosemite, with John Muir. Of course of all people in the world he was the one with whom it was best worth while thus to see the Yosemite. . . . The first night was clear, and we lay down in the darkening aisles of the great Sequoia grove. The majestic trunks, beautiful in color and in symmetry, rose round us like the pillars of a mightier cathedral than ever was conceived even by the fervor of the Middle Ages. Hermit thrushes sang beautifully in the evening, and again, with a burst of wonderful music, at dawn. I was interested and a little surprised to find that, unlike John Burroughs, John Muir cared little for birds or bird songs, and knew little about them. The hermit thrushes meant nothing to him, the trees and flowers and the cliffs everything. The only birds he noticed or cared for were some that were very conspicuous, such as the water-ousels—always particular favorites of mine too. The second night we camped in a snow-storm, on the edge of the canyon walls, under the spreading limbs of a grove of mighty silver fir; and next day we went down into the wonderland of the valley itself. I shall always be glad that I was in the Yosemite with John Muir and in the Yellowstone with John Burroughs.

A Trip to the Dismal Swamp

Paul Bartsch (1871–1960)

There are many parallels between the lives of Elliott Coues and Paul
Bartsch. Both were ornithological prodigies in their boyhood and both
achieved preeminence as professional scientists through the Smithsonian
Institution, Coues as an associate in the study of birds and Bartsch as curator of mollusks. Both had a broad knowledge of natural history that enabled them to contribute to branches of zoology outside their specialties
and to botany as well. Both studied and wrote about local natural history.
Bartsch's "A Trip to the Dismal Swamp" was published in 1901 in *The Osprey*, a magazine he later edited. It catered to the professional ornithologist and the sophisticated amateur naturalist; it is the only periodical that
Elliott Coues ever edited.

Throughout his fifty-year career at the Smithsonian, Bartsch worked to
strengthen the Washington scientific community. In addition to playing a
leading role in professional and conservation organizations, he taught for
thirty-seven years at Howard University Medical School and for forty-six
years at the George Washington University, where he founded the graduate
program in zoology in 1912.

Bartsch and his second wife transformed Lebanon, the home of his mature years, into a wildlife and wildflower sanctuary and botanical garden.
Located at Mason's Neck on the Potomac south of Washington, Lebanon's
458 acres had been a colonial plantation; under the Bartsches's care, it became a private nature center where Boy and Girl Scouts, Audubon groups,
and individual nature lovers were welcomed.

"A Trip to the Dismal Swamp" is unusual among the nineteenth- and
twentieth-century selections in this volume in that the spelling is erratic.
We have preserved the original orthography as a memorial to Elliot Coues,
whose editorial hand was obviously absent at the time of Bartsch's writing.
It was Coues's great pleasure to humiliate ornithological adversaries
should they lapse from his high standard. While editing the journals of
Lewis and Clark, Coues corrected their punctuation, spelling, grammar,
and even choice of words, not only in the published version, but on the
original manuscripts.

In his evocative description of evening at Lake Drummond, Bartsch
mentions the Lady of the Lake, the ghostly heroine of Thomas Moore's

1803 poem, "The Lake of the Dismal Swamp." The swamp and the lake itself are associated with much legendary and historical tragedy: Former
North Carolina governor William Drummond, after whom the lake is
named, was executed in Virginia in 1677 for his part in Bacon's Rebellion;
a party from William Byrd's boundary survey was lost there in 1728. The
memory of these unfortunates gives psychological substance to Moore's
romantic image of the lover who will hide himself and his beloved from
death in nature's heart:

They made her a grave too cold and damp
    For a soul so warm and true;
And she's gone to the lake of the Dismal Swamp
Where all night long, by firefly lamp,
    She paddles her white canoe.

And her firefly lamp I soon shall see,
    And her paddle I soon shall hear;
Long and loving our life shall be,
And I'll hide the maid in a cypress tree,
    When the footsteps of death are near!

The Audubon Naturalist Society has memorialized Bartsch's life of
service and professional accomplishment in the Bartsch Award, given to
individuals whose outstanding careers in natural history and conservation
merit association with his name.

From *The Osprey* 5, no. 3 (1901); as reprinted and augmented in *The Wood Thrush*—
now *Atlantic Naturalist*—5, no. 1(1949)

IN THE MIDDLE of June, 1897, a party of five, of which I was a member, paid
a visit to the Great Dismal Swamp of Virginia. We camped in the hotel at
the mouth of Jericho Ditch, on the edge of beautiful Lake Drummond, and
spent a week full of enjoyment and profit in this little frequented home of
solitude.

The pleasant memories and perhaps the desire to add a specimen of that
rare Warbler, *Helinaia swainsonii* Aud., which inhabits this region, to my
collection, prompted a second pilgrimage to the shores of the dusky lake
and it is of this second trip that I wish to speak.

On the eve of the 2d of June, 1899, Mr. William Palmer, Chief Taxider-
mist, U.S. National Museum, and myself embarked on the Washington and

Norfolk Steamer Norfolk, and arrived at the city of the same name the following morning. Our steamer was somewhat late, and failing to make connections, we were obliged to take a somewhat later train for Suffolk than we had intended; however, we finally reached this place where our supplies for a week's trip were to be purchased.

I wish I might devote a chapter to Suffolk and describe the effect this little city produces upon a man from the energetic north or west, but I fear this would require more space than is allotted to the entire sketch—hence, suffice it to say that here the automobile has as yet not superseded the ox-cart; nor the desire for wealth, and the power of the almighty dollar closed the hospitable doors of its inhabitants to the stranger, nor diminished the native's love of leisure. Quaint historic Suffolk! even you, like your gloomy neighbor, have charms all your own, and your memory invites again and again a closer and longer acquaintance.

We supplied our commissary department with everything that experienced hands deem necessary for such a trip as the one we were about to undertake, and did this to an admirable degree, forgetting only that most needed article, the staff of life—our bread.

After a drive of some two miles through a country devoted largely to truck gardening, we reached Jericho Ditch, one of the three possible entrances to the swamp, and by two o'clock p.m. we were ready to push off, down the canal, for the lake ten miles to the southeast.

Profiting by our former experience, we had this time chosen the little flat bottomed, double-bowed boat in preference to the clumsy, heavy, water-soaked, hollowed-out log, ordinarily termed "dugout," which caused us no end of trouble in '97, due, no doubt, in a large measure to a lack of training on the part of the occupants. Whatever the craft, there are but two ways to propel it; one by means of the paddle, the other by pole, each method requiring some experience. The ditch is not wide enough to permit the use of oars, and the way is frequently obstructed by sphagnum and other aquatic vegetation. But withal, the ditch is a dream of a place, and I long to be there again! Now that the memory of hardship and toil have faded in part, or at least, have moved into the background, the pleasure of its beauty stands out all the more charming and vivid, and I can imagine myself reclining in comfortable ease while Uncle Joshua, that dusky dweller of the lake, slowly and with measured stroke drives my canoe silently through the long aisle toward the enchanting lake on trip number three.

Voices of familiar birds greeted us on every hand; the swamp is filled with musical sound. There are the notes of the Maryland Yellow-throat, the

Yellow-breasted Chat, and the ever noisy White-eyed Vireo, greeting you and calling to you long before you push your canoe from its moorings, and as you proceed down the canal, still other familiar sounds will reach your ear, for the fauna of the adjacent region mingles strongly with the birds which are confined to the Swamp proper, and such notes as those of Prairie Warbler and the Chewink [towhee] will linger for a long time.

For some distance the heavy timber has been cut away and brought out from the swamp by way of the ditch, sometimes as floating logs, sometimes as sections ready to be cut into shingles or fence posts, . . . and frequently as the finished article itself. Both Washington and Jericho Ditch were made with no other end in view than to reach the valuable timber of the region and bring it to market. Formerly a towpath was kept in repair on one side of the canal, but to-day this has been reclaimed by swamp vegetation, and in many places all traces of it have vanished. For a number of miles therefore we do not have heavy timber bounding the canal, but a dense almost impenetrable second-growth of brush and shrubbery, which extends its branches and vainly attempts to overarch this watery way. On these arching branches the Acadian Flycatcher finds a place where he may place his nest and cradle his young, away out of reach of the many reptiles which infest the region. This bird is a very abundant summer resident throughout the swamp, and its peculiar note is an ever conspicuous feature of the ditch. Its relative, the Great Crested Flycatcher, is also present, and its note is always more or less in evidence, but yet the Acadian outnumbers him at least ten to one. Here and there the banks of brush give place to heavy beds of fern extending for some distance where the soil of the towpath furnishes them a foothold. Not unfrequently, too, the sides are bordered by a rank growth of cane, a welcome retreat of the Yellow-throat. This bird assumes more and more the characters of the Florida variety *roscoe* as one gets deeper into the interior, and I have found it necessary to bestow this varietal name upon the specimens taken about the lake and the surrounding country. These forms are easily distinguished from typical *trichas*, even in the field, on account of the differences in their notes. The specimens, however, are not typical *roscoe*, but belong to a form intermediate between true *trichas* and *roscoe*, favoring the variety more than they do *trichas*.

The two most characteristic birds of the swamp make their appearance soon after one sets out from the landing, becoming more and more abundant as one approaches the lake. These are the two Swamp Wood Warblers, the Prothonotary and the Hooded, both abundant summer residents of the region. I can think of no fairer picture than such as we beheld on many an occasion during our stay. A narrow, straight, clear, glossy, stretch of dark colored water, bounded by vegitation so rank that it appeared like a veritable wall, with a strip of clear blue sky above and perfect reflection beneath; so perfect in fact, that you will turn the photo taken, over and over before you will satisfy yourself as to which is its correct position? Here green Smilaces (*rotundifolia* and *laurifolia*) bound the whole which in places consisted largely of Swamp Azalea (*A. viscosa*), Wild Cherry, (*P. virginianus*), Swamp Huckleberry, (*V. straminium*), and that splendid shrub with its pendent racemes of showy waxwhite flowers (*Leucothea racemosa*) all decked with fragrant blossoms at this season while their shady bases were ensconced in stockings of green moss among which sparkling Sundews might be seen or perhaps a colony of that pretty Orchis (*Pogonia ophioglossoides*), peeping forth from its deep green setting with beauteous blush of pink, while midst the Sphagnum of the ditch dwelt harmoniously the delicate little Bladderwort (*Utricularia vulgaris*), raising on slender pedicel its tiny, delicate, rosy cup of a blossom up above the watery home of its submerged stem. It is amongst scenes like these that I learned to appreciate the beauty of the Golden Swamp Warbler most, for here indeed, his brilliant plumage seemed in accord with its surroundings. As he appeared for a moment like a blazing meteor passing down this gorgeous aisle to be swallowed up the very next by the sheltering wall of foliage, or perhaps as sometimes happened a pair would be observed in full chase, then indeed is when the Prothonotory Warbler appears at his best, for extreme animation is added, and the effect of the white in his tail feathers comes into play.

He is at all times a sprightly fellow, full of activity and music, and considerably on the wing, gliding rapidly from one place to another, rarely rising high above the lower vegetation, for he is essentially a bird clinging closely to the proximity of mother earth and water, and yet he is truly arboreal. In his movements he differs from all his relatives. He does not possess that gleaning nature characteristic of so many members of his family, but seeks his food upon and among the abundant decaying moss-covered logs and stumps, which have been accumulating here for ages, flitting from one to another, and extracting from them the insect food constituting his daily fare. Here again we must pause and comment upon his beauty. For what fairer picture could one imagine than a Prothonotary clinging to a moss-covered cypress knee, perhaps only a foot above the water, with his head partly lowered and tilted as if gazing and admiring the reflections of his brilliant form in the enchanting scene mirrored beneath.

As nesting site, the Prothonotary chooses any convenient cavity. This may be in an old stump a few feet from the ground, or some ten to fifteen feet above it. We even found one neatly tucked away in a hollow made by the twisting of a cypress knee, only a foot-and-a-half from its base. The greater number however seem to be placed in small decayed trees at a height easily within the reach of one's hand. It is possible that nests so placed are more conspicuous, and hence more easily noted than others, which would account for the fact, that by far the greater number found were thus situated. In almost every case the stump was decidedly rotten, and one could easily break away the outer protecting wall with one's fingers, if desirable, and thus expose the structure proper, which in all instances consisted of a base, of varying depth, made almost exclusively of the tree trunk investing mosses while the superstructure or nest proper consisted of a neat cup formed entirely of fine rootlets.

The Hooded is of a wholly different temperament, apparently frequenting all parts of the swamp, and not like the Prothonotary partial to the borders of the large tracts of water. You may find him near the ground or in the tree tops, but usually at an elevation half way between these two extremes. He is of an extremely cheerful disposition and your attention will no doubt be called to him by his notes, for he is ever saying something, as he moves about, searching for his food, repeating it again and again with varied emphasis. The syllables most frequently heard sound something like weee weee wo-ee-tsee rendered in a most pleasing manner, with the sweetest of accents which belong wholly and alone to our little swamp inhabitant the Hooded Warbler. This bird indeed, more than any another, tends to enliven these scenes, which without avian chorus, would certainly seem steeped in deepest gloom. All the nests which we found of this warbler were placed in crotches of cane, and contained four young. The nest is not a model of architecture; but one well suited for its purpose. Dead leaves of cane to which a few of the oak and other trees were added, composed the rough exterior, the inside or lining being of slender grass stems neatly turned to line the mould.

So much for these two warblers, and now again to our task. We arrived at our hotel toward dusk, and finding no one at home lifted the latch and stepped inside the only cabin which commands a view of Drummond's Lake.

The hotel is placed upon a bit of elevated ground on the left side of the ditch, about a hundred yards north of its junction with the lake. Formerly there were two buildings in close proximity, but now the one to the south is gradually being consumed for kindling wood. The main structure, though made of rough boards, is nevertheless built after the most approved sanitary style. First of all it is raised upon sections of logs, some four feet from the ground, to keep the house from being damp; however light and ventilation are its two strong points, for there are chinks between the boards as well as between the shingles, each of which contributes its little mite to produce an airy whole, to say nothing of the additions which come by way of the places in the windows which seemed to have parted, long ago, with the once embraced glass.

The interior is divided into five compartments. A central one, extending from one side to the other, forming a more or less square space some twenty feet in diameter, serves as kitchen, dining room, library, parlor or whatsoever use you choose to put it to. It is furnished with a long, wide table made of rough board, and a long wooden bench, on either side of this, an iron stove, which dates back quite a number of years, and a few long shelves on the wall which were destined to hold all the household effects which Joshua called his own. To the north and south of this room are two sleeping apartments, each of which is furnished with a double bunk of spacious size, filled with straw, every stem of which spoke of pressure well applied.

We claimed as our quarters the west side rooms, to the south and north, and were quite comfortably housed, and at peace with our inner man when the shades of night stole softly upon us.

By far the most attractive part of this dwelling is the large porch on its west side, whose outer railing serves admirably well for a back to the board bench which extends its entire length. Here we seated ourselves to rest awhile from toil, and talk over the experiences of the day, while good Mother Nature silently lowered the dusky curtain, and proclaimed a change of scene. How delightful to be seated thus and watch this gradual transformation of day to eve, to twilight, and dusk to night, each scene bringing with it its own events. The little frog who has occasionally during the day announced his presence by rapping his shingles together, with a vigorous whack, whack, whack, whack, whack, (for indeed there is no sound to which his note might be more properly likened than the forcible rapping together of two shingles,) has now grown quite vociferous. For a little while the Chimney-swifts mingle with the bats in their common pursuit; then the large Dragon flies (Epiaeschna heros Fabr.) which have been whirring up and down the ditch all day come in to roost beneath the house or underneath its projecting eaves; the Woodcock seeks her favorite bog, and the graceful Great Blue Heron sails quietly to his stamping grounds, for such I took the promontory at the junction of the lake and ditch to be; judging from the number of visiting cards he had deposited there. No doubt he comes here to join the frogs in their chorus and note the doings of Uncle Joshua, but he decidedly declined an interview which Mr. Palmer planned a little later.

As dusk deepens to darkness, and the starry orbs one by one appear until their full count has answered to the call of roll, countless fireflies flash their brilliant torches midst the deep shadows of the woods, until one might well believe himself transported to a fairy-land where Nymph and Dryads are at play. One's voice gradually sinks midst scenes like these until it is lost, and you gaze in silent admiration, and listen to the sounds all atune to-night; peacefully calm and contentedly happy, you dream, and as the hours pass, you people the scenes and would scarcely be surprised if the Lady of the Lake herself would appear "paddling her white canoe."

We were astir early the next morning, and had visited our traps and counted our night's catch of small mammalia, consisting chiefly of Peromyscus leucopus [the white-footed mouse] and P. nuttalli [the golden mouse], long before the sun appeared upon the scene. In the swamp every leaflet is steeped in dew in early morning, and dense fog envelopes everything, rendering the fragrant atmosphere most pleasantly cool. Breakfast over, I took a stroll along the path leading into deep woods back of the house. On our former visit we had paid Joshua to cut this path through the jungle that we might the more easily pursue our way. For some reason he seemed to have taken a fancy to it himself, and to have kept it in repair. A brilliant Redstart flashed his colors and was skipping about the lower vegetation adjoining the building. Maryland Yellow-throats scolded as they moved through the moist tangle. Both were busily intent upon procuring food for their young. After passing some fifty yards back of the house into the timber, to where the undergrowth appears as a dense tangle of briars, cane and ferns, I stopped and squeaked; just one note, reminding me of that of the Water-thrush, followed by a swift swish of the wing, and a Swainson's Warbler sat perched upon a slender twig not five feet from me. We gazed at each other for a moment; then he departed as suddenly as he had come. His position, manner of flight and attitude reminded me strongly of that of the lesser thrushes. This and another equally close and short glimpse were all that I managed to see of Swainson's Warbler on this trip. The bird is very shy and seclusive, and though I visited the locality again and again, and squeaked my most seductive squeak till my throat was hoarse and sore, I failed to call him from his hiding. I knew he was present, for his sweet clear burst of melody, pure as that of the Water-thrush, but sweeter far in theme and execution, came to us now and then from his favorite place of hiding. We added but a single specimen of this Warbler on this trip, one that Mr. Palmer persuaded to come to the edge of the thicket bordering a boggy road, several miles from the place where I had observed my bird.

The fifth was a day whose memory will cling for many a year to come. We crossed the lake early in the morning, paddled along its southern shore, visited the Outlet Canal at the east end, and returned along its northern margin late in the afternoon.

The lake is a very shallow basin, some two and one-half miles in diameter, with a maximum depth of sixteen feet. During the summer months its waters become quite warm. On this day our thermometer registered a temperature of 96° Fahr. near the margin and 92° at the greatest depth we sounded, the water of its tributaries being somewhat lower. The lake seemed to be swarming with minute organisms, for every little floating leaf which we picked up from its surface was found to shelter a host of invertebrate forms from the direct rays of the blazing sun.

In spite of the many praises and curative properties accredited to this dusky liquid, my internal anatomy absolutely refused to harbor any of the stuff on this memorable day. I was feeling all but well when we left in the morning, and became less and less so as the hours slipped by, and oh, how I did long for a single drink of pure water, just a little cooler than that about us, and though we tried each little tributary, luke warm or warmer it always proved to be, and a single taste of it would suffice to cause me to turn away from it with a shudder.

About two o'clock in the afternoon we arrived at the Outlet Canal; here we landed our canoe and walked down the path along its high embankment to the lock where we were greeted by Mr. Marsh, the keeper of the lock. I asked him immediately if he had anything cooler to drink than ditch water, and he replied that he had a well, which he said was located a couple hundred yards back in the timber. I was too tired to join them in their trip to the precious fountain so stretched out under the shady trees and waited, long, longing, minutes for their return. How I loved that pitcher as it came nearer and nearer, and finally poised over my cup. At last I was to have that drink which I had craved so many hours—but, even as the liquid fell into the glass my spirits sank and my frame weakened—dark! the same old dark, swamp flavored fluid only a few degrees cooler than that which had mocked me all day. Mr. Palmer paddled me home to the hotel that afternoon, limp and despondent, ready to give up all for a single drink of pure, cool water. It required two days of rest to get myself in shape for further explorations. The first of these was spent upon my bunk, the second in taking care of collections and capturing butterflies, which appeared abundantly about the hotel. They seemed to be partial to the dumping ground and judging from the manner in which a number applied their long probosces to the carcass of a small mammal which had been deprived of its skin, sipping up the fluid brought to the surface by decomposition, they were not disinclined toward a carnivorous diet. By far the greater number seen here were *Papilio turnus*, and *P. palamedes*; though *P. ajax* and individuals of a number of other genera were by no means rare. [*Papilio* is the genus of the swallow-tails.]

On the eighth we again visited the east end of the lake and camped for a night at the Outlet Lock.

When the first white men visited the lake many years ago, immense cypresses skirted its margin. To-day we have only a fringing line of stumps, which plainly mark the handiwork of civilized man, with here and there a hollow cypress shell which was too thin, even to furnish shingles. These natural chimneys furnish nesting sites to the Swifts, and almost every one fit for such use appeared to be tenanted by a pair or more of these dusky individuals. Not solely by them however, for we found several species of bats, *Lasiurus borealis*, *Nycticeius humeralis*, and that curiously large-eared species *Corynorhinus macrotis* taking refuge within their walls, while upon their wide spread partly submerged roots sundry species of water snakes found a pleasant resting place. A pair of Great Crested Flycatchers appeared to be nesting in a cavity in one of the upper branches of one of these trees, while in another a pair of pretty Parula Warblers had concealed their neat home in a bunch of grey Tillandsia [Spanish moss] which drapes these silent sentinels of the lake. Toward noon these trees and bordering stumps were visited by strings of Turkey Buzzards which would stop for a drink and perhaps a bit of a bath before resuming their graceful searching flight. We spent the greater portion of the day collecting plants, amongst them a beautiful lot of a new fern, since described as *Dryopteris goldiana celsa* by Mr. Palmer, and many Prothalial fronds and young stages of a number of species, which were growing abundantly in the rich, moist, peaty soil exposed by the deep cut made for the Outlet Canal. The Red-bellied and Pileated Woodpeckers seemed to be quite abundant in the large timber bordering the canal, and the loud buoyant notes of the latter were very pronounced as they went laughing from place to place. Red-shouldered Hawks, perhaps of the Florida variety, were also quite abundant, and judging from the hooting at night *Syrnium nebulosum alleni* was well represented in the swamp fauna. [*Syrnium nebulosum* is now *Strix varia*—the Barred Owl.]

We returned to the hotel on the morning of the ninth and remained only long enough to dispose of some of our collections and to replenish our larder for a trip up Washington Ditch.

This water way takes its name from the fact that Washington himself supervised its construction. It is between four and five miles in length extending from Jericho Ditch near its union with the lake, in a west of northwesterly direction. It is a beautiful path, passing through dense timber almost throughout its whole extent. Tall trees to the right and left stretch their long branches across this watery trail and thus leave the canopy o'er head almost unbroken. Only here and there where a tall cypress with its few trim branches decked with slender needles rears its towering top, does one get a clearer view of the heavens above for the needles form a veil-like canopy not at all dense, like that of the broad leaved trees. Hooded Warblers and Prothonotaries are conspicuous features of this region; while the Tufted Tits and Carolina Wrens yodeled their jolly songs as they moved about among the lower vegetation.

The scene was a most charming one and presented all that could be desired upon our first trip. This time, however, we found more than we had bargained for and all of this in the entomological line. In '97 I made my first acquaintance with the Black Flies, and this only on the last day of our visit. I was greatly disappointed in their size. The stories I had heard had led me to believe these little bull dogs to be at least as large as a good-sized Horse-fly and now they proved to be of almost microscopic proportions; but if their size was small their appetite certainly was large enough and their persistency a thing to be admired. They appeared to be all jaws, ever busily engaged in digging. While at the lake we had occasionally been visited by a large ferocious fly of flat form and more or less transparent wings, whose visit usually meant a piece of skin gone and a painful bleeding spot. No matter how little time elapsed between your discovery of the intruder and his expulsion you were sure to be left bleeding if he touched you. On this trip up Washington Ditch, I killed seven, at one time, as fast as I could strike. They belonged to two different species, and I believe we failed to bring specimens back with us for identification, our mode of collecting being too severe to permit of preservation. These pests, together with countless Black Flies and Mosquitos, made it necessary for one to brush his face with each stroke of the paddle, and I remember well that as we withdrew the paddle from the water we would brush our face and neck with the hollow of our arm in order to keep these beasts of the forest from devouring us then and there.

The water in the ditch was quite low and necessitated considerable pushing and poling, occasionally, to slide our boat ahead over the slimy bottom until we would reach a deeper stretch of water.

We arrived at the end toward evening and established ourselves for the night in the corn crib belonging to the colored family at the head of the ditch. In the mean time it had grown dark, but being anxious to have a drink of pure water and some bread, neither of which had been ours since we left Suffolk I persuaded one of the little colored urchins to act as my guide on a trip to the nearest store, which was at Sanders, Va., some three miles distant.

Heavy thunder clouds marked the western horizon and the flashes of lightning became more and more vivid and lighted our way as we proceeded along winding paths, over boggy roads across this outlying member of the swamp. Owls were very abundant and at one time I even felt tempted to collect a specimen with my twenty-two calibre revolver, the only gun I had taken with me, but my aim was poor in the uncertain light and this Bubo may still be enjoying his nightly raids and serenades.

A little further along a fox ran across our path and trotted leisurely along a short distance ahead of us. The ball which was intended to add his skin to our collection simply increased his speed.

While we were purchasing our provisions and satisfying my thirst, which seemed to be everlasting, the storm broke loose most violently and this caused me to accept Mr. Sanders' invitation to spend the night with him, which I gladly did. A good clean bed is at all times preferable to a corn crib floor, particularly on a rainy night, doubly so, when the roof of the crib is leaky.

We returned early the following morning and were just in time to join Mr. Palmer in the cup of coffee he had prepared and add crackers and sweets to the meager bill of fare.

We found a pair of Kingfishers at this end of the ditch and I am puzzled as to the whereabouts of their breeding grounds, there being no bank anywhere near this place. Pine Warblers, birds we had not noted in the interior of the swamp, were also quite abundant in this place.

The return trip was much easier owing to the increase of water in the ditch due to the rain of the previous night. The coolness of the atmosphere seemed also to somewhat lessen the activities of mosquitos and flies, for which we were duly thankful. We succeeded in getting a good ducking from a sudden shower, just before we reached the hotel, but our spirits were good and we really enjoyed this bit of experience.

That night we packed our contraptions, and the following morning found us paddling with a steady stroke up Jericho Ditch to meet the appointment with our driver. It was a drizzling day, a day well suited for a long pull, provided you are dressed lightly enough not to mind the moist garments, and we were.

We arrived in due time, adding a female Wood Duck, with her flock of young ducklings, to our list of swamp inhabitants, just before we left its bounds.

We were well pleased with our week's sojourn in this part of the country and sorry indeed to part from the region which had given us so many delightful moments as well as experiences to the contrary, and almost wished that we might return to this home of solitude and simplicity, to camp again on the edge of beautiful Lake Drummond.

We now append a list of birds observed on the two summer trips into the swamp.

Florida Cormorant, Wood Duck, Great Blue Heron, Green Heron, Woodcock, Turkey Buzzard, Red-shouldered Hawk, Florida Barred Owl, Great Horned Owl, Yellow-billed Cuckoo, King Fisher, Red-bellied Woodpecker, Downy Woodpecker, Hairy Woodpecker, Pileated Woodpecker, Chimney Swift, Ruby-throated Hummer, Kingbird, Great Crested Flycatcher, Acadian Flycatcher, Wood Pewee, Crow, Towhee Bunting, Cardinal, Barn Swallow, Purple Martin, Waxwing, Red-eyed Vireo, Warbling Vireo, White-eyed Vireo, Black and White Creeper, Prothonotary Warbler, Swainson's Warbler, Worm-eating Warbler, Parula Warbler, Yellow Warbler, Yellow-throated Warbler, Pine Warbler, Prairie Warbler, Oven Bird, Louisiana Water Thrush, Maryland Yellow-throat, Florida Yellow-throat, Yellow-breasted Chat, Hooded Warbler, Redstart, Cat Bird, House Wren, Carolina Wren, Nuthatch, Tufted Tit, Carolina Chickadee, Wood Thrush.

Birds seen on Audubon Society Trip to Dismal Swamp May 27–31, 1949

Green Heron, Turkey Vulture, Killdeer, Spotted Sandpiper, Mourning Dove, Yellow-billed Cuckoo, Chimney Swift, Ruby-throated Hummingbird, Pileated Woodpecker, Red-bellied Woodpecker, Red-headed Woodpecker,

Downy Woodpecker, Kingbird, Crested Flycatcher, Acadian Flycatcher, Wood Pewee, Rough-winged Swallow, Blue Jay, Crow, Carolina Chickadee, Tufted Titmouse, Carolina Wren, Mockingbird, Catbird, Brown Thrasher, Wood Thrush, White-eyed Vireo, Red-eyed Vireo, Prothonotary Warbler, Parula Warbler (Southern), Yellow Warbler, Wayne's Warbler (Black-throated Green), Black-poll Warbler, Prairie Warbler, Louisiana Water-thrush, Maryland Yellow-throat, Hooded Warbler, Redstart, Cardinal, Towhee.

Epilogue—1949

The Dismal Swamp, isolated and inaccessible as it must have appeared to the early explorers, has, thanks to advances in modern technology and the white man's greed, rapidly fallen from its unique floristic and faunistic state. Civilization has pressed its pursuits all around its edge and pushed the native biota farther and farther into the interior. Lake Drummond is no longer the beautiful shallow stretch of water that 50 years ago—when I first visited it—was fringed by a rim of gigantic Bald Cypresses that stood in the lake at the same distance from the shore as outposts and sentinels of the magnificent forest stretching inward. Desire for lumber and shingles, yielding shekels to the purse, has been responsible for the removal of the accessible marketable timber. A rather commonplace vegetation is left as its successor.

The deepening of the Deep Creek ship canal and Feeder Canal for the purpose of maintaining the water supply in this inland waterway at sufficient depth for navigation has so drained the swamp area that no longer can one paddle through Jericho Ditch or Washington Ditch in a dugout canoe, for these ditches are now largely claimed by brush and cane. The shore of beautiful Lake Drummond has become a common picnic ground not foreign to the carousing and sousing of certain human elements of adjacent cities; for they can now easily reach the lake in motorboats—a thing impossible when the water table was as it stood in 1907. However, I am happy to report that I saw a notice that drastic restrictions have recently been placed by the companies owning the region to protect it from possible fire hazard.

The changes in the avifauna are also very apparent. The Prothonotary Warbler, once a superabundant species, is still present in numbers but appears to have suffered a decided reduction, and so does the Hooded Warbler. We were able, however, to add Wayne's Warbler to our list. The Parula

Warbler should be listed as the Southern Parula, which breeds in the Spanish Moss *Tilandsia*. The Chimney Swifts are also reduced about the lake, having lost their natural nesting site—the hollow fringing Bald Cypresses.

Gone is the solitude where many times in the olden days I sought refuge from the nerve-chafing things that constitute the daily grind. For in that solitude it was possible to weigh and sort the worth-while things from the dross and chaff and restore to the mind peace and contentment.

Birds *and* Magnolia Bogs

Waldo Lee McAtee (1883–1962)

During his forty-three year career with the Biological Survey (later the U.S. Fish and Wildlife Service), McAtee published some twelve hundred papers on nearly every biological subject from entomology and ornithology to evolutionary theory. Like Paul Bartsch and many other government scientists, he studied local natural history as an avocation and worked to preserve local natural areas.

McAtee's *The Natural History of the District of Columbia* is the first and only attempt at a comprehensive description of the natural history of the region surrounding the nation's capital. Basing his discussion on a historical summary article which he had previously published, McAtee enumerates the elements of the region's past and present biota and contrasts the coastal plain and the piedmont as floral and faunal provinces. This important record possesses two unusual and interesting features: U.S. Geological Survey maps from about 1917, and McAtee's comparative analysis of the New Jersey pine barrens and Washington's now nearly extinct magnolia bogs. Although the general reader may find McAtee's listing of the flora of the magnolia bogs rather dry, the botanist—professional or amateur—will mourn the beautiful and rare plants that have been lost to urban sprawl.

Both selections from *The Natural History of the District of Columbia*, Bulletin of the Biological Society of Washington, no. 1 (Washington, D.C.: Biological Society of Washington, 1918)

Birds

SOME OF THE earlier references to the birds of the region are of interest. We are informed that one of the Indian names for the Potomac was Cohonguroton or river of swans. It is said, however, that Occoquan was the farthest up river feeding place of the swans; but flocks of as many as 300 were seen there and of two kinds, both trumpeter and whooper. There is no later record of the trumpeter swan, however, and the whooper in modern books is called whistling swan to distinguish it from the European bird.

The Potomac was a noted resort for the canvasback duck, the favorite ground for the species extending from Analostan Island to Craney Island 25 miles below. It is said that myriads of them were present, fairly covering the stream. As if in prophecy one author (Elliot) deprecates the shooting with large guns, especially at night. As we now know, it is due to this and similar practices that such large gatherings of these splendid birds are things of the past.

Evidently it was not necessary in those early days for hunters to journey far from the city. In 1797, Francis Baily remarks:

"Game is plenty in these parts, and, what perhaps may appear to you remarkable, I saw some boys who were out a shooting, actually kill several brace of partridges in what will be one of the most public streets of the city." "In 1836 a flock of 30 to 40 wild turkeys flew over Georgetown going toward Chain Bridge and a man on the bridge killed 9 of them."

In the Proceedings of the National Institute for the Promotion of Science are various interesting notes relating to the birds of the District. The donations announced at the meeting of September 12, 1842, especially are noteworthy. Four specimens of Leach's petrel, one of Wilson's petrel, and one Audubon shearwater were presented. The birds were taken the preceding month, August, 1842, and the records in each case are the first for the District. This incursion of maritime species is undoubtedly that referred to by Haley, who says "during a violent easterly storm a few years ago, the Potomac was covered with multitudes of Mother Cary's chickens (*Thalassidroma leachii*) which had been forced out of their usual course by the gale."

In the bulletin of the National Institute also are earlier records for the surf scoter, the double-crested cormorant, old squaw, snow bunting, and yellow rail than are cited in later publications, and the only record for the ivory gull.

Of birds which once frequented the District but which now are gone we may mention: the passenger pigeon, now wholly extinct, the sandhill crane, Carolina parakeet, and prairie chicken. The wild turkey and the ruffed grouse no longer find congenial haunts within the District, but occur sparingly in some of the wildest adjoining territory. Practically the same is true of the pileated woodpecker, although this species being of a more roving disposition may, occasionally, be detected within our limits. The wood duck, once a breeder within the District, now nests only in the more secluded parts of nearby stream valleys, but still occurs within the District during migration. These species have been driven away, either by direct persecution by man, or by the destruction of habitats essential to their welfare. Another bird, the black-throated bunting or dick-cissel, has departed for reasons of its own. Much territory here is suited to its needs, but the bird has withdrawn from much of its former eastern range, including the District of Columbia. On the other hand, certain species have become more common in recent years. Among them we may mention the crow blackbird [common grackle], orchard oriole, Cape-May warbler, butcher-bird [loggerhead shrike], robin, and the mockingbird. To replace the lost black-throated bunting another finch, Bachman's sparrow, is gradually occupying this region as a breeding home. The starling, a new-comer, sometimes abundant in winter, has also begun to nest in small numbers.

The English sparrow was introduced into Washington in 1871. The following contemporaneous account of the matter may not be entirely pleasing to those who have had disagreeable experience with this hardy little stranger. "A flock of imported sparrows was set at liberty in the public grounds in 1871, for the destruction of insects. Each year new cages are placed in the trees for the accommodation of their increased numbers. These useful birds are fed regularly every morning during the winter in Franklin, Lafayette and other squares." [Both the pileated woodpecker and the wood duck have returned to the District and now nest in the vicinity of the National Zoo and elsewhere.]

Magnolia Bogs Near Washington, D.C.

In treating the types of collecting grounds in the District of Columbia region, . . . it is easiest to begin with an account of the most strikingly characterized areas. In the writer's opinion this distinction clearly belongs in this region to the white sand and gravel bogs, or magnolia bogs, found only in the Coastal Plain formations.

The name Magnolia Bogs is selected for the areas about to be discussed, because it has a certain currency, and because the swamp magnolia or sweet bay (*Magnolia virginiana*) probably is not absent from one of them (of any size), something which is not true of any other equally conspicuous plant. These bogs are restricted to Coastal Plain formations, for it is only among those that the surficial deposits give the proper basal conditions. Where a surface layer, usually of coarse white gravel, or of gravel and sand mixed, is underlaid by an impervious layer of clay and flushed by a constant flow of spring water, there grows without exception, and only there, some combination of the plants which characterize what are here called Magnolia bogs.

Such bogs exist at a number of points along Indian Creek and its continuation the Eastern Branch. . . . On the other side of the valley and flowing into Paint Branch are the four Powdermill bogs (others now drained once existed here). . . .

I will begin with the general surroundings of my favorite group—the Powdermill Bogs. These lie near the here sharply defined inner border of the Coastal Plain, and two of the four indeed lie on top of what is really a Piedmont Hill. The Coastal Plain country here is strikingly different from the Piedmont, in the preponderance of sandy and gravelly soils. For instance, this region is the nearest to Washington, where one can walk long distances in soft sandy roads—an experience which on some of the hottest days makes a lasting impression concerning the geological and other peculiarities of the Coastal Plain.

As to the general flora of the area, the common oaks are *Quercus marilandica, stellata* and *alba* [black jack, post, and white oak]. The pines include *Pinus rigida* and *virginiana* [pitch and Virginia or scrub pine], the latter more common; chestnut and chinquapin abound, as do also sweet gum, dogwood and sassafras. The commonest shrubs are mountain laurel, pink azalea, blueberries and huckleberries. Among the herbs, *Cypripedium acaule* [pink lady slipper], *Polygala incarnata* [a milkwort], *Baptisia tinctoria* [wild indigo], *Sarothra gentianoides* [now *Hypericum gentianoides*—orange grass or pine weed] and *Chrysopsis mariana* [Maryland golden aster] are the most characteristic of the indigenous species. The growth immediately surrounding the Magnolia bogs includes red maple, alder*(Alnus rugosa)*, sour gum, holly (*Ilex opaca*) and *Pinus virginiana*.

The bogs are fringed, or dotted with clumps of *Magnolia virginiana*, Myrica, swamp azalea, sheep laurel, *Gaylussacia dumosa* [huckleberry], *Vaccinium corymbosum* [high bush blueberry], *Viburnum nudum* and *cassinoides* [swamp-haw and wild raisin] and other shrubs. . . . Around the bases of the shrub colonies are deep cushions of sphagnum in which grow some of our showiest orchids as *Pogonia ophioglossoides* and *Limodorum* [now *Calopogon pulchellus*—the grass pink]. The open centers of the bogs, or interspaces between the shrub islands give a view of the surface stratum of these areas—the white gravel, or gravel and sand, flush to the surface or slightly overflowed with clear, cool spring water. In the water grow algae, and the lycopods, *Utricularia* [bladder wort], Sundews, *Xyris* [yellow-eyed grass], *Tofieldia* [false asphodel] and many other of the plants mentioned below. On the slightest elevations of the gravel are clumps of lichens of the genus *Cladonia*, here growing in water, though elsewhere seen in the dryest possible situations.

The aspect and the plant associations of the Magnolia bogs as well as some of their animal inhabitants are unique in our region, and make these areas the objectives of pilgrimages by devotees of all branches of natural history.

Color in Virginia *and*
The National Forests

Wallace Nutting (1861–1941)

Retired Congregationalist clergyman Wallace Nutting devoted his talents
to the appreciation of the picturesque landscape of the eastern United
States and the British Isles. He illustrated his books in the *America Beautiful* series with his own photographic images, which he also sold as hand-
colored silver prints. Although his style may seem somewhat exaggerated
now, it is typical of much of nineteenth-century travel and landscape writing. "Color in Virginia" is one of his less flamboyant pieces and yields a
painter's insight: The soil is a major landscape element and one of its basic
sources of color. "The National Forests" records the rebirth of interest in
the eastern woodlands as a protector of watersheds and a recreational resource. The Shenandoah National Forest is now the George Washington
National Forest.

Both selections from *Virginia Beautiful* (Framingham, Mass: Old America Company,
1930)

Color in Virginia

THE GORGEOUS red clay of Virginia is the most striking feature of color. In
places where the roads have been cut through the hills, the effect is almost
trying to the eyes, it is so brilliantly, and so extensively, and uniformly red. A
great part of many of the counties is composed of this wonderfully colored
soil. How beautiful it is and how effective appears at once when we happen
to pass into a region of blue or white clay which becomes at once dreary.
There is a warmth about this rich color so that a plantation formed of it
has in spring either rich greens, or rich reds over the entire surface. Is it
iron, which gives this effect? When the delicate evergreens begin to send
out their new shoots, when the great leaves of the sycamore spread over the
spring brooks, the poplar and the young pale oak leaves appear with all the
other harbingers of the season, such a medley of green above the patches
of red!

There are those who object to yellow color in the streams, but it does not bother me at all. It adds one more tint, striping the landscapes. Of course there are streams in other soils which are clear, and reflect shades of the arch above.

We have elsewhere mentioned the glory of the color that arises from the blossoms of the numerous flowering trees in Virginia. Probably the most superb effect, however, of color is that of a ripened grain field. Poets have done their best in describing it, and that best is never good enough. The corn, also, has a beauty in all its stages of growth, whether in summer or autumn, and the tobacco fields with their strong green, touched with olive, add their note. All told, the earth beneath the varied skies, and the tints that rush up the mountains, crowd the entire range of vision until there is nothing left to be imagined or desired. Even the russet of the early autumn, which indicates the rest of natural forces, has a mellowness and charm, for all things are beautiful in their time, and something is beautiful all the time.

The National Forests

Forest districts set aside as parks by the national government form a very respectable area in Virginia. The proximity of Washington favors such projects, as also that in connection with Williamsburg-Yorktown-Jamestown. One should understand forest in this connection more in the Latin than in the English sense. That is, an outside district, more or less wild, and not necessarily wholly or even mostly covered by trees.

Thus the Natural Bridge district of course includes roads and farms, and parcels of land left in private ownership. The government is able to prevent, in one way or another, the bringing of objectionable features into the limits of the forest. The natural resources are conserved; the timber is cut only by way of keeping the forest in prime condition.

Roads are constructed from time to time as appropriations are secured, and probably private rights may gradually be extinguished in the process of the generations.

The Natural Bridge is under private management, and well conducted. No doubt any attempted destruction of fine natural features there or elsewhere would be resisted by the government.

The West, owing to the marvelous natural features like the Yellowstone, the Yosemite and so forth, has in the past properly received greater attention from the government, in the way of securing national ownership than the East. But the greater populations in the East are now receiving attention, since parks within a few hundred miles are of so much more practical value than those that are thousands of miles away. Thus the park taking its name from the Natural Bridge has been made to extend many miles north of that wonderful phenomenon, nearly to Waynesboro.

In the southwest is a region set apart, beginning at Ivanhoe in Wythe county and extending in a long reach into Tennessee.

The Shenandoah National Forest is, in minor part, in West Virginia. It begins in Bath county and runs northeast to Strasburg, not many miles south of Winchester. It is now proposed to add to these forests what is to be called the Shenandoah National Park, extending from Waynesboro northeast to Front Royal and including the Blue Ridge as the Shenandoah Forest includes the Alleghanies. It should be understood that the shapes and directions of these reservations are based on the mountain ranges. The area included is largely land too high or rough to serve for agriculture, and will not therefore subtract markedly from the productive capacity of the state. The largest natural resource in the reservations is the timber.

Sometimes we hesitate to provide far enough in the future. Now it may seem a vast area to segregate and pay for. But fifty years from now the grandchildren will bless us for every square mile thus forever secured to beauty and incidentally to hold the rainfall and prevent destructive freshets. The beauties of these districts are mostly in the mountain contours, and the silences of forest seclusion.

Two or three roads in this region we show. Camping, under wise restrictions, thus permitting long vacations among these mountain glories, is feasible.

In addition to Washington, Baltimore and Richmond and lesser populations near at hand, east of the mountains, we may well note that the great and populous state of Ohio, in a plains country, is not far away, and will have benefits arising from its nearness.

These reservations form the only mountain districts till we cross the entire Mississippi basin and reach the Rocky mountains.

With the rapidly developing means of moving about, these mountain parks, for such would be a proper name for them, are nearer our front door than the next county was a hundred years ago.

Revels Island

George Shiras (1859–1942)

George Shiras's first interest in natural history was the outgrowth of hunting. Responding to the obvious overexploitation of game and commercial wildlife, he became a conservationist, a serious and competent naturalist, and a photographer. The wealthy son of a Supreme Court justice and a practicing attorney himself, he served a term in Congress, where he was one of Theodore Roosevelt's stalwarts in the battles for wildlife protection and resource conservation.

Shiras was the inventor of flashlight techniques for wildlife photographs. His pictures won the gold medal at the 1900 Paris Exposition and the grand prize at the St. Louis World Fair, an indication that they were as pleasing as they were innovative.

Many of his *National Geographic* articles were republished in the two-volume *Hunting Wild Life with Camera and Flashlight*. From that work comes "Revels Island," his depiction of the abuse of barrier-island wildlife by local foragers and sportsmen. This piece is the second in the sequence on avian conservation on the Central Atlantic coast.

From *Hunting Wild Life with Camera and Flashlight* (Washington, D.C.: National Geographic Society, 1936)

Eastern Shore of Virginia—Earlier Visits to Revels Island

REVELS ISLAND, partly marsh and partly a low ridge overgrown with pines and cedars, is surrounded by extensive salt marshes and shallow bays. It lies about a mile to the southward of Little Machipongo Inlet, and the same distance inland from the sand dunes along Parramore Beach, on the Atlantic coast.

It is one of a group bordering the eastern shore of Virginia, between the open beach and the mainland. The islands are in Accomac County, one of the two counties forming the eastern shore of Virginia, and terminating the peninsula that also borders the eastern shore of Chesapeake Bay.

Revels Island, owned by the Revels Island Shooting Club, of which I became a member in 1894, comprises several thousand acres. It contains two large, nearly land-locked bays, sufficiently shallow to form feeding-places for ducks, geese, and brant; a few fresh-water ponds which are visited by black ducks; and many mud flats and sandy beaches attractive to shore birds. Several navigable channels give access by motor boat to most of the property, and at times of high tides many creeklike waterways penetrate other parts of the island otherwise inaccessible by boat.

Just south of the clubhouse is a long, broad, sandy beach, extending a mile west, and terminating in a sandy point. Across the water a similar point on Sandy Island combines with it nearly to enclose Revels Island Bay, which is the best feeding-place for ducks, geese, and brant in this region.

Nearly a mile north of the clubhouse is a long narrow ridge covered with yellow pines, cedars, and several kinds of bushes. At intervals of two or three years a very high spring tide occurs, and all the property except the ridge is covered with a foot or two of water. Once when I visited the island, the clubhouse and cottages were surrounded by the tidewaters, and no land was visible for many miles except the pine ridge and the distant main shore.

Because of these occasional floods, predatory animals, as a rule, avoided the area, although once or twice a pair of foxes appeared and made a den on the ridge, from which place they were easily dug out by fox hunters. The ground-breeding birds, therefore, had no four-footed enemies, and those nesting in the trees apparently were rarely disturbed by owls. The only resident hawk was the osprey, which always lives on friendly terms with its neighbors. Bald eagles were not uncommon, but they lived mainly on fish taken from the ospreys, or on dead fish and dead or wounded ducks.

To the southward lies the long, ocean-washed Hog Island, which helps to enclose Broadwaters, a part of the eastern shore of a wide bay or sound that was once the favored shooting resort of Grover Cleveland.

The nesting birds had, however, one enemy that was present throughout the breeding season, and caused great havoc by destroying thousands of eggs and many of the nestlings. This was the fish crow. Members of the species apparently timed their coming to arrive on the island at the beginning of the period when food of this kind became abundant.

In May, under one tall pine, I found about 500 eggshells, most of them having a large puncture in one end. They were chiefly the eggs of the laughing, or black-headed gull, and the marsh hen, or clapper rail, but included, also, those of the green heron, grackle, red-winged blackbird, skimmer, and willet.

Other enemies of some of the breeding birds were the "eggers," including a large proportion of the natives of the Eastern Shore. Under local law it was permissible to collect newly laid eggs at the beginning of the nesting season. The eggs so taken were largely those of the laughing gull and the marsh hen. Gull nests were often closely grouped over several acres; consequently the eggs were easily collected.

One day I spoke to Jonah, the colored chore boy at the clubhouse, about a breeding colony of laughing gulls, and was surprised at the interest he displayed. I understood this a week later, when, on visiting the back yard at his request, I found a rounded heap of gulls' eggs, some four hundred in number. Dismayed at this sight, I voiced my disapproval.

Whether or not such annual pillage has any serious effect on the number of young raised each season, the Federal bird law has outlawed the practice, although I do not doubt that eggs in considerable numbers are still collected each year. . . .

The clapper rails, called locally marsh hens, were abundant on Revels Island, but they lived such secretive lives in the tall grasses that, despite their harsh, cackling notes, they were rarely seen except when one made a painstaking search for them. Each spring they returned from the South in extraordinary numbers, and skulked about among the grasses, rising and flying only a short distance when startled. At such times their weak flight makes them an easy target for the hunter. Their nests, neatly hidden under the overarching grasses, contain from 10 to 18 pale eggs that are comparatively large for so small a bird.

As was the case with the black-headed gulls, thousands of the eggs of these rails were taken when they were freshly laid. Trained dogs were sometimes used to help find the artfully concealed nests. In seasons when heavy tides raised the water level of the marshes, an enormous number of eggs of the clapper rail floated from the nests and formed a drift line along the shores of the marshy areas. After the tide had receded, the birds lost no time in laying new clutches, and their great numbers appeared to continue undiminished.

The eggers argued with apparently demonstrated justification that a general robbery of the nests of the rails and the black-headed gulls for a short period under local regulation had no effect upon the numbers of the young birds reared each year. The robbed parents promptly proceeded to lay new sets of eggs. If the nests were repeatedly despoiled, the effect would unquestionably be harmful.

The wild-fowl shooting in the tidal waters close to Revels Island never equaled that in the sounds farther south. The peculiar shortage was due largely to the absence of fresh-water ducks, the black duck being the only one in this class found in abundance.

When I first visited Revels Island, many geese, brant, and broadbills (scaups), with occasional flocks of redheads, and a fair number of golden-eyes and buffleheads, or butter balls, frequented the region. This club was the first, I believe, to introduce floating blinds made of green cedar boughs stuck in buoyant wooden frames large enough to admit a ducking boat. Within these floating blinds a narrow, flat-bottomed scow was sometimes left during the shooting season for the use of the sportsmen.

Such a contrivance, when anchored, was always headed up wind, so that the decoys could be placed out to advantage. The hunter needed to watch only for the approaching birds, which, according to their habit, came in against the wind. Moreover, these floating blinds rose and fell with the tide; whereas it was difficult to shoot from stuck blinds at low tide, and an exceptionally high one exposed the boat and hunter. The floating blinds were set out before the arrival of the birds, which, in consequence, regarded the clump of cedars as a part of the landscape.

In those days no baiting was done, and it was essential to have the blinds located on good feeding-grounds or along narrow flyways. At first the shooting was satisfactory, but it gradually became poorer as the shallow bays were leased for oyster planting, and the near-by guardhouses, which were continuously occupied by watchmen in the fall and winter, became nuisances.

When naphtha launches, and later those propelled by gasoline, displaced the sailboats, these bays were kept in a state of continual disturbance, for with motor craft the lack of wind was no obstacle, but tended to increase activities.

On the eastern shore marshes of Virginia, many of the black ducks have learned the danger of going to their feeding-places in fresh-water ponds by day, and seek them as the shades of night are falling. Taking advantage of this, the hunters have devised an unusual method of outwitting the wary birds. They make a high mound of marsh grass or seaweed near the side of the pond toward which the ducks usually come. Before the evening flight begins, the hunter, dressed in dark clothing, takes his place in front of the blind instead of behind it, for the approaching birds would see his projecting head if he were looking over the blind from behind. Sitting in front, he blends into it and is invisible.

For many years some market hunters on the marshes of the eastern shore of Virginia have used the destructive method of netting black ducks at night. Both the netting of the birds and their sale have long been outlawed, but persistent efforts to break up this nefarious practice have not yet become entirely successful.

Nets have about a two-inch mesh, large enough to permit a duck's head to pass through, but not to be withdrawn easily, since the feathers catch on the sides of the mesh. The nets are staked horizontally along the surface of the shallow water of natural or artificial channels, leading out from ponds frequented by the birds. Corn is then scattered in front and under the nets. The ducks, following the bait heads down, swim slowly under the nets as they feed. When their heads are raised they slip through the meshes and are held fast. Sometimes almost an entire flock will be taken by this means. The outlaws who do this are so well acquainted with the marshes and work so slyly that they are difficult to apprehend.

The marshes and mud flats about Revels Island were famous for the number and variety of shore birds that visited them during migration. Even when an alarming decrease in the numbers of these birds was noticed along the greater part of the Atlantic coast, these marshes were apparently the stopping place of all the survivors.

It is not strange that eventually a tremendous decrease in shore birds was observed during migrations; for in the spring when the local shore birds were either nesting or mating every clubhouse from Virginia to New Jersey was filled with members intent on hunting shore birds at a season when all other shooting was prohibited.

Day after day I have seen otherwise reputable sportsmen bring in 200 birds, and when the weather was warm it was practically impossible to keep such birds from spoiling. In the later years, convinced of its wastefulness I gave up spring shooting, but, having substituted the camera for the gun, I was doubtless less tempted than some of the others.

In an article published some years ago, I related an incident of one of my May hunting trips with a camera. I was accompanied by a shooting companion, who fired at a clapper rail as it arose. When the wounded bird was retrieved by the spaniel, a blood-splotched egg was laid in the sportsman's hand. The incident immediately made another convert to the creed opposed to spring shooting.

After watching for many years the shore birds in their daily flight along the beaches and mud flats or about marshy ponds, I often wondered how they passed the night. Undoubtedly in the breeding season most of these little waders are more or less concealed about the nests, but during their migrations they remain near the open water.

To test this question on Revels Island, I made two trips with a jacklight to the places much frequented by these birds in the daytime. The Hudsonian curlews I found massed in considerable flocks on flats just above high tide, where at one time they were shot by natives with the aid of a kerosene torch or lantern. Flocks of sandpipers, turnstones, robin-snipe [knot], and a few black-breasted plovers were seen squatting on the sandy shore, or on mud banks, while dowitchers were in the scanty grass a few yards farther back. Species that did not gather in large flocks by day, such as the yellow-legs, willet, ring-necked and semipalmated plover, were not seen. Being more or less solitary in habits, they were probably concealed in the vegetation back from the shore or about marshy ponds.

In the course of my visit to Revels Island a marked transition took place in the oyster industry. In the early years I saw oysters dredged from the deeper waters of the small bays and channels, but these shell fish gradually decreased until the business was threatened. The wild oysters varied greatly in size, and it became increasingly difficult to find a sufficient quantity of the standard sizes to meet the requirements of the market.

Finally the State of Virginia leased the best oyster grounds to individuals, although some of the beds were barren of oysters at the time. An abundance of old shells and some living oysters were strewn on the bottom to afford attachments for the oyster spawn, and this method of water farming soon proved so successful in producing desirable shell fish that a state of warfare developed between the lease holders protecting their property and those called "oyster pirates," who believed they had an inalienable right to anything produced by the sea. In order to protect the planted oyster beds it finally became necessary to station guards armed with rifles along the shore during fall and winter. Small houses were built near by for their accommodation.

The establishment of the guards in all the best bays of the region had a disastrous effect upon the wild-fowl shooting. Geese, brant, and ducks were accustomed to feed and rest in the bays, especially in rough weather. No sooner did a flock of birds settle on the water, however, than the nearest guards would send rifle balls into their midst, driving them out to sea or into the big bays, where they would remain until darkness enabled them to return in safety. In the same period the few sailboats were displaced by many noisy motor boats that kept the birds in constant alarm.

On the Eastern Shore there was as a rule no noticeable increased migratory flight on the approach of cold weather, but the birds arrived in easy stages from the North, as the waters there were gradually chilled. This was in contrast to the movement in spring when the wild fowl passed in almost continuous flights to their northern breeding grounds.

One afternoon in November, 1896, I was occupying a floating blind in Revels Island Bay. A strong, cold north wind, the first of the season, foretold the coming of freezing weather. Looking toward the north, I saw what appeared like a cloud in the otherwise clear sky. Soon it was apparent that an immense flock of ducks numbering thousands was approaching high in the air.

When the travelers sighted the broad shallow waters ahead, they swooped downward with a roar almost like that of a western cyclone. From a great height the birds descended in a graceful spiral. Three times this vast flock of scaups, for such they were, hurtled over the blind, dropping several hundred yards at each turn, making a sound with their wings resembling the sighing of a high wind in the treetops. Finally the visitors passed low over my decoys and alighted all about me with a tumultuous splashing, some almost striking the brush blind in which I sat.

Although tempted to shoot into the crowded ranks, with the prospect of dropping half a dozen birds, I restrained the impulse in order that the hungry and tired ducks could enjoy a period of rest, and thereby be induced to remain a day or two longer. It was a delightful experience to sit concealed in their midst. Some of the scaups splashed about vigorously, taking refreshing baths, some immediately began diving in search of food, and some faced the wind in little groups with heads drawn down on their shoulders, weary from the long flight.

No doubt among this flock were many ducks that were familiar with the attractions of this locality through visits during former seasons. They guided in the inexperienced youngsters of a new generation, even though they may previously have seen many a companion fall before the gun, an inevitable peril that these migrants must face wherever may be located their winter quarters.

As the wind and the tide forced the flock toward the opposite shore, I quietly withdrew, content in not having collected any toll from these newly arrived wanderers.

Aunt Caroline, a faithful and proficient colored cook, had charge of the club kitchen for more than a generation. She was always appreciated and was regarded as one of the club's valuable assets. Living in a State famous for its culinary art, she had few equals. The making of delicious clam chowder was one of her greatest accomplishments, and large clams were always available on a sandspit only about 100 yards away.

Early in the fall a goodly supply of oysters would be gathered from distant bays and placed in the shallow water on both sides of the long dock. Sometimes between meals a guide would wade out and get a basketful of them, which would be opened and eaten by us on the sunny side of the boathouse. Aunt Caroline served the oysters in several ways.

In the winter months, eels speared in their hibernating places in the mud at the heads of creeks were another delicacy on the bill of fare. In the hunting season Aunt Caroline produced the most appetizing dishes of perfectly cooked ducks and shore birds, besides stewed terrapin and snipe potpies. The memory of her pastries, including apple and pumpkin pies, puddings, doughnuts, and other tasty products of her skill, still remains with me. Even the little tin lunch pails that were sent out to the blinds with us were like little Christmas boxes with their varied assortment of good things to allay the hearty appetites we had sharpened by hours in the open air. . . .

Last Days at Revels Island

Like many other members of the Revels Island Club, in the middle nineties, I visited the shore in the spring not so much for shooting at a time when other game was protected as for enjoying the beauty of Nature throwing off her drab winter garment and replacing it with green, swelling buds and unfolding leaves. This beauty, the gentle warmth of the sun, and the soft spring breezes constituted a welcome change to residents of more northern latitudes who loved the out-of-doors.

To Revels Island during these balmy days came nearly all the species of shore birds that inhabit our Atlantic coast. Some were en route from their winter homes in South America to their breeding grounds beyond the Arctic Circle. There were others that nest in less distant places, as well as those that remain to rear their young along the Eastern Shore. Though the different species arrived at different times, each form had its special schedule of arrival and departure.

First to appear were the jacksnipes, or grass snipes [buff-breasted sandpiper?], which usually kept to the mainland, for the fresh-water meadows were to their liking. These were followed successively by Hudsonian curlews (many of which had wintered in South Carolina), willets, greater and lesser yellowlegs, numerous species of sandpipers, plovers (ring-necked, Wilson's, and black-breasted), turnstones, dowitchers, and knots or robin snipe.

In those days the wastefulness and cruelty of shooting birds that were already mating, or those that were actually in the midst of their nesting activities among the broken shells of the seashore or in tussocks of grass in the marshes, were not appreciated until several species were approaching extinction.

Because of the large number of species, each with its peculiar habits, shore-bird shooting at the island afforded a far pleasanter and more varied form of sport than did the wildfowling in the adjacent bays, where the salt water appeared to have attractions mainly for scaups, golden-eyes, geese, and brant. Comparatively few kinds of waterfowl were to be found in the vicinity of the island, although not much farther to the south, on Back Bay and Currituck Sound, were millions of marsh and deep-water ducks, together with tens of thousands of greater snow and Canada geese and whistling swans.

An ample supply of wooden and tin decoys, shaped and painted to resemble the larger or more desirable species of shore birds, was available at the club. In a catboat with a large leg-of-mutton sail the gunner was conveyed by his guide from the clubhouse to a blind, which, the direction and force of the wind being considered, was best located for the purpose in view.

In hunting curlew, fowlers often dug a pit at the edge of a sand point in the marsh where the birds were accustomed to feed as the receding tide exposed the mud flats. When the tide was rising, the curlews followed the narrow channels through the island, alighting to rest on the grassy flats along either side. In such places, the hunters, well concealed behind grass blinds, could enjoy flight shooting.

These birds were favorites with many sportsmen because of their size and slow, steady flight. Their large, compact flocks could be seen a mile or more away, as they came in to their feeding or resting places. If the hunter wished to shoot yellowlegs or willets, he would occupy a bush blind close to the edge of a little fresh-water pond, in the mud and shallow water of which the decoys would be placed in such spots as these birds commonly frequented when feeding.

The turnstones gathered on the mud banks bordering the larger bays in company with the smaller sandpipers that preferred the open shores. Because of the small size of these birds and their habit of flying in compact flocks, the gunners were able to bring them down in such numbers, sometimes a dozen or more at a shot, that they provided the material for many a delicious potpie, a welcome relief from the products of the frying pan.

Toward the end of the season, about the middle of May, flocks of robin snipe frequented the exposed sea beaches, and for years they afforded excellent shooting. After a time I became seriously alarmed about the future of these handsome birds, for they began to decrease rapidly in numbers, and late in May, 1904, I made a special trip to Revels Island to obtain pictures of what I feared might be a doomed species.

All day I remained in a blind with my camera before a flock circled over the decoys. The marked difference between hunting with a gun and with a camera was here demonstrated. Had I discharged a gun at this flock, a few birds might have been dropped, and the rest would have hurried on in wild alarm toward their far northern home. As it was, I obtained a fine series of pictures of the entire flock as its members circled back time after time to satisfy their innocent curiosity concerning the strange wooden counterfeits.

During the days I passed in the blinds I was much interested in noting the skill with which some of the local guides imitated the notes of these birds. Often when the birds were passing on their northward flight, or were merely seeking new feeding grounds after having been disturbed by a rising tide, they would pass our decoys, which were strung out near shore, without paying them the least attention.

The guide at my side in the blind would imitate the note peculiar to the species that was passing, and very commonly the flock would respond by swinging in on a graceful curve that would bring them within gunshot. If we did not shoot, they would alight among the decoys, where we could photograph them at our leisure.

Nature photographers, especially beginners, find much enjoyment in picturing the nests and eggs of birds to be found so readily in most country places. The more ambitious of them photograph the parent bird on the nest, or when it is feeding its young. In many cases the notes made by these amateurs have proved of value to ornithologists concerned with the home life of our birds.

At first, being interested mainly in game animals and birds, I neglected opportunities to get pictures of the nests, even of rare birds. Moreover, I was seldom in the forests in May or June, my outings occurring usually at a time when the birds were already hatched and on the wing.

After many visits in spring to the island as a sportsman, I went there to make photographic records of the birds and their nests. Once on going to photograph the northern flight of the robin snipe, I found that the movement had not yet begun, and after waiting a day or two, I decided that it would be interesting to look for the nests of breeding birds. Such a search should result in a fairly complete census of the summer-bird residents of the Eastern Shore. How fascinating this endeavor proved.

On the first morning of my quest I left the cottage with a small camera affixed to a tripod for use in taking pictures of stationary objects at close range. This was the outfit that I had used in photographing fungi in the forests of northern Michigan. First I went down on the sand beach that extended for nearly a mile along the southern end of the island. . . .

I had never hunted on this beach but had often walked its entire length for exercise after a day in the cramped confines of a shooting blind, and frequently had brought back a basket of clams for Aunt Caroline to convert into one of her famous chowders. In addition to sanderlings, turnstones, and other migrants, the birds that inhabited this beach in the spring included a number of species that remained to breed, and it seemed quite certain that on the sand above high tide some nests could be found.

After I had gone a few hundred yards along the beach, I saw the black and white figure of an oyster catcher near the edge of the water, but it took wing as I approached. Closely examining the upper beach near the place where it had appeared, I found two heavily splotched eggs in a little hollow where the sand had been scratched out. The eggs were surrounded by a number of broken sea shells as if an attempt had been made to outline a crude nest or to camouflage the eggs. I photographed the eggs and continued my walk.

Soon afterward I discovered three dark-colored eggs with dark spots in a depression in the bare sand, but no parent bird was visible in the neighborhood. As I was focusing the camera on this new find, the identity of the owner was established by the arrival of a common tern, which flew over my head protesting loudly.

As I approached the end of the sandy point, I observed a pair of black skimmers on the beach, but I doubted that they were nesting there, since these birds had a large breeding colony on Hog Island, on the opposite side of the channel. I was pleasantly surprised, therefore, to find their nest in this unexpected place.

After I had photographed it, I retraced my steps to the clubhouse along a line of small sand dunes covered with bunches of grass, from the direction of which the notes of Wilson's plover had sounded as I came down the beach. In that vicinity I had frequently seen these pretty little ring-necked plovers. After a considerable search I found a set of their eggs on the sand and added a photograph of them to my collection. . . .

I returned to the clubhouse, in the vicinity of which I hoped to obtain another picture. The buildings were surrounded by several acres of tall, thin grass that . . . harbor[ed] myriads of mosquitoes that could not be dislodged, even by the heaviest winds off the ocean. If a person wearing black garments passed through this grass in the spring, in a few minutes the black on his back would turn to a uniform brown from the host of mosquitoes alighting on it. Fortunately, in the day-time these insects were not very vicious, and at night well-screened windows prevented them from being annoying.

This grassy locality was the resort of a pair of meadow larks that could be seen flying about at all hours of the day, and heard singing musically mornings and evenings. That these birds were nesting on this little island, surrounded by miles of salt marshes, and so far away from the mainland, would have seemed unlikely to me had not their actions indicated that they were housekeeping.

Several times I had observed one of the birds descend into the grass near a small cedar. Approaching the spot, I searched carefully and at length discovered a pyramid of grass tops, like a little Indian tepee, under which was a nest containing four eggs. Parting the grass, I photographed the cleverly concealed nest and then restored the canopy to its original position. . . .

The next to my last trip to the island was made to photograph the robin snipe and the Hudsonian curlew, for it seemed to me as if they were going the way of the wild pigeon and would soon be exterminated.

My last visit to the island was in May, 1923, at which time I was accompanied by Dr. E.W. Nelson, then Chief of the Biological Survey of the United States Department of Agriculture. The purpose of the trip was to check up on the reported increase of shore birds as a result of their protection under the Migratory Bird Law.

The launch had no sooner put out from the little town of Wachapreague, on the mainland side of Wachapreague Inlet, north of Parramore Island, than Hudsonian curlews began springing up on all sides, and we observed nearly a thousand on the six-mile trip. Yet this bird had nearly become extinct ten years before.

In our several days on the marshes and mud flats we found that the protection given the birds by the Federal law had resulted in an increase in the numbers of most of the shore birds, including the willet, the black-breasted and the smaller plovers, the knot or robin-snipe, dowitcher, calico-backs, or turnstones, and many varieties of sandpipers. The yellow-legs, however, were scarce, since an open season still permitted shooting of this species.

Subsequently the Advisory Board, of which I was a member, a committee of game commissioners and sportsmen appointed to offer recommendations for drafting regulations relative to the administration of the Migratory Bird Law, advised that the season be closed on yellow-legs. This suggestion was adopted by the Department of Agriculture in 1927.

Fernald's Ecstasy! Fernald's Chagrin!

Cecil C. Frost (b. 1942)
Lytton J. Musselman (b. 1943)

Of all twentieth-century botanists, Merritt Lyndon Fernald (1873–1950) of Gray's Herbarium at Harvard University was the most influential and the most prolific in publication. Yet he had—rarity of rarities in such men—a sense of humor. In their technical paper, "History and Vegetation of the Blackwater Ecologic Preserve," Frost and Musselman treat us to the thrill of Fernald's discoveries and his chagrin at preemption, all in one of the most ecologically significant and unusual Central Atlantic botanical sites, the Zuni Pine Barrens in Suffolk County, Virginia. In 1985, the Union Camp Corporation created the Preserve by donating its 319-acre holdings in the Barrens to Old Dominion University through the Nature Conservancy.

We hope that the botanically inexperienced reader will enjoy the fun of finding rarities with Fernald and forgive the editors for leaving the scientific names of plants in Latin; the music of Fernald's diction would be destroyed by inserting common names in the text. A list of common names of mentioned species, genera, and families appears at the end of the article.

Cecil C. Frost is professor of biology at the East Carolina University at Greenville, North Carolina. Lytton Musselman is professor of biological sciences, eminent scholar and curator of the herbarium at Old Dominion University in Norfolk, Virginia. All bracketed interpolations in this selection are Frost's and Musselman's.

From *Castanea* 52, no. 1 (1987)

History and Vegetation of the Blackwater Ecologic Preserve

Botanical Exploration

Botanical exploration of southeastern Virginia came remarkably late, considering the long history of settlement in the area. The Zuni Pine Barrens are less than 30 miles south of John Smith's 1607 settlement at

Jamestown. Substantial plantations appeared along the south side of the James River within 25 years after original settlement, but the divide between the James and the Blackwater represented a substantial barrier in colonial times when most transportation was by water. . . .

In the three centuries preceding the work of M. L. Fernald in the 1930's, a number of botanists may have collected south of the James, including the Rev. John Clayton, John Bannister, Mark Catesby, John Clayton of Gloucester, John Mitchell, John Bartram, James Greenway, M. A. Curtis, and Frederick Pursh. Through a remarkable series of accidents and lost or unfinished works, little information has filtered down to the present other than a few specimens in herbaria. . . .

Fernald's exploration of southeastern Virginia was exhaustive. It commenced in 1933 and covered 14 field seasons, spanning the years of his life from around age 60 to 73. He published more than 1,200 pages of botanical literature on Virginia, mostly centered on the area south of the James River, from the coast inland to Brunswick County. The last trip to Virginia was in 1946. Harvill et al (1977)* commented: "Some of Fernald's most famous plant locales have already been destroyed, and were it not for those fourteen years of persisting and masterful field work we would never have known of many of Virginia's most ecologically and phytogeographically significant habitats, with their many rare and fastidious species."

On a warm July evening in 1936, three botanists and an entomologist had become lost on the last day of a collecting trip in southeastern Virginia. Fernald, Bayard Long, R. J. Smart, and Carroll Williams found themselves unexpectedly at Franklin.

"The obvious way home for most normal individuals was via Courtland, 10 miles away, thence by the very familiar Jerusalem Plank Road; but, having set our faces this last day in another direction, we could not tolerate further anticlimax and defeat. Consequently we chose to drive after dark by a dirt road northward to Zuni, a back road that was destined on our next two trips to be our most used artery through the country. Near Walters we suddenly realized that we were passing through as beautiful and unspoiled pineland as we had anywhere met. It was dark but, getting out to investigate, we promptly walked into a carpet of the tropical *Crotalaria rotundifo-*

*Harvill, A. M., Jr., C. E. Stevens, and D.M.E. Ware. 1977. Atlas of the Virginia Flora. Part 1. Pteridophytes through monocotyledons. Virginia Botanical Associates, Farmville. 59 p.

lia [= *C. angulata*], here at its northern limit. Obviously the region must be explored on the next trip." Fernald returned on August 19, this time with his colleague from Cambridge, Ludlow Griscom. Meeting Long and Williams at Richmond the party reached Zuni on the 20th. Since the afternoon was spent botanizing the short distance along SR 614 from Antioch Swamp to the edge of the Zuni Pine Barrens, their progress to the site and its location are well documented.

"Taking the road south from Zuni, we soon came to the dammed up brook in the woods. [This small mill pond in Antioch Swamp on SR 614 is still extant]. Here we tried our luck, getting a few desirable but scarcely notable plants. Along the road here, however, as in open woods near Kilby and near Yorktown, where Long, Fogg and I had collected it a year before, there was a fruiting species of Privet. Its small, membranous, and (when dried) caducous leaves show it to be *Ligustrum sinense* Lour., recorded by Small as an escape in southern Louisiana. Much farther north, in southeastern Virginia, it is making itself quite at home. A little farther on we stopped to investigate the roadside ditches, where *Lipocarpha maculata* and a complex series of species of *Hypericum* abound. Among the latter was *H. dissimulatum* Bicknell, apparently not previously found in Virginia, though next day we found it abundant at the station of *Juncus brachycarpus* near New Bohemia. Long and Griscom wandered across some swales while I followed a wood road, where, mixed with the common *Juncus repens* in a pocket of *Sphagnum*, *Proserpinaca pectinata* abounded. We have met it nowhere else in eastern Virginia nor is it represented in the Gray Herbarium from the state; it was, however, collected in Virginia by Clayton, his material, according to Asa Gray's memorandum, being a mixture of *P. palustris* and *P. pectinata*. Kearney also reported it from Northwest in Norfolk County. The party of two brought in a series of *Xyris*, *X. difformis* and *X. ambigua*, and a few plants of the new one which Long and I had got in July near New Bohemia. We all went back for more and during the quest found *Desmodium tenuifolium* T. & G., which has not been recorded from north of North Carolina.

"Moving on to the south we came to extensive white sands in the open, suggestive in their small way of the dunes of the outer coast, in Princess Anne County, toward 50 miles away. [This would be the sandy area along SR 614, just south of the low place where Horse Swamp crosses the road.] And here, in the interior, *Panicum Commonsianum* and *Cyperus filiculmis*, var. *oblitus* Fern. & Grisc. of Cape Henry and, new to us, the southern *Aris-*

tida virgata. Searching the dry woods for novelties and collecting variations of *Panicum lancearium* and *Paspalum setaceum* which were here very abundant, and the first ordinary northern (even Hudsonian) Sheep Laurel, *Kalmia angustifolia*, we had ever seen on the Coastal Plain of Virginia, we were soon rewarded by great clumps with lilac pink heads suggesting those of *Liatris* but in broad corymbs, the stems of the plants cespitose and without bulbous bases. This was surely something novel for us, our first representatives in the manual range of the southern genus *Carphephorus*, in this case *C. bellidifolius* (Michx.) T. & G" (Fernald 1937).[†]

The party returned to the area on August 22. Previous collecting had taken place only along the road, but the barrens are about a mile wide at this point, extending from the road, west to the Blackwater River. Following directions from a local farmer, Fernald left the main road, entering this tract to discover the heart of the Zuni Pine Barrens, now the Blackwater Ecologic Preserve.

"At the next farm the description of the country was confirmed and, following the cart-road to which we were directed, we entered one of the botanical paradises of the summer, and confirmed an often forgotten axiom: 'it pays to ask the native.'

"The thin woods of *Pinus taeda* and *Quercus laevis* Walt. (*Q. catesbaei* Michx.) were carpeted with white sand, with a dense thicket of the usual shrubs of sandy woods, but wherever there was an opening exciting herbs were growing. *Carphephorus bellidifolius* abounded and on the more open sands *Euphorbia Ipecachuanhae* occurred. . . . I was happy to collect these plants, which seemed interesting to me; but, while I was thus wasting time, Long shouted 'Here's Pyxie' and Griscom replied 'Here's another *Liatris*-like thing'; and, before I could reach either of them, there came the report: '*Seymeria cassioides* again.' And so it went. We had stumbled into what we had sought for four years, real unspoiled pine barren in Virginia. *Pyxidanthera barbulata* literally carpeted the ground in many areas, at the first station discovered between southern New Jersey and North Carolina; *Carphephorus tomentosus* (Michx.) T. & G. was a second species of a genus, which, two days before, had been 'new to Virginia,' *C. tomentosus* not represented in the Gray Herbarium from North of Bladen County in southwestern North Carolina; *Seymeria cassioides* already found with *Schwalbea americana* in Greensville County, was here very abundant; its recorded

[†]Fernald, M. L. 1937. Local plants of the inner Coastal Plain of southeastern Virginia. Rhodora 39:321–366.

northern limits otherwise in eastern and southeastern North Carolina. The wonderful cespitose *Xyris* of white sands, true *X. flexuosa* [=*X. caroliniana*], as shown by Harper, the plant with large spiraling castaneous bulbs, stiff and slender spiralling leaves and large acutish spikes of showy flowers (*X. arenicola* Small) soon appeared, again at its first station between New Jersey and North Carolina. In sphagnous depressions and thickets *Zigadenus glaberrimus* and *Sarracenia purpurea* var. *venosa* were both scattered, *Panicum Clutei* [=*P. dichotomum*] was frequent and *Habenaria blephariglottis*, var. *conspicua* was just flowering.

"Where the cart-road leads through an extensive sphagnous depression (undoubtedly one of the pondholes of early spring) two plants specially pleased us: *Rhynchospora distans* (Michx.) Vahl [=*R. fascicularis*], heretofore recorded only from the West Indies and Florida to South Carolina; and *Juncus abortivus* Chapm. a beautiful tall relative of the northern *J. pelocarpus* with coarse rhizomes (*J. pelocarpus* var. *crassicaudex* Engelm.), primarily of Florida but known, very rarely indeed, northward to a single station in Darlington County, South Carolina. Long epitomized the situation as we were all conceiving it: 'This is real botanizing!' Thirst, hunger and heat had been forgotten, though toward 3 o'clock we returned to the car, but, still wanting more, the insatiable hunter of rarities poked into one of the open bare white patches and brought us a collection of *Arenaria caroliniana* the first from between New Jersey and southeastern North Carolina" (Fernald 1937).

So ended a sterling day of collecting in the Zuni Pine Barrens. The botanists were rewarded with nine state record plants from this specific location, seven of them in one day. In all, Fernald recorded dozens of rare species from the natural area and the immediate surrounding area from Zuni to Walters. At least one more state record was to be obtained from the site. Here is Fernald's account (Fernald 1937) of the discovery of *Polygonella polygama* (October-flower) upon his return with Long and Williams on October 16, 1936: ". . . we found *Zigadenus glaberrimus* more widely dispersed than we had supposed, and with it *Sarracenia flava*, which we had not seen in August. *Carphephorus tomentosus*, too, proved to be fairly abundant; and just at dusk, when we could hardly see, I came upon a single plant which puzzled me. Obviously of the *Polygonaceae*, it looked like *Polygonella*, but not any known in the 'manual range.' I had found one plant, and Long, for obvious reasons, wanting another, we sought in the increasing darkness on hands and knees, repeatedly returning, as a check, to the site of the original plant. Finally, with Long's jocose reproof, 'You've destroyed the locality,' following me, I gave up and went as far as darkness would permit in

". . . we were startled and grieved to hear Mrs. Correll announce: 'Why there's Long-leaf Pine right there!' And there it was!" "Longleaf Pine," from *History and Vegetation of the Blackwater Ecologic Preserve.* Reprinted from Castanea 52(1): 16–46. March 1987

search of something different. Returning after half-an-hour, I heard Long's gleeful shout: 'I've put up 17 sheets so far.' There, fully occupying one of the open plats of sand, and apparently only one, was a solid carpet of *Polygonella*. It proved to be *P. polygama* (Vent.) Engelm. & Gray, and this is the first station for it north of southeastern North Carolina (the Wilmington region). Again our great find was at twilight!". . .

The presence and condition of longleaf in the Zuni Pine Barrens was not initially reported by Fernald, who made few notes on canopy species, since the trees of the region were well known and he was interested in discovering new species. The irrepressible Fernald ruefully described how this shortcoming was called to his attention on New Year's Day, 1939 (Fernald 1939).[‡]

"After the scientific meetings at Richmond, where, in conversation, doubt was raised by Dr. Roland Harper as to the exact status of *Pinus palustris* (Long-leaf Pine) in Virginia, Long and I induced Mr. and Mrs. Donovan S. Correll to drive with us to Harper's supposed station (seen from a train). December 31st was spent in wading in ice-water, for fruit of the various gentians of the bogs and flat pine-lands. On New Year's Day, Long and I started to exhibit some of our choice habitats. Slowing down at our old parking-spot in the pine barrens south of Zuni, we were startled and grieved to hear Mrs. Correll announce: 'Why there's Long-leaf Pine right there!' And there it was! Intent on *Carphephorus, Polygonella polygama, Pyxidanthera, Juncus abortivus* and the other pine-barren herbs and low shrubs new to Virginia, we had half-a-dozen times brushed by the great columnar young pines without their 'registering.' Not only young columns were there; plenty of old fruiting trees occur. We have not yet got over our chagrin, for we promptly remembered Long-leaf Pine south of Cleopus in Nansemond County; we later collected it from specimens we had several times jostled in passing, south of Franklin in Southampton County; and in western Nansemond (near the Blackwater) we now have an area where it and *Chamaecyparis* are rapidly coming back after intensive cutting. Long and I can't jeer each other by mentioning Long-leaf Pine; that score is even! The mention of it simply makes us sad and humble."

Scientific and common names of the plants mentioned above, taken from *Manual of the Vascular Flora of the Carolinas*, by Albert E. Radford,

[‡]Fernald, M. L. 1939. Last survivors in the flora of Tidewater Virginia. Rhodora 41: 465–504.

Harry E. Ahles, and C. Ritchie Bell (Chapel Hill: University of North Carolina Press, 1968).

Arenaria caroliniana: Pine Barren Sandwort
Aristida virgata: a needle grass
Carphephorus bellidifolius and C. tomentosus: Blazing Stars—in the daisy family
Chamaecyparis thyoides: White Cedar
Crotalaria rotundifolia (= *C. angulata*): Rattlebox, Rabbit Bell—a legume
Cyperus filiculmis: a sedge
Desmodium tenuifolium: Beggar's Ticks, Tick-Trefoil
Euphorbia ipecachuanhae: Wild Ipecac
Habenaria blephariglottis, var. *conspicua*: a terrestrial orchid
Hypericum dissimulatum: a St. John's-wort
Juncus abortivus, Juncus brachycarpus, J. pelocarpus, Juncus repens: rushes
Kalmia angustifolia: Sheep Laurel
Liatris: the Blazing Star genus in the daisy family
Ligustrum sinense: Privet
Lipocarpha maculata: an annual rush
Panicum commonsianum, Panicum lancearium, Panicum clutei [=*P. dichotomum*]: panic grasses
Pinus palustris: Long-leaf Pine
Pinus taeda: Loblolly Pine
Polygonaceae: the Buckwheat family
Polygonella, Polygonella polygama: Jointweed, October Flower
Proserpinaca pectinata, Proserpinaca palustris: Mermaid Weed
Pyxidanthera barbulata: Pyxie
Quercus laevis: Turkey Oak
Rhynchospora distans [=*R. fascicularis*]: Beak Rush
Sarracenia flava: Pitcher-plant
Sarracenia purpurea var. *venosa*: Pitcher-plant
Schwalbea americana: Chaffseed
Seymeria cassioides: Mullein-Foxglove
Sphagnum: moss
Xyris: the type genus of yellow-eyed grass family
Xyris ambigua: Yellow-eyed Grass
Zigadenus glaberrimus: White Camus, a lily

The Barbarians

Maurice Broun (1906–1979)

Each autumn, thousands of migrating hawks fly low over Pennsylvania's Kittatinny Ridge where Hawk Mountain Sanctuary is located. Since the 1870s, local sportsmen visited the mountain to shoot the passing hawks. In 1934, Rosalie Edge purchased the property to establish the world's first sanctuary dedicated to birds of prey. Broun, a young ornithologist from New England, was hired to be the first manager of the sanctuary. He and his wife moved in to establish a presence on the mountain and bring an end to the wanton killing of hawks there. In October 1934, the stage was set for a clash of cultures. Broun describes this confrontation in "The Barbarians," which is excerpted from his autobiographical book about Hawk Mountain, *Hawks Aloft* (1942). Broun's experience is a real-world example of the conflict between traditional values and the growing conservation movement. Broun managed Hawk Mountain Sanctuary until his retirement in 1966. Under his stewardship, it became a world-renowned location to observe hawks and study their migration. In 1992, thanks to Rosalie Edge and Maurice Broun, the one millionth bird of prey flew by unmolested.

From *Hawks Aloft* (Kutztown, Pa: Kutztown Publishing Company, 1942)

IT WAS A BLESSING to be comfortably settled with the Kochs. At last we could relax; it had been utterly impossible to do so on the mountain, at "Schaumboch's." And Mrs. Koch's food! Her large square table groaned under weight of a variety of foods, which included several kinds of meat, chicken, eggs, relishes, jams, pies, cake and cookies; and we came to know those traditional Pennsylvania Dutch achievements: shoo-fly pie, apple butter and scrapple. Irma said it was like a visit to a foreign country. Mrs. Koch beamed and told us not once, but many times, how "proud" she was that we enjoyed her food. To be "proud" was to be pleased.

Walter Koch was not so "proud," however. He had just returned from Marberger's store where, late in the day, many of the neighbors foregathered for cracker-barrel chatter of current events. The *fahricht* (crazy) couple from Massachusetts had become a sensational current event, and the air in Drehersville was charged with the hottest kind of argument. The menfolk did not approve of the Kochs providing us with board and shelter. So the Kochs found themselves the center of a stormy discussion, all because of the "foreigners." But Walter Koch, a man of courage and independent mind, was our stanch ally; at the risk of becoming most unpopular with his neighbors, he defended our position. He warned us that we were in for a lot of trouble; possibly the coming week end.

The following morning I found that every single one of my sixty-odd posters along the road had been removed. It began to rain, for which I rejoiced, since no one was likely to venture up the mountain to make trouble. I drove into Hamburg, the nearest large town, to obtain more posters, and to make contact with game wardens and the State Police. I thought, naively, that I could obtain official protection on week ends.

"You can't keep gunners off that land, and I wouldn't take your job for a hundred dollars a day!" exclaimed Game Protector Dressner as I interviewed him in his home. I explained that I was doing the job for nothing— "just expenses." Dressner was dumbfounded. After a minute of silence, he phoned another game warden, who came promptly. The situation was so novel and amusing to both wardens—outsiders protecting hawks, and in control of a whole mountaintop to do so—that they guffawed. They were as sympathetic as crows that had discovered an owl. Since they, too, joined in the hawk-shoots, it was useless to appeal to them for help. Then how about the State Police? I went over to the police barracks and learned that the police had their hands full with strikes in the local industries. Dressner had assured me that the police had been known to participate in the hawk-shooting.

(I did not see Dressner again for thirteen years. Then, on a Sunday in November, he and his family appeared at the Sanctuary summit rocks. I recognized him instantly, which so surprised Dressner that he was again dumbfounded. When he recovered from his surprise, we reminisced pleasantly. Dressner had long since given up shooting hawks, and game protection, too, for fruit-growing. He confided to me that on that first meeting he was sure we were crackpots, certain to have a brief and violent career on that mountain.)

The rain came down steadily, a comfort. I returned to the Koch farm, to rest in our large, inviting room. But I could not rest. I was worried and I had a queasy, inadequate feeling, which did not, however, derive from lack of experience. I had had abundant experience with trespassers and game-law violators, at various wildlife refuges in New England. But this situation was far more complex; it involved the interests of hundreds, possibly thousands, of organized, politically-ruled men who were certain to boil up in anger and resentment at the intrusion of a small, to them unheard-of, organization which had suddenly seized "their" entire mountain. Though we possessed maps and land titles, the location of the twelve miles of boundaries of the wilderness property was anybody's guess. Were we sitting on a powder keg? To withdraw was unthinkable. Glumly I pondered the whole picture, and the words of Shakespeare: "Wrens make prey where eagles dare not perch."

The week end was upon us. I drove up the mountain after breakfast and in a drizzling rain I managed to nail up an entirely new set of posters. The weather cleared in the early afternoon. A few hawks passed low over the road. Only two cars appeared, each emptying gunners—five in one car. These men asked if they could walk to the pinnacle, and I allowed them to do so, without their guns. Returning, an old man in the group had this to offer: "A fellow doesn't want a gun up there; he should bring a pair of field glasses and a camera." These were the first heartening words I had heard on the mountain since our arrival.

Sunday brought raw, nasty weather, which suited me immensely. At 5 a.m. I was at my post of duty on the mountain road, expecting hunters and the promised trouble. It began to rain again, so I returned to the Kochs' for breakfast. And back up the mountain after breakfast. In those days I was cursed with a New England conscience. Nothing happened, except the weather, and obligingly it poured all through the day. While I guarded the road, Irma attended the local (Lutheran) church with the Kochs. Some seventy natives were in attendance, and how they stared at my wife. From then on she was known as the "hawk-woman."

Looking back on those early, disquieting experiences, I marvel at our great good luck with the weather. Providentially, torrents of rain fell on three successive week ends, and the anticipated hordes of hawk-killers did not materialize. The game wardens had warned me, however, that early October would bring plenty of hawks and plenty of trouble in the form of toughs from the coal region.

Mrs. Edge and her son Peter came out to the mountain in the middle of the second week to see how everything had been going. The situation was well in hand, and we had had no trouble—not yet—but it behooved us to engage a deputy sheriff, I advised Mrs. Edge. Obviously we must secure the services of someone who was authorized to make arrests, if necessary. I had already begun to cast around for the right man and, through the help of a sympathetic notary in a near-by town, I hoped to engage Bob Kramer, if Mrs. Edge approved. And she did. The cost of maintaining Kramer for ten weeks was another worry for Mrs. Edge, but she did not hesitate.

Bob Kramer, of near-by Auburn, a sturdy man of forty-two, good-humored and dependable, possessed an important weapon which I lacked: the Pennsylvania Dutch tongue. He had been engaged in police work for years. Kramer would have agreed to work for us on week ends only, but we took him on daily, beginning the end of September. I also engaged a surveyor, who successfully determined our important west boundary, the one nearest the hunters of Drehersville.

Meanwhile I continued my vigil, day after day, at the entrance to the Sanctuary, where few hawks are seen unless the wind is in a southerly quarter. All sorts of men with high-powered rifles and shotguns came to indulge in the old "sport," only to learn that on *this* mountain it was a thing of the past. A few hunters came from New Jersey, and two from Delaware. My tongue wagged incessantly those first few weeks. It was no fun trying to convince those men of the folly of shooting hawks. Many were surly, and some went off with pent-up truculence. My only weapons that entire season were a ready tongue and a bold front—under which I sometimes quailed! But Kramer had a gun which was respected.

The evening of the seventeenth two young men dropped in at the Kochs' and said they had been gunning a few miles up the ridge, during the afternoon. They asked me whether I had seen the big hawk flight. No, I had not. Then I learned that they had counted almost two thousand hawks passing high over the ridge that afternoon; a broad-wing flight, I gathered. I was chagrined that I had missed the spectacle. Not until October 7th did I make daily visits to the mountain summit to observe the wonderful hawk-flights, while Kramer patrolled the road.

The possibility of an "invasion" of hunters now became very real. Kramer's daily presence had deterred the local hotheads from forcing their way; but Walter Koch, who always knew what was going on and warned us accordingly, advised me that it might be necessary for me to stand guard at the old shooting-stands on the crest of the mountain. From there it was possible to observe the various approaches to the summit, through the woods from the north or from the west.

One day I learned from Mr. Koch, almost with disbelief, that a certain obstreperous character in Drehersville, who worked cheek by jowl with the officials of the numerous hunting clubs, had been obtaining sworn affi-

"This same man killed a red-tailed hawk and, to taunt us, he hung the bird, with wings spread, from the girders of the little bridge over which we passed twice daily." Drehersville Bridge, S. Finnegan, after a photo in *Hawks Aloft*

davits from many of the local farmers that the hawks often came down and carried off young pigs! This same man killed a red-tailed hawk and, to taunt us, he hung the bird, with wings spread, from the girders of the little bridge over which we passed twice daily. There the bird hung for about ten days. I took a picture of it which helped us in our money-raising campaign.

Now a great hullabaloo was raised in gunning circles throughout two counties against the out-of-state "chiselers." The farmers in the vicinity made the loudest squawk. They not only resented us and our assumed arrogance in taking over "their" mountain, they resented the name "Hawk Mountain" and claimed that there never had been such a place. Local newspapers belabored us and carried the usual stale message that the hawks were killing off the game. A great to-do was made by the Pottsville merchant "sportsman" who used to come up the mountain on week ends, his truck loaded with cartridges to sell. We learned that the local sportsmen's clubs, representing 15,000 hunters, had engaged a lawyer to search all land titles and find loopholes which might break Mrs. Edge's lease, and to buy the mountain, if possible. The hunters were holding frequent meetings to decide what to do.

A few days later, the agitated hawk-shooters, though still contemplating the purchase of "Hawk Mountain," leased a considerable tract of land near Port Clinton. I saw their advertisement in a newspaper, urging gunners to kill hawks in this new place, about four miles down the ridge, and offering gunners "a new line of shells, at .60 a case." Kramer investigated the Port Clinton hawk-shoots. These could be serious on days when the wind was easterly, but at no time was the slaughter comparable to that which had occurred formerly on our mountain. The place was also much more difficult of access.

Most of the hunters that I encountered had been killing hawks on this mountain for many years. Most of them were obdurate in their opinion of hawks in general and, they insisted, all hawks should be exterminated. It was useless to argue that the hawks do not feed while migrating, and that the food habits of the birds of prey involved mainly rodents. One farmer, in spite of his carping, allowed his large flock of white leghorns to roam the fields at the foot of the mountain. Why, I asked the gunners, were there so many grouse drumming in these upland woods? Here, at the greatest concentration point for hawks in the entire country, the ruffed grouse abounded; one day I had counted thirty-three of the birds in different parts of the Sanctuary. Rabbits, quail and pheasants were plentiful in the excellent cover of the old fields in the vicinity of Drehersville. But perhaps I was "seeing things," for the hawks kill off the game!

In early October much of the opposition had quieted, but it looked like the calm before the storm, and throughout the month Kramer and I anticipated trouble daily. Mr. Koch shook his head apprehensively. (I think that during that whole season Walter Koch did more worrying about the "hawk people" than we did about ourselves.) The fourth week end was approaching, and Mr. Koch was sure that this week end we would have trouble. A group of local hunters was planning to mob Kramer and me and force their way to the summit.

Late Friday afternoon two husky young men, built like fullbacks, appeared without guns at the Sanctuary. I was pleasantly surprised to learn that they had been recruited by Richard Pough to help us protect the place for a week or so. Pough, one of the "discoverers" of the hawk-shoots, had been in constant touch with Mrs. Edge. Knowing only too well what we might be up against with the lawless elements among the hawk-shooters, Pough generously arranged to have Charlie French and Dudley Wagar, both of Philadelphia, help us. Mrs. Koch cheerfully provided accommodations for the two young men.

The following day it poured again—the fourth soggy Saturday! The four of us, Kramer, the newcomers and I spent a few hours on the mountain road, nevertheless, hunched in our cars. We even turned away a few hunters who had come from Reading. Back at the farmhouse I asked Mr. Koch if he thought the weather would clear. "Maurice, it always has," said he with a chuckle. In the evening he returned from Marberger's store with a twinkle in his eyes and a knowing grin. It was being bruited around the village that we had engaged two detectives.

Sunday, October 7th, brought beautiful weather and ideal hawking conditions. Kramer and Wagar took the road, while French and I posted ourselves at the summit rocks. It was a day of many surprises, and some drama—but not the drama we had expected. We had plenty of company, some of it very talented. Ten members of the Delaware Valley Ornithological Club, of Philadelphia, including Richard Pough, Samuel Scoville, Jr., the writer, Julian K. Potter, the ornithologist, and Jacob B. Abbott, the artist, were among the observers at the Lookout that day. The hawk flight was disappointing—only a hundred birds of thirteen species. But to me it was tremendously exciting to see so many kinds of hawks. A special feature was an adult golden eagle. The great bird came obligingly close, an eye-opener to the ornithological gathering—and the first of many golden eagles that were to lure bird watchers from all over the country.

Early in the afternoon we heard some shooting on the ridge-top, about a half mile directly behind us. Charlie French and I and one of the D.V.O.C. men took off through the woods and presently we reached the west boundary of the Sanctuary. There, on the edge of our line, marked by no-trespassing posters, were ten men, two of them perched high in a tree, blazing away at occasional hawks passing just out of shotgun range. The men were just off the Sanctuary property. There was nothing I could do, except perhaps to wait until they might kill a protected species (ten ospreys and a bald eagle were the only "protected" birds that passed), and then I would prosecute the killer. So we leaned against a tree and waited, silently. The shooting stopped, the men were maddened that we just stood there and stared at them. Each passing minute increased the tension till one of the men snapped, "Well, watcha goin' to do about it?" I replied, "Just stay here and see what you fellows might do." The fellow lowered his gun, came up to me menacingly and said, "I'll knock your————block off." For a moment it looked like a fight—and it might have been bad business, three unarmed men against ten with guns and hot tempers—but the fellow suddenly stopped and spluttered, "You damn hawk-lovers; you're just a bunch of barbarians." How we three unarmed men laughed! I warned the men not to be caught trespassing, and I withdrew with my companions.

Returning to the Lookout, I found more visitors. A "mob" had indeed come! That day seventy-four men, women and children climbed to the Lookout to enjoy the beautiful scenery and birds. It was an inspiring sight, and it augured well for the successful outcome of our "new deal for the hawks." At the entrance, Kramer had turned away thirty-two gunners, including a few women. Ten times that number of gunners might have been on hand that day had we not spent the previous weeks impressing the hunting elements that we meant business on the mountain. Pleasant week ends thereafter brought increasing numbers of bird-students and protectionists to enjoy the hawking.

Hawk-hunters, some of them hard-bitten fellows who looked as though they would as soon shoot a mother-in-law as a hawk, continued to come late into November—a month *after* the opening of the small game season—so deep-rooted was the urge to follow this perverse and cruel "sport." But in spite of all the threats and warnings and the hubbub of the shotgun squads, we had a singularly peaceful time of it along the old mountain road. At the summit, in the few weeks that it was possible to observe the hawk-flights, we had the satisfaction of seeing more than ten thousand hawks pass safely; not a single bird was killed. Not a single untoward incident occurred in that birth-year of the Sanctuary.

Mrs. Edge's coup in obtaining the mountain and our efforts in safeguarding it were an undreamed-of success. Kramer's help was a godsend, my wife's patience and courage were an inspiration, the Kochs were a blessing (especially invaluable was Walter Koch's tapping of the grapevine), and Mrs. Edge's financial and moral support insured victory. In the end, Mrs.

Edge remunerated us generously, though we had not expected a cent be-yond our expenses. The National Audubon Society, the Massachusetts Audubon Society, the New Jersey Audubon Society, the Linnaean Society of New York, and many individuals, of whom the most openhanded was Dr. Willard G. Van Name, came to Mrs. Edge's aid with needed funds. So ended in triumph our initial adventures in conservation at Hawk Mountain Sanctuary.

Flood Tide *and* Chincoteague: A National Wildlife Refuge

Rachel Carson (1907–1964)

Rachel Carson is the most significant nature writer of the twentieth century: *The Sea Around Us* and *Silent Spring* are landmarks in the reawakening of America to nature and to conservation. The success of these two books was due in part to Carson's facility in communicating both emotion and information through language that is accessible to any literate person. Her intricate merging of sensory images and precise scientific facts creates "a sense of wonder" at the complexity of the natural world. During her employment as a biologist and writer at the U.S. Fish and Wildlife Service, her style evolved from an essentially nineteenth-century opulence of expression into the lyrical parsimony that Thomas J. Lyon has called "deceptively simple." The Central Atlantic is fortunate to be the setting of two pieces that demonstrate the change: "Flood Tide" from *Under the Sea Wind* (1941), which was Carson's first book; and *Chincoteague: A National Wildlife Refuge*, a 1947 U.S. Fish and Wildlife Service booklet.

Under the Sea Wind contains many stylistic experiments and influences. Prime among the influences is the English novelist and nature writer Henry Williamson, whose *Tarka the Otter* and *Salar the Salmon* Carson admired. Williamson personalized his animal characters through the device of calling an individual animal by the generic name of its species or by some other Latin or descriptive word. Carson adopted this technique throughout *Under the Sea Wind*; the portion of "Flood Tide" excerpted below features Rynchops, the black skimmer in his breeding season home on North Carolina's Outer Banks. This selection is best read as an homage to Williamson, for Carson experiments with his cast of characters, his timing of animal interactions, and his vocabulary.

Rachel Carson was the first woman to be chief editor of the U.S. Fish and Wildlife Service publications. In this capacity, she inaugurated the service's *Conservation in Action* series with her own twenty-page booklet describing Chincoteague Refuge on Assateague Island, Virginia. Written in Carson's deceptively straightforward style, this document informed its audience about the refuge and its place in the natural and human world. Today, it interests us not only as an example of her writing but also as a record of the changes that have taken place in conservation. In 1947, the refuge was seeking visitation, offering public recreation opportunities, and even supporting subsistence and commercial uses. Now, the refuge's mission has been extended to the safeguarding of endangered species: Delmarva fox squirrels inhabit mature mixed forests, and piping plovers and least terns nest on the beach; peregrine falcons have nested in a hacking tower built for them; and a rare orchid, the southern twayblade, hides among the loblolly pine needles. In order to protect breeding terns and plovers, public access is restricted six months a year to the interpretive drives and trails and to the small Assateague National Seashore portion of the beach.

From *Under the Sea Wind* (New York: Simon and Schuster, 1941)

Flood Tide

THE ISLAND lay in shadow only a little deeper than those that were swiftly stealing across the sound from the east. On its western shore the wet sand of the narrow beach caught the same reflection of palely gleaming sky that laid a bright path across the water from island beach to horizon. Both water and sand were the color of steel overlaid with the sheen of silver, so that it was hard to say where water ended and land began.

Although it was a small island, so small that a gull might have flown across it with a score of wing beats, night had already come to its northern and eastern end. Here the marsh grasses waded boldly out into dark water, and shadows lay thick among the low-growing cedars and yaupons.

With the dusk a strange bird came to the island from its nesting grounds on the outer banks. Its wings were pure black and from tip to tip their spread was more than the length of a man's arm. It flew steadily and without haste across the sound, its progress as measured and as meaningful as that of the shadows which little by little were dulling the bright water path. The bird was called Rynchops, the black skimmer.

As he neared the shore of the island the skimmer drifted closer to the water, bringing his dark form into strong silhouette against the gray sheet, like the shadow of a great bird that passed unseen above. Yet so quietly did he approach that the sound of his wings, if sound there were, was lost in the whisper song of the water turning over the shells on the wet sand.

At the last spring tide, when the thin shell of the new moon brought the water lapping among the sea oats that fringed the dunes of the banks, Rynchops and his kin had arrived on the outer barrier strip of sand between sound and sea. They had journeyed northward from the coast of Yucatán where they had wintered. Under the warm June sun they would lay their eggs and hatch their buff-colored chicks on the sandy islands of the sound and on the outer beaches. But at first they were weary after the long flight and they rested by day on sand bars when the tide was out or roamed over the sound and its bordering marshes by night.

Before the moon had come to the full, Rynchops had remembered the island. It lay across a quiet sound from which the banks shouldered away the South Atlantic rollers. To the north the island was separated from the mainland by a deep gutter where the ebbing tides raced strongly. On the south side the beach sloped gently, so that at slack water the fishermen could wade out half a mile before the water came above their armpits as they raked scallops or hauled their long seines. In these shallows young fishes swarmed, feeding on the small game of the waters, and shrimp swam with backward flipping of their tails. The rich life of the shallows brought the skimmers nightly from their nesting grounds on the banks, to take their food from the water as they moved with winnowing flight above it.

About sunset the tide had been out. Now it was rising, covering the afternoon resting places of the skimmers, moving through the inlet, and flowing up into the marshes. Through most of the night the skimmers would feed, gliding on slender wings above the water in search of the small fishes that had moved in with the tide to the shelter of grassy shallows. Because they fed on the rising tide, the skimmers were called flood gulls.

On the south beach of the island, where water no deeper than a man's hand ran over gently ribbed bottom, Rynchops began to wheel and quarter over the shallows. He flew with a curious, lilting motion, lifting his wings high after the downstroke. His head was bent sharply so that the long lower bill, shaped like a scissor blade, might cut the water.

The blade or cutwater plowed a miniature furrow over the placid sheet of the sound, setting up wavelets of its own and sending vibrations thudding down through the water to rebound from the sandy bottom. The wave messages were received by the blennies and killifish that were roving the shallows on the alert for food. In the fish world many things are told by sound waves. Sometimes the vibrations tell of food animals like small shrimps or oar-footed crustaceans moving in swarms overhead. And so at the passing of the skimmer the small fishes came nosing at the surface, curious and hungry. Rynchops, wheeling about, returned along the way he had come and snapped up three of the fishes by the rapid opening and closing of his short upper bill.

Ah-h-h-h, called the black skimmer. *Ha-a-a-a! H-a-a-a-a! H-a-a-a-a!*

His voice was harsh and barking. It carried far across the water, and from the marshes there came back, like echoes, the answering cries of other skimmers.

While the water was reclaiming inch after inch of sandy shore, Rynchops moved back and forth over the south beach of the island, luring the fishes to rise along his path and seizing them on his return. After he had taken enough minnows to appease his hunger he wheeled up from the water with half a dozen flapping wing beats and circled the island. As he soared above the marshy eastern end schools of killifish moved beneath him through the forests of sea hay, but they were safe from the skimmer, whose wingspread was too great to allow him to fly among the clumps of grass.

Rynchops swerved out around the dock that had been built by the fisherman who lived on the island, crossed the gutter, and swept far over the salt marshes, taking joy in flight and soaring motion. There he joined a flock of other skimmers and together they moved over the marshes in long lines and columns, sometimes appearing as dark shadows on the night sky; sometimes as spectral birds when, wheeling swallowlike in air, they showed white breasts and gleaming underparts. As they flew they raised their voices in the weird night chorus of the skimmers, a strange medley of notes high-pitched and low, now soft as the cooing of a mourning dove, and again rising and falling, swelling and throbbing, dying away in the still air like the far-off baying of a pack of hounds.

The flood gulls circled the island and crossed and recrossed the flats to the southward. All through the hours of the rising tide, they would hunt in flocks over the quiet waters of the sound. The skimmers loved nights of darkness and tonight thick clouds lay between the water and the moon's light.

On the beach the water was moving with soft tinkling sounds among the windrows of jingle shells and young scallop shells. It ran swiftly under heaps of sea lettuce to rouse sand fleas that had taken refuge there when the tide ebbed that afternoon. The beach hoppers floated out on the backwash of each wavelet and moved in the returning water, swimming on their backs, legs uppermost. In the water they were comparatively safe from their enemies the ghost crabs, who roamed the night beaches on swift and silent feet.

In the waters bordering the island many creatures besides the skimmers were abroad that night, foraging in the shallows. As the darkness grew and the incoming tide lapped higher and higher among the marsh grasses, two diamondback terrapins slipped into the water to join the moving forms of others of their kind. These were females, who had just finished laying their eggs above the high-tide line. They had dug nests in the soft sand, working with hind feet until they scooped out jug-shaped holes not quite so deep as their own bodies were long. Then they had deposited their eggs, one five, the other eight. These they had carefully covered with sand, crawling back and forth to conceal the location of the nest. There were other nests in the sand, but none more than two weeks old, for May is the beginning of the nesting season among the diamondbacks.

As Rynchops followed the killifish in toward the shelter of the marsh he saw the terrapins swimming in the shallow water where the tide was moving swiftly. The terrapins nibbled at the marsh grasses and picked off small coiled snails that had crept up the flat blades. Sometimes they swam down to take crabs off the bottom. One of the two terrapins passed between two slender uprights like stakes thrust into the sand. They were the legs of the solitary great blue heron who flew every night from his rookery three miles away to fish from the island.

The heron stood motionless, his neck curved back on his shoulders, his bill poised to spear fish as they darted past his legs. As the terrapin moved out into deeper water she startled a young mullet and sent it racing toward the beach in confusion and panic. The sharp-eyed heron saw the movement and with a quick dart seized the fish crosswise in his bill. He tossed it into the air, caught it head first, and swallowed it. It was the first fish other than small fry that he had caught that night.

The tide was almost halfway to the confused litter of sea wrack, bits of sticks, dried claws of crabs, and broken shell fragments that marked high-water level. Above the tide line there were faint stirrings in the sand where the terrapins had lately begun to lay their eggs. The season's young would not hatch until August, but many young of the year before still were buried in the sand, not yet roused from the torpor of hibernation. During the winter the young terrapins had lived on the remnant of yolk left from embryonic life. Many had died, for the winter had been long and the frosts had bitten deep into the sands. Those that survived were weak and emaciated, their bodies so shrunken within the shells that they were smaller than when they had hatched. Now they were moving feebly in the sands where the old terrapins were laying the eggs of a new generation of young.

About the time the tide was midway to the flood, a wave of motion stroked the tops of the grasses above the terrapin egg bed, as though a breeze passed, but there was little wind that night. The grasses above the sand bed parted. A rat, crafty with the cunning of years and filled with the lust for blood, had come down to the water along a path which his feet and his thick tail had worn to a smooth track through the grass. The rat lived with his mate and others of his kind under an old shed where the fisherman kept his nets, faring well on the eggs of the many birds that nested on the island, and on the young birds.

As the rat looked out from the fringe of grass bordering the terrapin nests the heron sprang from the water a stone's throw away with a strong flapping of his wings and flew across the island to the north shore. He had seen two fishermen in a small boat coming around the western tip of the island. The fishermen had been gigging flounders, spearing them on the bottom in shallow water by the light of a torch which flared at the bow. A yellow splotch of light moved over the dark water in advance of the boat and sent trembling streamers across the wavelets that rippled shoreward from the boat's passing. Twin points of green fire glowed in the grass above the sand bed. They remained stationary until the boat had passed on around the south shore and had headed toward the town docks. Only then did the rat glide down from the path onto the sand.

The scent of terrapin and of terrapin eggs, fresh laid, was heavy in the air. Snuffling and squeaking in excitement, the rat began to dig and in a few minutes had uncovered an egg, had pierced the shell, and sucked out the yolk. He then uncovered two other eggs and might have eaten them if he had not heard a movement in a nearby clump of marsh grass—the scrambling of a young terrapin struggling to escape the water that was seeping up around its tussock of tangled roots and mud. A dark form moved across the sand and through the rivulet of water. The rat seized the baby terrapin and carried it in his teeth through the marsh grasses to a hummock of higher ground. Engrossed in gnawing away the thin shell of the terrapin, he did not notice how the tide was creeping up about him and running deeper around the hummock. It was thus that the blue heron, wading back around the shore of the island, came upon the rat and speared him.

Chincoteague: A National Wildlife Refuge (Washington, D.C.: GPO, 1947)

Chincoteague

CHINCOTEAGUE, like other waterfowl refuges, is needed because birds migrate, and because in so doing they expose themselves to great dangers. The migration of birds is one of the ancient spectacles of earth, and one of the most mysterious. But while we know little about why birds migrate or how they find their way over enormous distances, common sense tells us this:

like human travelers, birds must have places where they can stop in safety for food and rest.

Once there were plenty of natural hostelries for the migrants. That was before our expanding civilization had drained the marshes, polluted the waters, substituted resort towns for wilderness. That was in the days when hunters were few. In those days our waterfowl probably numbered 200 million. Now only a small remnant of this number is left.

If we are to preserve the remaining waterfowl, and the sports and recreations which depend on them, we must set apart for the birds refuges like Chincoteague, where they may find these simple and necessary creature requirements: food, rest, security. . . .

Two things determined the location of the Chincoteague Refuge: its physical features, combining beaches, dunes, marshes, woodland, and protected waters; and its position with relation to the flight lanes of the birds. . . .

About nine thousand acres in area, the refuge occupies the southern third of Assateague Island, separated from Chincoteague Island by a narrow channel. Assateague is one of the barrier islands typical of the Middle Atlantic coast, never more than three miles from shore to shore, lying between Chincoteague Bay and the sea. Seen from the air, as the migrating waterfowl coming in from the north must see it, its eastern border is a wide ribbon of sand that curves around in a long arc at the southern end of the island to form a nearly enclosed harbor.

Back from the beach the sand mounts into low dunes, and the hills of sand are little by little bound and restrained by the beach grasses and the low, succulent, sand-loving dune plants. As the vegetation increases, the dunes fall away into salt marshes, bordering the bay. Like islands standing out of the low marsh areas are the patches of firmer, higher ground, forested with pine and oak and carpeted with thickets of myrtle, bayberry, sumac, rose, and catbriar. Scattered through the marshes are ponds and potholes filled with wigeongrass and bordered with bulrushes and other good food for ducks and geese. This is waterfowl country. This is the kind of country the ducks knew in the old days, before the white man's civilization disturbed the face of the land. This is the kind of country that is rapidly disappearing except where it is preserved in wildlife sanctuaries. . . .

The changing seasons at Chincoteague are reflected in the changing populations of the birds. The summer months are quiet. Except for a few black ducks and a handful of blue-winged teal, the thousands of waterfowl that wintered on the refuge have gone north. They are now dispersed over an immense area, from Greenland to Alaska. The migratory flights of waterfowl from the south have paused briefly at the refuge and now they, too, are gone.

Up in the marshes around Ragged Point the black ducks have been nesting. In April you might have found their nests here and there under the bayberries; in June the broods of ducklings, with their mothers, begin to appear in the slashes. Around the Levels there are a few broods of the blue-winged teal, making its first slow comeback as a nesting bird in this region after years of scarcity. And early almost any morning of the summer you could see a bittern slinking through the tall salt meadow grass or hear the sharp clatter of the rails.

August passes into September, with its briskly cooler nights and shortening days. Since July the shore birds have been returning from the north, and now the beaches and the mud flats are crowded with them. September brings the first of the returning waterfowl, and toward the end of the month flocks of small land bird migrants appear. One morning tree swallows by the thousand are lined up, wing to wing, on the Coast Guard telephone wires for miles along the beach. Heavy flights of robins and flickers pass through; hawks—mostly the narrow-winged falcons and the accipiters—sweep down the coast toward the south. Then in October, when the marshes are silvered with frost in the mornings, the waterfowl begin to pour in from the north. Crossing the Levels, you see flights of pintails circling the marshes, dropping down into the ponds. After a night of heavy migration, the refuge suddenly takes on new life as flocks of canvasbacks, redheads, teal, and baldpates rise into the air in noisy thousands.

Offshore, beyond the white lines of breakers, great numbers of sea ducks appear. Rafts of scoters parallel the beach from one end of the refuge to the other. Old squaws and goldeneyes congregate in the nearly landlocked harbor of Assateague Anchorage, following the oyster dredgers. These sea ducks flock around the boat so closely they are almost run down, diving for the small sea creatures and plants stirred up by the dredges. Canada geese are increasing day by day, flocking in to the Levels and Toms Cove, a few settling in around the marshes of Ragged Point and Sheep Ridge.

Through October, November, and into December the flights of waterfowl increase. Brant gather in the Anchorage, a few whistling swans appear in the Levels. The snow geese drift in, having made the long flight from Greenland and the islands of the Arctic Sea, with only one or two stops anywhere on the continent of North America.

Some of the waterfowl and all of the shore birds continue south after resting and feeding on the refuge. Other waterfowl remain, some of almost

"The snow geese drift in, having made the long flight from Greenland and the islands of the Arctic Sea." Snow Goose at Chincoteague, K. L. Howe, from *Chincoteague: A National Wildlife Refuge*

every Atlantic coast species. At Chincoteague the winters are not, as a rule, severe. The blizzards and the heavy freezes that sometimes lock the Chesapeake in ice from shore to shore are here tempered by the bordering sea, and it is a rare winter when there is not plenty of open water on the refuge where the ducks can get at the wigeongrass and the sea lettuce, and plenty of snow-free marsh where the geese can pull up the roots of the salt meadow grasses.

The turn of the year finds about 30,000 ducks wintering on the refuge itself, another 10,000 or so on the bordering ocean and Chincoteague Bay. As for the geese, a fairly mild winter may see nearly 10,000 of them on the refuge—perhaps 5,000 snow geese, several thousand brant, a thousand Canadas. Black duck, baldpate, and pintail are more numerous than any other kinds of fresh-water ducks; scoters and scaups outnumber all other sea ducks.

March is the time of transformation, the month when the great migrations start. Flock after flock, the ducks, geese, and swans leave for the north. Others come in from the south, linger briefly, move on. By late April, all the waterfowl are gone, except for a few black ducks, teal, and baldpates.

April is the month of the shore birds. Although on an occasional day in March you may hear the high, clear whistle of the yellowlegs, the full tide of the shore bird migration does not reach the refuge until April. The piping, Wilson's, and killdeer plovers, the willet, the spotted sandpiper, and the oyster-catcher stay throughout the summer as nesting birds. There are also little colonies of nesting terns, laughing gulls, and black skimmers on the beach at the southern end of the refuge, known as Fishing Point. But for the most part the activities of the refuge have reached their lowest point by midsummer—the ebb between the flood tides of migration.

Bird banding, an important activity at many Federal waterfowl refuges, helps trace the intricate pattern of bird migration. In the short time since the Chincoteague Refuge was established, banding done on this refuge has revealed many interesting and useful facts about the birds. These records are supplemented by the results of earlier banding in this area, carried on chiefly by John H. Buckalew, manager of the refuge.

Many different methods, all of them harmless, are used to capture birds for banding. Waterfowl usually are taken in a large, cagelike trap baited with corn. Once captured, the bird is banded by placing a numbered aluminum band around its leg. The band carries an inscription: "Notify Fish and Wildlife Service, Washington, D. C."

So far, most of the birds banded at Chincoteague have been black ducks and pintails. But during the winter of 1945–46, ten different species of ducks, totaling 1,617 individuals, were banded on the refuge.

How migrating waterfowl make use of the chain of refuges along their flyways is clearly illustrated at Chincoteague—first, by recoveries of birds banded there, second, by recoveries at Chincoteague of birds banded elsewhere. The recoveries so far link Chincoteague with the following Federal waterfowl refuges: Parker River, Mass.; Bombay Hook, Del.; Mattamuskeet, N.C.; and Cape Romain, S.C.

Banding of black ducks has showed us how the migrating birds come down from Canada and New England; it has also given interesting information about the way the ducks move about during the winter. Apparently they roam about over an area with a radius of a hundred miles or more. For instance, two black ducks banded at Chincoteague in December 1945 were recovered the following month, one in Salem County, N.J., more than

100 miles away, the other at Chesapeake City, Md., a distance of 115 miles.

As for the pintails, banding shows that the migrants that stop over at Chincoteague may continue all the way down the Atlantic coast. Pintails banded at the refuge have been recovered from North and South Carolina and Florida.

The most distant recoveries so far of any Chincoteague-banded birds are these: a common tern recovered in Puerto Rico, and a black duck at Tracadie, Nova Scotia. . . .

Economic uses of the land included within the Chincoteague Wildlife Refuge continue as before the establishment of the refuge.

The famous shellfish country of the Eastern Shore of the Chesapeake surrounds the Chincoteague Wildlife Refuge. Chincoteague oysters have a widespread reputation for quality; perhaps the fact that they grow in water that is almost as salty as the open ocean accounts for their distinctive flavor. Although the region is best known for its oysters, clamming, carried on throughout the year, probably brings a larger income to local fishermen than the oysters do.

The establishment of a wildlife refuge has not interfered with the use of the area for shellfishing. The refuge itself contains about 250 acres of shellfish grounds. These consist of a narrow strip of flats between the tide lines, running in a long arc around the inside of Assateague Anchorage, and bordering the channel between the islands.

About 184 acres of these grounds are under cultivation. Before the refuge was established, the shellfish area was leased from the former owner of the property. It is now leased from the United States Government. One-fourth of the rental is paid to Accomac County, in which the refuge lies. The balance goes into the United States treasury.

Cultivation of oysters as it is practiced in the Chincoteague area consists of bringing in small, "seed" oysters, planting them on leased grounds, protecting them from natural enemies, harvesting the oysters when they have reached good market size. Fishermen go "down the bay" to dredge the seed oysters from public oyster rocks, then bring back barge loads of the baby oysters and sell them to growers in the Chincoteague area. After getting the best price they can for their load, the fishermen then plant the oysters for the purchaser, on whatever part of his grounds he directs. These planting operations begin in the spring, continue all summer and into the fall. Fishermen spend many days—sometimes several weeks—dredging a saleable quantity of oysters. During the spring and fall they run the risk that a sudden freeze may kill their barge loads of oysters before they have disposed of them.

Clamming is practically a year round occupation in the Chincoteague area. At low tide the clammers work the exposed mud flats in the marshes and scattered through the channels between the islands. The clams lie buried in the mud, in warm weather only a short distance beneath the surface.

Common methods of clamming during the summer are "signing"— watching for the signs of a clam's presence in the mud and quickly digging it out with a short-handled, pronged hoe—and wading. An experienced wader, working in water neck-deep, feels a clam under foot, quickly slides it up his leg, and tosses it into his sack. During the winter clams are taken by tonging.

Cultivation of clams is simple. Clam dealers who lease growing grounds save the smallest sizes—called "buttons"—out of each load they buy. They plant these small clams, allowing them to grow before marketing them. Clam culture does not require planting of shells and elaborate protection against enemies as oyster culture does; on the whole, therefore, it is less expensive and the returns to the grower are larger.

The wild ponies of Chincoteague have made the name of this small Eastern Shore island familiar to people all over eastern United States. Chincoteague Island itself is no longer inhabited by feral stock; the herds graze on Assateague, Wallops, and a few other uninhabited coastal islands. But on the last week end of July, in the annual wild horse round-up, animals from nearby islands are brought to Chincoteague to be sold, so this island still gives its name to the wild horses of the entire region.

Although historical facts about the origin of the horses are scanty, there is no dearth of legend. Some say they swam ashore from a vessel shipwrecked off this coast long before there were permanent white settlements in the region. Others will have it that pirates, systematically plundering coastwise shipping, used to put their horses ashore to graze on the islands.

From whatever stock the ponies descended, they are a rugged lot. Smaller than an average horse, larger than an average pony, their coats a bit shaggy and long, they bear the stamp of their wild seacoast environment. They live most of their lives within sight or sound of the surf, they crop the sparse marsh grasses, they shelter wherever they can when wild storms sweep up the coast. Once each year, men from Chincoteague Island come ashore, and the annual Chincoteague pony round-up begins. The animals

are driven together on the beach; at low tide they are herded across Assateague Channel, swimming through water shoulder high to a man, to
Chincoteague Island and into a 20-acre enclosure. There the annual pony
sale is held, many of the buyers coming from hundreds of miles. The Chincoteague pony business is now largely in the hands of the town firemen,
who own most of the stock, prepare for and manage the annual pony pen-
ning carnival and sale.

The establishment of a wildlife refuge on the southern end of Assateague Island did not interfere with the generations-old custom of grazing stock. Permits to graze 300 head of horses and cattle within the refuge
property are now held by residents of Chincoteague. One-fourth of the annual rental for this economic use of the refuge land reverts to the counties
in which the refuge lies. The presence of these grazing animals is not detri-
mental to the waterfowl for which the refuge was established. From the
standpoint of the owner of the stock, the refuge has proved a better grazing
ground than an uninhabited island. The refuge manager, patrolling the
grounds, keeps a watchful eye on the stock and more than once has come to
the rescue of a pony mired in the marshes, saving it from drowning on the
high tide.

Use of the Chincoteague Refuge for recreational purposes may be
arranged through the refuge manager, who will give permission to visit the
refuge at any time that the proposed use of the property does not conflict
with the needs of the birds.

Spring in Washington

Louis Halle (b. 1910)

Spring in Washington by John Burroughs Medal–winner Louis Halle is the crown jewel among the many postwar gems of regional nature writing. Of all the books written about urban nature, none has a greater intimacy and none a more diverse and unspoiled subject. A political scientist at the State Department, Halle was one of the many government workers brought to Washington by the war; an amateur naturalist and birder, he sought out the natural areas and aspects of the capital and its environs on early-morning and weekend bicycle rides. Thus he escaped the "preoccupations of the hive [that] fill us, driving out all memory of the universe into which we were born" (p. 31).

Through the Audubon Society of the District of Columbia, Halle met Smithsonian scientist Paul Bartsch, whose wildlife sanctuary-home on the Potomac was often the destination of his rides. Another Auduboner, Roger Tory Peterson, became his birding mentor and later wrote the introduction to the second edition of *Spring in Washington*. Another colleague was Rachel Carson, whom, Halle bemusedly remembers, he ventured to instruct on literary technique at their first meeting. (Carson had already written *Under the Sea Wind* and had her own distinctive style.)

Spring in Washington is a round of seasonal sketches that blends birding experiences, natural history observations, landscape appreciation, and some of the most sensitive responses to weather ever written. Halle had won the Burroughs Medal in 1941 for *Birds against Men* and so was precluded from receiving it for the even more deserving *Spring in Washington*.

From *Spring in Washington* (New York: Harper and Row, 1957; Baltimore: Johns Hopkins University Press, 1988)

THE MATHEMATICIANS reckon that spring begins March 21, but the mathematicians are a month behind the season the year around. For those who observe the first signs, spring comes earlier than others know. Before the end of January, while the scenery remains desolate and the sun leaves no warmth, the first sparks are already being enkindled in the breasts of songbirds. As I left my home at daybreak January 22, under a cloud rack becoming visible, in a dead tree across the street a cardinal was singing *cue-cue-cue-cue-cue-cue*, rapidly, all on one pitch and without variation. Up to that moment, for many silent months, I do not recall that my mind had been occupied with other than the indoor thoughts of the hive. In its dark winter quarters it had survived entirely on a diet of paper: official documents provided by the government, supplemented by such reading as I had time for. The out-of-doors meant the weather, and the weather was a wintry nuisance with which one put up in those daily excursions to and from the office. One forgot about the seasons; the passage of time was measured by the unchanging flow and accumulation of paper; eternity was a pension in the future. Then the cardinal sang, waking me up, or at least penetrating and disturbing my sleep. Like the ground hog emerging from his burrow, I blinked at the sky through the opening and snuffed the wind. It was still winter, except for the cardinal who had his own inner stirrings.

On the 28th, a Sunday, the temperature rose to freezing and the sun shone all morning through such a delicate haze as softens the horizons of spring. The same cardinal at daybreak, from the same tree, was singing *toowee toowee toowee toowee toowee*, then again *cue-cue-cue-cue-cue-cue*. The time for monitoring the arrival of spring was manifestly at hand, and I set off by bicycle to do so.

The river, when I came to it, was mainly frozen, but a few scattered flocks of gulls were busy about black openings in the ice. From the shrubbery close by the statue of William Jennings Bryan a white-throated sparrow unexpectedly sang the slow, high notes of his song, sweet and languid. Having finished, he did not repeat the performance, perhaps, for a week. On the other side of Memorial Bridge you could smell spring in the air, never so intoxicating as in this first whiff of the year. I unbuttoned my coat to it. I should say that I began unbuttoning my soul or inner man for the first time in an age of months. On my left hand was the river, bordered by a line of leaning poplars and willows with shrubbery about their feet. On my right, the sward that would again be green was sodden where the warm sun thawed it. By the memorial of flying gulls done in bronze, a cardinal and a song sparrow sang. The cardinal was repeating his full spring song, two musical syllables going downstairs into the cellar. The song sparrow tried the first few notes of his own song, experimentally, but never got beyond them. He reminded me how early it still was for spring. A red-tailed hawk, sitting heavily in a tree by the river, was still in winter quarters. At Roaches Run the open water was crowded with wintering pintails chiefly, plus a few black ducks, a few mallards, and four coots. Out on the river opposite, some mergansers, red-breasted and American, were swimming and diving in a wide-open seam of the ice. By this time the haze had become cloud and overcome the sun. I buttoned up my coat against the chilling air, thinking: it's going to snow.

To me the bicycle is in many ways a more satisfactory invention than the automobile. It is consonant with the independence of man because it works under his own power entirely. There is no combustion of some petroleum product from Venezuela to set the pedals going. Purely mechanical instruments like watches and bicycles are to be preferred to engines that depend on the purchase of power from foreign sources. You can be more independent, and therefore more of a man, in a sailing vessel than in a power-driven boat. In the former you can still keep going if the national or international economy breaks down. You need not trouble yourself about legislative enactments for the exchange of goods and services, about international treaty arrangements for which your life is hostage. The price of power, on the other hand, is enslavement.

Bicycling, furthermore, is the nearest approximation I know to the flight of birds. The airplane simply carries a man on its back like an obedient Pegasus; it gives him no wings of his own. There are movements on a bicycle corresponding to almost all the variations in the flight of the larger birds. Plunging free downhill is like a hawk stooping. On the level stretches you may pedal with a steady rhythm like a heron flapping; or you may, like an accipitrine hawk, alternate rapid pedaling with gliding. If you want to test the force and direction of the wind, there is no better way than to circle, banked inward, like a turkey vulture. When you have the wind against you, headway is best made by yawing or wavering, like a crow flying upwind. I have climbed a steep hill by circling or spiraling, rising each time on the upturn with the momentum of the downturn, like any soaring bird. I have shot in and out through stalled traffic like a goshawk through the woods. The best way to ride, especially downhill, is with both hands in your pockets and leaning backwards. This is not so hard as it looks; like a bird, you control your direction perfectly by unconscious shifts in your balance. Especially on the long downslopes, this is to know the freedom of the wind. The air rushing past your ears reminds you that the birds must be partially deafened by their own speed.

Because you move under your own power, bicycling is to be compared rather to walking than to automobiling. By this standard, the ease and speed with which you encompass great distances seem miraculous. In an hour on the way to work I have covered ten or twelve miles, gone clean out of the city to look for signs of spring and come back into it untired and, in fact, refreshed for the day's work. In four or five hours of a Sunday I have covered fifty miles, visiting strange lands in Virginia or Maryland. . . .

Every morning now is a fresh wonder, no two quite the same. Thursday, March 1, a cloudless day, the west wind blowing easily across the city. By the time the sun rises now, about a quarter to eight, I am likely to be across the bridge and into Virginia, having myself arisen in the starlight. On a morning like this I have knotted a woolen scarf about my neck and tucked it into my jacket, for it is frosty and clear and the wind cuts. Looking across the river, I see the sun rise brilliantly between the silhouettes of the Monument and the Capitol dome, and feel its warm rays flash across the land at the same moment that the countryside about me is transformed into light and shadow. The trees at Roaches Run and the marsh grasses stand in relief, flooded by radiance from the horizon. All the birds are sparkling and ebullient in the sharp dawn. A redwing at the top of a tree is singing *conqueree-ee-ee*, shaking out his black-and-scarlet wings and spreading his tail at each utterance. Three grackles are clucking and grating to one another in the thicket. This is life beginning all over again, emerging from the darkness and damp into the new day. It is spring in microcosm. The tide is out, and where an area of marsh grass is exposed in the middle of the lagoon a great blue heron stands motionless. Another comes in from behind the island like a drifting feather, the sun illuminating it from below, drops its legs, uncurls its neck, and alights silently near the first. A horned grebe sits by its solitary self across the water. Two coots swim about the edge of the grasses, pumping their heads. I have already formed a nodding acquaintance with them.

On one side of the wooded island that is almost connected with the near shore, right up to the bank at my feet, the water is crowded with pintails beyond counting. Some sit on floating logs preening, others swim about in groups, holding their heads high on their curved stems to view me. Perhaps they think me a sign of spring, with my binoculars, as indeed I am. A few in closest to shore take alarm, leap from the surface, and flap out to put down with little splashes among their fellows beyond. Mixed in with them, or preening along the shore of the island, are big black ducks and a few mallards. Farther out, in open water, is a flock of American mergansers. This completes the picture except for a score of herring gulls, some wailing mournfully. One gull, with a prize in its bill, flies zigzag, dodging to escape a rabble of suitors at its tail. When it finally drops the prize another picks it up and the chase continues, like boys playing tag in the freshness of morning. Occasionally there is a great outburst of wailing and screaming among them.

Before dawn on Saturday, after a night of heavy rain, I went out into a saturated world, no stars showing. The wind was from the south, as warm as buttered toast, heavy and smelling of rain. Coasting down the dark, glistening road through the park, I caught the wild odor of the tidal marshes downriver, a smell of the ocean itself, of fish, of decaying vegetation and pungent marsh ooze, of wilderness. . . .

Winter or summer, if you wish to match yourself against a wilderness, I can recommend nothing better locally than the tidal marshes around Dyke, a couple of miles below Alexandria. I daresay the open marsh here, excluding the swampy woods that extend up- and down-river from it, does not cover an area half so large as that of the airport, which is a mile and a half in its greatest length, but the difficulty of making your way through it gives it size enough. At low tide you may struggle step by step through marsh grasses that rise to your shoulder, sinking at every few steps above your knees into some unseen hole or into the smooth and treacherous ooze.

"This abundance of life, virile and variegated, expanding over the countryside with the change of season, was worth an amphibious excursion from the highway." Dyke Marsh, F. L. Jaques, from *Spring in Washington*

Only a determined man can make his way across these marshes. They are deceptive, for they hide the existence of innumerable water inlets until he stumbles upon them. Then he must work his way up their banks until, God willing and the tide remaining low, he finds them narrow enough to risk a leap, when he again sets forth to the next obstructing channel. These inlets penetrate the marsh everywhere, a network through which the tide flows in and out with the slow regularity of an animal breathing. We have tried a flat-bottomed boat too, pulling and pushing it at high tide through the inlets; but the ooze soon clings to its bottom and the reeds block its way. The man carries the boat more than the boat the man. Vultures, marsh hawks, and sometimes eagles sweep past like shadows, ducks whistle by like grapeshot, herons flap their great cambered wings and trail their legs over the grasses; but a man has to struggle like Laocoön for every yard gained.

It is so late in the season when the new grass appears in the marshes, after the woods are already in leaf, that its springing may almost be taken as a sign of summer. Although the elm trees had flowered this week all over Washington, and we had just had an April day in which sprinkles of warm rain swept through the sunlit city as from an accidentally diverted garden hose, the bleached and broken grasses of last year still covered the marshes on Sunday, March 11. The wind was in the west and the sun shone. Where an inlet passes under the highway, a mixed company of ducks burst up from the hummocks where they had been preening, when I stopped my bicycle, and swept out into the open marsh, black ducks and mallards quacking, a female wood duck crying *oo-eek oo-eek oo-eek.* . . .

Just beyond the inlet is as good a place as any to enter the marsh. A path leads into the woods and becomes lost in swampy thickets choked with brambles. I pushed my way through them, like the Prince coming to the rescue of the Sleeping Beauty, thinking myself alone until an invisible orchestra struck up and I was surrounded by ringing melody. It was the richest kind of bird music, coming in chorus from every direction, but wholly unfamiliar to me. Then I saw that the underbrush and brambles were full of fox sparrows, all singing. After a minute or two they stopped as abruptly as they had begun, and did not resume for all my waiting. A dozen yards more brought me to the edge of the open marsh, into the sunlight once more.

For two hours I struggled through the marsh, filling the sky with ducks that took off from the inlets ahead of me, sometimes only two or three, sometimes fifteen or twenty at once. The quacking black ducks and mallards were heavy on the wing, circling in masses all about the horizon.

Alongside them, the smaller baldpates, pintails, and wood ducks flew in swift, compact groups. They rose high in the air, circled, and came sweeping down in long curves over the reeds. They circled away again, exploring the whole marsh with its myriad veins, before they decided it was safe to put down and, on suddenly set wings, scudded all together over the grass-tops and disappeared into some inlet hidden from view. When they put into the smaller inlets, they backed their wings and dropped vertically from fifteen or twenty feet. Several times I flushed ducks no larger than pigeons, the green-winged teal, swiftest of all, sweeping like sandpipers over the marshes, here and away again before you knew it.

I could never hope to stalk any of these surface-feeding ducks for a close view of them on the water, but the little groups of American mergansers on the two broadest inlets were not nearly so wary. I crept up to spy on their privacy from the rushes, until one of them would spy me. Then, croaking softly, they would all taxi along the inlet, splashing with wings and feet, at last rising from the water and, stretched taut, make off like arrows to the open river. On one inlet a horned grebe, when it saw me, sank down like a rock and did not reappear. On another, a coot pattered away from me about the bend. A greater yellowlegs flew across the outer edge of the marshes on its way north, far in advance of schedule according to the bird calendar (although that evening I saw half a dozen more migrating in a flock across the airport). Though it was not a warm day, little companies of gnats were to be seen about the wooded edges of the marshland.

To complete the picture, you have not only singing blackbirds and song sparrows to add: two eagles with white heads and tails were beating back and forth or soaring aloft; turkey vultures and a single female marsh hawk were circling or sweeping by; a red-shouldered hawk hung overhead; great blue herons traversed the grassy pastures with wings beating slowly and easily, alighting on their long stalks by the borders of inlets, taking off again with the peculiar slow buoyancy of their flight, as if they were not altogether heavier than air. Crows struggled into the wind. Gulls flapped past or circled out over the river. This abundance of life, virile and variegated, expanding over the countryside with the change of season, was worth an amphibious excursion from the highway. . . .

This week, however, was bountiful chiefly in its flowers. The City of Washington might have been deliberately decked for a flower festival, as when the citizens hang out their flags because it is Flag Day. The lilac clusters came out in profusion overnight, among the young leaves, freshening the air. So did the azaleas, in all their variety, transforming the woodland parks and dooryards. A man from Mars might have stopped passers-by to inquire in what god's celebration the city was so garlanded.

This is the height of spring—or one of the heights, to be followed by others. Yet it would be improvident to find only spring in springtime or fall in autumn. There is no better time than winter to enjoy a summer day, no better time than spring to savor the fall. If you observe the progress of the seasons carefully, you will find them all present the year around. They are interwoven themes in this continuing symphonic utterance, each becoming dominant in its turn without ever wholly vanquishing the rest. Listen carefully and you will hear on the cellos, throughout this first movement, the theme of fall; subordinate, awaiting its eventual turn to be announced on the brasses and taken up by the violins, but there nevertheless. Occasionally and for a moment it emerges clearly, as if by accident, like a bird that sings out of season.

The day after the lilacs and azaleas came out full, I was awakened long before dawn by the wind lashing the trees outside and the rattling of my bedroom door. A gale from the northwest, blowing in gusts, tossed the river and Tidal Basin. Black clouds traveled overhead, intermittent showers drenched the earth. In East Potomac Park the ground was littered with twigs from the bobbing and tugging willows. About the Tidal Basin and on 17th Street the leaves were not falling but the elm seeds were, whirling down on the wind and drifting along the street. They drove into your face, as you pedaled against the wind, pelting it in showers. Who ever heard of being blinded by elm seeds? By afternoon the sky had cleared except for traveling powder puffs, the wind had steadied and came from the west, and it grew cold. A perfect fall day. The elm seeds, like some breakfast cereal, lay along the gutters in drifts. During the next few days the street cleaners were busy sweeping them up and carting them away—lest, perhaps, they sprout in the macadam and the streets become forested. The street cleaners were dutifully defending our civilization, guarding it from ruin, though they overlooked the threat of violets that I had happened to discover. . . .

I present here, as background to this account, a piece on the wood thrush and its kin that I wrote in 1942:

I have long had it in mind to set down some personal observations on the genus *Hylocichla*, which comprises the five species of spotted thrush inhabiting the forests of North America. The five species are: *H. mustelina*, the wood thrush; *H. guttata*, the hermit thrush; *H. ustulata*, the olive-backed thrush; *H. minima*, the gray-cheeked thrush; and *H. fuscescens*, the veery. They are all very similar, and yet distinctive too. All are inhabitants of the heavy shade, the perpetual golden gloom of the forest. They are at home in the lowest range of the woods, among the dead foliage and humus on the ground itself, or in the foliage of the undergrowth. Several of them prefer steep and generally damp slopes in the forest with outcrops of moss-stained rock. They belong to this habitat as the violets do, and are as much a part of it. In the East in springtime or summer these recesses of the forest would appear to have lost some natural quality if no *Hylocichla* were present. They are not rare, or even uncommon; they are not, like so many exceptionally distinguished birds, subjects for occasional delight only.

In the most diverse sorts of birds, even barnyard fowl, one sometimes catches a mannerism or appearance of the reptilian. This is especially true of the spotted thrushes, which will at times assume attitudes of motionless alertness remindful of lizards, with which they share a distant common ancestor. Of course they are not really like lizards, but one gets a touch of it occasionally, not only in these attitudes but also in a peculiar appearance or expression about the base of the bill and the eyes. It is such a humorless expression as to be laughable on occasion. You see the same thing in the robin, close to, when he holds up his head intent to catch a sound—something primitive and stolid, even harsh, in the expression of the face.

Above—that is, on the head, back, wings, and upper side of the tail—this genus varies from olive-brown to a richer rusty or cinnamon brown. Underneath it is spotted, darkly in the wood thrush, in the veery only faintly on the throat and upper breast. The tail is quite short and the legs long, as befits birds that hunt their living on uneven ground. But I have never seen the spotted thrushes scratch, like towhees and fox sparrows. They turn the leaves over, in their foraging, with a quick toss of the bill.

In all the woods of North America there are no singers to compare with these spotted thrushes. The mockingbird, which shuns the woods, compares in technical brilliance, but he does not have a song in the sense that these do. He specializes in notes and variations, in the production of striking and beautiful single tones or phrases, but lacks melody. He arouses delight and astonishment, but the singing of the wood thrush and the hermit thrush and the veery evokes wonder. It is hard to associate it with the mundane world. When one listens to their songs with an attentive spirit, at twilight from the depths of the forest, it seems at times as if one heard something more than a singing bird. This is especially true of the veery, which is a less brilliant singer than either the wood or the hermit thrush, but unearthly.

I have become so fond of hearing the various spotted thrushes that I should miss them acutely if I lived where none occurred. As each winter advances, as the lapse of time since I last saw or heard them increases, as the date for their arrival draws nearer, the suspense of my anticipation mounts steadily. The hermit thrush comes early, and may indeed spend the winter at Pound Ridge, my home near the Connecticut border above New York City. But he is a different bird under these circumstances, when the woods are bare. He is merely another brown winter bird, somewhat resembling the fox sparrow, quite silent except for an occasional *chuck* as he flits to a fallen branch or pokes among last summer's leaves. You would hardly think him capable of song.

The hermit thrush is the only one of the spotted thrushes that winters in the United States. The others spend the winter in Central and South America, the olive-back as far south as Argentina. It is strange that birds of such sheltered habitat should launch themselves overseas twice a year—flying close to the waves, I imagine, so that from a ship at sea the traveler might catch an occasional glimpse of a brown speck fluttering in the trough—and yet survive. Even wood thrushes, boldest of all in our parts, are easily confused and sometimes lose their heads altogether when they find themselves out in the open, away from the shelter of their native trees. . . .

Some commentators feel that the song of the wood thrush is marred, or brought short of perfection, by the light and seemingly impromptu phrases interspersed between the flutelike passages. They feel that these touches are often unmusical and somewhat harsh, and so take away from the perfect music of the flute tones. But to me there is extraordinary interest in these grace notes and trimmings, and a sort of uncanny beauty that is lacking from the purer tone of the main phrases, to which they serve as foils.

The ease and leisure of the wood thrush's song is one of its characteristics. The singer is never shaken with effort like a house wren. Usually he sits motionless on a branch, at rest. Every few seconds (with the regularity of some marvelous mechanical toy) he lifts his head, opens his bill, and delivers himself of a brief phrase; subsiding then until another phrase has formed and is ready to well up within him. The song is discontinuous and never finished. I like especially the little *hip hip* with which, like a cheer leader, he usually introduces the principal phrases. These phrases generally consist of three or four flutelike notes bound together. They are followed immediately, as a rule, by a muted trill—then silence. . . .

If you held the stuffed skin of a wood thrush in one hand and that of a veery in the other, you would not see any fundamental difference. They would not be exactly the same shade of brown, the veery would not be so heavily spotted below, the wood thrush would be slightly larger. In life, too, these species resemble each other closely, as do all the spotted thrushes. But there are differences of manner and attitude that are fully as great as those of color and marking—rather greater, in fact. The wood thrush is more stalwart, more excitable, more vocal, and more assertive. At the least alarm it puffs itself up, erects the feathers on top of its head, and utters its loud, ringing alarm notes—*pit-pit-pit*. The veery is silent, elusive, and retiring. It is not so much shy as secretive, and this gives it an air of mystery that the wood thrush lacks. A veery may be quite near you in the woods and you will not notice it at all, where a wood thrush would attract your attention with its bold ways.

The wood thrush, in keeping with its boldness, has accommodated itself to our cities. It is at home now, like the catbird, wherever there are shade trees and shrubbery. But it is the only one of the five. At Pound Ridge the veeries are invariably found in dank places, in the low swampy woods that border the large marshes. In June you can hear them just at dusk calling softly to each other across the marshes. You will not find them, ordinarily, unless you are looking for them, and they are apt to fall silent as you draw near. If they are alarmed at your presence, when you have crept up on them, it may be manifested only by a very soft sound, a sort of *whew*, that you will not hear unless you are very close indeed. It is deceptive, and I have sometimes had to watch the movement of a bird's throat to be sure it was uttering the sound at all. I have never seen a veery puff itself up, spread its chest, so to speak, and raise the feathers of its head like a wood thrush. It remains quiet and inconspicuous, no matter what the motive for alarm.

The song of the veery is a soft and continuous swirling sound that gives the impression of spiraling downward. Commentators are at variance over how it should be rated, and understandably so, for it is not comparable to the song of any other bird. It is not brilliant or spectacular, or notable for range and variety—these being the qualities that are usually dwelt on in thinking of birds as rivaling each other in song. This voice is merely uncanny and unearthly. It has a soft, reedy double tone, such as might conceivably be produced by a violinist drawing his bow across two strings at once; but no mechanical instrument could produce such thin, resonant chords. It has also a windy quality, and perhaps one could give an idea of it by comparing it to the sound produced by blowing across the top of a bottle. The overtone, the resonance, as if the bird carried its own echo within it-self, might make one think that the song was actually issuing from inside a bottle. It is a soft, tremulous, utterly ethereal sound, swirling downward and ending, swirling downward and ending again. Heard in the gloom of twi-light, back and forth across the marshes, it gives the impression that this is no bird at all but some spirit not to be discovered.

In my experience the season during which the song of the veery may be heard lasts less than a month out of the twelve. Like the wood thrushes, the veeries arrive at Pound Ridge about the first week in May. Then you may hear them calling, but you will not hear them sing. The call may be quite loud and carry far, but it is soft in quality. It is of two syllables that blend into each other, a sort of *weheu*—hence the bird's name. Sometimes you hear only the second syllable, very faintly.

It is close to the middle of May when the veeries begin to sing. Evening after evening, for the next three weeks, you can hear them if you go to the right places. Toward the end, however, the songs become intermittent, the singers no longer persist in them. By the middle of June there are young in the nests and the adults no longer have the leisure to sing, or even to call to each other. You will not hear them again, now, until another spring.

When, in the early winter of 1941–42, I moved to the city of Washing-ton, one of my few regrets was that I should be residing too far south to hear the song of the veery when spring came. Veeries do not breed south of central New Jersey, except in the mountains, and they do not sing except on their breeding grounds. Although my time in Washington was almost wholly occupied with other matters, I did not have to give up my pursuit of birds entirely, for I made it a habit to walk to work every morning through such a lovely bit of woodland as you would not look for in any city park. I had between a mile and two miles of this woodland to traverse, and it con-tained a greater density and variety of birds than you could find in most of the surrounding country. Even barred owls and black-crowned night herons and broad-winged hawks were present. By the middle of May the wood thrushes were in greater profusion than they ever are at Pound Ridge. They sang from all sides, bounded along the path ahead of me, called *pit-pit* in alarm at my passage. The bobwhites were profuse and vocal. I heard their tense, vibrant whistles incessantly and sometimes saw them moving stealth-ily through the deep shade of the ground cover. Almost every morning while they were in Washington on their way north I heard the olive-backed thrushes. Their song was soft and vibrant, but without the resonance of the veery's, ascending in a series of musical bounds.

On the night of May 20 it rained heavily, clearing at dawn. The woods were still absorbing the night's rain when I walked down in the morning. The sun was just about to make itself felt. Its rays showed against a woodland mist that remained as an aftermath of the rain, leaving patches and sparkles of light at odd intervals. The world, still so fresh and moist, seemed as though it had just emerged from the chrysalis of an age-old darkness.

At one point a small tributary stream tumbles through a ravine to enter the main creek. Back up the ravine the woods are dense and rise steeply on either hand. It is a place of big trees, many beeches with gnarled roots, tall tulip trees, sycamores, and ponderous oaks, all interlaced above so that you see only bits of sky. A soft golden light suffuses the scene. Although I had passed the entrance to this ravine every morning, I had never entered it. This morning, however, something made me pause in front of it. An Acadian flycatcher was uttering its explosive call at intervals, a pewee was voicing its long-drawn sorrow, and I could hear the perky buzzing of a parula warbler directly overhead. When I listened I could hear many other songs and calls farther off. Something, however, had brought the veery to my mind. I waited a moment, listening intently, heard nothing out of the way, and started forward again. I had to stop a second time. Again, some vibration amid all these voices had put me in mind of a veery. And each time I started forward the impression returned. At last I entered the ravine to investigate.

No sooner had I entered than all doubt vanished. Faint but clear, against the murmuring and buzzing of the woods and the roar of water, it came, the swirling, swirling, tremulous spiral of tone, over and over again. I found the delicate bird at the head of the ravine, singing in the forest mist, amid the long rays of golden light. He was moving from branch to branch, raising his head at intervals and opening his bill to release that lovely series of intertwining and falling phrases.

Morning and evening, after that, I took the path through the ravine, expecting every time that the veery would be gone on his way north. He was always there. As soon as I entered his precincts I would again hear the magic spirals of tone, coming as if from nowhere and permeating the forest. At the end of a week it had become apparent that the veery had taken up his territory far outside the normal breeding range of his species.

On June 1, in the morning, I found two veeries singing on the slopes of the ravine. My veery sang and was answered from close by, again and again. The second song, however, did not have the same quality as the first. It was rapid and perfunctory, lacking the full resonance. Hereafter there were three of us who observed the veeries from day to day, wondering whether we dared hope that they were a true pair and would stay to breed in Washington, so far from their native ground. It was hard to know what we should make of the second singer—perhaps a young male not yet in full voice. None of us could be sure the female of the species ever sang. But there was no doubt that the two birds were occupying one territory: several times we saw them chasing each other in play through the trees.

Occasionally, as the season advanced, we did not find either of the veeries for several days in succession. Their singing became less persistent. After June 15 they were no longer heard at all and, lacking the opportunity to hunt them out in the woods, we did not find a sign of them in the nine days that followed. It seemed likely that they had at last resumed their northward course. After all, the latest date we found on the record for Washington was June 2.

It was June 25, on my way to work, when I again saw one of the veeries. On the 26th, again, I found a veery carrying a caterpillar in its bill, not swallowing it, but retaining it in its bill while it continued to forage among the dead leaves. Then it flew off through the woods and I lost it. I said nothing of this to the others, but the following Sunday morning I put on old clothes and set off, determined to find out if the veeries were nesting or to assure myself that they were not.

I was almost three hours about the business. At long intervals I would come upon one or the other of the pair in some part of the woods, hunting food, sometimes swallowing it, sometimes carrying it in its bill. Always it flew off through the woods and I lost it. I could find no center or focal point of activity. The pair seemed to be ranging the woods indiscriminately and aloof from each other.

For their part, the veeries paid no attention to me. They showed no curiosity or alarm, even when I squeaked with my lips in imitations of ravished nestlings. Those squeaks would sometimes set the woods to ringing with alarm all about me. The wood thrushes would shout at me, the catbirds come mewing, the towhees drag their wings on the ground at my feet; Carolina wrens and house wrens would chatter angrily, even the warblers and titmice would come down from the treetops to see what it was all about. But the veeries remained heedless, and I took this for a sign that they were not nesting and consequently did not share the common motive for alarm.

I had actually given up the hunt and was on my way out of the woods when my eye was again caught by one of the veeries. It had a caterpillar in its bill and was uttering its almost inaudible single note, the faint *whew*. It flew toward some shrubbery on the slope, disappeared, returned without the caterpillar, and hopped in its peculiar bounding way among the dead leaves near the path, searching for another morsel. It found another, flew straight to a low branch, and remained there, watching me, uttering its plaintive note repeatedly. It flew to another branch, waited a moment, still eying me, then dropped to a low tangle of vine-clad shrubbery. I fixed it in my binoculars.

The veery was standing on top of the vine, in the open. As I studied it I noticed a stirring at its feet, there among the vine leaves. The bird dipped its head, then flew. An instant later I was looking straight down upon three half-fledged nestlings in an open cup among the leaves. The sensation that filled me at that moment could not have been more overpowering if I had stepped through the shrubbery to find the end of the rainbow.

When you have been out before dawn, when you have flown through clouds and primordial mists, when you have seen the earth created and have relived Genesis, when you have struggled through the primeval wilderness, when you have bicycled fifty miles and returned in the afternoon to the camp of man, you must be prepared to accept the sunset. The day is closing down. It makes no difference now whether the hopes of Paradise were realized or not. The world has grown old and is tired. Now the sinking sun has fallen behind the trees across the street; it is dusk; the world is fading out. At last there is only the "huge and thoughtful night." One wonders, does God still dwell in the tents of Shem in the darkness, or is this but the memory of an illusion? Soon there is only sleep. The cycle of existence is over.

In crossing April 8 off your calendar, you cross out spring and summer and autumn, the life of man, and the history of the world.

The Chesapeake Marshes

Gilbert Klingel (1909–1986)

A naturalist and yachtsman, Klingel wrote two books about his personal experiences with nature: *The Bay*, about the Chesapeake Bay, and *Inagua* (1940), which treats Great Inagua Island in the Bahamas, where he was shipwrecked. *The Bay* won the Burroughs Medal in 1953 and set the standard for later writers such as William Warner and Tom Horton. Klingel's writing is more personal and descriptive than that of his successors; there is more beauty and less science. Perhaps this is because the Chesapeake Bay did not seem endangered at the time he was working there. The book has become more popular today than when it was published thanks to the movement to "Save the Bay."

In this selection, Klingel sits and observes a Patuxent River marsh for twenty-four hours, giving us a perspective on an entire ecosystem rather than an in-depth study of an individual species. The complexity and beauty of life in the ever-changing marsh are evocatively described. This is what the marshes once were. Will they be this vital tomorrow?

From *The Bay* (New York: Dodd, Mead, and Company, 1951)

NEAR THE Tobacco Market town of Upper Marlboro in Maryland, the Patuxent River finds its way to the level of the sea. After a long tortuous journey from its source at the edge of the Piedmont Plateau and across the tumbled region of the Eastern Fall Line, it suddenly emerges from a narrow green valley overhung with trees into the broad reaches of the Patuxent marshes. Here it changes from a swift, tumbling stream, with rapids, eddies, and even waterfalls, to a slow, winding, lazy waterway. The change is complete, and as far as Holland Ferry, twenty miles below, the river is unlike either of its extremities.

These twenty miles of river constitute a sort of halfway zone, a place that is neither part of the open salty bay nor a portion of the upland country. The upper end of the swamp is steeped in the fresh water of the flowing river; farther down the water becomes more saline as it merges with and gradually becomes part of the Chesapeake.

In a sense, this lovely valley of wild rice and waving cat-tails, this midway region of water lilies and marsh grass, of narrow channels and mud flats is a place of struggle, although it is a strife which goes on so quietly and so peacefully as to be almost unnoticed. It is the scene of the never-ending battle between the ocean and the solid land.

Twice in a day the long fingers of the Bay creep in between the reeds and the cat-tails, flood the spaces between the grass hummocks, and fill the curving channels with a brackish inundation; twice the land regains what it has lost. As the ocean retreats it takes with it particles of mud and sand, bits of leaves, fragments of floating reeds, blades of broken grass. The land in its turn sends out roots and tendrils to anchor the soil more firmly; seeds fall on the bars exposed at low tide and secure themselves, grow, and extend their hold. The river sends down new ground; this falls to the bottom in the slack tide and creates new soil for green growing things. Everywhere, on a small or large scale, the struggle continues. The land fills up an old channel with tightly held earth; the waters cut a new one, etching out the grains one at a time or in big chunks, dragging them out to sea.

Similar strife is being waged all over the Bay country, wherever the sea meets the land. On the ocean front the battle is thunderous and is waged with big waves and giant combers; in the valley of the Patuxent and in other marshes of the Bay, the action is slow and stealthy, silent and furtive.

This alternate expansion and recession, this twice-daily drowning of the marshes and their drying out again sets the tempo for the life of the swamp and limits and controls the growth and character of the vegetation and of the swamp itself. Plants and animals, mammals, birds, fish, and serpents all lead their lives in accordance with the periodic invasion and retreat. Consciously or unconsciously, all the swamp beings fall into the pattern of the tides and become a part of the earth-sea struggle.

The Patuxent marshes are not greatly different from most of the Chesapeake marshes except that they are larger than many, and longer and more winding. The tidal marshes are a universal feature of the Chesapeake and those of the Patuxent are typical. Almost every estuary has its bordering swamp and the shores of the Bay are dotted with thousands of lagoon marshes. These are places varying from little patches, hardly a half acre in extent, to large areas covering miles of half-submerged land. They are formed, usually, when the currents create a sand bar or shallow ridge across an indentation in the shore line. This bar, building itself ever higher, soon affords protection for the shallow, still water inside. In time, in a few days, a few weeks, or months, seeds lodge in the exposed flats, take root, and anchor the soil. Leaves and branches fall from nearby trees; rain-washed silt from the neighboring land fills the interstices with soft, silky mud; plants grow, spread their leaves, and blossom only to crumple in the water and thus add their bulk to the total. In this way swamps are born.

These marginal swamps are places of surpassing beauty, and there is a quality of loveliness about them that is different from all else. Even when they occur in regions that are thickly settled, they are set apart in lonely fashion, protected from the world by their dense fringing vegetation or by their acres of yielding soil. In a world of busy, swarming human beings and whirring machinery they remain isolated and free of intrusion. It is, perhaps, this unspoiled character and their untrammeled natural appearance that make them most appealing. There is also a brooding air that is most entrancing, a vague somnolence associated with few other scenes.

The life of the swamps is one of cycles, of growth and recession, advance and retreat. This is not only daily, tide urged, and controlled, a sort of natural breathing, so to speak, an oft-reiterated systole and diastole of movement, a falling and rising of the waters; it is also the alternation of day and night, the waking and sleeping of the creatures of the swamp, and the evidence of their activities. It is the swing of the seasons, the turn of the spring to summer—fall to winter—the coming of the heat and of the cold, the burgeoning of the seemingly dead seeds and roots, and their return to brown lifeless substance again. It is the coming and going of the ducks and geese, the sandpipers, and the marsh wrens; it is the hum of insects and their later silence; the difference between the shimmer of heat waves above the green reeds and the crackling of ice between the broken brown fronds.

It is not possible to describe a Chesapeake swamp in one unhalting paragraph, nor in two or in two times two. My personal recollections are made of a host of separate and isolated remembrances, like the numerous pictures in an old-fashioned art gallery or the facets of a many-sided crystal. A Chesapeake marsh is a multitude of mind portraits done in a host of colors, but always with delicacy.

It is the sight of a white egret posed on one leg against a background of green reeds, waiting motionless and patient for a fish to pass; it is the opened chalice of a great white and purple, yellow-stamened mallow, or the equally beautiful vision of a water lily in full bloom beside oval lilypads floating on dark water. It is the somber green of overhanging pine trees reflected in the still pools; the widening and often-repeated circles of raindrops falling on the winding channels, making a soft hissing sound as they touch. It is the splash of fish and the liquid burble of a marsh wren rising in a burst of energy above all other sounds. It is sunshine and blue sky and sparkling waters; it is also grayness and dull brown; ice and a piercing wind; it is the noise of dried reeds clattering one against another, millions of minute rubbings and bumpings blending into one multitude of sound; it is the noise of ducks and geese gabbling to one another in the early morning; the sporadic clattering of rails; and the rustle of some unseen being creeping between the cattails. It is the gleam of moonlight upon a layer of mist lying close to the water, and the reflection of starlight; conversely, it is glare and heat of quivering hot air. It is the smell of dried mud and of decaying vegetation inextricably mixed with the aromatic scent of pine and the odor of long-dead fish and dried mussels. It is an expanse of waving grass turning golden and swaying and bending like wheat in the breeze, rippling and waving; it is the red glow of the setting sun and the faint clicking of bats in the long shadows; it is the dancing of swarms of hovering gnats and the drone and whine of mosquitoes in the gloom. It is the red, black, and yellow bodies of painted turtles sunning themselves on half-submerged logs; the V-shaped ripples that denote the heads of serpents gliding across a channel to seek frogs on the other side; frogs themselves calling in the dark, the shrill of toads, the deeper, solitary tone of the larger batrachians, and the massed chorus of thousands of spring peepers. It is the clustering of a glistening mass of dewdrops on a strand of marsh grass, and the patterned cracks of mud dried in the sun. All these things and many more, visual, sensory and aural, are a part of the mosaic that comprises the total picture of a Chesapeake swamp.

And so the portrait of a marsh is not an assemblage of water and soil and vegetation which may be coldly defined and catalogued. Like music, which is conceived of notes and scales, of chords and arpeggios, it is a never-ending series of compositions; of Bach and Beethoven, Strauss and Debussy, of Chopin and even Wagner. It is a processional of portraits, a series of dramas, some small, some large, a sequence of intransient masterpieces on a variety of scales; some are grandiose and majestic like the murals of Michelangelo; others are delicately and gently limned like the threads of a Chinese silk or the tracery of a Dresden porcelain.

Once I spent a whole twenty-four hours on a bluff overlooking the Patuxent River in the very heart of the swamp. In a canoe I had found the spot in the evening and had made camp among the pines and had spread my sleeping bag on the brown needles. Tired from a long paddle I decided to remain until the following day. The place was well chosen and quite isolated. From the height the full extent of the river valley was visible. The masses of reeds and wild rice and the winding course of the river itself, curving back and forth like some great glistening serpent, were spread beneath my feet; from the pines I could see but was unseen and unnoticed.

I awoke about three in the morning. It was dark and cool. There was no wind and a deep hush had spread over the world. Silently I pulled on a sweater and a pair of moccasins and softly, as though half afraid to mar the quiet, stepped over to the edge of the bluff and sat down with my back against a gnarled old pine. There was no moon and the marsh was dim and obscure. Very faintly, scattered stars peeped out between masses of dark clouds. Here and there a few caught the surface of the water and gleamed palely in reflection.

For a long while I listened and heard no sound. The night creatures, tired from the evening's activity, had ceased their calling and wanderings and had retreated into their hiding places, or drowsed invisible in the gloom. It was their hour of waiting before the change from night to day, when all the world was in suspense.

I must have drowsed because when I woke again I was shivering and a heavy dew saturated the grass and dripped from the leaves. It was still dark but the darkness was not quite so black as before. The swamp was still invisible and was still silent. But as I listened there came from far out in the center one low, clear note. For a long time it was the only sound, then I heard it again, stronger and more full. In the daylight, or at any other time, it would have passed unnoticed, drowned in a medley of other sounds, but in the night it arose alone and unnamed, and because of its loneliness dominated the dark.

The note reached its full pitch and then softly died away. Somehow I was reminded of a rocket I once saw at sea, a single pinpoint of light that soared up out of the blackness, blazed into brilliant illumination at its zenith, and then vanished from the earth. This single note was the signal for which the marsh had been waiting. Once again it came; then far off in the distance another pierced the gloom, then another. The spell was broken. In a steady progression other voices added themselves to the first until the air was throbbing. And all the while the night retreated, giving way to gray-black, to gray, and then turned soft rose.

With the beginning of light the whole swamp came alive. There was the rustling of thousands of wings as the hungry flocks began to feed and to go about their early errands; unseen splashes betrayed the activity of small fishes schooling, and the querulous voices of hidden ducks echoed back and forth across the valley.

The amount of life that is hidden and becomes evident only in these early-morning hours is surprising. The sunlight had hardly touched the tops of the distant trees when large groups of red-winged blackbirds were wheeling and streaming back and forth from their favorite feeding places; flocks of sandpipers coasted just above the mud flats, then settled at the water's edge and tripped over the sand bars looking for food exposed by the low tide. Like brown shadows the henlike bodies of rails could be seen threading between the reeds, occasionally one punctuated the morning air with its clatter; coots paddled in small groups of two or three along the river's brim; several flocks of crows crossed the valley cawing as they went; one of these suddenly turned and dived out of sight along the distant bank; hosts of diminutive sparrows swayed on the tops of old reed stalks or undertook short trips between the swamp and the shore; myrtle warblers clustered about the bushes and low shrubs or swirled in miniature flights between points of land, descending on the bordering trees like leaves blown by an October wind.

The sequence of events ushered in by the coming of the day followed a slow but definite pattern. The first joyous activity caused by the departure of night reached its climax as the rays of the sun passed the distant tree-tops and then stole downward, catching first the very tips of the reeds, leaving the bases in shadow. At this moment every feature of the swamp was accentuated, cast into vivid high light. Every reed carried momentarily a crest of flame; and the dew that saturated every fiber caught the color and cast it back with a brilliance reminiscent of the shimmer of old silk.

With the advent of full daylight the activity slackened; the flocks still moved, though in smaller numbers and with less vivacity. As the dew disappeared and the heat of the sun began to temper the morning cool, the voices abated, diminishing steadily, almost imperceptibly. The fish no longer jumped as merrily and their splashings were less frequent. The sand bars and the bobbing figures of the sandpipers began to disappear one by one as the rising tide stole their feeding places and crowded them against the reeds.

By ten o'clock the scene had changed, the mood altered. The marsh was then drowned in sunlight and the thermometer had climbed; heat waves were beginning to rise. It was no longer the hour of the ducks and coots, of the red-winged blackbirds or the rails. They were nowhere to be seen, nor were their voices to be heard. Instead, a low steady drone rose from the marsh, a vibrant monotone that persisted minute after minute. It so permeated the air and it came into being so slowly and unobtrusively that at first I did not notice it, and I was unaware that it had not been there before. Only when the coarser sounds had been eliminated did it come to attention.

It was the sound of millions of insects, the drone of hundreds of bees, the hum of countless flies, the beating of the elytra of beetles, the stirring of all the legions of arthropods. There were individual sounds that rose slightly above the general hum as some insect passed close; the high-pitched whine of assassin flies; the peculiar rustle of dragonfly wings and the irritating singing of tiny, almost invisible diptera. But it was the bees that dominated the ensemble. One does not usually think of a salt marsh as filled with bees; they are more reminiscent of clover, timothy, and meadows of verdant grass. But they were everywhere, swarming about the just-opened mallows and other swamp flowers. Yet there must have been some other attractions, for the bees were many and the flowers few.

The hours of the insects were long and as the sun approached the zenith they persisted and their ceaseless monotone increased in volume until it overcame all other sounds.

By then the tide was high and the *Littorina* snails, those gray comical periwinkles which spend all their lives on grass stalks hovering between successive inundation and dehydration, were soaking up the brine and had emerged from their lime houses where they had been waiting tightly sealed for the coming of the water. Their life is one monotonous succession of wettings and dryings, of slow creeping movement while they are feeding and long periods of sleep between times, tightly closed to keep from drying out. They are truly midway creatures in a midway world; their lives are limited to within a foot or so of tide lines; in their slow methodical way they have partly broken from their ancestral ocean, yet have not quite achieved a life on dry land. They may stray just so far; beyond a certain point is death by dehydration. The full tide is their necessity, and although they no longer need to spend all their hours in the water they are held to it as though bound by prison chains.

The division of the day into the hours of the events of the swamp is a much more meaningful method of keeping time than our mathematical chronology. The Chinese have long used this poetical technique in the designation of the years and the seasons. To have lived in the year of the Dragon or of the Tiger is far more entrancing than to have existed through

1936 or 1943. It may be argued, of course, that such a method is unscientific, and so it undoubtedly is. But to attempt to describe the passing of a day in a Chesapeake marsh by cataloguing the arithmetical hours is an uninspiring business. How much more descriptive it is to speak of the Dark Hour of the First Voice, the Time of the Wakening of the Birds, the Interval of the Rising Tide, or the Hour of the Leptorrhine! The creatures of the swamp do not live by arithmetic; they are moved by events, are actuated by sun and tide, by light and darkness, by heat and cold, by hunger and fullness, and by the movements of the life about them.

And so the time of the *Littorina* was succeeded by the hours of somnolence and of the falling tide. The sun passed the zenith and began its earthward trip. The heat increased and waves of hot air caused the distant shore and the reeds to quiver. The birds vanished, all except the vultures which endlessly soared high in the sky. Although they were the only moving, living things, they increased the feeling of drowsiness. For a long time the swamp lay still, quiet and deserted.

Such periods of calm always precede times of great activity. It is as though nature, asleep, is gathering force once again to show a burst of energy. The calm before a storm, the deceptive warmth of Indian summer, the slow gathering of the clouds before a northeaster are phenomena in kind. The heat of the day beats down the feathered things and the glare drives the mammals to shelter. Even the serpents seek the shade and the turtles retire to sheltered nooks. Only man is foolish and sweats and toils in the fields. But with the passing of the hot hours the burden is lifted and the world once again breaks into activity.

But there is no comparison with the alteration from dark to dawn. There is no time of the opening voice, no sudden ushering in of animate existence. Slowly as the heat declines and the rays of the sun grow longer, as the shadows steal in, the creatures of the place come out of their hiding and go about their errands. Serpents cross and recross the winding channels looking for food; ducks and grebes appear as by magic; the rails resume the clattering they halted in the early morning; the rush of wings is heard again; fish splash; the little green herons stalk daintily in the shallows spearing minnows. From the bordering pines mourning doves call plaintively. There is a different quality about these sounds and movements. The spontaneity is gone; the bird calls are superficially the same, but the vivacity is missing, a certain joyous timbre lacking. There is activity, but it is activity dictated by need alone; stomachs must be filled and preparation made for the coming of the night. Muscles are tired, the day has been long; there is a brief resurgence of energy but little is left over for joyous singing or carefree romping. The swallows are an exception. Their flashing bodies turn and twist over the marsh in endless gyration; their small-voiced twittering seems as sprightly as ever.

There is no sharp cleavage between day and night. The two worlds merge imperceptibly; the creatures of the day disappear singly or in flocks; their places are taken by the myriads of the evening. The alteration is not readily visible; even from my vantage point overlooking the swamp all the details were not revealed. As the shadows spread out and enveloped the earth, one became conscious that the red-winged blackbirds were no longer moving, that the mourning doves had ceased their interminable calling, that the sky was free of the last vulture, that the warblers were not to be seen nor were their songs to be heard. Only the *Littorina* remained impassive on the grass stalks waiting patiently for the coming of the tide. All over the marsh and in the bushes countless heads were being thrust under countless wings, countless pairs of eyes were closing, dropping into that half-sleep which characterizes the uneasy rest of the wild.

And, as imperceptibly as the day creatures disappeared, so did the night animals begin their activity. Seemingly out of nowhere, the twisting, fluttering shapes of bats appeared, replacing the swallows. Their darting forms silhouetted momentarily against the sky, then became invisible against the hovering shadows. The soft whisper of their tissue wings and the strange clicking they make sounded temporarily as they passed close, subsided, and then rose again.

I could not have told when the first frog voices made themselves heard. They were almost in full volume before I thought of them. In the nocturnal chorus the individual species could be readily distinguished; there were the shrill reiterated notes of the spring peepers, the deep "chug" of the great bulls, the protracted shrill of toads, and the similar but more musical song of the swamp tree frogs, the bright green, waxy-looking, big-eyed *Cinereum*. So gradually did the amphibians take up their chorus that it was not until the gloom was pierced by a frightened, almost childlike cry that I became aware of them. Somewhere in the maze of reeds a brown water snake had seized one of their number, and in quick terror the frog had cried out. Suddenly every frog voice in the whole vast extent of the swamp was stilled. For a long minute the silence persisted; then in the distance a frog called softly, then louder. Another took up the notes and soon they were in full chorus again. Frogs forget easily.

The sun had been gone only a short while when the whippoorwills started. The swamp echoed to their repeated pleas to "whip-poor-will." Every Chesapeake marsh has its quota of whippoorwills; they do not live in the swamp itself, but on the borders, preferably in the pines; and in the appropriate season, when they are calling, they set the tempo and timbre for all the marsh sounds. One seldom sees them, for they are habitants of the dark; during the day they remain quiet, motionless, sitting lengthwise on some log or branch, mottled or speckled, invisible against the wood. But as soon as night comes they begin their feverish calling, over and over, endlessly admonishing the world to "whip-poor-will," then again and again to "whip-poor-will," "whip-poor-will," "poor will."

The time of the calling of the whippoorwills is a long one. They must derive a sheer joy out of it, some type of avian ecstasy that drives them on and on, or they are impelled by some vital, uncontrollable urge to communicate their message to their kind and to the wide, wide world. They are sort of a Temperate Zone "brain-fever" bird, and indeed their repeated calling drives some urban and unornithological souls nearly frantic.

The life of the early-evening hours is as busy as the corresponding burst of activity in the early morning. This is the time of the muskrats, the period when they go about the canals in search of food or sit on top of their feeding platforms or on their conical reed houses and survey their darkened domain. It is also the hour when the owls are soaring over the swamp looking for those same muskrats and for their lesser cousins, the mice. These latter beings occur in legions and their down-lined nesting places are found wherever there is a dry space.

The doings in a Chesapeake marsh at night can only be inferred; our eyes are too ill designed to give the needed vision. It is as well, for the twin senses of sound and smell are neglected human attributes. The call of the whippoorwill is more potent than the sight of one; the wonderful smell of dried mud, sun-baked reeds, decaying vegetation and the ever-present aura of salt water that drifts out of the marshes carries as many connotations as visual appearance. So, from my observation place upon the bluff, I could picture the events of the night without seeing.

The sudden slap of some object upon the water followed by a splash would be the hurried retreat of a muskrat aware of danger, perhaps in the form of a hovering owl. All over the swamp similar slaps and splashes indicated that the warning had been heard and was being passed along. Out in the open water between the grass islands a rapidly reiterated pattering sound accompanied by a pulsating whirring marked the place where some duck or other wild fowl was blundering into the night, literally walking on the top of the water, trying to take to the air. Something had startled it, and it was frightened, was seeking escape from its enemy, real or imagined.

Most of the night sounds are soft and must be listened for; they occur as undertones to the din of the frogs and the heavier sounds of the swamp. There are multitudes of tiny scrapings and raspings, little scratching noises which are difficult of definition, the sound of dripping, and the barely audible "plop" of bubbles of marsh gas rising to the surface and bursting. Back of all these is a faint clattering, an infinitesimal banging and bumping, in tune and associated with a delicate sighing. At first this is indefinable but then, as the categories of sound separate and take their proper places, it becomes plain. It is the sound of the night wind; the sighing caused by the passage of air through millions of grass stems, between the close-packed blades; the clattering and banging is the hitting of the individual reeds and stems, as they nod and bend to the pressure.

Slowly the hours of the night wore on. At some ill-defined point the whippoorwills ceased their calling. The frogs sounded less enthusiastic and presently the reeds and cattails were quiet again. Even the splashings and patterings were heard no more, for the wind had died, gently and gradually. Then came the most entrancing time of all.

From the top of a strong-scented myrtle bush close to a starlit pool a lone mockingbird began its song. Clear and sweet it poured out its whole repertoire to a silent world. Note after note went pealing across the quiet reeds, some soft, some low, some strong and full. What had wakened this dull gray bird and caused it to burst into song, there is no way of knowing. There was no answering call or another sound. Alone and for nearly an hour the melody continued and all the while the hush prevailed. Perhaps the very quiet, and the opportunity to be the sole actor in a midnight show caused this bird to break into melody. More likely, the song was created by some inner need for expression, some strange desire to fill the silent spaces with sound or to give vent to a sense of well being. Whatever the cause or whatever dreams prompted the song, it continued until long after the stars had reached the zenith and were dipping downward. Then on a last clear note it ended.

It was the final act of the day. The cycle had come to completion. For I drifted off to sleep and when I awoke, the dew was heavy on the grass, the morning chorus had begun.

May at Monticello

Edwin Way Teale (1899–1980)

After a successful thirteen-year career as a feature writer for *Popular Science Monthly*, Edwin Way Teale freelanced as an author, editor, and photographer, winning the John Burroughs Medal for *New Horizons* in 1943. He made his mark on nature writing with a series of books in which he depicted the seasons through America, beginning with *North With the Spring* (1951); followed by *Autumn Across America* (1956) and *Journey into Summer* (1960); and ending with *Wandering Through Winter* (1965), which won the Pulitzer Prize for General Nonfiction. Perhaps his most significant contribution as an editor is *The Wilderness World of John Muir*, which has been in print for forty years.

From *North with the Spring* (New York: Dodd, Mead, and Company, 1951)

OUR SPEEDOMETER touched 11,000 miles on that eighty-sixth day of our trip. We had been running west through Virginia where May had turned locust trees into creamy clouds of white and fire-pink blazed along embankments and lions and tigers bared their teeth on billboards that marked the trail of the earliest circus of spring. Now, in midmorning, we were climbing the wooded mountain road that led to Monticello.

Automobiles with license plates from more than twenty states had already mounted the road ahead of us that morning. They had brought people of varied interests and diverse outlooks to do homage to the many-sided genius of Thomas Jefferson. Most were attracted by the patriot, the statesman, the humanitarian. Some were interested by the architect, the inventor, and we—in addition to all these—by the naturalist. An often-overlooked facet in the life of this extraordinary man is his not inconsiderable contribution as a pioneer naturalist in America.

Thomas Jefferson published the first accurate and extensive list of birds in this country. He kept careful meteorological records for decades. He set down detailed facts about the trees of Virginia. He classified its animals. He recorded the comparative weights of red, gray, and black squirrels. He was the first American to make a scientific report on the fossils of the New World.

In 1787, when Jefferson published his celebrated *Notes on Virginia*, he listed all the birds known in the area. The total was fewer than 130 species. Today, according to Dr. J. J. Murray, of Lexington—editor of *The Raven*, official organ of The Virginia Society of Ornithology—the state list includes 400 species and subspecies—344 of the former and 56 of the latter. In all the United States east of the Rockies the number of full species is well under 450. So Virginia's 344 indicates the richness of bird life in that state. Driving across it, we noted down the different kinds of birds we saw as we rode along. By the time we came to Monticello our list had reached 85.

And at Monticello, birds were all around us—wood thrushes, towhees, brown thrashers, ovenbirds, yellowthroats, ruby-crowned kinglets, catbirds. We saw—to use the terminology of the Jefferson list—the lettuce bird or the goldfinch; the Virginia nightingale or the cardinal; the fieldfare of Carolina or the robin. We did not see, and no one will ever see again, two of the species on the list. Both of them—the passenger pigeon and the Carolina paroquet—have in the intervening years become extinct. But we saw two other birds not on the list and unknown in America when it was made. These were the comparatively recent introductions, the English sparrow and the starling. Jefferson, however, was one of the few Americans of his day who would have recognized them. In all probability he had seen them abroad while representing his country in Europe.

On that May morning one hundred twenty springs had passed since Jefferson died on his mountaintop overlooking the valley where he was born. One hundred sixty years had gone by since he published his *Notes on Virginia*. Yet the natural history of Monticello remained virtually unchanged. Bluebirds sang on the fence posts. Phoebes flitted in and out of the open doors of the old stables. A robin had built its nest at the top of one of the white columns of the west portico. And brown thrashers ran across the grass beneath an ancient linden tree that once provided shade for the third President of the United States.

Off to the east, beyond the mountainside where spring-clad trees stretched in a tumbling sea down the slope toward the Piedmont, a trio of turkey buzzards swung slowly, curving on the wind, hanging on the updrafts, drifting far out over the valley above tiny fields snipped from the plush of wooded hillsides, then sliding back to go riding low above Monticello. And all that morning the brilliant blue sky was filled with the metallic crackling of the chimney swifts.

Beside Jefferson's grave, we watched a chipping sparrow tilting its rusty cap this way and that as it fed on dandelion seeds. Fluttering into the air, it would alight on a bending stem and ride it to the ground. Occasionally, as it plucked the seeds, it would lift its head for a quick survey, with dandelion fluff projecting like a scraggly white mustache on either side of its bill. Before swallowing each seed, it clipped off the parachute, which floated to the ground. At the end, beneath the denuded stem the accumulated fluff looked like a little windrow of foam clinging to the grass. How many thousand dandelion seeds never take root because of the feeding of a single sparrow!

The birds of Monticello provide one of the outstanding memories of a naturalist's visit. The trees provide another. Here, rooted where Thomas Jefferson had planted them in the eighteenth century, stood ancient tulips, lindens, copper beeches, sugar maples, European larches. Here were noble trees, patriarchs that brought to mind Sir Thomas Browne's observation of long ago: "Generations pass while some trees stand and old families last not three oaks."

In beginning one of his Socratic dialogues, Plato wrote:

"Scene: Under a plane tree . . . "

Under a tree . . . That phrase recurs frequently in the history of human thought. Thinkers as diverse and as far removed as Gautama beneath his Bo tree in the Far East and Ralph Waldo Emerson under a New England pine have been associated with trees. "He spake of trees, from the cedar tree that is in Lebanon even unto the hyssop that springeth out of the wall." So the Book of Kings in the Bible describes King Solomon, whose wisdom was proverbial in his time.

Around us, on this May morning, rose trees that had been associated with the thoughts of Jefferson. He had walked beneath their boughs, rested in their shade, seen them against blue sky and red sunset, watched them in wind and rain. They were part of his life when the author of the Declaration of Independence was evolving and strengthening his own eloquent philosophy of justice and human rights.

Now they were clothed in a new installment of green. For the leaves, life was new. For the trees, the events of spring represented merely an old, old sequence. One hundred twenty, one hundred fifty times, or more, a fresh mantle of leaves had taken the place of those which had fallen in autumn. Their green varied from tree to tree, almost from branch to branch. And beyond, along the mountainside, the shadings of spring were manifold. At no other time of year, except in autumn, is there greater variety of color in a woodland than in spring. A thousand and one subtle shadings of green, lost in summer, characterize the new foliage. Autumn colors are flaunting; they catch the eye. Spring tintings are delicate and often overlooked.

Every hour, under that brilliant morning sun, each square yard of outstretched leaves was manufacturing something like one fiftieth of an ounce of sugar. The broad ribbon leaves of an acre of growing corn will produce, in a single summer day, as much as two hundred pounds of sugar which is converted into the material of the plant. Leading to all the leaf factories of the trees around us was the running transportation system of the sap. Spring had increased its volume, had stimulated its flow. Coursing through the channels of trunk and branch and twig, it moved often under surprising pressures. In one laboratory experiment, scientists found that even the lowly tomato plant can produce pressures ranging up to about one hundred pounds to the square inch—sufficient to carry sap to the topmost twig of a California sequoia. Each tree at Monticello, beech, linden, maple, tulip, was being nourished by its own particular kind of sap. As in human blood groups, the fluid within tree trunks is specialized. Oak sap, for example, will not nourish a birch tree nor maple sap a beech.

From the tops of all the trees that Jefferson had planted, lightning rods project upward. This wise precaution protects them from thunderbolts in their exposed position on the mountaintop. In other ways, good sense has prevailed in keeping the house and grounds unchanged. The gardens have been laid out from sketches Jefferson made. The same fine and simple flowers he planted in the different beds—columbine, Virginia bluebells, phlox drummondi, tulips, and stock—grow there still. On this spring day—hundreds of butterfly generations after Jefferson's desire, expressed in the words: "All my wishes end where I hope my days will end, at Monticello," had come true—tiger swallowtails drifted among the garden flowers. And all along the edge of the restored fishpool, honeybees were alighting to drink the brick-red water.

We spent a long time within that noble house whose designing and building might be called Jefferson's lifelong avocation. He began it in his twenties; he was in his sixties when it was done. Everywhere we delighted in evidences of his brilliantly original mind. In turn, we became interested in his revolving study table, his "Petite Format" library, his clock that marked the days as well as the hours, his octagonal filing table with its pie-piece drawers. We had just emerged and were standing near the spot where Jefferson used to set up his telescope to watch the progress being made in building the University of Virginia, at Charlottesville in the valley below, when all the small birds feeding in the open dashed pell-mell into the bushes.

A swift gray shape skimmed past us. It was a Cooper's hawk scudding low among the trees. As it went by, from the bushes around us there arose a

"... good sense has prevailed in keeping the house and grounds unchanged."
Monticello, S. Finnegan

confused babel of bird voices. Instead of remaining silent in the presence of the hawk, all the hidden birds joined in a twittering crescendo. We were in the midst of that curious phenomenon sometimes referred to as the "confusion chorus."

The psychology of the bird of prey directs it toward an individual which it pursues. By flocking together in the air, small birds are able to divide the attention of the hawk, to distract it by many shapes in motion. As long as they keep together, and the hawk is unable to cut one individual from the flying mass, all escape. The confusion chorus appears to be a kind of flocking by sound. The calls, coming from all sides at the same time, apparently disconcert the bird of prey. At any rate, the Cooper's hawk swept on without pausing, reached the edge of the mountainside, and slid down out of sight. The twittering chorus ceased. The little birds, mostly chipping sparrows and English sparrows, flitted out of the bushes into the open. Their fright was over. The appearance of danger had set off a sequence of instinctive acts. Now that the danger was past there remained no visible remnant of haunting fear. Monticello in May was once more a place of sunshine and of peace.

In the Forest of Fountainebleau, which Jefferson often visited while American minister to the court of France, the green woodpecker is known by the apt name of the "awakener of the woods." An American bird deserving the same title is the familiar flicker, the "yucker" of Jefferson's bird list. Directly above our heads, as we were starting down the road on leaving, one of these woodpeckers burst into its strident, rolling cry. It filled all the space between the trees and was flung far out over the valley. Then, with that disconcerting suddenness that ends a flicker's call, the sound ceased. This was the last bird voice we heard at Monticello.

A hundred miles by road to the south and west, down the Blue Ridge Mountains, we came to Virginia's famed Natural Bridge, once owned by Thomas Jefferson. George Washington first surveyed it in 1750. Jefferson first called the attention of the world to it in his *Notes on Virginia*. In 1774, just two years before the American Revolution, he acquired it from King George III, of England.

The sum he paid, ironically, was almost exactly the amount we were charged for admission. Commercial interests have fenced in this natural wonder—which ages of running water and not commercial interests produced—and have turned the spot—intimately associated with great men of the nation's founding—into a moneymaking enterprise. Like Niagara Falls, the Grand Canyon, and the geysers of the Yellowstone, all such scenic marvels of the land are part of the country's heritage. The natural wonders of the nation should belong to the nation. They should be part of the park system, open for the enjoyment of all and not closed for the enrichment of a few.

Depressed by this commercialization of natural beauty, we wandered along the paths, past the oldest and largest arborvitae tree in the world—a 1,600-year-old patriarch with a trunk 56 inches in diameter—and under the great stone arch, higher than Niagara Falls, where rough-winged swallows shuttled back and forth and Louisiana water thrushes ran among the rocks, hunting for food in the shallow stream. Nellie compared the short call-note of the water thrush to the striking together of pebbles and we fell to listing in our minds the birds we knew whose voices suggested sounds in their surroundings—from the liquid, gurgling notes of the redwing in the swamp to the call like tinkling icicles made by the tree sparrow that comes down from the Far North in winter. Thus beguiled, by and by we began to feel better.

That evening, outside a little Virginia town, the day ended with a pleasant adventure. Dusk was far advanced when a small boy came trudging down the dusty road outside our cabin. Bird voices seemed to accompany him, surrounding him and moving with him as he advanced. Whistling to himself, he was imitating robins, cardinals, orioles, bobwhites, meadowlarks. Like Thomas Jefferson, this country boy was more alert, more observant, more richly alive than most of those around him. We envied him this springtime of his interest in wild singers. "The birds of the naturalist," John Burroughs had written half a century before, "can never interest us like the thrush the farmboy heard singing in the cedars at twilight as he drove the cows to pasture or like that swallow that flew gleefully in the air above him as he picked stones from the early May meadows."

We never saw the passer-by except as a small dark shape moving through the dusk. But we have often remembered that whistling boy. I fell asleep wondering about him—who he was, what he was like, what adventures life had in store for him—and wishing him well.

C & O Canal

William O. Douglas (1898–1980)

Supreme Court Justice William O. Douglas was loved and respected throughout America for his tireless advocacy of the rights of people and of nature. An outdoorsman on the order of Theodore Roosevelt, he combined an easterner's sophisticated love of plants and animals with a westerner's zeal for "the vigorous life." Of his many books, at least four can be considered primarily nature and conservation writing: *The Three Hundred Year War: A Chronicle of Ecological Disaster* (1972) sets out Douglas's understanding of the environmental crisis. In *A Wilderness Bill of Rights* (1965), he states the case for America's need for and right to wilderness and proposes a cabinet-level office of conservation directly responsible to the president. *My Wilderness: The Pacific West* (1960) and *My Wilderness: East to Katahdin* (1961) are collections of geographically arranged essays on the landscape and natural history of America.

In "The C & O Canal," Douglas describes one of the favorite retreats of Washingtonians, which owes its continued natural state to his intervention. When the National Park Service planned a four-lane road in the canal right-of-way, his outspoken objection brought together conservationists and citizens in a successful campaign to preserve what became the nation's first linear park. Now, the C & O Canal National Historical Park protects the Potomac's undeveloped shoreline from tidewater at the District of Columbia to Cumberland, Maryland.

The sequence of this selection was rearranged to place Douglas's historical background material at the beginning.

From *My Wilderness: East to Katahdin* (Garden City, N.Y.: Doubleday and Company, 1961)

IT WAS IN March that I once hiked the canal from Cumberland, Maryland, to Washington, D.C.—roughly 180 miles. Bob Estabrook, Merlo Pusey, and I had planned the hike; but the number grew until there were thirty-seven. These were mostly outdoor men with some special claim to distinction in the wilderness—Olaus Murie, biologist; Irston Barnes, ornithologist; Harvey Broome, Wilderness Society; Sigurd Olson and Tony Smith, National Parks Association; and so on. A plan was afoot to turn the canal into a superhighway. Those who loved this long thin ribbon of wilderness along the Potomac protested. The result was an eight-day hike—a Gandhian protest against the highway. It rained every day, sometimes in torrents; but luck was with us, for it never once rained on us. The air was cool, making walking a pleasure. We averaged between twenty and twenty-seven miles a day.

The Potomac is the shortest route between East and West. Its name tells the story. It is derived from an Algonquian word meaning "to bring again, they go and come." It is, indeed, a river of travelers. Early trails ran up it, headed for the rich Ohio country that beckoned. . . .

The towpath of the old canal meanders, following the river in long graceful loops that often travel ten miles to go only one or two. From a height of land or from the air, the Potomac looks indeed like a gigantic snake, twisting and turning as it works its way eastward from the Alleghenies. The river built its serpentine channel millions of years ago, when it ran across fairly flat country. Water, like man, is nervous and restless. When the Potomac flowed across an ancient plateau, it twisted and turned, taking a tortuous path to the sea. When the earth's crust folded to form mountains, the ridges rose slowly enough to let the river keep the pattern of its early course. The famous Blue Ridge, a formidable barrier, rose across its path just above Harpers Ferry. But the Potomac cut through it too.

For one who hikes the towpath, every quarter-mile or so brings a new view—a sharp cliff, a flat meadow, a rough hillside, a narrow gorge. The stretch of the river from Cumberland east to Harpers Ferry is ridge-and-valley country, not marked by any distinct range. The ridges rise a thousand feet or more, each bearing a name—North, Sleepy Creek, Cacapon, Town, South, Bear Garden, Sideling. They abound with deer, wild turkey, fox, possum, quail, and some grouse and woodcock. These hills are shales, sandstone, quartz, and limestone. Originally they were covered with hardwoods. A new forest has taken over—some pine and cedars, much locust, alder, box elder, and red maple. The wild grape grows luxuriantly, forming stout ropes an inch or more thick. Occasionally poison ivy has an even larger diameter, clinging like a snake to an old sycamore that it has succeeded in climbing. The valleys are farmed for cereals, vegetables, and fruits, especially apples. There is rolling pasture land for cows and sheep. The river bottoms have magnificent sycamore. And in the damper places are thick stands of the river birch that give life and color to the woods even in Winter.

The river birch stands in muddy flats along the water's edge. Floods plague the Potomac, sometimes raising the water level thirty feet or more. I have seen new drift, ten feet high on river birch—signs of fresh flooding. The old trunks of the river birch are dark red-brown and covered with thick scales. All of them—old and young—have papery scales. Most of the trunks are straight and unbranched, rising fifty feet or more; and they stand almost as thick as jack pine in northern Minnesota. The wood of this tree has never enjoyed much of a reputation with lumbermen; and it has no real commercial value today. But it stands in quantity along the upper reaches of the Potomac. Its seeds ripen in late Spring, when the river is high. Some trees depend on wind and animals for the spread of their seeds. The river birch depends on the waters of the river for propagation. They carry the seeds downstream, leaving them on muddy banks. Mud seems necessary for their germination. The new shoots come up fast—in a matter of a few weeks. This riverbank tree performs a great service. It holds the banks against the swirl of the current. River birch serves a high function in the cause of conservation. . . .

The bright days of Indian summer are choice along the Potomac. Maples are crimson; sumac and dogwood, a rich dark red; gum trees and pawpaw, yellow; willow oak, a dull gold. There are fall days when the leaves have not yet fallen and when no breeze touches the trees. Then it's as if the woods were holding their breath, lest a leaf be lost. On such a day I was headed west along the C & O Canal towpath. There was hardly a sound in the woods—none but the cawing of a raven and the scolding of a squirrel as our dog Sandy—the Shetland sheepdog who travels the woods with me— scouted the thickets where the hawthorn and honeysuckle entwine. Suddenly a gust of wind touched a stand of sycamores. Down came scores of leaves. They were no longer flat and pliant, but dry and slightly cupped. They came whirling down like flying saucers. They scattered far, the wind spinning them in gentle gyrations. Each kept a horizontal plane, landing bottom down in the waters of the canal and dancing in the soft waves like dainty skiffs.

Out of Washington going west there is water in the canal for the first twenty miles or so. This waterway, built by black powder, mules with scoops, and men with picks and shovels, was finished in 1850. President John Quincy Adams turned the first spade of dirt in Georgetown (then Washington, D.C.'s, suburb) on July 4, 1828. This canal was part of George Washington's dream. It connected Cumberland, Maryland—about 180 miles to the west as the Potomac flows—with Washington, D.C., and it brought mostly coal to tidewater on the Potomac. The railroads soon followed, and the competition became intense—too severe for the canal. But it

continued in operation until 1923, when stubborn economic facts inter-
vened. The barges—90 feet by 13 feet—pulled by mules have now disappeared. The locks with gate beams made of oak still stand.

The canal has whitewashed stone lock houses where the lock tenders
once lived. There is one on the Washington end over which two great
sycamores tower. This bright fall day the white of the house, the mottled
bark of the sycamores and their yellow leaves made an exquisite pastel. I
stopped for the grandeur of the scene when a flock of blackbirds whirled
overhead. They moved in unison, swooping and turning en masse before
settling in treetops to chatter in a lively community meeting. A dozen
turkey vultures caught a current of air as they soared high over a stretch of
woods. They would stay with us all Winter. So would the white-crowned
sparrow, the junco, the redheaded woodpecker, and the wrens. But the
robin I saw in a walnut tree was headed south. So was the blue jay who
quickly disappeared in a huge tulip tree. This tulip tree was a blaze of yellow. The tulip is called popple by the country people. It's a magnolia that
rises in the Potomac region over a hundred feet in height and lives over two
hundred years. It is perhaps our stateliest eastern tree, measuring eight feet
or more in diameter and rising straight and high, having at the top a slight
bulge that gives it a queenly grace.

This was the ebb tide of Autumn. The oak and walnut had dropped
their nuts. So had the numerous hickories that flourish in the valley—bit-
ternut, pignut, and mockernut. The towpath was littered with them. The
papery, transparent husks of the box-elder maples were empty. The Siberian
crab apple, growing like a miniature shrub, was in fruit. Earlier it showed
white, handsome, long, and slender-stalked flowers. Now its yellowish fruit,
about three-quarters of an inch in diameter, was wrinkled and shrunken.
The common pokeberry was heavy with bunches of deep purple berries.
The scarlet berries of the dogwood had mostly dropped. Its silver-gray,
squarish terminal buds were conspicuous, conveying the illusion that
Spring was close at hand. The fruit of the pawpaw was black and wrinkled.
Inside was a delicious custard-like pulp that raccoons and possums like as
well as people do. The bell-shaped pods of the common perilla were full. So
were the spiny heads of the wingstem. The pigweed, chicory, viburnum, and
grape also had a full supply of seeds for the birds. They would be eaten in
part and scattered in part.

The birds now seemed tense and lonely. Only snatches of songs were
heard. Life did not have the zest it knew in the Spring. Then the birds had
mates to find, houses to build, families to rear. Those involved social re-
sponsibilities which took much energy. Then the woods fairly burst with

song. That was the season devoted to the organization of the group. With the coming of Fall, the family tasks were over and the challenge was the survival of the individual. Most of our feathered friends were now in migration. When they arrived at their southern destinations, they would not sing with the joy they express here in springtime. Nor would their plumage be as bright as it is here for the nuptials. Down South they would be defending no territory, building no homes, and, with few exceptions, searching no mates.

Only a few wildflowers remained. White and purple asters had survived. More conspicuous was the common pye weed with its pink flowers and serrated leaves which have a vanilla-like scent when crushed. This flower was named for the old Indian medicine man, Joe Pye, who practiced his art in Massachusetts in the late eighteenth century. He used this plant to cure typhus through "copious perspiration." Its roots were used by the earlier settlers for rheumatism. This October it added a delicate color to patches of the woods I crossed.

There were occasional bushes of the pale snapweed still showing yellow flowers. The dayflower—which many consider a weed—made a blue carpet over some edges of the towpath, its petals heart-shaped and clasping. Swamp smartweed showed a delicate raceme of whitish flowers. The water lilies in the canal were dormant. But growing high above them was the halberd-leaf rose mallow. Some of the flowers (shaped like the ancient halberd) were still in bloom; and their delicate flesh-colored petals with purple base were more in keeping with Spring than with Fall.

The clear November days when the temperature is in the low 30s have their own rewards. Then the leaves are down, rustling underfoot. The shining sumac—the one with resin dots on the branches and fruit—is heavy with bunches of seeds. The mimosa (the old silk tree from Persia introduced here over two centuries ago) stands like a plume, its pods hanging forlornly. The pods of the honey locust are turning black underfoot. The red berries of the Virginia hawthorn are brilliant in distant woods. The sweet gums—their star-shaped leaves fallen—now stand in splendor. This tree—whose gum long served man through the salves and medicines it produced—is at the peak in November. Its woody spiny balls hang from every twig like some Christmas decoration; there they stay most of the Winter long, even after the winged seeds have escaped.

The sycamore catches the eye when the forests are barren. Its smooth bark looks as if it is in sunshine even when clouds hang low. On a bright November day the sight of a stand of naked sycamore lifts the heart. Quite often one great horizontal limb extends over the canal in a protective gesture. But most of the branches, slightly twisted, reach for the heavens. The bark flakes off in irregular patches—light gray, pale tan, and chalky white. In any weather it leaves a mottled effect. In November the limbs hang with balls that burst and scatter seeds far and wide. It is from them that the tree gets the name buttonwood. This tree—the largest deciduous hard tree in North America—made a great contribution to the early pioneers, though the wood was almost impossible to split. Cross sections were once used for oxcart wheels. Many of the old trees along the Potomac—well over a hundred years old—have hollow hearts. A section from a hollow tree made a good hogshead once a board was nailed across one end. A man can sit out a storm in a hollow sycamore. Hundreds of swifts still make their home there. It is the tree the pileated woodpecker seems to prefer.

The white oak on a November day is a study in grace and strength. It is as broad and sweeping as the tulip tree is high. It long was the mainstay of our Navy. White oak was the best all-around hardwood the pioneers knew—the heaviest of all our oaks. It was the most durable wood when used in the ground. It is the state tree of Maryland, reaching a spread of nearly 150 feet. I know a white oak along the old canal that has spanned the years from Thomas Jefferson to Franklin Roosevelt and more. Whenever I pass it, the whole panorama of American history seems to stand in review.

On a bright November day one leans into a sharp wind out of the west. Freezing weather has come; little life is abroad. The waters of the Potomac are low and sluggish. The muskrats are holed up for the Winter. So are the turtles, the friendly black snakes, and the less friendly copperheads. One seems to have the woods all to himself. A gray squirrel scolds from a sweet gum. A blue heron, perched on a limb that overlooks the waters of the canal, flaps lazily away. A flock of pigeons, descendants of the Mediterranean rock dove, turns and disappears down a ravine. This is the time to be alone—surrounded by the stark grandeur of naked trees.

By November the persimmons that flourish in the Potomac Valley are just right. The trees are so widely scattered, one has to search them out. The bark of the persimmon is deeply divided into so many square plates that local people call it alligator bark. The tree is easier to locate in Fall and Winter than at other times, for its leaves are similar to those of the black gum, with which it is often associated; and the two grow to about the same height. The fruit turns from green to amber to dark orange and becomes edible when the frost touches it. By November the skin is so wrinkled that the fruit looks unappetizing, but the pulp is mushy and sweeter than it is astringent. The skin always has a tannic taste. So it is avoided. When I eat the fruit in November my hands and face need washing afterward. There are special trees along the old towpath that people search out in Winter. Some of the fruit is still on the branches; some is on the ground.

One clear cold January day I joined a couple under a lofty persimmon tree and had a true feast. "It's the fruit of gods!" I shouted.

"It's name is *Diospyros*," said the man. "And that means 'fruit of Zeus.'"

"Think of finding it so sweet and mushy in January," his wife added.

Late Winter has its charms along the old canal. There was a crisp January morning when I started a twenty-four-mile hike from Seneca, Maryland, to Washington, D.C., following the serpentine Potomac all the way. Two inches of snow lay bright and fresh over the country. The granite cliffs that line much of the Potomac were never more beautiful. The red cedars that stud them—the cedar whose berries are loved by the birds and who gave its name to the cedar waxwing—had been sprayed white. Every twig, every leaf was touched with powder snow. In two hours the temperature rose and an inch of new snow fell in large, wet flakes. Then came a southeast wind with sleet on its wings. I leaned into the storm, my coat collar buttoned close. The only life I saw were two mergansers flying at water level over the dark and murky Potomac. The snow balled up on my heels and under my arches. It was like walking on short stilts. It took over eight hours to negotiate the twenty-four miles. And when I got home, wet, chilled, and lame from the ordeal, I thought there must have been more than one barred owl snug in his nest who had seen me go by and wondered what mission would summon man on such a vile day. . . .

Some winter days have shown the Potomac wilderness in sheer splendor. I remember a bright, breathless day when the temperature was below 20° and fresh snow three inches deep lay crisp on the land. It powdered trees and shrubs alike and stood stiff like frost on the branches of the hawthorn. The Potomac was white with frosted ice, not showing the channels that keep it open most of the time. The canal was frozen. But the hour was too early for the skaters who would come up from Washington, D.C. I was the only one abroad. At least I thought I was, until I saw the fresh tracks of a rabbit. Later there were signs of a squirrel who had been foraging. When I reached Widewater—a pond about a mile long through which the barges once passed on their way up and down the canal—a host of starlings swooped down over the glistening ice as if to land, only to turn upward in a wide spiral and disappear over the river.

The starlings that Washingtonians find objectionable in Summer and Fall had moved on to western New York. The host of starlings cavorting on this winter day were newly arrived from down South, perhaps from the Carolinas. A hawk streaked across Widewater. A bald eagle soared at great heights. A cardinal hopped from limb to limb in a willow oak, whose nuts are bitter to our taste but liked by squirrels and some birds. All was silent, except the crunching of the snow underfoot. When I stopped, I could almost hear my heart beat. Yet I was less than a dozen miles from the heart of Washington, D.C. My wilderness, though small and confined, was real. It was in miniature the immense northland stretching to the Arctic Circle and beyond. I walked the length of Widewater and stopped on some huge granite rocks that were warm in the sun. The din of the city, the roar of its traffic, was behind me. So was the squalor of its slums. The schemes and machinations of the little men who possess the place seemed far away. I did not have to go far this winter morning to reach this wilderness of solitude and quiet. Only a few miles. That's what the cities need, I found myself saying. A wilderness at their back door, where a man can go and once more find harmony and peace in his inner being. Now a brisk west wind came up, shaking the powdered snow from the trees. I bent into it, lost in my thoughts as I headed for my take-out point, nine miles distant.

The Washington, D.C., area has known erratic storms in March or even April that left a foot or more of snow. One March, eight inches fell; and a thirty-mile wind out of the northwest built drifts several feet deep along the towpath. It was powder snow, excellent for skiing. But Sandy and I went on foot, expending as much energy in five miles as we usually do in twenty. There were, however, special rewards. Though we were on the edge of a great city, we were completely alone. No other human was in sight. It was as if we had moved the clock back a hundred years or more and found the Potomac grinding ice and singing to itself in a wilderness hardly known to man. The day was brilliant, showing off each bit of woodland floor in a naked forest. On exposed points the wind whistled in the tree-tops. Around the next bend in the river, all was quiet. In another mile two trees were rubbing together to break the deep silence. Then somewhere deep in the woods an unseen red-bellied woodpecker gave his noisy call—"Cha, cha, cha-churr, churr, churr." The water in the canal had frozen during a high wind that left gentle riffles on the ice's surface. Now the birds descended on it by the dozen. The deep snow had made foraging difficult. The birds took to the ice, feeding on specks too small for me to see. Some went out too fast for me to identify. But the others seemed to enjoy our company. Some were white-throated sparrows who often sing to me in New England—"Old Sam Peabody, Peabody, Peabody." The others were the goldfinches, which some call wild canaries. On warm days they drop in flight as if they were riding roller coasters, singing all the while, "Per-chik-o-ree." This snowy March day their voices were also mute as they hopped about the ice, looking for specks of food.

Late Spring and early Summer also give glorious days along the canal. The first shrub to come is the forsythia, whose bright yellow gives character even to a stand of weeds. The redbud is next. It is sometimes called the Judas tree, from the legend that it is the tree on which Judas Iscariot hanged himself. Its flowers, once said to be white, turned red with blood; and they grow right out of the branches. Today they are purplish-pink, bringing the Potomac Valley alive in the springtime by painting brilliant streaks in a bare forest of monotones. On bright days when a branch of redbud hangs over the water of the canal, it is hard to tell whether the branch or the reflection is the real one.

Once in April when the redbud was out, several inches of snow fell. The redbud gleamed like rubies and amethysts on frosted branches. The red-bud is soon followed by the dogwood, whose creamy white brings the woods to life. This is the state tree of Virginia, one extensively used as a decorative shrub. It is diminutive; and along the Potomac it leans out from the hillsides, as though making a dainty curtsy.

The black haw—a species of viburnum—comes into bloom at about the same time. It's a tall shrub whose white flowers (destined to turn into black, oval berries) lie in flat, circular clusters. With it bloom the pawpaws. Farther south the pawpaw is often a tall tree with a trunk that is a foot or more thick. But in the Potomac Valley it is an understory tree with delicate trunks and branches, and leaves about a foot long. Its spring blossoms are small and somber. They measure about an inch across, emerge as green, turn to brown, and end up maroon. And when the rich wine color arrives it brings a winy odor with it.

Early to bloom is a tree which in the Far West we call juneberry but which the people along the Potomac have dubbed the "shadbush," because its white blooms come when the shad run the river. The mountain laurel, wild roses, and white rhododendron arrive later. When the hawthorn shows its clusters of flowers in late May, the bees seem to go virtually crazy. Among the last to bloom is the honeysuckle, the bane of the farmers in the Potomac Valley. It forms a tough, durable carpet, hard to remove. It smothers shrubs and chokes great trees. It seems so unsure of life as to cling with great tenacity to anything it touches. It comes to full glory in early June. Its white and yellow bloom, which lasts for three weeks or more, fills the valley with perfume. It's a sweet, almost pungent, odor that hangs in the air, pervading the woods.

Among the first flowers to arrive is the bloodroot, whose juice the Indians used to paint their faces. Its white petals rise tenderly to form a delicate cup with a yellow base. This flower comes quickly and may shrivel and disappear in a few hours. Its fleeting presence makes bloodroot our choicest spring flower. . . .

Most of our spring flowers along the Potomac are more durable, such as the squirrel corn, kin to Dutchman's-breeches, that arrives with the bloodroot. Its light green leaves are lush and its stems are covered with pinkish flowers formed like miniature hearts, with delicate lips curving downward. . . .

By the first of May, Spring has arrived in the upper reaches of the Potomac as well as lower down. The spring migration of the birds is almost complete. A spring hike will bring over sixty, perhaps eighty, species within range. They are busy making new homes and claiming territory of their own. We camped once in an opening above Paw Paw tunnel and, between the first sign of dawn and sunrise, identified about two dozen. Before the day was done, fourteen different species of warbler were noted on our check list.

City in the Woods

Roger Tory Peterson (1908–1996)

James Fisher (1912–1970)

Roger Tory Peterson was the most famous of all American birdwatchers. His *Field Guide to the Birds* and subsequent field guides to a wide range of wildlife were major factors in the resurgence of interest in nature after World War II. Peterson, who was awarded the Presidential Medal of Freedom, was renowned as an author, bird artist, and lecturer whose enthusiasm for his subject was infectious. In *Wild America*, Peterson escorts his colleague, James Fisher, across North America, from Florida's Dry Tortugas to Alaska's Pribiloff Islands, looking at birds and the condition of the American wilderness. Fisher was a noted British ornithologist whose skill and field knowledge were equivalent to Peterson's, but he was seeing America for the first time. "City in the Woods" describes their brief stay in Washington. We can marvel through Fisher's eyes at the proximity of wilderness to the city and at every new bird, plant, and frog. "Roger, is that a———?" From Peterson, we learn of the conservation problems facing the city in the mid-1950s, and the struggles by conservationists to protect our heritage. From both, we can renew our pride in the beauty of our capital city and its natural places.

From *Wild America* (Boston: Houghton Mifflin, 1955)

THE CHESAPEAKE Bay Bridge, four and a half miles long, rose to its crest against a Peter Scott evening sky and dropped in a long sweeping curve toward the distant dark woodlands. Fifty miles of rural and suburban Maryland lay between us and my home, where Barbara would be waiting. From the roadsides, ditchsides, pondsides came a chorus that had begun tuning up, somewhat tentatively, in the afternoon and was now swelling to its nighttime climax, a chorus that had started in New England and was to accompany us until we reached the Gulf of Mexico—the music of the frogs and toads.

James had met his first spring peepers in a pond behind the Drurys' house in Rhode Island, four nights ago. After dinner that evening we had walked across the damp fields toward the clear plaintive birdlike peeping until the myriad voices almost shouted at us from the dark pool and then fell silent. To easterners this nostalgic sound more than any other—more than that of any bird—is the true voice of spring. It is a voice of resurrection: "Spring is come!" Everyone knows the voice and is glad, but few have ever seen the tiny inch-long singer. Tonight, with the peepers, there were multitudes of cricket frogs rasping out their strident notes, and here and there a green frog gave its single croak, like the plucking of a loose string on some instrument. But James found it hard to believe that the peepers were, in reality, frogs and he seemed even more dubious when I told him that the long pure trill that purred on a high pitch from some of the ponds was also made by a batrachian, the American toad. It sounded, he thought, like a blend of bird-trill and insect-trill. At one roadside stop we heard both it and the song of a brother gnome, Fowler's toad, a more nasal trill that started with a *w* sound—*waaaaaaaaaaaa*.

These sounds that pipe and trill from a hundred throats on evenings in spring are love songs of the swamp. They are ancient music, for the frogs sang their songs ages before the birds did; they were here first. The amphibians were the first class of backboned animals to climb out of primordial seas onto the land. The ardent males puff out their throats like bubble gum, and bleat, trill, peep, click, quack, or croak, depending on their kind. This orchestration of frogs and toads is one of the outstanding things about spring nights in eastern North America. True, one can hear frogs in Europe too—I have heard as many as four kinds on still nights in the Camargue reed beds in southern France. But in England there is only one native frog, and two toads. Now two Continental frogs are invading the south of England and one of them, the marsh frog, is accused of giving the British ones a rough time of it.

This evening was windless—perfect for night sounds. Once we heard the squeaking of flying squirrels, nearly overlooked among the more frequent, almost supersonic squeaks of pipistrelle bats coursing overhead in the darkness. A whip-poor-will chanted from the dry oak woodlands, beating out its name rhythmically, endlessly. Certainly, no other bird pronounces its own name more distinctly—or monotonously. I started to count (trying for John Burroughs' old record of 1088 *whip-poor-will* calls in succession without a breather) but had only got up to thirty when a car coming down the road cut the sequence short with an emphatic *Whip!*

How much sound there is at night around the nation's capital—and how oblivious is the average Washingtonian to it! His ears, attuned to motor cars and traffic seldom detect the music of nature—the voices of birds, frogs, or of insects—or the whispering of wind in the leaves. How often, at an outdoor barbecue, or when having drinks on the terrace after some Washington dinner party, have I heard, above the buzz of conversation, night herons quawking overhead on their way from Rock Creek Park to the Potomac, or the distant hooting of barred owls or the rasping snore of barn owls. Barn owls, symbols of wisdom, have lived in the northeast tower of the old Smithsonian building continuously for nearly ninety years. Over downtown roof-gardens the "peenting" of cruising nighthawks can often be heard above the hum of traffic, and in one suburban area, I have even listened to the moon-larking of that long-nosed recluse, the woodcock. The season opens in early spring with the aerial singing of the woodcock and the chorus of frogs, gives way by midsummer to the nocturnal stridulation of katydids and crickets, and ends in autumn with the lisps and chips of unseen birds hurrying southward on the cool northwest winds.

When James and I pulled into the driveway at Glen Echo on this warm April evening the barred owls were whooping it up down in the swamp by the canal.

April 26

More than any other large city in the world, Washington is a city of woods and parks; fingers of the wilderness penetrate nearly to its heart. Roger's home lies just outside the District of Columbia, on the slopes above the towpath of George Washington's Chesapeake and Ohio Canal, separated only by woodland from the Potomac River. The house was once the slave quarters of a larger neighbor, and hides in the wood edge, so that the spring flush of advancing warblers can be heard from indoors, and an opossum comes at night to the feeder. The drawing room has a big picture window framing an ingenious indoor garden and many living plants which creep about, so that nature seems continuous inside and out. Barbara said that the little striped ground squirrels (chipmunks) once burrowed under the baseboard of the house and into the indoor garden, to be followed a week or so later by a rodent-hunting pilot blacksnake that came in through their tunnel and made itself at home among the ferns. Much as she likes wildlife this was too much: flying squirrels could enter the open windows at night if they wanted to, and could even spend the day sleeping in the folds of the curtains—but snakes must go!

The excitement this day, Sunday, was a luncheon picnic of the ancient Washington Biologists' Field Club. Every year, when the shad fish run into Chesapeake Bay and up the Potomac, this eclectic body has an open-air shadbake (and in the autumn, an oyster roast), on its treasured islet in the river, Plummer's Island—one of the most intensively botanized, zoologized, ecologized wild islands in the world, I suppose. Roger and I walked along a narrow path through riverside woodland densely carpeted with blue phlox until we reached an arm of the fast muddy river where a captive rowboat awaited us. By means of ropes and pulleys we pulled ourselves over to Plummer's Island, and scrambling up the wooded hill to the hut at its top, we found it already stiff with prominent biologists. There were mammalogists, botanists, ornithologists, herpetologists, entomologists; many were federal employees, associated with the Smithsonian Institution, the Fish and Wildlife Service, the National Parks, and the National Herbarium. The dedicated men assembled here represented the core of the hundreds of wildlife technicians, biologists, and conservationists whose job it is to keep wild America wild.

It was very difficult to meet, at the same time, life-birds such as Clarence Cottam and the red-bellied woodpecker, John Aldrich and the American redstart, Howard Zahniser and the parula warbler, let alone those already on my tally, like Alexander Wetmore and the downy woodpecker, Frederick C. Lincoln and the black and white warbler. It was a delightful and informal occasion, upon which I found a kind sympathy from those with whom I was conversing, for my more-than-occasional "Oh, just a minute," or "Do you mind?" or "Roger, is that a———?" The novelties came so quickly for me. Delicately sailing across the canal, folding up wings and legs into sudden immobility by the bank, came the little green heron; soaring over the riverwood, the black vulture; lurching boldly through the new leaf and laughing loud, the pileated woodpecker. The yellow-bellied sapsucker at last was no longer just a name. And how big the crested flycatcher; how spotty the wood thrush; how tame the Carolina chickadee; how tiny the blue-gray gnatcatcher.

We sat, we talked, and we raised our field—or beer—glasses from time to time. Deft professional hands turned the fillets of shad over the grill, while a pretty remarkable selection of the finest biological thinkers of the U.S. queued up with cardboard plates like hungry schoolboys. I, mindful as I was of the honor of my invitation to this exclusive club, felt like a fourth-former who, asked to tea with the sixth-form fagmasters at the end of the term, finds them human after all. And most human of humans, if he does not mind my saying so, was a past president of the International Ornithological Congress and President of the American Ornithologists' Union and Secretary of the Smithsonian Institution, Alexander Wetmore. He had a ticket in his pocket for the morrow, for Barro Colorado Island, that incredible oasis of tropical bird life in Panama; and could scarcely disguise

his excitement at the prospect of some interesting birding on his old stamping ground.

On the day of the picnic the woodlands along the Potomac were like
flower gardens. The new green leaves of the trees had expanded sufficiently
to block some of the sunlight, therefore many of the early flowers of the
forest floor—the trailing arbutus, hepatica, spring beauty, trout lily, and
bloodroot—were already past. But the paths and grassy glades were showy
with beds of woodland phlox, their large pale lavender-blue blossoms clustered at the top of foot-tall stems. Violets looked up shyly; there were at
least three species of blue ones, a creamy white one, and a yellow one. North
America, with nearly eighty species, is abundantly blessed with violets. Wild
geraniums added their purplish-pink to the floral color scheme, and the
golden ragwort a touch of strong yellow. The flower that seemed to intrigue
James most was the Jack-in-the-pulpit, which he recognized as a sort of
arum. He examined the tubular greenish "pulpits" with their striped can-
opies and commented, "A wizard plant!"

When Europeans come to America they quickly notice one thing about
the flowers: a large percentage of those growing along the roadside are
plants that they already know, adventive plants which have come from Europe. A roadside is a roadside the world over. A farm is a farm—and a vacant city lot is much the same in Brooklyn as in Liverpool. Plants which
through the centuries have become reconciled to disturbed soils in the Old
World find no difficulty establishing a beachhead here. Their seeds arrive
as stowaways on cargo boats; they hitchhike inland along the railroad tracks
and highways; some have been deliberately introduced. Hundreds of
species—no one knows exactly how many, because new ones are constantly
being noticed—are now part of the American flora. The list is long: dandelion, black mustard, spearmint, peppermint, forget-me-not, mullein, field
daisy, several clovers, several hawkweeds, several buttercups, bouncing Bet,
white campion, butter-and-eggs, burdock, chicory, Queen Anne's lace,
yarrow, teasel, tansy, and many, many others. On the outskirts of New York
City, entry port for millions of human immigrants, 40 per cent of the flora
is of Old World origin.

The woodland flowers, on the other hand, are mostly new to Europeans.
The genus may be familiar, but the species is not. However, along the wood-
land edges this day there were several flowers that were old friends to James
Fisher. The garlic-mustard (hedge garlic) with its heart-shaped leaves and
clusters of small white blossoms would be in bloom now near his home in
Northampton, England. And Sweet Cicely, too, or something rather like it.
These familiars were growing not only in the low "flood forests" along the

Potomac, but also in Rock Creek Park, which we visited late in the afternoon.

The National Zoological Park, located midway along the length of Rock Creek Park, the long wooded ravine that probes deep into the city, acts as a sort of decoy to wildlife. Some years ago night herons, flying over Rock Creek, discovered the great flying cage where ornamental wading birds are kept. Stimulated by the nesting activities of their captive brethren they built their own twiggy nests on branches of the trees overhanging the enclosure. Basically, they were one colony, separated only by wire: inside were the tame birds, outside were the wild ones. The growing heronry splattered the sidewalks below with excrement. When park officials cut off some of the overhanging branches most of the herons (but not all) started another colony on a wooded slope nearby. This Rock Creek Park heronry has expanded a great deal since the day, more than twenty years ago, when Bill Mann, the zoo's director, first showed it to me. Now, there must be at least 400 nests among the high tops of the maples and oaks. James and I tried to count, but we soon decided that the time to make an accurate census is a bit earlier in the season, before the new leaves are out.

Nearby, over the flying cage of the birds of prey, sat a half-dozen wild black vultures, hungrily eying the chunks of raw red meat which the captive birds were wolfing. These six unemployed vultures were all that remained of the winter roost; the others were nesting now—in rock ledges and in hollow logs up and down the Potomac Valley. In winter I have seen as many as 100 black vultures roosting above the flying cages and fully 300 turkey vultures in the woods nearby. The aggressive black vultures keep their red-headed relatives in their place; there is almost complete segregation. On the roof of one of the nearby apartment buildings on Connecticut Avenue the turkey vultures often warm their toes on the ventilators—lending a touch to the Washington scene reminiscent of one that London once knew in medieval times when kites and ravens scavenged London's streets. (We are not implying anything about the District of Columbia's department of sanitation.)

Two things set Washington apart from other American cities—its gracious municipal architecture and its trees. The original plan of the French designer, L'Enfant, envisaged a stately city, reflecting the eighteenth-century Age of Reason. The fine buildings would be set off by broad vistas, accentuated by avenues of trees. In the ensuing years, natural woodland parks were set aside to insure breathing spaces for the growing city. But today there are certain city planners who seem to have forgotten this ideal of beauty and repose.

One Sunday several winters ago, when crossing the Connecticut Avenue bridge, one of the high bridges over Rock Creek, my companion, a news photographer from Texas remarked: "Look at all that land going to waste down there—all that valuable real estate."

I suggested that natural or "inspirational" values were important too—in fact, beyond price; but his only response was a blank stare.

Although many men—far too many—have this blind spot, Washington has always known leaders with vision. More than one president have paraphrased the thought that "men will not take as elevated a view of the national destiny working in the basement of a warehouse as they will on the heights of an Acropolis."[*] If the environment is drab or shabby the thinking and impulses of statesmanship are likely to become shabby.

John Quincy Adams, speaking of Rock Creek Park, said that after a round of trying official duties as President, he would seek relaxation in "this romantic glen, listening to the singing of a thousand birds . . . " Theodore Roosevelt recalled with pleasure that when he was chief executive he often took long walks, "perhaps down Rock Creek, which was then as wild as a stream in the White Mountains." Even foreign diplomats have sung the praises of Rock Creek. Viscount Bryce, the British Ambassador, exclaimed: "What city in the world is there where a man . . . can within a quarter of an hour and on his own feet get in a beautiful rocky glen such as you would find in the woods of Maine or Scotland?"

And yet this park which has served almost as a place of worship for statesmen is threatened with a new express highway. There has also been much recent talk of building one the length of the Chesapeake and Ohio Canal, the historic old canal which was conceived by George Washington and later built for the purpose of opening up the lands beyond the Appalachian mountains to settlement and trade. When a Washington newspaper ran editorials advocating the construction of a modern parkway along the canal the defenders of wilderness rose up in defense. Most powerful spokesman was Justice William O. Douglas of the Supreme Court of the United States, who challenged the writers of the editorials to walk the length of the canal with him so that they might see for themselves the wisdom of keeping the historic waterway with its picturesque lock houses as an unspoiled area.

The newsmen accepted the challenge. Starting at Cumberland, Mary-

---

[*]*Washington—City in the Woods* (Washington, D.C.: The Audubon Society of the District of Columbia, 1954).

"The locks with gate beams made of oak still stand." The C&O Canal, R. T. Peterson, from *Wild America*

land, on a cold gray morning, the last day of winter, they stepped briskly away from an old stone lock house toward Washington, 189 miles away. Close on their heels followed thirty-four other woods-walkers of every hue and stripe—bird watchers, photographers, conservationists, reporters, a radio broadcaster (who made tape recordings of birds and other sounds along the way), and also two stray dogs. When the motley collection of hikers approached Washington eight days later (some had dropped out) they were greeted by groups all along the path. Canoeists in the canal carried signs such as: LESS CARS—MORE CANOES. A Park Service sight-seeing barge drawn by two mules met the foot-weary travelers, who swarmed aboard, and the last five miles into the city became a triumphal procession—suggestive of Cleopatra's retinue on the Nile. While the good Justice sat in state on the poop of the barge with a twig of wisteria in his hand, crowds ran along the banks and waved from overhead bridges. Observers noted that somewhere along the line Douglas had got his chin into some poison ivy, but he was jubilant, for he had seemingly won his point: during the long hike the newsmen—in spite of their blisters—agreed that at least parts of the canal, the towpath, and its wild border of woodlands, should be preserved against the intrusion of highways. Let us hope that Douglas's effort proves not to have been a quixotic one.

Washington is a very satisfying city for the naturalist—if he does not mind the humid, almost tropical, summer climate. Here the facilities for those of his guild are second to none: wild country almost at the city's door; vast study collections in the Smithsonian and the National Herbarium; stacks of reference books—some almost priceless—at the Library of Congress; experts by the dozen, all willing to help, in the offices and laboratories of the Fish and Wildlife Service, the National Park Service, the National Forest Service, and the National Museum. Here, influential conservation organizations such as the National Wildlife Federation, the Nature Conservancy, the National Parks Association, the Wildlife Management Institute, and the Wilderness Society have their headquarters, as do magazines such as *The National Geographic Magazine*, *Nature Magazine*, *American Forests Magazine*, and *The Living Wilderness*. Of the local natural history societies, the Audubon Society of the District of Columbia is by far the largest, with 1200 members. It publishes *The Atlantic Naturalist* and is, perhaps, the most effective local Audubon group in the country.

If we had only one more full day, I said to James, we could run out to Patuxent, the research center of the Fish and Wildlife Service, and see the bird-banding setup.† James told me to forget that word *if*. We just couldn't do everything. There was a visa we must get for him at the Mexican embassy, some shopping to do, and some more packing.

James, the expert, directed the packing of the station wagon. Into it went our duffle bags, field clothes, sleeping bags, a bird blind, cooking equipment, a tape recorder, photographic gear, and even a portable refrigerator, in which we stored our film. We took so many books and maps that the car, now quite full up, was almost a traveling library. After strapping the big parabolic reflector (for the sound equipment) to the roof we were ready to go, ready for the next twenty thousand miles.

As we pulled out of the driveway a high wiry *zi-zi-zi-zi-zi-zi-zi* on one pitch sounded in the big oaks overhead. The first blackpoll warbler had arrived; spring migration was already nearing its climax.

---

†More than 7,000,000 North American birds have been banded (or ringed); 500,000 are added yearly. The little aluminum leg-bracelets carry numbers which are duly recorded on punch cards and kept on file at Patuxent, near Laurel, Maryland.

Fire Tower

Maurice Brooks (b. 1900)

Maurice Brooks, a former professor of wildlife management at West Virginia University, has been a renowned spokesman for the Appalachians for over fifty years. His book, *The Appalachians,* was selected to launch Houghton Mifflin's *The Naturalist's America* series. It covers the entire area both geographically— from Gaspe to Georgia—and ecologically—from forestry practices to salamanders.

Following is the chapter on the fire tower at Gaudineer Knob. Most serious natural history enthusiasts in the Central Atlantic have visited Gaudineer Knob, probably several times. Brooks's book may have provided the incentive to visit there. It certainly gave its readers new insights into the history, beauty, and ecology of the area. Although modern fire control methods have replaced the tower and its watchers, to us and to a multitude of fellow nature enthusiasts, the fire tower remains the symbol of the central Appalachians, a beautiful and unique area.

From *The Appalachians* (Boston: Houghton Mifflin, 1965)

A FIRE TOWER is a comforting sight, in settled country or in the wilderness. It stands as evidence that someone cares about the forest, and has made plans to keep it growing—green and productive. When fires start, and they will, the lookout in his tower sets in motion a chain of action, a planned attack that sooner or later will lead to the control of any blaze. This is a welcome thought to conservationists.

I invite your attention to Gaudineer Knob in southeastern West Virginia, and to the tower the United States Forest Service has erected on its summit. Don Gaudineer, for whom the peak was named, was a ranger on the Greenbrier district of the Monongahela National Forest. When fire threatened his family he gave his life to save them, and so a fine mountain bears his name.

The tower area is about thirty minutes in latitude south of Washington, a strange place for the red spruce forest that covers slope and crest. Elevation, however, tells the story. At the base of the tower Gaudineer Knob is 4445 feet above sea level. In average temperature and length of growing season this mountaintop is climatically a part of northern New England or eastern Canada. Plants and animals respond to these conditions; many of those present would be at home in New Brunswick, or north of Lake Superior. Here is a precious bit of Canada which spills southward along Appalachian ridges.

Cheat Mountain range, of which Gaudineer is a part, is well watered, and so for most of the year fire danger is minimal or nonexistent. During spring and fall, however, things are different, and there is the ever-present threat of a blaze that runs wild. From March to May and from October to December the tower will be manned, a lookout in the glass-walled cabin that stands above a young spruce forest.

From his platform above the trees a lookout approaches the condition of the cliché: he comes near to being master of all he surveys. He is higher than any other nearby object, and so for long distances his view is unobstructed. The safety and welfare of thousands of acres are in his keeping; he knows his job and accepts his responsibility. By the way, the gender of my pronouns would often be wrong; a good many girls and women serve the Forest Service and the states as lookouts.

Gaudineer Tower is strategically located. It stands on three divides, one political, two topographic. A portion of the tower is in Randolph County, the remainder in Pocahontas County. Westward Shavers Fork of the Cheat River gathers its waters for a journey northward to the Monongahela, and to Pittsburgh's Golden Triangle, where the Ohio is born. East of the tower is the Greenbrier, whose waters, before they too eventually join the Ohio, will have become a part of the New River, a stream that flows northwestward from Ashe County, North Carolina. To the west of the tower, mountain peaks are jumbled and mountain ridges deeply dissected. This land is a portion of the Allegheny Plateau, the topography of which is broken and unsystematic. To the east, however, the ridges are long and remarkably smooth. They form a part of the Ridge and Valley Province where streams in the valleys have a trellised pattern, and mountain folds are oriented to a northeast-southwest axis.

In the panoramic sweep from Gaudineer there are few cleared areas. A short distance away is the small opening of White Top, where, during the Civil War, Union forces built Fort Milroy to guard the Staunton-Parkersburg Turnpike, thus establishing the highest permanently occupied army camp that the long war knew. Toward the Greenbrier there are some glady areas, a few of which are flooded by beaver dams. Most of the landscape is forested, though, with second-growth spruce on the heights, and northern hardwoods—beech, birch, and maple—on the lower slopes.

Two miles south of the tower a paved highway, U.S. 250, crosses the mountains, but the road is out of sight. Beyond it is an authentic wilderness, a ridge known locally as Back Allegheny, with an elevation always above 4000 feet. In almost twenty miles no road nor trail follows its crest, and none crosses it except one lumber railroad. The original spruce forest was cut in the early 1900's, and a second harvest is being taken after fifty years.

A mile or so north of the tower is West Virginia's one remnant of original spruce forest, a 130-acre tract purchased at the insistence of Arthur Wood, who believed that future generations should know what an Appalachian spruce stand was like. Wood served as Supervisor of the Monongahela National Forest, and he left his imprint on many good things. In striking contrast to the ancient forest, one of man's newer ventures in space probing is nearby. At Greenbank is one of the world's great radio astronomy stations, and here the astrophysicists have been swinging the huge disk of their receiver to intercept possible signals from other sentient beings in outer space.

The lookout in his tower is not completely isolated. At hand is a telephone, and its ringing is an incongruous sound in a wild area. He also has companionship of a sort in other lookout stations. To the west he can see the tower on Barton Knob. Its management and ownership are different, since it is state-owned, but its purpose is the same. Farther north and west on clear days he may just make out Bickels Knob Tower, and to the east Smokecamp Tower is within easy sighting. Any of these may be helpful when there is a fire to locate.

Ordinarily the lookout is no Saint Simeon Stylites on a pedestal. He goes to ground level for water and to meet his body's needs. On days and nights of blessed rain he checks out with the ranger and returns to his own home. There are many times of low fire danger, and during these his vigilance is relaxed. Should conditions become threatening and high-class fire days develop, he is on the job with little respite. He knows, and disregards, the regular sources of smoke: portable sawmills here and there along a stream, the waste dump at Durbin, and the tannery at Frank. But let a strange smoke appear, particularly if it has the characteristic light color imparted by burning wood, and things begin to happen. On a platform in his cubicle is a circular map, oriented as to direction and with his own tower at its center.

Above the map is mounted an alidade which swings throughout the great circle of 360 degrees. He moves the alidade, sighting along its top, until a cross-hair squarely covers the smoke. Then he reads the bearing in degrees shown by the graduated margin of his map-holder. Next he estimates the distance from his tower to the smoke, not always an exact process, but helpful. Then and not until then, he telephones headquarters. He has done his job, and the responsibility passes to other hands.

In the meantime, if the smoke is a sizable one, lookouts on one or more neighboring towers will have sighted it and will be reporting their data. Soon headquarters can do some triangulating, establish the approximate location of the fire, and dispatch a crew to investigate and begin suppression if that is necessary. It's a good system and it works. In an area that suffers from frequent fires, the Monongahela National Forest is justly proud of its record. The average yearly burn is less than / of 1 percent—about three acres in each thousand.

The Forest Service welcomes visitors to Gaudineer Knob. For business uses, and for the public's convenience, their engineers have built a gravel-surfaced road to its summit. Here there are picnic areas beautifully screened by dense spruce hedges, and in these are tables and outdoor grills. Near the base of the tower a well provides cold water. And, *mirabile dictu*, there are few biting flies, even on a warm June day.

Visitors may climb to a platform surrounding the glassed-in cubicle on top of the tower, even when the tower is not manned. When the lookout is on duty it is good forest manners to ask his permission before climbing. No salutes of the quarter-deck are necessary, but the visitor is coming aboard what is temporarily the lookout's home craft. The similarity of a fire tower to a crow's nest will not escape old navy hands.

There is an interesting layering of living things apparent in the sixty-foot climb. At ground level the characteristic Gaudineer birds in summer are juncos and winter wrens. A dozen feet from the ground magnolia warblers are abundant. Red-breasted nuthatches search along the higher branches, and golden-crowned kinglets hunt tiny insects in outer twigs. The thirty-foot level is a good place for Blackburnian warblers; I found my only nest of these birds by looking squarely into it from halfway up the tower. The tallest of young spruces bear cones, these nearly always near treetop. When red crossbills are abundant, as they are some years, they feast on spruce seeds, using their crossed mandibles as chisel-like tools to open cone scales. The fortunate climber may watch them at their own level.

Above treetop, the view is likely to claim first attention, but a visitor

"Visitors may climb to a platform surrounding the glassed-in cubicle on top of the tower." Fire Tower, L. and L. Darling, from *The Appalachians*

might do well to take a long look at the young spruce forest below him, and to reflect on the cause of its being there. It is the result of one of those conjunctions of time and chance that have always fascinated the thoughtful.

Harvesting a spruce forest presents special difficulties to lumbermen. Spruce is a shallow-rooted tree, and it needs the support of nearby trees if it is to resist severe wind. When selection cutting is attempted, residual trees in the stand often blow down, a waste of wood and a major fire hazard. Clearcutting seems to be the only feasible lumbering procedure; but this cutting of all trees in a stand leaves none to produce seed. Much too often a fine spruce stand is followed in succession by ferns, briers, and such low-grade woody plants as aspens, fire cherry, and other species which foresters call "weed" trees. That this type of succession did not occur on Gaudineer is due to a narrow belt of tall spruces growing on the Greenbrier side of the mountain, just below the break of the first steep slope.

Some years before the Civil War a speculating land company bought a tract of 69,000 acres on the slope of Shavers Mountain. Their tract fronted for about seven miles along the eastern side of the mountain. To survey and mark their holdings the company hired a crew of men who must have found rough going in this wilderness. The crew did a good job, but its chief forgot one thing—the fact that a compass needle points to magnetic, not true north. In this area the angle of declination is about four degrees, a significant source of error on a seven-mile front.

An experienced Virginia surveyor, in checking the data, discovered the error but said nothing about it. Presently, however, when the sale was being concluded and the deeds recorded, he brought the error to light, and under a sort of "doctrine of vacancy" claimed the wedge of land left by a corrected survey. His title was established, and he and his heirs found themselves owner of a seven-mile strip of forest, aggregating almost 900 acres. While timber above and below the wedge was cut, this narrow holding was undisturbed. Its thickest end, a fringe of tall spruces on the near horizon, is just east of Gaudineer Tower. From these trees came seed to produce a new forest, a happy result of a hundred-year-old mistake. Northern birds, mammals, and plants are here because the young spruces, hundreds of acres of them, provide food and shelter.

Some of West Virginia's finest mountain country surrounds Gaudineer Tower. Just eastward is the long range of Middle Mountain, and along its crest the Forest Service maintains a road, forty miles through high country, most of it wooded and all a delight to the biologist. There is no better place in the state to look for wild turkeys, particularly in early morning of a late-summer day. Large areas on this mountain ridge were planted by Civilian Conservation Corps workers; new forests of spruce and pine are in being.

Beyond Middle Mountain, a distant, smooth line on the horizon is the Allegheny Backbone, here a secondary continental divide separating waters that flow down through the Potomac to Chesapeake Bay from those which join the New, the Great Kanawha, the Ohio, and the Mississippi on their way to the Gulf of Mexico. Spruce Knob, only a little higher than the remainder of the ridge around it, but still West Virginia's highest point at 4860 feet, is just visible on clear days.

To the south, Gaudineer Tower overlooks the upper reaches of the Greenbrier River, rich in the lore of logger and woodsman. Down through a valley sheltered by high mountains on either side, the Greenbrier flows through a southern extension of the great white pine forest. Thousands of acres of fine timber were here, and this was not long in coming to the attention of lumbermen. And then came an interesting discovery. The timber was here, with the water to carry it to mill, but mountain people were entirely without experience in log-driving. They could fell the trees and skid them to streambanks, but they could not ride them down the flood.

So here began one of the gaudy periods in mountain logging. Rivermen from northern streams, Maine and New Brunswick woodsmen, were imported to do the job, and for some years they labored, cutting timber and building splash-dams in winter, then awaiting the spring thaw and flood to carry their cargo to the mill. These men did not know Paul Bunyan (he was a Great Lakes creation, after all), but they had their own Bull of the Woods, Tony Beaver, whose exploits were limited only by the imagination of the storyteller. Lower Greenbrier towns saw lively days when the log-drivers arrived. And many a "Mc" or "Mac" on a valley name is evidence that some of these New Brunswick Scotsmen chose to settle along the river.

To the north and west, Gaudineer looks down on Cheat River country, a land of heavy second-growth forest, all of it high, and much of it roadless. So abundant is precipitation that vegetation from ground cover to forest crown grows in layers, each of which shelters its appropriate animal species. This makes for richness and variety in populations of living things.

The Gaudineer region is climactic in the mid-Appalachians, at the center of the highest and most extensive mountain mass between the White Mountains and the southern Blue Ridge in Virginia, North Carolina, and Tennessee. To a remarkable degree, it combines the qualities and characteristics of these widely separated ranges. It partakes of both North and South, and therein lies much of its attraction for naturalists. At times all the bird voices seem to be those of the North Woods, but suddenly one also hears a yellow-breasted chat, a hooded warbler, or a blue-gray gnatcatcher. The whole effect is delightfully confusing.

This mountain area is fast becoming something of a center for biologists and other outdoors people. The list of visitors is impressive—some of our foremost scientists, authors, and artists have known and enjoyed Gaudineer and its environs. Unlike so many of these wild areas, Gaudineer had its own resident observer, on the ground here for almost fifty years. His name was Harvey Cromer, and he began his working career as a lumberman, first in West Virginia, then in the Great Smokies. Still a young man, he returned to West Virginia, settled at Cheat Bridge, became a scout for a pulp and paper company, and, as the years passed, a mentor of the outdoors for all who would listen.

Harvey Cromer was never a scientist, and he would have shunned the name naturalist, but those living things around him which he hadn't seen and didn't know about were few indeed. I liked to visit him, and to ask all sorts of questions. If he didn't know he was quick to say so, but he usually came up with information, some of it astonishingly perceptive and accurate. He told me more about varying hares (he called them "snowshoe rabbits") and the mysterious disease which periodically strikes these mammals than I ever learned from any other field observer. He showed me a Bonaparte's gull which he had shot, identified, and had mounted—a strange bird to appear in this forested region. He was a calendar of outdoor events; he knew when and where things happened on the mountain. Some of his observations puzzled me as he told me about them, and they still do. I don't know what to say about his story of panther tracks in the snow on Gaudineer's slopes. He was usually careful and accurate, but if these big cats still occur, even casually, in West Virginia, why has no wildlife biologist been able to find trace of them?

I derive a certain comfort and satisfaction in thinking that these mountains still hold their secrets—not all the discoveries have yet been made. One summer a warbler (even that is an assumption) sang in the big spruces near Gaudineer's top. I heard it many times, I looked for it, unsuccessfully, I never have heard, there or elsewhere, another one like it. Some day I might know—but not yet.

Leaving the unknowns, it remains abundantly evident that, no matter what the season, there is always something worth seeing round and about Gaudineer. In autumn the lookout is on duty in his tower, and the foreground of his view is a sea of young spruce tops. In nice counterpoint to this dark green is the blaze of color on maple, birch, beech, and basswood just downslope. On fair days monarch butterflies—hundreds of them—drift southward, perhaps to winter in the Everglades. Occasional hawks pass over, although the tower is not on the side of the mountain most favored by migrating raptors.

Fall warblers, just as confusing as they are supposed to be, find much food in aphids that infest spruce twigs. There is constant scurrying among the chipmunks, and red squirrels are busy cutting and piling cones which will be their winter's food supply. Wild turkeys, safe enough from the hunter so long as they stay in rhododendron tangles, gobble at dawn and dusk.

This is a season of bright fruits, much of the color being supplied by deciduous hollies. Many people who admire evergreen American holly, with its Christmas associations, neglect the hollies which shed their leaves but leave a harvest of red fruits. There are three such species in the Gaudineer area, two of them widely distributed and well known. These are mountain holly (*Ilex montana*), the opalescent red fruits of which are at their best against the blue October skies, and winterberry (*I. verticillata*), a scarlet-berried shrub with fruits persisting into late winter. The third member of the holly group is long-stalked holly (*I. longipes*), a plant of limited distribution from West Virginia southward. It bears tremendous crops of large cerise fruits, each on a pedicel that holds it well away from the twig. It prefers to have its roots in water; in the Blister Swamp just below Gaudineer's summit there are thousands of these shrubs, and they provide one of autumn's most colorful effects. Like some other hollies, this one has a yellow-fruited form, the only known station being near White Top, about three miles from Gaudineer Tower.

Winter is a silent season on the heights. Few birds can find food under heavy snow and ice, and few care to weather arctic storms that sweep the crests. Every spruce needle acquires a coating of frost crystals, sparkling decorations that may last for weeks. Varying hares, now in spotless white pelage, search for the highbush cranberries, a favorite food at all seasons. A few ravens live on discards that other creatures overlook or reject.

Snow often piles deep, drifted by driving winds. This, too, has produced its story. Before the Civil War, mail was carried along the old Staunton-Parkersburg Turnpike from the upper Shenandoah Valley to Ohio River Settlements. Along the way were taverns and coach houses, a famous one, Traveler's Repose by name, a few miles from Gaudineer. One fall a new carrier took over the job, stopped at Traveler's Repose, liked the hospitality there, and stayed for the winter. After a while the people in Parkersburg, becoming impatient, managed to get word to Pittsburgh, thence to Washington, and a tracer was sent out to locate the missing carrier and his mail. Thereupon, he penned a famous letter, addressed to the Postmaster General. It concluded, "If the floodgates of hell were to open, and it were to rain fire and brimstone for six straight weeks, it wouldn't melt all the snow on Cheat Mountain, so if the people in Parkersburg want their damned old mail, let them come and get it!"

Spring comes slowly, and with many false starts. Along the south foot of Gaudineer Knob is a narrow swampy area, the Blister Swamp already mentioned. Here northern balsam fir grows, exudations on its trunk causing blisters, and accounting for the local name of the area. On warm nights, perhaps in April, spotted salamanders emerge from hibernation, seek forest pools for their mating, and deposit there the cottony egg masses that per-petuate their kind. As frost leaves the ground, earthworms become active, and woodcocks arrive to probe for them. Early nests of these birds will be built while there still is danger that snow will cover the eggs.

Farther up the slopes, where snow lingers, it will be May before spring wildflowers open under bare branches of northern hardwoods. Toward the last of that month, painted trilliums and pink lady's-slippers blossom just as leaves are opening on the trees. Among the spruces, flowers are few: oxalis and Canada mayflower are most common, and here and there heartleaf twayblades, tiny orchids of the north country, show their cleft-lipped blooms in early June.

Birds, too, are slow in reaching the high places. Until insects hatch, there is little for birds to eat in a spruce forest. Juncos need make only a short al-titudinal migration; they arrive with the first snowless days. Hermit thrushes also are hardy, and they are often scratching for food in early April, a month before the other nesting brown-backed thrushes—wood, veery, and Swainson's—appear. Northern waterthrushes begin singing in April, at home here on the heights well away from water. Most other summer resi-dents are on their breeding grounds by mid-May. Frost or even snow may yet come, but the birds are ready to set up housekeeping.

The summer visitor to Gaudineer must divide his time. He cannot af-ford to miss the massed beds of mountain laurel and rhododendron, these at their best as June turns to July. He must allow enough hours for wood warblers: from foot of mountain to its summit twenty-two warbler species are summer residents, more kinds than are known to nest on any other Ap-palachian peak. If he has an interest in the cold-blooded vertebrates, he will want to see the little gold-flecked Cheat Mountain salamander, a creature not known to occur outside this mountain range.

Just at dusk varying hares, now in summer brown and white, come out to eat grass beneath the fire tower. The platform above affords good views of their feeding and playing. Forest Service men like to see them, and try to encourage their presence. Ephe Olliver, Supervisor of the Monongahela Na-tional Forest, carries a sack of fertilizer in the back of his car, and when he visits a tower he scatters handfuls to promote grass growth.

Dusk also brings out the flying squirrels, here the larger northern species, near the southern limits of its range. Sometimes one will pause for a moment on an exposed snag near the tower. Winter wrens will still be singing, juncos chirping, and magnolia warblers giving querulous notes as though they were scolding the children.

But the dusk really belongs to the thrushes. Their full chorus begins earlier; at first most of the birds are well downhill, where wood thrushes will remain. As shadows creep upward, veeries and hermit thrushes seek the light toward the summit. Veeries usually keep to the undergrowth, but hermits like to sing from the highest tip of a spruce. Closest of all in approach to the tower are Swainson's thrushes. They seem reluctant to miss one daylight moment, one ray from the summer sunset. As the tower is on the highest point, so are the birds drawn to it in the dusk. Finally, singing must stop, there are a few sleepy chirps—then silence. The June day has ended.

This is fine country, and I keep returning to it. I am happy that it is protected—the tower is a symbol and a promise. This bit of the northland is a rare thing. It enables me to visit Canada or New England without leaving the boundaries of my native state. Strongly as one may feel the north-country atmosphere at Gaudineer, it is pleasant to have confirmation from others. When one of the international ornithological societies met in West Virginia, we arranged a field trip to the Cheat Mountain range. I walked along a trail with friends from Ontario, Doris and Murray Speirs. They looked at the spruce forest and the plants growing within its shade. They listened to the birds and watched the butterflies. They absorbed the atmosphere of the region, and reacted to its charm. Finally Doris turned to her husband and said, "Why, Murray, we're back home."

Down the Coast to Assateague

Charlton J. Ogburn Jr. (b. 1911)

A birdwatcher since childhood, Charlton Ogburn has written several books
on natural history subjects: *The Winter Beach*, which won the Burroughs
Medal in 1979, *The Southern Appalachians* (1975), and *The Adventure of Birds*
(1975). Observations of birds even appear in *Marauders* (1959), the story of
his World War II experiences with Merrill's Marauders in Burma. "Down
the Coast to Assateague" provides not only a description of the Eastern
Shore coast in winter but also the progress of conservation: the need, the
controversy, and the results.

The objections to the creation of the Assateague National Seashore
raised in the 1960s are the same as those raised elsewhere today under the
banners of property owners' rights and economic progress. The inadvis-
able development of central Assateague may be an extreme example of
disregard for natural forces, but the story remains relevant today.

From *The Winter Beach* (New York: William Morrow and Company, 1966)

IF YOU ARE following the changing vegetation and making that your
criterion, you will find that the South begins at Delaware Bay. (Another geographical fact little realized is that Delaware is almost entirely south of the
Mason-Dixon Line.) There the pitch pine finally gives up the coast, having
descended it from Maine and on its way dominated Cape Cod and much of
Long Island before coming even more fully into its own in New Jersey: the
famous Pine Barrens, whence the American armies of the Revolution and
the War of 1812 were supplied with weapons forged of local bog-iron
smelted over fires of pitch pine and which, after the exhaustion of the virgin
timber a century ago, were for years a virtual lost world, occupy more than
two thousand square miles behind the coastal marshes in the southern part
of the state.

The loblolly, which replaces the pitch pine on the coast of Delaware, is a
much taller tree with longer needles and cones and in maturity with a massive head of foliage borne on a bole that may rise straight and branchless for

from thirty to fifty feet; where the pitch pine is picturesque and meager, the loblolly is statuesque and lordly. With the loblolly comes the wax myrtle, a more-delicate-leaved, smaller-berried, evergreen sister of the bayberry. On the beach, behind the dunes, where the loblolly is as stunted and depressed as the pitch pine farther north, the wax myrtle grows the same low, dense clumps as the bayberry, which it wholly replaces below North Carolina, but in the woods it forms open shrubs ten feet tall and farther south becomes a small tree. Also on the coast of Delaware you begin to come up with birds that in the north are considered harbingers of spring. In a field near a commemorative stone marking the site of a Dutch settlement of 1631 on an inlet below Cape Henlopen, I saw grackles feeding in the stubble, and a little farther on, red-winged blackbirds. (The Dutch settlement, which was wiped out by Indians the next year and re-established the year after that, was something else I had never heard of.)

On the beach at Cape Henlopen itself came Bonaparte's gulls. In the graduated series of the family *Stercorariidae*, running from the swallowlike least tern to the great black-backed gull, which puts one in mind of an albatross, the Bonaparte's gull stands less than a quarter of the way along, a most engaging little gull, white on the leading edge of its pearly wings, almost as light and lively in the air as a tern and with a habit of flying with its small, black beak pointed down, tern-fashion. I had seen a few on Shinnecock Bay, but here there were six or seven hundred. They were stretched out on the water just behind the surf for a quarter of a mile along the outer, leeward side of the point. When the waves carried those in front into the breakers they would rise like a flock of white pigeons in a city square and settle elsewhere. Many were looking down and dabbling in the water. Evidently a churning-up of sea-lettuce from the bottom explained the congregation. The lovely creatures in their numbers and behavior seemed tinged with mystery, however, as if this were a visitation from another world, purer and gentler.

The pretty sight was one I felt I had earned, for the incessant and nerve-racking northwester in which I had been walking scorched the face; the temperature did not rise above 25 degrees all that day. The wind was driving straight down the bay, herding the crowded, frothing waves toward the sea, with the result that those along the southern shore broke directly upon the beach on the inner side of the Cape, which juts up into Delaware Bay like a lower incisor tooth in an open mouth. The result was also to illustrate a principle of wave action I had heretofore only read of. Where one might have expected that on the other, leeward side of the Cape the waves would be rushing away from the shore, still obedient to the wind that created them, the peninsula so bent them that all around it they were coming in directly upon the beach, those on the far side squarely into the wind, having been turned completely around. . . . Two calico-patterned shore birds called turnstones, plump, pink-legged and dovelike, took off in the guise of flying chocolate sundaes, emitting katydid cries.

Did it matter that this was rather far north for the turnstone in winter, or what the behavior of Bonaparte's gulls may be, or how the pitch, loblolly and longleaf pines divide up the coast, or that the sand on the beach at Brigantine is dark grey and fine? I thought a bit about the question as I drove along.

The shore in winter is rather spare, to say the least. It is nature with few concessions to the human need for comfort. Its emptiness, where the beach is devoid of any marks of human habitation, will take you back to a past before man appeared on earth and perhaps give you an inkling of what it would be like to find yourself returned to that past beside an ocean that had never known a keel, the only one of your kind in existence. On the other hand, the tokens elsewhere at the shore of man's visitation do not much temper the sense of your isolation. The snow-fencing erected to hold the sands (of which there must be a thousand miles along the Atlantic coast), the interminable lines of telephone poles with the wires sagging between them, the uninhabited and dissipated-looking cottage warrens created a more sordid desolation. The seasonal ebb of the human sea from the shore leaves hundreds of miles of resorts nine-tenths deserted.

Cape Henlopen presented a special case of dereliction. There was a sentry-box and then one barracks after another and street after street of other barracks and smaller houses—officers' quarters—all deserted and silent. This was Fort Miles, now decommissioned and acquired by the State of Delaware. It was, I am glad to say, to be converted into a park which would include the whole cape and the coast for two and a half miles south of it, but the conversion had not yet started. The street signs, beginning to rust, still stood at the intersections. Of a few buildings, only charred ruins remained. Evidently vandals had got to them. One authorized demolition crew was at work. Of other sign of life there was none except for a man climbing a concrete tower overlooking the point. This stark, cylindrical structure, cut with a slot or two like those in a knight's visor, was incongruously capped with an endearing little clapboard cottage which, to judge by the wind vane and anemometer atop it, was a weather station.

Similar towers, resembling concrete silos, stood at intervals down the coast, relics of the war like helmeted giants still gazing out through those narrowed apertures across the sea, too mindless to grasp that the danger had passed. On the coast of Maryland the summer cottages, many in pastel shades, overshadowed by big apartment motels, occupied the shore five ranks deep, mile upon mile, back from an ocean and beneath a sky that alike were hard, bright and cold as the bitter wind that still was blowing. I have never beheld a scene of human abandonment on such a scale as that from Bethany Beach to Ocean City—not that it was not greatly to be preferred to the same scene in summer when, I understand, proclamation-bearing aircraft and boats blaring through loudspeakers patrol off shore advertising local night spots. Locked-up churches and empty gas stations witnessed the completeness of the evacuation.

So it is that traveling along the shore in winter by yourself you are apt to discover your capacity for loneliness. If at the same time you discover that your interest in the nature of the outer world is undiminished you can account yourself fortunate. That was the answer that came to me to the question of whether the succession of plants and birds, the physics of wave-motion and the varying structure of beaches were important; if you thought they were, you had much to be grateful for—and whether you did was likely to depend (to be realistic about this) upon whether you had associates who thought they were and would willingly listen to what you had to report about them. In that, I knew myself to be especially well off.

But of course the question could be pressed further. Suppose the circumstances of the wintry shore were carried to their logical extreme and one found oneself at sea in a sinking ship beyond hope of rescue. Would one then have an eye for the processes of the universe? I should have liked to think that, failing an ability to execute in the time remaining a stanza of verse that would epitomize man's experience on earth, I had it in me to absorb myself during that final ordeal in taking notes on the performance of such birds as might be present (shearwaters would be a possibility even in mid-Atlantic) with a view to plugging them in a bottle addressed to the Secretary of the Smithsonian Institution before the waters closed over me. My recognition that I should be as little up to the one as capable of the other did not perturb me as it should have done for the simple reason that I had grounds for more immediate concern. I fell far short at the best of times of such reasonable standards as those set by Sir Thomas Browne. My observation of nature was desultory in the extreme. I had engaged in precious little "judicious enquiry" into God's acts or "deliberate research into his creatures." I had not been one of those—much as I applauded them—who in doing so "highly magnifie him." We are not all equal to exacting disciplines. I was one of "those vulgar heads that rudely stare about, and with a gross rusticity admire his workes." Still, it could be argued that admiring his works with a gross rusticity is preferable to not admiring them at all. And I could testify that finding them admirable makes a difference in the state of mind of a traveler in the realm of the winter sea, even if it might not alone sustain him in the final pass—since, as Sir Thomas points out, "the long habit of living indisposeth us for dying."

On Assateague Island, I found, admiration came easily from the moment of my arrival. When I had marched through the dunes to the beach the ocean lay before me like a deep-blue plain, quieted beneath the stroke of the daylong, offshore wind, its surface disturbed only by the low swells from the far distance that appeared as darker lines upon it and spent themselves on the beach with a small, last-minute crack or a mere tired collapse. It was quiet enough for a flock of gulls to be settling upon the water, apparently for the night. Across the whole expanse of the ocean the front of each wavelet reflected evanescently the indescribable soft orange that glowed above the horizon before fading into the azure. It was a sea of molten gems which fluidly expanded and contracted in the agitation of its surface, a sea of fable beside which one might have expected a mounted knight to appear to contemplate it, casque in arm. Behind, the thinnest paring of a moon hung over the darkening woods. These were part of the great loblolly and dense deciduous forests rich in hollies up to thirty feet tall of the mainland coast of Maryland. In passing through them on the road from Berlin there had been a feeling of remoteness—the first I had since leaving Maine—by which I had known that I was truly in the South.

Assateague is a southern Fire Island. The similarities are remarkable. Both are thirty-three miles long, though the former, being wider, contains 18,000 acres (almost thirty square miles) to the latter's 5,700. Both are edged on the outer side by an excellent beach (Assateague's magnificent in its breadth) and on the inner, along the bays they enclose, by salt marshes, ragged in shoreline. Both islands had been separated from the barrier beaches above them, of which they had previously formed a part, by a storm, and the storms that cut the new inlets occurred within two years of each other, in 1931 and 1933. Both have since then been accessible until recently only by ferry, which impeded their settlement. The lower tip of each, for four miles, is a state-operated public recreational area, a state park in the case of one and, in the case of the other, Federal land leased to an agency of the state—the Chincoteague-Assateague Bridge and Beach Authority. But here is a difference: the lower nine miles of Assateague, comprising all the portion in Virginia and half the acreage of the whole, has been in Federal ownership for some years—since 1943, to be exact—having been purchased with the proceeds of duck-stamps and designated (by a misnomer) the Chincoteague National Wildlife Refuge. In the past several years, both islands have been connected with the mainland by two bridges each, and in each case one bridge is a few miles from the lower tip and the other about a fifth of the way down from the upper. In both cases a local park was created at the end of the upper bridge—a small county park in one, a two-mile-long Maryland state park in the other. In both cases the major bridge was opened in 1964. In both the plans for the bridge precipitated the question of the island's future and joined conservationists and exploiters in a battle that resounded across the country. The objective of the former in both cases was the designation of the island as a National Seashore. In both, private interests pressed for building permits till the eleventh hour and by recourse to the courts defeated the efforts of the state executive to deny them. Fewer permits were issued for Assateague, but they included permits for a motel and a $100,000 tavern.

But there have been significant dissimilarities. The occupation of Fire Island was started several generations ago but remained confined mostly to the lower half of the island. Only in the 1950's did real-estate promotion begin on Assateague—but it got under way then with a vengeance. Buying up the land at a reputed fifteen to thirty dollars an acre, a developer laid out a fifteen-mile-long subdivision consisting of 6,000 half-acre lots (1,268 zoned commercial) and occupying the middle half of the island. Calling the development Ocean Beach, he constructed a sand-asphalt road through it with a spur to a ferry-landing. Prospects, a bitter witness recalled to a Congressional subcommittee, "were swayed by high-pressure advertising, whole-page advertising, Mister, 'God is love; love thy neighbor as thyself,' at a cost of $2,000 to $5,000 per page." The developer, he recalled, "used to have a prayer meeting every time he held a sales meeting." Whether by these or other methods, lots were disposed of to 3,200 buyers and summer cottages began to be built. The hope of bringing the island into the National Park system, which went back thirty years, would surely have been doomed but for the intervention of Providence. In March 1962 a violent storm struck the coast, inundating much of Assateague, destroying thirty-two of the houses so far constructed and damaging seven of the remaining eighteen. The doubtful feasibility of the kind of settlement of the island called for by the planners of Ocean Beach seemed to be demonstrated; said a survey prepared by the Bureau of Outdoor Recreation, "A large part of the central section of the island is 1.5 feet above mean sea level (only a few inches above mean high tide) which would seem to indicate that in times of rough weather a substantial portion of the island is awash." Circumstances which led to the suicide of Ocean Beach's developer gave the conservationists a second chance.

The battle was to run for three and a half years. Whereas Fire Island's inhabitants stood to gain by the creation of a National Seashore which would be confined to the largely unsettled portion of the island and supported it, the lot-owners of Assateague would be prevented from becoming inhabitants by a National Seashore which would necessarily require their holdings, and they fought it. In the metropolitan area of New York, where open space is a rarity, a sophisticated and informed public could appreciate the value of a seashore park. In rural Worcester County, in which the Maryland portion of Assateague is situated, opinion was formed by small businessmen and property-owners concerned for the tax base.

The verdict of the storm was by no means accepted by the local interests. They contended that the seaside resorts to the north had been hard hit by the storm but had weathered the damage. They were unmoved by the rejoinder of the publisher of *The Worcester Democrat*, who pointed out that in Ocean City, which had the benefit of over seventy-five years of private development, the damage had been repaired only at a cost of a million dollars in state funds and of hundreds of thousands in the work done by the Corps of Engineers in the restoration of the dune line. They were not interested in the opinion of the Maryland Board of Public Works that to render Assateague suitable for a development like Ocean Beach, between seventeen and nineteen million dollars would have to be spent in installing utilities, raising elevations and erecting dunes—for which six hundred waterfront lots would have to be sacrificed—and that this figure would not include the 50 per cent of the cost of erecting the dunes that the Federal Government would be asked to pay.

At bottom, the issue was what it always is when conservationists and local investors clash: what kind of country are we going to have? The Worcester County Commissioners made no bones about their preference. They asserted that "the overwhelming part of the public which desires ocean front entertainment is invariably drawn to large population centers where comfortable hotel and motel accommodations are available, as well as shopping facilities and evening entertainment activities such as nightclubs, shopping areas, and amusement areas. . . . Worcester County believes that Assateague Island should be privately developed with private capital, initiative and energy in the American way, and not by socialistic bureaucrats desiring public ownership for the satisfaction of those few who do not have the industry and energy to provide for themselves." The Commissioners did not believe that the National Seashore "would become anything but a barren wilderness useful only to bird watchers." Even appeals to their enlightened material self-interest were futile. Congressman Roy A. Taylor of North Carolina spoke fruitlessly of the economic benefits that Cape Hatteras National Seashore had brought to adjacent communities. Senator Daniel B. Brewster of Maryland reminded them in vain that "estimates by competent independent economic consultants show that if the National Seashore is established, there would be an increase in the assessed valuation of the surrounding country that would add $20 to $25 million to the tax base of Worcester County. Even the most optimistic estimates of private developers presuppose an increase of only $18 million."

With the lot-owners themselves it was impossible not to sympathize, up to a point. "These people feel they're being cheated," a local businessman declared. "They're being cheated just after their bridge has been completed which, incidentally, they worked long and hard to get, and finally, when they thought that they'd at last be able to build on land they purchased some fifteen years ago, they are stopped." He added that he did not think they would be cheated monetarily by the Government, but, as one of the lot-owners exclaimed, "There's no price tag that you can hang on my dream." It was the American dream, certainly: a place of one's own away from it all. But we cannot eat our cake and have it too. If the lot-owners correctly identified the cake-eaters—those responsible for the increase of our population by three million a year and for the annual racking-up of 10,000 or 20,000 miles on ever more millions of motorcars, among whom are doubtless included many of the lot-owners themselves—they did not indicate it. Yet just as the interests of those who "might otherwise have had an opportunity to see a small portion of the land as the forces of nature originally shaped it"—as Robert L. Dwight of the Citizens Committee for the Preservation of Assateague Island put it—would have been sacrificed had the lot-owners been able to realize their piece of the American dream, so their piece of the dream must also have been sacrificed in time to the spreading human swarm. Indeed, at a public hearing in Baltimore, as Mr. Dwight recalled, "the spokesmen for the property-owners, themselves, pictured the ultimate creation of another Ocean City or perhaps even a Miami. They said it would just take a little time. The 3,000 houses would then get torn down to make way for this."

Had the prospects for the Assateague National Seashore been poor in February 1965 I could not have brought myself to visit the island. As it was, half-a-dozen bills authorizing the Seashore had been introduced in Congress and their objective had the active support of sportsmen's organizations, garden clubs, civic associations, labor unions, every conservation body in the country, local opinion in Chincoteague, both Maryland Senators and the Maryland and Virginia Congressmen concerned. The expectation that Assateague would be preserved gave one license to enjoy it.

I parked the bus overnight at the edge of the parking plaza in which the highway ended immediately after crossing the new 1.5-million-dollar bridge at the Maryland end. After breakfast by lamplight I was off before the sun had cleared the horizon, encouraged to see it rise large and orange above an ocean dappled with the peach color of the eastern sky. The inevitable telephone poles led off in both directions and the sandy lane beneath them was rutted with car tracks—to be expected even on a barrier island where footprints are few. In the distance in either direction one or two houses were in view. But on the whole the island seemed wild and unaltered; and with no other human figure to be seen on that broad, flat strand I felt like a castaway. The thermometer stood at 12 degrees and my hands and feet were like stones. Even if my binocular had not been as stiff as a single casting I could not have manipulated it for a better look at the horned grebes off shore, forty-five in one flock, more than I had ever seen before in one place. (An habitué of the coastal waters in the cold half of the year, the horned grebe in its drab winter garb might be likened to a delicate, diminutive Canada goose with its markings faded out and the suggestion of a beret on its head.) Everything was frozen: the silvery beach where the retreating waves had left it wet and the salt marshes on the other side. A few song sparrows keeping company with a band of myrtle warblers were puffed up against the cold. But the whole universe seemed united, as under the baton of a supreme conductor, in that dayburst, and the icy air, making one more appreciatively conscious of the warmth harbored within one's overcoat, made one also more aware—as the severity of the winter beach generally did—of how little to be taken for granted is the gift of life and how greatly therefore it is to be esteemed, not for what rare and exotic confections it may bring but as a moment-to-moment boon in itself. If the shore at its bleakest tested one's spirits it also invigorated what it tested. Perhaps Sir

Thomas Browne would have been less prone to count the world, as he said he did, "not an Inne, but an Hospitall, and a place, not to live, but to die in," if research into God's creatures had required of him more physical exertion in an intractable out-of-doors.

The sun must soon have made a difference in the temperature. At least I cannot remember thinking about the cold very long after the start of the three-hour walk I took down the island. I might not have gone so far but for the unexpected sight at a distance, by some loblolly woods, of a large, conventional, two-story house with gable roof and attic, paintless and, as my glasses showed after another ten or fifteen minutes, its windowpanes gone and its roof partly fallen in. I was told by two other visitors to the island whom I encountered that it was a former hotel, from half a century back, which had failed and been abandoned. These two, men in their sixties, were driving a fifteen-year-old, soft-tired sedan and had been stopping every quarter of a mile or so to get out and walk off into the brush, hallooing in a puzzling fashion; we had alternately been overtaking each other. They explained that they were looking for an eight-month-old, black-and-tan foxhound which had strayed from a pack they had been out with the evening before and asked if I had come upon him. But all I had seen were some of the famous Assateague ponies, eight of them, including a white and several piebalds, small, short-necked and with forelocks hanging down their foreheads; rather listless, they seemed.

I found the old hotel gutted and the interior strewn with lath and plaster. In the surrounding scrub growth were a rusting bedstead or two and similar hardware. Sitting on a fallen beam in the warming sun with a cup of coffee from a vacuum bottle and a package of graham crackers, I felt on extraordinarily good terms with the world, lighthearted and carefree, as I had on the road to Sankaty Head. One more degree of liberation and I should have dissolved in the limpid ether.

One might have hesitated to take it on oneself to decree the bankruptcy of the hotel and the destruction of the cottages hit by the storm of 1962, but that did not mean one had to repine over the wreckage, and I spared myself the distress of doing so. I am afraid I beheld even with composure the remains of the asphalt road that made Ocean Beach possible; they resembled strips of tread from a gigantic, blown-out tire. One cottage in this section, built on stilts just back from the beach, had survived intact to do disproportionate damage to the landscape, but the others were in ruins in various degrees. The best-preserved of these was a kind of town hall by the pinewoods which had been only displaced and left at an angle. The pines themselves, though twenty to thirty feet tall and a third of a mile from the sea, were browned from salt burn or dead at the top. Of some of the cottages, only pipes and other metal parts remained, maybe a hot-water-heater or the electrical connections. A ruptured wooden-stave water tank on low pilings with the rusting corpse of a Jeep pickup truck at its feet, evidently caught there by the storm, recalled photographs of the dust bowl of thirty years back.

Despite the cold, this was clearly a southern beach, and there was a jungly feeling about the dense hummocks of wax myrtle and stunted pines with a few bear oaks among them that rose behind fields of pale, silky, knee-high grasses.

After I had returned to the mainland to drive to the lower end of the island, signs of the South multiplied. I had hardly crossed the bridge before I ran into a flock of tens of thousands of grackles pouring through the woods and alighting on the grassy shoulders of the highway. (It was probably as many birds as I had ever seen at one time, and in the rustling of the myriad sable wings I must say there was something a little disturbing.) Even while the frosty air nipped your face and the glazed snow glistened in the furrows of the plowed fields you knew that this was a hot country in summer. It may have been the turkey vultures balancing on the air currents like tightrope artists with arms outstretched as they coasted over the treetops, or the sheen or pallor of the blue winter sky or the strength of the sun even on a freezing day. . . . On the other side of the Virginia line the woods were green with holly, wax myrtle and red bay—a skimpy little tree with leaves like the mountain laurel's. The curious farmhouses of eastern Virginia, only one room deep but two broad and two stories high, put in an appearance, and with them occasional plain white, lonely churches. The town of Chincoteague itself greeted one with a shabbiness that economic adversity in many forms has made also characteristic of much of the South. This was made more evident by contrast with the depersonalized, affluent neatness of the distant barracks, office buildings and huge saucer antenna of the Wallops Island missile-launching site which you see before the highway takes off across the marshes for Chincoteague Island. (The succession of islands below Chincoteague is Wallops, Assawoman.)

Lined up along the bay and the channel separating it from the marshy island over which one crosses from the mainland, Chincoteague is a well-sited town. Had it, like so many fishing ports, had the benefit for the past two or three generations of a well-to-do population of devoted summer-home-owners, it might today remind one of, say, Wellfleet or even of a minor Provincetown. As it is, it has had to depend on the harvest of oysters and clams, from which the returns are not great or easily come by. (Oysters are grown mostly on private beds planted with seed oysters dredged from public rocks by commercial fishermen. Clam beds are also seeded, the adults being garnered by dredging in winter and in summer by waders who locate them by signs in the mud or by feeling them underfoot.) In urging his constituency's need of the Assateague National Seashore, Congressman Thomas N. Downing stated that "when Chincoteague Naval Air Station moved out in 1959, this just put a blight, an economic blight, on the entire countryside." He went on to say that 55 per cent of the families in the area have an income of under $3,000 a year, that farms in the area were reduced by 25 per cent from 1950 to 1960 and the population by 13 per cent. What the National Seashore could mean, Chincoteague has in recent years had a chance to discover in the annual windfall of tourist dollars the July roundup of ponies brings. This nationally-reported event, managed by the Chincoteague Volunteer Fire Company, attracts more thousands every year to see the several hundred surplus animals herded, swimming, across the channel from Assateague to Chincoteague, where they are put up for auction.

On the waterfront at Chincoteague were piles of oyster shells like centuries-old middens, one the size of a two-story house. (Actually the shells are redistributed on the beds every season to give the young something to attach themselves to.) But the yards of the dealers, which dominate the main street, were trashy with bottles and papers, and the wharves and fishing boats, while they could be respected as genuine—they were not the toys of the idle rich—seemed run down and ill kept.

Chincoteague being famous for its oysters, particularly those of Tom's Cove (now part of the Refuge), I decided to suspend my rule of eating in the bus and have half a dozen of the delicacies. But the plump waitress behind the counter in a restaurant advertising sea-food specialties seemed bewildered by an order for raw oysters. "Oysters on the half-shell?" she asked. "That or any other way they come uncooked," I said. She went and consulted with the owner, who pulled down the corners of his mouth and shook his head. In a booth two teen-agers sat with mouths agape listening addlebrained to a jukebox that thundered like the organ of a movie cathedral; one would have thought the instrument an artificial heart on which they depended for their lifeblood. . . . Another restaurant boasting that it served "all kinds of sea-food" was closed for the winter. I gave up.

But I should not construe too much from this experience. Thanks to the efforts of fifteen women of the town, an oyster museum is now planned for the Chincoteague waterfront. The museum will tell the full story of the oyster biologically, historically and commercially, with living exhibits, and the embassies of other oyster-producing countries have promised cooperation. Chincoteague, it would seem, is getting the idea. It could well be transformed by the National Seashore.

Meanwhile, if the town has the shortcomings of a community in the South bypassed by prosperity, one must acknowledge that it has also the virtues of a Southern community. The girls on the street were trimmer and prettier than those I had seen in comparable towns in the north, including Mount Desert and Cape Cod. And while the municipal dock was earth-filled and crude (I had developed a pretty taste in municipal docks) the policeman who directed me to it took me fatherly-fashion by the arm and made me welcome to spend the night there most cordially. More surprisingly, there was a clean, heated public toilet; the public toilet in the park at Bar Harbor was disdainfully closed for the season and I had seen none other anywhere.

In the South you are generally nearer the traditional or the primitive than you are in any other part of the country I know. This can be for the better and it can be for the worse. It is for the worse in my view, since I do not care to live in the atmosphere of a battlefield, in the persistence of the widespread Southern addiction to hunting, in which many rural Southerners are little disposed to suffer the interference of the law. The Ranger who drove me around the Chincoteague Wildlife Refuge—a tall young man with a narrow build and a narrow face, from Memphis, Tennessee, a graduate of the University of Mississippi—did not like to dwell upon the trouble caused by poachers; it was the business of the Refuge to get along with the public and win its good will. He could not, however, conceal his regret for his days in the Northwest where, as he said, the level of education was high and public support for game regulations strong. And from an acquaintance of mine who was informed about the local situation I had heard something of the lawlessness of the gunners in the area. Shooting over baited fields was habitual—even state legislators in Maryland, as I knew, being repeatedly caught in this practice. Shooting out of season and shooting in the Refuge were also common, and the Refuge wardens were in real danger. One had been shot a few years before and would have been killed by his assailant had not the latter's gun misfired when he came up to deliver the *coup de grace* by discharging it into his victim's head. For his offense he had been sentenced by the local court to a year in jail and was now to be seen in the streets of

Chincoteague, an accepted citizen of the community. It was my friend's opinion that anyone who killed a warden in this part of the state would have popular opinion on his side. I asked if the hunters could not see that it was to their advantage for wildfowl to have sufficient protection to provide hunting in the future. He scoffed. "If the world's last female duck were in range of one of these pot-gunners he'd shoot it without a moment's hesitation."

The Ranger escorting me admitted that the use of fixed traps in the Refuge for catching ducks for banding had to be abandoned owing to the frequency with which the captives would be lifted by some of the local inhabitants who also—illegally—set traps of their own. There was a lively black market for game and a delicacy like a black duck would bring four dollars, which was well worth stealing for, or otherwise breaking the law to get. Perhaps in this too the opportunities the National Seashore will bring will make a difference. At least I can imagine that law-enforcement may be more difficult when a quarter of the labor force is unemployed, as Congressman Downing says it has been at times in the Chincoteague area. Anyway, the Refuge now relied upon cannon-traps in snaring waterfowl for banding. These, by means of a bank of mortars, fired a net over a baited area. A few days before, 446 birds had been captured at one time with this device. The Canada geese had to be handled with care. The trick was to grasp their wings together at the base and hold them away from you. Their bite was not so bad but a blow from one of their wings could hurt. The herring gulls, on the other hand, had a bite that drew blood. Like other wildfowl men, the Ranger had little liking for the gulls.

At its lower extremity, Assateague ends in a hook much like the one in which Cape Cod ends at its upper. Just before the start of the hook it achieves its greatest width, one of over two miles; the end of the island rather resembles an open harness-clasp. Debouching from the bridge onto this part you come to a pine forest which in beauty is second to none I have ever seen, though admittedly I saw it at probably its uncommon best, with a low sun flooding it from the side with a ripe, rich light and glistening on the ice-encrusted snow, turning it to citron. A circular trail has been laid out through it. The terrain is steeply hilly, being formed of old dunes which rise to a maximum height of forty-seven feet, and some of the loblollies that largely make up the forest have a forty-or fifty-foot spread of massive limbs and trunks too big to encircle with your arms; for trees on a barrier beach these are giants. Among the hollies, myrtles and bays of the understory are bear oaks, some of which have trunks you can barely encompass with your two hands, which makes them giants too, of their kind. The forest might be the grounds of a Buddhist temple.

The pines extend northward along the inner side of the island but in diminished size, and the ones I saw where the land was narrower were browned like those at the Maryland end. The storm of 1962 had been the most damaging in thirty years. The former Coast Guard station up near the Maryland line, which had been in use by the Refuge, was wrecked. Where the seas had poured in on the southern portion, the island was bare and gaunt, a place of desolation. A line of dunes had now been constructed behind the enormous beach to stand off future storms—though of course no such defense-works could be wholly proof against the assaults of the sea.

In addition to the dunes, miles of dikes had been erected to create impoundments of fresh water and were being extended. It cannot have been much fun working on the dragline—a cranelike machine with a free-swinging bucket at the end of a boom which I saw parked by a ditch and which made me think of the picked-over carcass of a brontosaurus. "The sand gets in your hair, your clothes, your teeth, everywhere here," said the Ranger. His heart was unmistakably in the Northwest, even more in Alaska, to which his passion for wildfowl had led him to work his way before he had enlisted in the Fish and Wildlife Service and to which he was pining to return. "You ought to see the Mississippi Flyway," he said. "You can see a hundred thousand ducks at a time there. Lakes the size of these are covered solid." I had exclaimed over a dense line of black ducks on an unfrozen part of the impoundment. To me at least their thousands were impressive, as were the twenty snow geese and ten whistling swans that were with them. The male swans, their mating instincts already awakening, were sparring with each other. Two would stand erect in the water face to face, enormous wings flailing the air, magnificent as embattled stallions. They recalled, too, figures in a coat of arms; one saw them supporting a shield between them. Even the Ranger was moved by the sight we had from the tip of the hook, wondering for a moment if we were really seeing what we thought we were—a low-lying cloud of birds a mile away across the bay. It was indeed a flock of birds, immense as their numbers had to be to account for the mass. They were brants. When they put down on the opposite shore, the Ranger, after counting a minute fraction of the flock through his binocular and multiplying it by the denominator, came up with an estimate of fifteen thousand birds.

The nearly five-mile-long hook was the most monstrous unrelieved sand-waste I had yet met with. There was virtually nothing on it but whelks, but it was whelks from end to end, such a littering of whelk shells as one was stumped to find an explanation for—whelk shells the color of peach ice cream deepening to orange-pink on the inside of the coil and others dark grey with peach showing through. And they were all of full size, eight inches long and five wide at the maximum extent of the spiral.

In summer, according to my guide, the sand of the hook was so rutted with the tracks of beach-buggies it was hard to walk over. One can imagine the damage that must have been done to Assateague if the Refuge had not been in existence to seal the island off when the bridge from Chincoteague was built in 1962. As it is, just above the complex at the base of the hook, where the road from the bridge ends—restaurant, bathhouses and souvenir shop, all under the Bridge and Beach Authority—a fence across the beach keeps the buggies out of the Refuge proper, admission to which requires a permit. Robert Murphy, the writer, told me that when he had been there in August he had found it like Times Square on New Year's Eve.

We drove back to this spot at a good clip, it having been noticed that the needle of the pickup truck's gas gauge stood at "E." We made it as far as, but no farther than, the deep sand of the ramp over the dunes leading to the paved road before the engine commenced to falter. The Ranger turned it off at once, observing that if you ran a car to the last drop of fuel you could wear the battery out getting it started again after you had replenished the supply. Snapping on the radio transmitter in the dashboard, which gave out with a raucous blast, he reported our situation to headquarters. Replied a waggish voice from the receiver, "By the restaurant, eh? Ummm. I can't seem to find a map that would show where the restaurant is. Why don't you just walk back?" Nevertheless, a truck with a can of gas soon arrived.

Do not feed the ponies, said a sign beside the road. Why not? I asked. "For one thing, the ponies bite," the Ranger said. "For another, feeding them from cars would cause them to congregate on the road. They have pretty thin pickings and don't need much temptation. You notice how their ribs show." They were, to be sure, a somewhat lackluster lot. Here and there were some of them standing about, seemingly always well apart from one another and apathetic. They did not much suggest the thundering herd, wild with the love of freedom that one has been led to picture. But the actuality is not what counts. Thanks partly to a rather loosely imagined novel about the ponies by a writer of popular juveniles and the motion picture that followed it, they are championed by children all over the country, and consequently by adults as well. Though they compete with the native wildlife for forage, eking out a living on marsh grasses, the Refuge is stuck with them.

The bill to make a National Seashore of Assateague introduced in the new Congress by Thomas N. Downing, about which I heard on the radio at Chincoteague, expressly stipulated for the preservation of the ponies. And there can be no doubt, as the past chairman of the Chincoteague Fire Company's Pony Committee testified, that "the tourists who come to the Chincoteague area to see these pony herds contribute greatly to the economy of this depressed area." In 1965, no less than fifty thousand were reported to have come to see the roundup and sale. One wonders how many, by contrast, came to see what is native to the country: the waterfowl from millions of square miles of the northern half of the continent hard-pressed for the food and shelter offered by the Refuge, which is strategically located at the neck of the funnel of the great Atlantic corridor; the shorebirds for which Assateague is a concentration point on their astonishing hemisphere-to-hemisphere migrations, on which many fly fifteen thousand miles a year. Before Cape Hatteras National Seashore was created there were also wild ponies on Ocracoke Island, their origin explained by similar romantic stories (their ancestors were put ashore by Sir Walter Raleigh, or by pirates, or had swum ashore from a wrecked Spanish or Portuguese galleon), but there the Government got to the animals before fame did and rounded them up to keep them from destroying the grasses then being planted to stabilize the dunes; their descendants may be seen in a corral maintained by the Boy Scouts, for whom they make possible the novelty of a mounted troop.

I found myself much more drawn to another hoofed animal introduced to Assateague which, though less celebrated than the horses, seems to thrive better on what the island has to offer. At least the sika deer give that impression and seem to fit more naturally into the habitat, which is doubtless why I feel differently about them. If you keep your eyes open in the woods or along the edge of the woods you are more than likely to see a family-sized group of them. They are the size of the native white-tailed deer and have the whitetail's habit of standing stock-still and staring at you, inoffensively. But the sika is a quite different beast, of the genus *Cervus*, to which the American elk also belongs. Its face is shorter than the whitetail's, its eyes wide apart like a cow's, and it has a deep body and a dense furry coat with white spots down the spine and a white patch around the tail. The Ranger observed that as a result of the Imperial Japanese partiality toward sikas as gifts, the species is now found around the world. Partly because they are very thrifty feeders—as I could believe, seeing one browsing on wax myrtle—they quickly build up much larger and denser populations than the native deer, he said. Even heavy hunting may not keep their numbers down, for which reason their importation into Maryland is forbidden. Because the Chincoteague Wildlife Refuge was becoming overcrowded with sikas, an open season had been declared the preceding fall and 246 bucks, does and fawns been killed by local gunners. The Ranger approved of the hunt, being in favor of all "compatible" uses of refuges which would demonstrate their value to local sportsmen and win public support. (The Chincoteague Refuge is ordinarily completely closed to hunting because of its narrowness.) Given the inadmissibility of reintroducing wolves or even cougars— the preferable means of dealing with the overabundance of deer anywhere, in my view—I did not know what solution I should have proposed. But I was glad not to have been on hand to hear the cannonading and to see the faces of those who thought the sport enjoyable.

Speaking of the bill to create the Assateague National Seashore, Senator Brewster said on July 23, 1965: "If Congress fails now to complete action on this measure, there is little likelihood that private development can be longer forestalled. The American people will have lost the largest remaining undeveloped seashore between Cape Cod and Cape Hatteras and one of the very few remaining such areas in this country."

In September an Assateague National Seashore was authorized—but at a heavy price. In addition to the southernmost four miles of the island, which will remain leased to the Bridge and Beach Authority, and the two miles at the upper bridge, which will remain a Maryland state park—both these areas to be developed for "intensive use"—another six hundred acres below the state park will be leased out for commercial development, *and* the construction of a highway running the length of the island between the bridges is mandatory. Congressman Rogers C. B. Morton of Maryland stood on his "insistence" that the road be built. Such a road, said Congressman Downing, "would mean that those fifty million Americans we have been talking about [to whom Assateague would be accessible] could travel by automobile and really enjoy the island."

Heaven and Earth in Jest
and The Present

Annie Dillard (b. 1945)

Annie Dillard learned her craft in the writing program at Hollins College in Roanoke, Virginia, where she earned both a bachelor's and a master's degree. In her first book, a collection of poems titled *Tickets for a Prayer Wheel* (1974), she introduced many themes and images that she later incorporated into her essays, autobiographical prose, and fiction.

Published first in *Harper's* and then as a Book-of-the-Month Club selection, her second book, *Pilgrim at Tinker Creek*, brought her national acclaim and won the 1975 Pulitzer Prize for General Nonfiction. Although it is often classed as nature literature, the book is a poet's investigation of the possibilities for religious meaning in life within the intellectual confines of modern biological science's understanding of human nature. Sequestered in southwestern Virginia, Dillard prepared for writing, as Thoreau had at Walden, by creating a journal of impressions and ideas. She later transformed these into a seasonal record of her strange and wonderful quest for personal truth through the canons of western philosophy, science, and literature. The ideas that she encountered in round-the-clock bouts of reading were refracted through her experiences of the rural countryside, producing a mix of poetic response to nature and emotional and intellectual alarm at the realization that those ideas are inadequate explanations of her responses. Her resulting cry, "We don't know what's going on here," echoes the existential loneliness of the modern soul, reminding us of Raskolnikov's tortured mind. But unlike Dostoyevsky's fictive foil who must kill and suffer before he can love, Dillard improvises her own salvation in a gentle act of poetry: In one marvelous image she creates and justifies the deity that her spirit requires, *The poet is a bell rung by God*.

The success of *Pilgrim at Tinker Creek* earned Dillard a contributing editorship at *Harper's* and a scholar-in-residence position at Western Washington University at Bellingham where she taught creative writing and poetry. Her post-*Pilgrim* writing has added fiction to her continuing production of essays, poetry, and autobiography. She now resides in New England.

Both selections from *Pilgrim at Tinker Creek* (New York: Harper and Row, 1974)

Heaven and Earth in Jest

I LIVE BY a creek, Tinker Creek, in a valley in Virginia's Blue Ridge. An anchorite's hermitage is called an anchor-hold; some anchor-holds were simple sheds clamped to the side of a church like a barnacle to a rock. I think of this house clamped to the side of Tinker Creek as an anchor-hold. It holds me at anchor to the rock bottom of the creek itself and it keeps me steadied in the current, as a sea anchor does, facing the stream of light pouring down. It's a good place to live; there's a lot to think about. The creeks—Tinker and Carvin's—are an active mystery, fresh every minute. Theirs is the mystery of the continuous creation and all that providence implies: the uncertainty of vision, the horror of the fixed, the dissolution of the present, the intricacy of beauty, the pressure of fecundity, the elusiveness of the free, and the flawed nature of perfection. The mountains—Tinker and Brushy, McAfee's Knob and Dead Man—are a passive mystery, the oldest of all. Theirs is the one simple mystery of creation from nothing, of matter itself, anything at all, the given. Mountains are giant, restful, absorbent. You can heave your spirit into a mountain and the mountain will keep it, folded, and not throw it back as some creeks will. The creeks are the world with all its stimulus and beauty; I live there. But the mountains are home.

The wood duck flew away. I caught only a glimpse of something like a bright torpedo that blasted the leaves where it flew. Back at the house I ate a bowl of oatmeal; much later in the day came the long slant of light that means good walking.

If the day is fine, any walk will do; it all looks good. Water in particular looks its best, reflecting blue sky in the flat, and chopping it into graveled shallows and white chute and foam in the riffles. On a dark day, or a hazy one, everything's washed-out and lackluster but the water. It carries its own lights. I set out for the railroad tracks, for the hill the flocks fly over, for the woods where the white mare lives. But I go to the water.

Today is one of those excellent January partly cloudies in which light chooses an unexpected part of the landscape to trick out in gilt, and then shadow sweeps it away. You know you're alive. You take huge steps, trying to feel the planet's roundness arc between your feet. Kazantzakis says that when he was young he had a canary and a globe. When he freed the canary, it would perch on the globe and sing. All his life, wandering the earth, he felt as though he had a canary on top of his mind, singing.

West of the house, Tinker Creek makes a sharp loop, so that the creek is both in back of the house, south of me, and also on the other side of the road, north of me. I like to go north. There the afternoon sun hits the creek just right, deepening the reflected blue and lighting the sides of trees on the banks. Steers from the pasture across the creek come down to drink; I always flush a rabbit or two there; I sit on a fallen trunk in the shade and watch the squirrels in the sun. There are two separated wooden fences suspended from cables that cross the creek just upstream from my tree-trunk bench. They keep the steers from escaping up or down the creek when they come to drink. Squirrels, the neighborhood children, and I use the downstream fence as a swaying bridge across the creek. But the steers are there today.

I sit on the downed tree and watch the black steers slip on the creek bottom. They are all bred beef: beef heart, beef hide, beef hocks. They're a human product like rayon. They're like a field of shoes. They have cast-iron shanks and tongues like foam insoles. You can't see through to their brains as you can with other animals; they have beef fat behind their eyes, beef stew.

I cross the fence six feet above the water, walking my hands down the rusty cable and tightroping my feet along the narrow edge of the planks. When I hit the other bank and terra firma, some steers are bunched in a knot between me and the barbed-wire fence I want to cross. So I suddenly rush at them in an enthusiastic sprint, flailing my arms and hollering, "Lightning! Copperhead! Swedish meatballs!" They flee, still in a knot, stumbling across the flat pasture. I stand with the wind on my face.

When I slide under a barbed-wire fence, cross a field, and run over a sycamore trunk felled across the water, I'm on a little island shaped like a tear in the middle of Tinker Creek. On one side of the creek is a steep forested bank; the water is swift and deep on that side of the island. On the other side is the level field I walked through next to the steers' pasture; the water between the field and the island is shallow and sluggish. In summer's low water, flags and bulrushes grow along a series of shallow pools cooled by the lazy current. Water striders patrol the surface film, crayfish hump along the silt bottom eating filth, frogs shout and glare, and shiners and small bream hide among roots from the sulky green heron's eye. I come to this island every month of the year. I walk around it, stopping and staring, or I straddle the sycamore log over the creek, curling my legs out of the water in winter, trying to read. Today I sit on dry grass at the end of the island by the slower side of the creek. I'm drawn to this spot. I come to it as to an oracle; I return to it as a man years later will seek out the battlefield where he lost a leg or an arm.

A couple of summers ago I was walking along the edge of the island to see what I could see in the water, and mainly to scare frogs. Frogs have an inelegant way of taking off from invisible positions on the bank just ahead of your feet, in dire panic, emitting a froggy "Yike!" and splashing into the water. Incredibly, this amused me, and, incredibly, it amuses me still. As I walked along the grassy edge of the island, I got better and better at seeing frogs both in and out of the water. I learned to recognize, slowing down, the difference in texture of the light reflected from mudbank, water, grass, or frog. Frogs were flying all around me. At the end of the island I noticed a small green frog. He was exactly half in and half out of the water, looking like a schematic diagram of an amphibian, and he didn't jump.

He didn't jump; I crept closer. At last I knelt on the island's winterkilled grass, lost, dumbstruck, staring at the frog in the creek just four feet away. He was a very small frog with wide, dull eyes. And just as I looked at him, he slowly crumpled and began to sag. The spirit vanished from his eyes as if snuffed. His skin emptied and drooped; his very skull seemed to collapse and settle like a kicked tent. He was shrinking before my eyes like a deflating football. I watched the taut, glistening skin on his shoulders ruck, and rumple, and fall. Soon, part of his skin, formless as a pricked balloon, lay in floating folds like bright scum on top of the water: it was a monstrous and terrifying thing. I gaped bewildered, appalled. An oval shadow hung in the water behind the drained frog; then the shadow glided away. The frog skin bag started to sink.

I had read about the giant water bug, but never seen one. "Giant water bug" is really the name of the creature, which is an enormous, heavy-bodied brown beetle. It eats insects, tadpoles, fish, and frogs. Its grasping forelegs are mighty and hooked inward. It seizes a victim with these legs, hugs it tight, and paralyzes it with enzymes injected during a vicious bite. That one bite is the only bite it ever takes. Through the puncture shoot the poisons that dissolve the victim's muscles and bones and organs—all but the skin— and through it the giant water bug sucks out the victim's body, reduced to a juice. This event is quite common in warm fresh water. The frog I saw was being sucked by a giant water bug. I had been kneeling on the island grass; when the unrecognizable flap of frog skin settled on the creek bottom, swaying, I stood up and brushed the knees of my pants. I couldn't catch my breath.

Of course, many carnivorous animals devour their prey alive. The usual method seems to be to subdue the victim by downing or grasping it so it can't flee, then eating it whole or in a series of bloody bites. Frogs eat everything whole, stuffing prey into their mouths with their thumbs. People have seen frogs with their wide jaws so full of live dragonflies they couldn't close them. Ants don't even have to catch their prey: in the spring they swarm over newly hatched, featherless birds in the nest and eat them tiny bite by bite.

That it's rough out there and chancy is no surprise. Every live thing is a survivor on a kind of extended emergency bivouac. But at the same time we are also created. In the Koran, Allah asks, "The heaven and the earth and all in between, thinkest thou I made them *in jest*?" It's a good question. What do we think of the created universe, spanning an unthinkable void with an unthinkable profusion of forms? Or what do we think of nothingness, those sickening reaches of time in either direction? If the giant water bug was not made in jest, was it then made in earnest? Pascal uses a nice term to describe the notion of the creator's, once having called forth the universe, turning his back to it: *Deus Absconditus*. Is this what we think happened? Was the sense of it there, and God absconded with it, ate it, like a wolf who disappears round the edge of the house with the Thanksgiving turkey? "God is subtle," Einstein said, "but not malicious." Again, Einstein said that "nature conceals her mystery by means of her essential grandeur, not by her cunning." It could be that God has not absconded but spread, as our vision and understanding of the universe have spread, to a fabric of spirit and sense so grand and subtle, so powerful in a new way, that we can only feel blindly of its hem. In making the thick darkness a swaddling band for the sea, God "set bars and doors" and said, "Hitherto shalt thou come, but no further." But have we come even that far? Have we rowed out to the thick darkness, or are we all playing pinochle in the bottom of the boat?

Cruelty is a mystery, and the waste of pain. But if we describe a world to compass these things, a world that is a long, brute game, then we bump against another mystery: the inrush of power and light, the canary that sings on the skull. Unless all ages and races of men have been deluded by the same mass hypnotist (who?), there seems to be such a thing as beauty, a grace wholly gratuitous. About five years ago I saw a mockingbird make a straight vertical descent from the roof gutter of a four-story building. It was an act as careless and spontaneous as the curl of a stem or the kindling of a star.

The mockingbird took a single step into the air and dropped. His wings were still folded against his sides as though he were singing from a limb and not falling, accelerating thirty-two feet per second per second, through empty air. Just a breath before he would have been dashed to the ground, he unfurled his wings with exact, deliberate care, revealing the broad bars of white, spread his elegant, white-banded tail, and so floated onto the grass. I had just rounded a corner when his insouciant step caught my eye; there was no one else in sight. The fact of his free fall was like the old philosophical conundrum about the tree that falls in the forest. The answer must be, I think, that beauty and grace are performed whether or not we will or sense them. The least we can do is try to be there.

Another time I saw another wonder: sharks off the Atlantic coast of Florida. There is a way a wave rises above the ocean horizon, a triangular wedge against the sky. If you stand where the ocean breaks on a shallow beach, you see the raised water in a wave is translucent, shot with lights. One late afternoon at low tide a hundred big sharks passed the beach near the mouth of a tidal river in a feeding frenzy. As each green wave rose from the churning water, it illuminated within itself the six- or eight-foot-long bodies of twisting sharks. The sharks disappeared as each wave rolled toward me; then a new wave would swell above the horizon, containing in it, like scorpions in amber, sharks that roiled and heaved. The sight held awesome wonders: power and beauty, grace tangled in a rapture with violence.

We don't know what's going on here. If these tremendous events are random combinations of matter run amok, the yield of millions of monkeys at millions of typewriters, then what is it in us, hammered out of those same typewriters, that they ignite? We don't know. Our life is a faint tracing on the surface of mystery, like the idle, curved tunnels of leaf miners on the face of a leaf. We must somehow take a wider view, look at the whole landscape, really see it, and describe what's going on here. Then we can at least wail the right question into the swaddling band of darkness, or, if it comes to that, choir the proper praise.

At the time of Lewis and Clark, setting the prairies on fire was a well-known signal that meant, "Come down to the water." It was an extravagant gesture, but we can't do less. If the landscape reveals one certainty, it is that the extravagant gesture is the very stuff of creation. After the one extravagant gesture of creation in the first place, the universe has continued to deal exclusively in extravagances, flinging intricacies and colossi down aeons of emptiness, heaping profusions on profligacies with ever-fresh vigor. The whole show has been on fire from the word go. I come down to the water to cool my eyes. But everywhere I look I see fire; that which isn't flint is tinder, and the whole world sparks and flames.

I have come to the grassy island late in the day. The creek is up; icy water sweeps under the sycamore log bridge. The frog skin, of course, is utterly gone. I have stared at that one spot on the creek bottom for so long, focusing past the rush of water, that when I stand, the opposite bank seems to stretch before my eyes and flow grassily upstream. When the bank settles down I cross the sycamore log and enter again the big plowed field next to the steers' pasture.

The wind is terrific out of the west; the sun comes and goes. I can see the shadow on the field before me deepen uniformly and spread like a plague. Everything seems so dull I am amazed I can even distinguish objects. And suddenly the light runs across the land like a comber, and up the trees, and goes again in a wink: I think I've gone blind or died. When it comes again, the light, you hold your breath, and if it stays you forget about it until it goes again.

It's the most beautiful day of the year. At four o'clock the eastern sky is a dead stratus black flecked with low white clouds. The sun in the west illuminates the ground, the mountains, and especially the bare branches of trees, so that everywhere silver trees cut into the black sky like a photographer's negative of a landscape. The air and the ground are dry; the mountains are going on and off like neon signs. Clouds slide east as if pulled from the horizon, like a tablecloth whipped off a table. The hemlocks by the barbed-wire fence are flinging themselves east as though their backs would break. Purple shadows are racing east; the wind makes me face east, and again I feel the dizzying, drawn sensation I felt when the creek bank reeled.

At four-thirty the sky in the east is clear; how could that big blackness be blown? Fifteen minutes later another darkness is coming overhead from the northwest; and it's here. Everything is drained of its light as if sucked. Only at the horizon do inky black mountains give way to distant, lighted mountains—lighted not by direct illumination but rather paled by glowing sheets of mist hung before them. Now the blackness is in the east; everything is half in shadow, half in sun, every clod, tree, mountain, and hedge. I can't see Tinker Mountain through the line of hemlock, till it comes on like a streetlight, ping, *ex nihilo*. Its sandstone cliffs pink and swell. Suddenly the light goes; the cliffs recede as if pushed. The sun hits a clump of sycamores between me and the mountains; the sycamore arms light up, and *I can't see the cliffs*. They're gone. The pale network of sycamore arms, which a second ago was transparent as a screen, is suddenly opaque, glowing with light. Now the sycamore arms snuff out, the mountains come on, and there are the cliffs again.

I walk home. By five-thirty the show has pulled out. Nothing is left but an unreal blue and a few banked clouds low in the north. Some sort of carnival magician has been here, some fast-talking worker of wonders who has the act backwards. "Something in this hand," he says, "something in this hand, something up my sleeve, something behind my back..." and abracadabra, he snaps his fingers, and it's all gone. Only the bland, blank-faced magician remains, in his unruffled coat, barehanded, acknowledging a smattering of baffled applause. When you look again the whole show has pulled up stakes and moved on down the road. It never stops. New shows roll in from over the mountains and the magician reappears unannounced from a fold in the curtain you never dreamed was an opening. Scarves of clouds, rabbits in plain view, disappear into the black hat forever. Presto chango. The audience, if there is an audience at all, is dizzy from head-turning, dazed. . . .

The Present

CATCH IT IF YOU CAN.

It is early March. I am dazed from a long day of interstate driving homeward; I pull in at a gas station in Nowhere, Virginia, north of Lexington. The young boy in charge ("Chick 'at oll?") is offering a free cup of coffee with every gas purchase. We talk in the glass-walled office while my coffee cools enough to drink. He tells me, among other things, that the rival gas station down the road, whose FREE COFFEE sign is visible from the interstate, charges you fifteen cents if you want your coffee in a Styrofoam cup, as opposed, I guess, to your bare hands.

All the time we talk, the boy's new beagle puppy is skidding around the office, sniffing impartially at my shoes and at the wire rack of folded maps. The cheerful human conversation wakes me, recalls me, not to a normal consciousness, but to a kind of energetic readiness. I step outside, followed by the puppy.

I am absolutely alone. There are no other customers. The road is vacant, the interstate is out of sight and earshot. I have hazarded into a new corner of the world, an unknown spot, a Brigadoon. Before me extends a low hill trembling in yellow brome, and behind the hill, filling the sky, rises an enormous mountain ridge, forested, alive and awesome with brilliant blown lights. I have never seen anything so tremulous and live. Overhead, great strips and chunks of cloud dash to the northwest in a gold rush. At my back the sun is setting—how can I not have noticed before that the sun is setting? My mind has been a blank slab of black asphalt for hours, but that doesn't stop the sun's wild wheel. I set my coffee beside me on the curb; I smell loam on the wind; I pat the puppy; I watch the mountain.

My hand works automatically over the puppy's fur, following the line of hair under his ears, down his neck, inside his forelegs, along his hot-skinned belly.

Shadows lope along the mountain's rumpled flanks; they elongate like root tips, like lobes of spilling water, faster and faster. A warm purple pigment pools in each ruck and tuck of the rock; it deepens and spreads, boring crevasses, canyons. As the purple vaults and slides, it tricks out the unleafed forest and rumpled rock in gilt, in shape-shifting patches of glow. These gold lights veer and retract, shatter and glide in a series of dazzling splashes, shrinking, leaking, exploding. The ridge's bosses and hummocks sprout bulging from its side; the whole mountain looms miles closer; the light warms and reddens; the bare forest folds and pleats itself like living protoplasm before my eyes, like a running chart, a wildly scrawling oscillograph on the present moment. The air cools; the puppy's skin is hot. I am more alive than all the world.

This is it, I think, this is it, right now, the present, this empty gas station, here, this western wind, this tang of coffee on the tongue, and I am patting the puppy, I am watching the mountain. And the second I verbalize this awareness in my brain, I cease to see the mountain or feel the puppy. I am opaque, so much black asphalt. But at the same second, the second I know I've lost it, I also realize that the puppy is still squirming on his back under my hand. Nothing has changed for him. He draws his legs down to stretch the skin taut so he feels every fingertip's stroke along his furred and arching side, his flank, his flung-back throat.

I sip my coffee. I look at the mountain, which is still doing its tricks, as you look at a still-beautiful face belonging to a person who was once your lover in another country years ago: with fond nostalgia, and recognition, but no real feeling save a secret astonishment that you are now strangers. Thanks. For the memories. It is ironic that the one thing that all religions recognize as separating us from our creator—our very self-consciousness—is also the one thing that divides us from our fellow creatures. It was a bitter birthday present from evolution, cutting us off at both ends. I get in the car and drive home.

The Search for Betula Uber

Eugene Kinkead (1906–1992)

The Central Atlantic is not normally thought of as a hot spot for botanical rarities, but as we have learned from Fernald's experience in the Zuni Pine Barrens, what you find is often limited only by what you know. The great field botanists find interesting plants wherever they are. Yet, as much botany is done in the herbarium as in the field, for it is in the herbarium that the collected specimens are stored and studied and new species named. It was in the herbarium that the round-leaf birch got species status and there it was lost for fifty years. "The Search for Betula Uber" is the story of the rediscovery of what is probably North America's rarest tree still growing in the wild, told by master journalist Eugene Kinkead.

During his fifty-eight-year career as a "The Talk of the Town" columnist and editor with the *New Yorker* magazine, Kinkead wrote on every subject from society to war, but his favorite topic was always nature. The titles of two of his last books indicate how a city man with a country man's heart can find nature wherever he is: *Wildness Is All Around Us: Notes of an Urban Naturalist* (1976) and *Central Park* (1990).

From "Our Footloose Correspondents," *New Yorker,* January 12, 1976

PUBLIC LAW 93-205, which is better known as the Endangered Species Act of 1973, and was passed by Congress on December 28th of that year, directed the Secretary of the Smithsonian Institution of Washington, D.C., to prepare, by the end of 1974, a report on United States plants that had recently become extinct or were deemed to be in danger of becoming so before long. The report, a monumental job of research, surveying the status of some twenty thousand plants in the forty-nine continental states (Hawaii was dealt with separately) and making recommendations for safeguarding those in jeopardy, was turned out, in the short designated time, under the supervision of Dr. Edward S. Ayensu, the chairman of the Smithsonian's Botany Department. Of the flora listed, some ten percent, or two thousand ninety-nine species, were found to be either in real danger or to have lately departed. Seven hundred and sixty-one plants were designated as "endangered," meaning their survival was in serious doubt, twelve hundred and thirty-eight were listed as "threatened," and an even one hundred were declared extinct—at least in the wild.

Of those plants labelled extinct, only two were among the largest—the trees. One of these, the "lost" Franklinia (*Franklinia alatamaha*), is a rather famous species in the world of botany. It was discovered during Colonial days: John Bartram, King's Botanist, and his son William found it in the year 1765 growing beside the Altamaha River, on the low coastal plain of southeast Georgia, in what is now McIntosh County, about thirty miles from the sea. Its finders described it as a shrub or small tree reaching a maximum height of thirty-odd feet, and they correctly placed it in the tea family. It had glossy green leaves somewhat resembling those of the magnolia. The large creamy-white flowers, renewing themselves in warm weather for weeks and even months, had the fragrance of orange blossoms. The original population is believed to have occupied a locale no larger at best than five acres, a tract of acid land composed of sandhill bog. The tree, the only species in its genus, was named in honor of Benjamin Franklin, in 1785, five years before he died. In 1803, a botanist reported only six or eight mature Franklinias left at the original site, though many cultivated examples were by then flourishing elsewhere. By 1806, no more were to be seen in the wild. Why the species vanished from its native habitat is uncertain. One theory is that the alkaline Altamaha River flooded the area, doing the plant in. A more likely cause, however, botanists think, is overcollecting. Soon after the discovery of Franklinia, the Bartrams, recognizing the tree's decorative qualities, began digging up specimens and dispatching them to Philadelphia and elsewhere. This practice was continued for decades by others. It produced at least one benefit. Now the tree, although it is gone from nature, exists quite widely in arboretums, public grounds, and gardens in both the Old World and the New. In fact, three rather scraggly examples stand before the National Museum of Natural History, in Washington— the Smithsonian building where the report on endangered flora was put together. A much more impressive representative, about twenty-five feet high, rises on the Senate side of the Capitol grounds.

The other tree on the extinct list was not a famous one. Nor did it have the early good fortune to be preserved by being planted in gardens. Indeed, in recent years botanists had begun to question seriously whether such a tree had ever existed. It was a birch, sometimes known as Ashe's birch. It was discovered in 1914 by William Willard Ashe, an experienced forester employed by the United States Forest Service, on the banks of a modest stream draining a part of Smyth County, in the rural, mountainous region of southwest Virginia—a section of the Appalachians that Ashe knew well. Some time later, Ashe, following scientific custom, sent materials from the tree—twigs, leaves, and female catkins (which bear the seeds)—to the United States National Herbarium, at the Smithsonian; to the New York Botanical Garden; and to two botanical adjuncts of Harvard University— the Arnold Arboretum, in Jamaica Plain, Massachusetts, and the Gray Herbarium, in Cambridge. Accompanying the specimens were labels in Ashe's handwriting stating that the tree, from twenty to twenty-five feet high, was found in the month of June, 1914, on the banks of Dickey Creek, in Smyth County, at an altitude of two thousand eight hundred feet, south of the Sugar Grove Station. This building, now vanished, was a depot of the Marion & Rye Valley Railroad, erected at a time when rail lines penetrated even to sections that were very sparsely populated, as Dickey Creek then was and still is. The tree, Ashe thought, resembled the black, or sweet, birch, also found in the area, both having a black, aromatic bark with a winter-green fragrance and flavor. The leaves of the two trees, however, were different. Black-birch leaves are pointed, like an arrowhead; those of Ashe's birch were rounded at the tip. In a paper published four years after his find—in the April, 1918, issue of *Rhodora*, the journal of the New England Botanical Club—Ashe formally named the tree *Betula lenta uber* n. var. (meaning "new variety," thus indicating that he believed it to be a new variety of the very common black birch). *Betula lenta* is the name of the black birch and "*uber*" is the Latin word for "fruitful" (rather a strange epithet, as it turned out, to tie to this tree); a variety is a biological form whose differences within the species are too slight to entitle it to true specific rank. Among the facts about the tree in the *Rhodora* article were the length and breadth of the leaf, the number of primary veins, and other leaf characteristics; the length of the leaf stalk; and peculiarities of the female catkins, fruit scales, and seeds. The tree was one of more than a hundred new species and varieties that Ashe botanically described and named in some forty years as a state and federal forester—a career that started in 1893 in North Carolina, where he was born. He placed the birch in a group (series Costate) that includes the black birch and the yellow birch (*Betula alleghaniensis*), both widely found in the Dickey Creek area.

It stayed in that niche for less than thirty years. In 1945, Dr. Merritt Lyndon Fernald, Fisher Professor of Natural History at Harvard, director of its Gray Herbarium, and one of the most eminent American botanists of this century, took a new look at the birches of eastern North America, and in the process his eye fell on *Betula lenta uber*. After seeing Ashe's specimens from both Harvard sources, Fernald, writing in the October, 1945, issue of *Rhodora*, raised the tree to full specific rank, calling it simply *Betula uber*. In his opinion, the plant, except for its aromatic bark, had little in common with the black birch. Because of the structure of its leaves and female catkins, it more nearly resembled, he thought, the birches in series Humiles—a group that includes the low, or swamp, birch (*B. pumila*), a plant of the northeastern United States and Canada, which, in its more northerly habitat, is sometimes a dwarf only a foot or two high. Since Fernald's pronouncement, Ashe's birch has remained a full species in series Humiles, although it appears to be widely separated in structure and habitat from the other members of the series and is the only one not found readily in nature.

Within a few years, a research fellow at Harvard decided to investigate this scarcity; Albert G. Johnson, a horticulturist, who is now with the University of Minnesota, was one of a number of botanists to search, over the years, for a specimen of Ashe's birch. In the winter of 1953, Johnson, supported by funds from the Maria Moors Cabot Foundation for Botanical Research at Harvard University, travelled to Dickey Creek—a watercourse that flows north through the little community of Sugar Grove into the South Fork of the Holston River, which, as a tributary of the Tennessee River, is part of the Mississippi River drainage system. Although the leaves were off the trees at the time of Johnson's visit, he wrote, in the June, 1954, issue of *Rhodora*, that he felt he would have no difficulty recognizing *Betula uber* if it had been present in any quantity in the area. Johnson walked south from Sugar Grove along the banks of the creek. Near town, he reported, these were mainly clear but occasionally bore an irregular fringe of shrubs and some trees. He pursued his search over a stretch of four miles, going well into the hilly region of the 617,533-acre Jefferson National Forest, through which the southern portion of Dickey Creek runs. He mounted considerably higher than the two thousand eight hundred feet at which Ashe said he had found the tree. But Johnson saw only black and yellow birch—the common ones thereabouts. Nor could the district ranger in the national forest, whom Johnson had queried and who had looked for the tree himself, give Johnson any leads.

Accordingly, in the last paragraph of his article Johnson wrote that the birch "probably no longer exists as an individual and very likely never did so in the form of a population. Ashe's birch has probably died or been destroyed in the process of urbanization of the community in which he found it forty years ago. It is probable that this birch variety was founded solely on an aberrant individual and certainly does not appear to deserve further consideration as a species." End of article. By that time, many botanists were of the opinion that, for some unaccountable reason, the tree might have been a freak.

Here the matter rested, in limbo, until the beginning of this decade. In the early nineteen-sixties, Peter Mazzeo, a research assistant at the United States National Arboretum, a unit of the Department of Agriculture, who was working on a proposed flora of Virginia, came upon the written spoor of *Betula uber* and found himself fascinated by reports of the discovery and subsequent apparent evaporation into thin air of Ashe's birch. In 1970, he decided to examine all the material from the tree that he could get his hands on, and to study everything available on it in print. Besides the material that Ashe had sent to the four herbaria, four other sets of botanical specimens had turned up in Ashe's effects following his death, in 1932. These went to his alma mater, the University of North Carolina, which is presumed to have sent one to the Carnegie Museum of Natural History, in Pittsburgh, and one to the herbarium at the National Arboretum.

Altogether, Mazzeo was able to look at seven of Ashe's specimens—the four from the institutions that had received them after Ashe's death, plus three of the original four sent out by Ashe in 1914. The latter were those at the Gray Herbarium, the Arnold Arboretum, and the New York Botanical Garden. The material sent to the Smithsonian had been lost, and lost rather early. In a letter written in 1922, Ashe complained that he had been unable to find the material he had shipped there. The specimen sent there was designated as the primary type (or holotype, meaning the single specimen designated by an author as the type of a species at the time of establishing the group) for *Betula uber*. Thus when Fernald wrote his paper, he had to base his observations on a duplicate (or isotype), selecting the one at the Gray Herbarium, which Mazzeo has since designated as the replacement for the lost holotype.

During his research, however, Mazzeo was able to find an eighth set of specimens, which had gone all but unnoticed for years. Searching the files of the Arnold Arboretum herbarium, he found a set of material on Ashe's birch with a label, in handwriting different from Ashe's, that said that the specimen had been collected by H. B. Ayres on Cressy Creek. This stream is not far to the east of Dickey Creek and, like it, feeds into the South Fork of the Holston River. Also on the label were the words "*Betula uber*" in Fernald's unmistakable script. According to Fernald's custom, his notation was undated. The assumption is that before writing his paper he had requested all birch materials from the Arnold to be sent to him at the Gray, had seen the Ayres specimen, had annotated the label, and had forgotten about it by the time he wrote his paper.

Ayres, an older man than Ashe by sixteen years, was a forester usually employed by private industry. He worked largely for railroads, appraising the timber on their lands; that is, he was what was known in the trade as a "timber cruiser." He was also an occasional collaborator of Ashe's. Among their joint works was a 1905 report for the United States Geological Survey entitled "The Southern Appalachian Forests." In it they evaluated the timber possibilities of the Dickey and Cressy Creek districts, among other areas. The report made no reference to *Betula uber*.

In 1973, in an article dealing with the dozen-odd species of the birch family present in Virginia, Mazzeo made brief mention of the mysteries of *Betula uber*. He mentioned the name Cressy Creek in print for the first time, albeit almost peripherally (and the paper misspelled it "Creesy"). The item was published in a quarterly called *Jeffersonia: A Newsletter of Virginia Botany*. A year and a half later, however, in the September, 1974, number of the botanical quarterly *Castanea*, edited at the University of West Virginia, Mazzeo devoted an entire paper, with photographic illustrations of *Betula uber* material, to what he had been able to learn in his several years' study of the birch. The paper noted that, after sixty years and many searches, no trace of living specimens of this shadowy plant had been found.

Mazzeo himself, meanwhile, tried to rectify this lack. He had made a special trip to the region solely to search for Ashe's birch. This turned out to be just another unsuccessful effort. But in February, 1975, the *Christian Science Monitor* carried a feature on Mazzeo's search for Ashe's birch, which I happened to see. As a result, I telephoned Mazzeo and said that if he planned another hunt I would like to go along. In my layman's ignorance, I said that if the tree had been found once, I thought it certainly could be found again. Mazzeo said that, as a matter of fact, he was planning another trip in the fall and would be glad to have me accompany him.

In the meantime, a reading of Mazzeo's 1973 paper had interested a twenty-six-year-old Virginia native named Douglas Ogle. He was a biology instructor at Virginia Highlands Community College, in nearby Abingdon, and was also in the Ph.D. program in botany at the Virginia Polytechnic Institute and State University, in Blacksburg. When Mazzeo's piece on the birch came out in *Castanea*, Ogle decided to map out a careful campaign of search for the tree, and to follow it in his 1975 summer vacation. His plan was a sensible one. Both Ashe and Ayres had reported their finds along the two creeks. Ogle decided that the tree, as a biological entity, might be restricted to such locales. Therefore, he thought there were a couple of likely ways in which the birch could have been discovered. Since there were only two access routes to the area, it could have been by someone walking along the railroad tracks, whose right-of-way cut back and forth across the streams; or by someone moving along the local wagon roads, which did the same thing. Ogle proceeded to trace out and follow the old rail beds, now devoid of their tracks, and the serpentine wagon roads, now also out of use in most cases, in the areas adjacent to the creeks.

Last August 22nd, Ogle found, growing among ordinary black birches along the west bank of Cressy Creek, on the property of Garland Ross, a retired schoolteacher and part-time farmer, a number of birches with odd-looking leaves. With Ross' permission, he collected some leafy twigs from the unusual plants. That same day, Ogle took his materials to the herbarium at the Virginia Polytechnic Institute, where Leonard Uttal, the herbarium's assistant curator, studied the find using Fernald's 1945 article and Mazzeo's article, with its photographs, detailed descriptions, and measurements. On August 28th, Uttal got Mazzeo on the telephone in Washington. "I think *Betula uber* has been found," Uttal said.

Plans were immediately begun for an expedition to determine whether this was so and also to seek other specimens—some of them, preferably, small enough to use for nursery purposes. Mazzeo notified his superior, Dr. F. G. Meyer, supervisory research botanist at the National Arboretum, who, not surprisingly, wanted to come along. I was alerted and happily agreed to appear. So, with the same result, were Ogle and Dr. W. H. Wagner, Jr., who became the group leader by virtue of his early interest in the plant and his professional eminence. He is chairman of the Department of Botany of the University of Michigan, at Ann Arbor, a professor in its School of Natural Resources (of which the forestry division is a part), a well-known specialist in the field of ferns, and a highly respected general botanist. For some months previously, he had been talking with Mazzeo about going with him in a search for *Betula uber*. The trip was set for mid-September.

On the appointed day, our contingent gathered, late in the afternoon, at the airport at Roanoke, Virginia. Wagner proved to be an acute, animated scholar in his middle fifties, with an easy social manner; Meyer, tall and spare, is about the same age; and Mazzeo, bearded and soft-spoken, is in his thirties. These two had motored down that day from Washington in a panel van bearing the logo of the Department of Agriculture. In the back of the van were various pieces of equipment, such as plant presses with felt blotters; newsprint, in which to press the specimens; cardboard ventilators, to hold them; and a pruner about twenty feet long, for reaching remote twigs on a tree. Because only federal employees are allowed to ride in a government vehicle, I rented a car at the airport, and Wagner and I followed the others, in their van, over a stretch of about a hundred miles to Marion, which is the seat of Smyth County. (The town is named after the Revolutionary general Francis Marion, known as the Swamp Fox.) There we were to spend the next couple of nights in a motel. Ogle was to meet us the following day.

At dinner that evening, to my considerable surprise, Wagner gave what was almost a lecture downgrading the chances of our project. He argued— quite convincingly, it seemed to me—that the tree we were about to see might well not be what we thought it was. Playing the part of devil's advocate, he brought up numerous reasons to suppose that it was a botanical aberration, not worthy of species rank—if, indeed, it was Ashe's birch at all. Perhaps, however, his stand was to have been expected. At the University of Michigan, I had learned, the botanists and the foresters had long questioned the existence of *Betula uber*. For one thing, in the summer of 1952 Walter F. Kleinschmidt, of the University of Michigan's Botanical Gardens, had carefully searched the area in Smyth County where Ashe had reported his birch, and had been unable to find any trace of it. At the end of Wagner's talk, the two other botanists disagreed with his objections. "We think the tree is as advertised," Mazzeo said. "I predict that tomorrow four new pairs of eyes will see *Betula uber*."

One thing the three botanists agreed upon completely was that if the object of our trip were generally known other botanists by the dozen would be camping around us in no time. As a matter of fact, our party, to my surprise, *was* substantially increased next morning. Following an early breakfast, we left the motel in the two cars under an iron-gray sky a little before eight for a rendezvous with Ogle at a point about halfway along the road that runs between Marion and Sugar Grove, a community in the hill country, about a dozen miles to the southeast of the county seat. At the appointed place, we met Ogle, a tall, heavyset, quiet man, who was alone in his car. Almost immediately, another automobile, with Leonard Uttal and Dr.

Duncan Porter, a systemic botanist at the Virginia Polytechnic Institute, joined us, and then came a third car, carrying two members of the Biology Department of Virginia Highlands Community College, where Ogle taught. A few minutes later, our caravan of five vehicles, led by Ogle, set off for the site on Cressy Creek where he had found the birch.

Along the way, it started to rain a little. After a drive of about ten minutes, we stopped south of Sugar Grove and parked along the shoulder of a blacktop road. The road ran along Cressy Creek, which bore on each bank a thin fringe of trees. As I glanced around me, I could see that we were at the bottom of a deep, overgrown valley. Empty, tree-covered hills rose on either side of us. The farmhouse of Garland Ross lay ahead to our right, that of Ray Haulsee behind to our left; both farms were adjacent to the boundaries of the Jefferson National Forest. The sounds of pigs and chickens and, from time to time, the lowing of cows could be heard. The rain, borne on flurries of wind, was heavier now.

The nine of us left our cars and, with Ogle in the lead, made our way through the roadside screen of trees to Cressy Creek. "Most of what we're looking for is on the other side," Ogle said. The stream was about fifteen feet wide and nine to twelve inches deep, and was strewn with rocks. We crossed by wading or leaping cautiously from rock to rock. When all of us had reached the west bank and were among the trees, Ogle suggested we look up. "Can you see leaves that are dissimilar to those of the black birch?" he asked. The leaves of the black birch were numerous all around us, but when I looked up, it was hard, with the rain pelting into my face, to see anything. Then Wagner, standing beside a nearby tree, cried elatedly, "Yes, yes, I see what you mean. The rounded leaf! The rounded leaf!" And, following his gaze, I saw what he saw—leaves formed like old-fashioned palm-leaf fans ranged in serried ranks above his head. That was the shape of the leaf that had been depicted in Mazzeo's article. After more than sixty years of botanical mystery, of doubts, of denials and fears of extinction, the living flora grew at mere arm's length before us. That gusty morning, not four but eight new pairs of eyes glimpsed for the first time the long-sought, elusive *Betula uber*.

Some days earlier, when my poetical daughter heard that I was venturing into the Southern mountains to search for a possibly extinct tree, she said, "I have visions of it deep in a great forest, draped in a golden net, with manifold birds singing on its boughs, and national foresters posted around it, holding guard dogs." However, the plant we were all gazing at was lean, birdless, and rangy—from three to five yards taller than the maximum height of twenty-five feet given by Ashe. It was crowded by similarly spindly black birches and other trees. Obviously, all of them were engaged in a struggle for sunlight.

Now, looking down the creek to the north, I saw several trees with orange plastic bands tied around their trunks. These proved to be more Ashe's birch, marked by Ogle. Altogether, we counted eleven mature examples of the tree. To a casual observer, they looked much like their black-birch neighbors except for the leaves. They were comparable in height and in trunk size, and the boles of both species bore mottled gray-and-black bark, spotted in places with lichen. With a penknife, I cut off bits of the bark of each species. Each, I found, had a wintergreen fragrance and taste, but Ogle felt that those of Ashe's birch were somewhat the weaker. "Like teaberry gum," he said. The largest *uber* in the grove had a circumference at breast height of about eighteen inches. I estimated it to be some forty-five years old, and Wagner said he thought that was probably close. "Birch grows slowly," he said.

Once we had identified the trees, Wagner set forth our next, equally important goal: "Have these trees been reproducing themselves? We must find that out now. We must look for seedlings." Soon our party had scattered over a wide area west of the creek. I roamed in the rain for fully half a mile, wandering over a meadow that sloped upward to the west, and stopping only when I reached the border of a thick wood where seedlings would not thrive. The job was not easy for any of us. We were on Ray Haulsee's farm, with cows foraging across it. Their range included the space under the trees along the creek's west bank, and they obviously found young birch trees of any variety to their taste, for we discovered many stumps of seedlings bearing merely a leaf or two. The rain continued intermittently in hard showers and slack-offs. The cows, whose numbers seemed to increase, regarded us in a bemused fashion, their heads raised from the ground and their large eyes reflecting curiosity about the unwonted band of strangers in their midst. For our part, we regarded them with outright animosity. Everywhere, we came upon evidence of their destruction of young birches.

Around noon, we drove back to Sugar Grove and ate at a lunchroom *cum* filling station *cum* general store, which served us some well-cured Virginia ham. Afterward, we drove back past the site on Cressy Creek and down the highway to the south. We branched off to the left, taking a dirt road that went up the side of a mountain. Part way up, we parked and got out to poke along its shoulders and into the woods in a survey for additional examples of Ashe's birch. Wagner was of the opinion that others might be found in the neighborhood. Ogle was not so sure. He said he had been up twenty adjacent valleys since late August without seeing any. In mid-afternoon, our search of the hillside having proved futile, we returned to Cressy Creek. The four botanists—Ogle, Mazzeo, Meyer, and Wagner— wanted to check the branches of the trees we had found for possible male and female catkins. Both normally occur on the same birch, and establishing their presence was necessary in order to determine whether they were fertile. Birch catkins combine to produce seed when windblown pollen from a male catkin falls on the ovary of a female catkin. The catkins start forming in late summer for the next season, the female more slowly than the male. In the spring, when both are mature, the wind does its job and fruits are formed which contain the seeds. These seeds are inside nutlets with narrow wings, forming fruits called samaras. (The best-known samara is the maple key, which is much larger than the fruit of the birch.)

The long pruner was taken from the van, and Ogle offered to climb a tree on a catkin reconnaissance. He seemed remarkably agile for a man of his size—he weighs more than two hundred pounds—and quickly began making his way aloft. After several minutes of activity in the branches, he said, "I think I see something. Hand me the pruner." It was passed up to him, and Ogle, carrying the awkward instrument easily, moved still higher and out onto a branch. We heard snipping, and down fluttered cuttings. Wagner pounced on them. For some moments, he examined what he had. Then he gave an elated cry. "It's fertile! It's fertile!" Mazzeo cried, "Oh, that's marvelous! You have the male catkin, too. It's never been seen before!" Their jubilation was caused mainly by a seed or two in a decaying female catkin and some immature pollen grains in a male.

Emboldened by the knowledge that the trees could have progeny, the rest of us, under Wagner's direction, began a spirited new search for more seedlings. This time, we went to a fenced-in meadow of about an acre directly across the road to the east. It was also on Ray Haulsee's land. And there we found the seedlings, from six inches to three feet high, of both the black birch and Ashe's birch. Actually, it was a logical place for them to be. The prevailing wind was from the west and would have blown seed there. As the botanists made a count of the seedlings of both species, I, at Wagner's request, stood by with paper and pencil and set down the score according to what was shouted at me by the botanists. The total was eighty-nine seedlings of *Betula lenta* and sixteen of *uber*. "That's about the same ratio found among the mature trees on the creek," Wagner declared.

It was then about five o'clock. The rain had stopped for the moment, and the sun had broken through the clouds. Ogle took us to the Ross house to meet the owner, whom he knew. The house was reached by a wide, rail-less plank bridge across Cressy Creek. After introductions, we were given permission to gather on the bridge for sorting and drying what seemed to me the enormous assortment of material we had collected. Ray Haulsee came over, and he, too, was introduced to us by Ogle. Both landowners were friendly men, quite interested in what we were doing. Ross took us a little way north of his house but some way south of where Ogle had found his *Betula uber*. There, close to a great pig that had earlier grunted his puzzle-ment at us, Ross pointed out two other examples of the birch—one mature, one a sapling—both also on the west side of the creek. This brought our total of adult specimens to twelve. When we told Haulsee about the seedlings we had found in his meadow and the damage that cows had done to those on the west side of Cressy Creek, he obligingly said, "I don't have to use that field for pasture."

Our dinner that night at the motel was late. Afterward, the jungle of collected material was unloaded from the van and piled onto the covered walkway in front of the adjoining rooms of Mazzeo, Meyer, and Wagner, who, along with Ogle, diligently sorted, pressed, mounted, and labelled what seemed to me an infinitude of specimens. They worked until midnight. Next morning, I asked Ogle, who had returned to help with the uncompleted labelling, his opinion of why no *uber* had been found along Dickey Creek, where Ashe had first reported it. "That's a question we'd all like to answer," he said. "I have a theory, which I'm trying to prove, that Ayres, not Ashe, found *uber*, and told his collaborator about it. Furthermore, it could be that the original trees were, in reality, found along Cressy Creek, not Dickey Creek. Ashe had a reputation in some quarters as a careless botanist, and certainly some of the data on his *uber* labels are incorrect. For example, one or two of them state that the tree was found at thirty-eight hundred, not twenty-eight hundred, feet. This at least lends some color to the possibility that he was wrong on other scores. However, assuming that the tree *was* collected by Ashe on Dickey Creek, there are several possible explanations for its disappearance from there during the last sixty years. Among these are the chance that only one or two trees existed there, and that these were competed out of existence, with no seedling survivors. I know that trees along the creek were culled for farmland. Or it is even possible that people distrusted the unfamiliar tree. Before Ray Haulsee was aware of *uber's* botanical value, he took down, on his property, what may have been the largest member of the Cressy Creek population, because, from the shape of the leaves, he thought the tree was diseased."

Ogle said that he and Mazzeo planned to collaborate on a scientific paper on the rediscovery of *Betula uber* on Cressy Creek, to be published in 1976. In it he expects to suggest that *uber* receive the common name of "Round-leaf birch." He also hopes, by some means, to get a high fence erected around the small population of trees.

Before Wagner left that afternoon, I asked him what he thought of *uber* now. "You were a doubting Thomas day before yesterday," I reminded him.

Wagner replied, "A serious botanist has to ask the questions I did. Here you have a tree that was invisible for decades following its discovery. Nobody could find it. Obviously, it was rare. Perhaps it was only a single tree. It might have been a variety created by nature—a distinctive part of a species but with different minor characteristics, such as the northern variety of the red oak, *var. borealis*, found in the colder parts of the United States. It might have been a solitary cultivar—a variety created through breeding by man but never existing in nature except as an escapee. It might have been a sterile hybrid, like a mule—a mongrel between two species of plants. Or it might have been an individual variant, a freak resulting from some genetic upset of the kind that produces the human examples seen in circus sideshows. A true species, however, has its own characteristic range on earth, its own habitat and associates. In terms of form, it has its own distinctive features, differing from those of all other species. Its individuals are more like its own race than any others. And, genetically, it is capable of creating similar offspring by fertile seeds. Although I properly came as a doubter, I now believe that *uber* has the qualifications of a true species."

Wagner said that something he planned to do at once in Michigan was to check the comparative fertility of the pollen grains from *uber* and those from *lenta*, several of whose male catkins he was also taking along. (Subsequently, he reported that *uber* seemed to be somewhat less fertile.) Mazzeo and Meyer, for their part, went back to the Sugar Grove area that afternoon to look for more *uber* and to gather more data, take more photographs, pick up more samples, and to gather a few seedlings for the National Arboretum.

A few days later, in Washington, I went out to the Arboretum to see whether any new developments had occurred. Mazzeo told me that while no new mature specimens had been found, Ogle had discovered five additional seedlings in Haulsee's meadow, bringing the total of these to twenty-one. Mazzeo said that considerable *uber* material had been sent to Wagner, and that one of the four seedlings brought back would also eventually go to him. The seedlings, then under the care of a competent gardener at the Arboretum, were doing well, I was told. Over the coming year, it was the Arboretum's plan to grow more *uber* from seed and cuttings and, in due course, supply healthy plants to its numerous arboretum correspondents around the world. Thus, even if *uber* in the wild state should ultimately die out, the plant would be preserved, as Franklinia had been. Today, it is the rarest birch in the country. It may be the rarest on earth.

Beautiful Swimmer

William W. Warner (b. 1920)

William Warner's *Beautiful Swimmers* won the 1976 Pulitzer Prize for
General Nonfiction. The book impressed everyone from literary critics
to the watermen who made their living on the Chesapeake Bay. Extensive
research, both in the literature and firsthand, fully understood and expressed in simple and straightforward prose is the hallmark of Warner's
writing. It epitomizes the recent trend in nature writing to personal experience integrated with scientific knowledge. As one of Warner's watermen
admirers put it, "He wrote it the way he learned it and he put it down the
way it was" (Grant Corbin, quoted in Michael Wentzel, Baltimore *Evening
Sun,* April 5, 1983, p. B2).

  In this selection, Warner describes the blue crab. Recent discoveries have
shown just what a remarkable and contrary creature it is; however, much of
its life cycle is still poorly understood. If any single creature is symbolic
of the Central Atlantic states, it is the blue crab—the basis of a unique industry and the staple of the local cuisine. Many bay-area residents will
measure the success of efforts to restore Chesapeake Bay by the crab
harvests of the future.

From *Beautiful Swimmers* (Boston: Little, Brown, 1976)

T HE ATLANTIC blue crab is known to scientists as *Callinectes sapidus* Rathbun. It is very well named. *Callinectes* is Greek for beautiful swimmer.
Sapidus, of course, means tasty or savory in Latin. Rathbun is the late Dr.
Mary J. Rathbun of the Smithsonian Institution, who first gave the crab its
specific name.

  Dr. Rathbun, known as Mary Jane to her Smithsonian colleagues, has
often been called the dean of American carcinologists, as experts in crabs
and other crustaceans are properly termed. Before her death in 1943, Mary
Jane identified and described over 998 new species of crabs, an absolute
record in the annals of carcinology. In only one case did she choose to honor
culinary qualities. History has borne out the wisdom of her choice. No crab
in the world has been as much caught or eagerly consumed as *sapidus.*

Whether or not *Callinectes* may justly be considered beautiful depends on whom you ask. Scientists tend to avoid aesthetic judgments. Many lay observers think the blue crab frightening or even ugly in appearance. They do not understand its popular name and often ask what is blue about a blue crab. The question betrays a basic ignorance of truly adult specimens. Most people see the species in the smaller back bays of the Atlantic coast; crabs never grow very large in these waters, since they are quite salty throughout and lack the brackish middle salinities that assure optimum growth in the Chesapeake and other large estuaries. The barrier beach islands and their back bays may provide our most dramatic seascapes, but they are not the place to see the pleasing hues of well-grown crabs. Large males have a deep lapis lazuli coloration along their arms, more on the undersides than on top, extending almost to the points of the claws. In full summer the walking and swimming legs of both sexes take on a lighter blue, which artists would probably call cerulean. Females, as we have said before, decorate their claws with a bright orange-red, which color is seen only at the extreme tips among males. Since females wave their claws in and out during courtship, it may be that this dimorphism is a sexually advantageous adaptation. If so, it is probably a very important one, since the blue crab is believed to be somewhat color blind.

Those who most appreciate *Callinectes'* beauty, I think, are crabbers and other people who handle crabs professionally. Some years ago in the month of October, I visited a clean and well-managed crab house in Bellhaven, North Carolina, a pleasant town on Pamlico Sound's Pungo River. In the company of the plant owner's wife I watched dock handlers load the cooking crates with good catches of prime sooks. As they should be at that time of year, the sooks were fully hard and fat, although relatively recently moulted. Their abdomens were therefore pure white, with a lustrous alabaster quality. (Later in the intermoult period crab abdomens take on the glazed and slightly stained look of aging horses' teeth; often they are also spotted with "rust.") The carapaces or top shells were similarly clean. Thus, gazing down at the mass of three thousand or more crabs in each crate, we saw a rich and fragmented palette of olive greens, reds, varying shades of blue and marble white.

"Now, tell me, did ever you see such beautiful crabs?" the owner's wife asked, quite spontaneously.

"Prettiest crabs I seen all year," a black dockhand volunteered.

I had to agree. Anyone would.

Still, as is often said, beauty is in the eyes of the beholder. We can but little imagine the sheer terror which the sight of a blue crab must inspire in a fat little killifish or a slow-moving annelid worm. The crab's claw arms will be held out at the ready, waving slowly in the manner of a shadow boxer. Walking legs will be slightly doubled, ready for tigerlike springs, and the outer maxillipeds—literally "jaw feet" or two small limbs in front of the crab's mouth—will flutter distractingly. The effect must be mesmeric, such as the praying mantis is said to possess over its insect victims. Perhaps not quite so hypnotic but of extreme importance to the crab in this situation are its eyes. Like most crustaceans, the blue crab has stalked eyes. When a crab is at peace with the world, they are but two little round beads. On the prowl, they are elevated and look like stubby horns. As with insects, the eyes are compound. This means that they possess thousands of facets—multiple lenses, if you prefer—which catch and register a mosaic of patterns. More importantly, simple laboratory tests seem to indicate that the stalked and compound eyes give the blue crab almost three-hundred-and-sixty-degree vision. Those who with ungloved hand try to seize a crab with raised eyestalks from the rear will have this capability most forcefully impressed on them. If at all, the blue crab may have a forward blind spot at certain ranges in the small space directly between its eyes. Perhaps this accounts for the crab's preference for shifting lateral motion, from which it is easier to correct this deficiency, rather than rigid forward and back movement. Whatever the answer, a blue crab sees very well. Although colors may be blurred, the crab is extremely sensitive to shapes and motions. It has good range, too, at least for a crustacean. I have frequently tried standing still in a boat as far as fifteen feet from cornered individuals and then raising an arm quickly. Instantly the crabs respond, claws flicked up to the combat position.

Beauty, then, to some. Piercing eyes and a fearful symmetry, like William Blake's tiger, to others. But there are no such divided views on *Callinectes'* swimming ability. Specialists and lay observers alike agree that the blue crab has few peers in this respect. Some carcinologists believe that a few larger portunids or members of the swimming crab family—*Portunus pelagicus*, for example, which ranges from the eastern Mediterranean to Tahiti—might be better swimmers. But from what I have seen of the family album, I rather suspect that these crabs would fare best in distance events in any aquatic olympiad, while the Atlantic blue and some of its close relatives might take the sprints.

Certainly the blue crab is superbly designed for speed in the water. Its body is shallow, compressed and fusiform, or tapering at both ends. Although strong, its skeletal frame is very light, as anyone who picks up a cast-off shell readily appreciates. At the lateral extremities are wickedly tapered spines, the Pitot tubes, one might say, of the crab's supersonic airframe. (These spines grow very sharp in large crabs; good-sized specimens falling to a wooden deck occasionally impale themselves on them, quivering like the target knives of a sideshow artist.) This lateral adaptation is as it should be, of course, for an animal given to sideways travel.

Remarkable as this airframe body structure may be, it is the blue crab's propulsion units that are most responsible for its swimming success. These are the fifth or last pair of appendages, most commonly known as the swimming legs. Beginning at their fourth segments, the swimming legs become progressively thinner and flatter. The seventh or final segment is completely flat and rounded like a paddle, ideally shaped for rapid sculling. Equally remarkable is the articulation of the swimming legs. Even knowledgeable observers are surprised to learn that a blue crab can bend them above and behind its back until the paddles touch. They are unaware of this extreme flexibility, no doubt, because the occasions to observe it are rather rare. One such is to steal up on a pair of courting crabs. Prominent in the male blue crab's repertoire of courtship signals is one involving the swimming legs. A randy Jimmy will wave them sensuously and synchronously from side to side above his back, with the paddle surfaces facing forward, as though tracing little question marks and parentheses in the water. Females show appreciation by rapidly waving their claws or rocking side to side on their walking legs.

But courting gestures are not the principal function of the powerfully muscled and flexible swimming legs. They mainly serve to propel the crab, of course, not only sideways, but also forward or backward, not to mention helicopter-style rotation which permits a crab to hover like a hawk. Most of the time all we see of these actions is a blur. As those who try wading in shallows with a dip net know, a startled blue crab bursts off the bottom in a cloud of mud or sand and darts away with the speed of a fish. Such rapid all-directional movement is of great advantage to swimming crabs. Consider the unfortunate lobster. Its rigid and overlapping abdominal or "tail" segments restrict it to dead ahead or astern. Of the two directions, it seems to prefer swimming backward. Such inclination coupled with dim vision is probably why lobsters are always bumping into things. But again this is probably as it should be. It is to the lobster's advantage to back into corners. Safely positioned in a rocky niche, the lobster is well-nigh invulnerable to frontal attack, thanks to its enormously powerful claws. By contrast,

"At courting time male blue crabs show some degree of territoriality, mainly by exhibiting a threat posture, or holding their arms out fully extended in a straight line with the claws slightly open." Male Crabs Courting, C. Hanks, from *Beautiful Swimmers*

open water speed and burying in soft bottoms are the swimming crabs' main escape tactics.

Less recognized are the blue crab's walking abilities. As befits an arthropod, *Callinectes* has many well-articulated joints. It has no less than seventy, in fact, in its five principal pairs of limbs. Three of these pairs are the walking legs; they permit the crab to scuttle along very nicely both on dry land and on sandy or muddy bottoms. It is true that a blue crab does not like dry land locomotion, yet it does rather well in emergencies. Each year the city of Crisfield, "Seafood Capital of the Nation," sponsors an event known as the National Hard Crab Derby, certainly one of our nation's more bizarre folk celebrations. At the crack of a gun, crabs are unceremoniously dumped from a forty-stall starting gate on to a sixteen-foot board track, very slightly inclined. Thus stimulated, blue crabs that are not stopped by distractions will scurry down the course in eight to twelve seconds. Terrestrial species like the nimble ghost crab, for whom running is a principal defense measure, do better, of course. Still, the Derby organizers, who have matched many species over the years, consider the blue crab's time entirely respectable. For those who cannot attend the Derby, a good way to see crabs moving out of water is to visit a loading dock. Crawling is scarcely the word for what happens when lively individuals escape from a barrel. They streak across the dock in rapid bursts, nine times out of ten in the direction of the water. Handlers have to jump to catch them.

With such advantages do blue crabs go about their life, which is an almost continual hunt for food. They will hunt, in fact, at the least opportunity and with great patience. A good place to observe their patience is at the ferry dock at Tylerton on Smith Island. The watermen here have the habit of dumping their worn-out boat engines right off the dock, asking any who criticize the practice what earthly purpose is served in lugging the heavy things any farther. Although their wives may complain about the impression created on visitors, the local marine fauna love the old engine blocks. Minnows and the fry of larger fish swarm through these rusty castles, swimming in and out of their numerous turrets and vaulted chambers. As might be expected, crabs are attracted. They hold themselves poised in the water, hovering perfectly, with arms rigidly extended. If the tide is not strong, it is another excellent opportunity to appreciate swimming leg flexibility; each leg can easily be seen whirling in medium-speed helicopter rotation, with the paddles serving as the variable pitch rotor blades. When choice minnows present themselves, of course, the crabs dart at them. They usually miss. But being mostly juveniles, they happily try again and again. I have watched this phenomenon at length and often, to the point, I am sure, that the Tylertonians think me strange.

Older crabs are said to be too wise to engage in such shenanigans; they prefer to hunt live prey by burying themselves lightly in sand or mud and seizing by surprise. We cannot say, however, what any blue crab may do in a pinch. Dr. Austin Williams of the National Marine Fisheries Service, an expert who has recently published a definitive reappraisal of the genus *Cal-*

linectes, tells of a singular occurrence which involved three-inch or virtually adult crabs, since at this length blue crabs are but one or two moults away from legal catch size.

"I was working down at the University of North Carolina's Marine Laboratory in Morehead City, and we had just built a series of experimental ponds," Dr. Williams recalls. "The ponds were new, with clay liners, and no established fauna to speak of. Not long after introducing the crabs, I was surprised to see them gathering in numbers near the outlets of the pipes supplying water to each pond. The crabs were highly agitated, stabbing away at nothing that I could see. On further investigation we found that our pumped water was not yet saline enough. We were breeding mosquitos, it seems. The crabs were actually snapping at mosquito larvae with their claws."

It was impossible to see if the crabs gained anything from this exercise. Dr. Williams does not rule out the possibility, since the crabs kept at it tirelessly. "Anyway, we decided we were very bad husbandmen to have our crabs doing this," he says. "They must have been nearly starving." Happily, the ponds soon produced more substantial fare, and the crabs were eventually seen to stop snapping at nothing.

How often crabs hunt and kill each other is a matter of considerable debate. Throughout history, the world has viewed crabs as unpleasant and bellicose animals. "Crab" is synonymous with a nasty or complaining disposition in a great many languages. Both *cancer* and *karkinos*, the Latin and Greek forms respectively, have been borrowed to describe the world's most deadly disease. Thus cancer and carcinogens, much to the annoyance of carcinologists who are forever receiving letters from medical libraries asking what stage of the disease they are investigating. From time to time *Crustaceana*, the International Journal of Crustacean Research, suggests a change to "crustaceologist," but nothing has come of this.

Most crabbers believe the crab's bad name is not fully warranted. Opinions vary, however. "Who knows?" asks "Chas" Howard of Crisfield's Maryland Crabmeat Company. "Only thing I know is they can crawl, swim and bite like hell."

"Oh, if they're hungry enough, they fight," Grant Corbin has told me. "Get too many crowded together and that's bad, too. You remember the day we went out in June getting pots half full, with maybe ten to twenty crabs? Well, then you remember there weren't neither dead one. More than that, though, and they start beating on each other."

"Undoubtedly, crowding is a big factor, as in the crab floats," says Gordon Wheatley, an experienced crab scraper who is also principal of Tangier Island's combined grade and high school. "But sometimes crabs are just plain belligerent for no reason. Nothing within clawshot is safe."

Beyond fighting, cannibalism per se is certainly not thought to be a favored practice among blue crabs. No one has ever seen one healthy hard blue crab purposely set out to eat another in its entirety. But let a fighting crab get a walking leg or other choice morsel from one of his brothers and he will of course eat it, provided other crabs do not first steal it from him. In nature a crab that has lost a limb has an excellent chance to escape. The nearby crab community invariably swarms around the victor, who will be hard put to defend his prize. The loser is thus ignored. He or she is free to wander off and will easily grow another limb by means of a remarkable crustacean attribute known as autogeny. (The opposite, autotomy, or dropping off the limb at the socket in the first place, is done even more easily.) This is not the case, however, within the restrictions of a crab float. Quite the contrary, a floated crab with a missing claw or other disadvantage attracts further attacks. Eventually it may be killed and consumed. Thus it happens, a cannibalism of opportunity.

Also arguing against complete cannibalism—necrophagism, I suppose I should say—is the blue crab's aversion to dead of the same species. Crabbers are unanimous in their opinion that a dead crab repels live individuals, as has been repeatedly demonstrated in crab pots. "No doubt about it," says Captain Ernest Kitching of Ewell. "Crabs has got more sense. I wouldn't want to go crawl into a place with dead people, would you?"

Ask the question often enough and you begin to get a guarded and qualified consensus. Persons who know the blue crab best say that it does not normally eat its own kind or go around spoiling for a fight at every opportunity. But given an emergency or crowded artificial conditions, it will. Crowding, in fact, can even touch off wild and indiscriminate fighting under natural conditions. I had an excellent opportunity to observe such combat late one August while driving down a doubtful road on the lonely peninsula in the Dorchester marshes known as Bishop's Head. In spite of difficulties in keeping to the muddy tracks, my attention was drawn to great numbers of *Uca pugnax*, or the mudbank fiddler crab, scurrying across the road. In an adjoining creek the water continually boiled with sizeable surface explosions. The disturbance, I thought, was nothing less than a school of wayward blues or more probably spawning rockfish. Quickly I began to think of assembling my fishing rod.

But, stopping the car and getting out, I was immediately aware that fish were not the prime cause of the commotion. What had happened was this. An unusually strong spring tide had all but emptied the creek, leaving largely dry its steep five-foot banks, which were riddled with crab burrows. The impression created was of an old fashioned high-walled bathtub with three quarters of the water let out. Conditions were obviously too extreme for the little mud fiddlers, who even less than their cousin *Uca pugilator*, or the sand fiddler, cannot stand too much drying out. Undoubtedly the fiddlers were marching across the road in search of more water and a calmer venue. But more fascinating than the fiddlers' retreat was the scene in the remaining sluiceway of water, which was very clear and not more than four feet wide and a foot or two deep. Too many large blue crabs had come far up this creek, as they commonly do in marsh creeks in August to mate, and now it offered them too little space. Quite simply, the crabs were getting in each other's way. Courtship practices undoubtedly further aggravated the situation, this being the peak mating period. At courting time male blue crabs show some degree of territoriality, mainly by exhibiting a threat posture, or holding their arms out fully extended in a straight line with the claws slightly open. Between bumping into each other and threat postures that failed to convey their message, therefore, the crabs fought hard and frequently. Being generally excited, they also lunged at anything that moved in the water. Small boils punctuated by a spray of tiny silver minnows broke the surface whenever a partially buried crab jumped at live prey. Larger boils came when crabs met head-on. For the most part they sought to avoid each other, backpedaling and sidestepping, claws at the ready, very much as good boxers bob and weave in the ring. But soon, or at least every ten seconds, little volcanos erupted as one or another crab got cornered and elected to fight. Most often when the mud settled and the water cleared, one of the combatants had the limb of another in its claws. Within seconds came larger eruptions as every crab within sight zeroed in to steal the prize.

Just as insects and a glaring sun began to dictate departure, I saw a female with claws folded into the submissive posture moving carefully to avoid all possible encounters. She was of good size, six inches or better, with the clean shell of grayish cast that is a sign of recent moulting, a sook in buckram condition, in other words. Being unsure of her still weak muscles, she wisely avoided the general fray. At one point, however, her caution went too far. She found herself half out of water behind a mudball cemented with weeds. A rusty looking little male—two-thirds her size, but hard and fat— suddenly materialized on the other side of the mudball with thoughts other than courtship obviously on his mind. Both crabs then tested the obstacle with their claws for firmness. Satisfied with its consistency, the male started to crawl up and over it. Immediately the sook climbed backward out of the water a full three feet up the steep bank and settled into a cavity excavated at full tide. There she sat motionless in the broiling sun for a long time, watching me and the little male. I was clearly the lesser of two evils, being close enough to touch her. Only when the male was out of sight did she climb down and re-enter the water. Instantly she buried herself in a quiet corner, until only her eyestalks were visible.

Blue crabs hate direct sunlight and cannot long tolerate it. Loose in a boat, they always run for the shade. The sook's evasive action therefore struck me as remarkable. I do not really know how long it lasted. It seemed like five minutes. I received about six mosquito and two green fly bites, in any event, having remained motionless so as not to scare the crab. As I finally left, the creek water continued to boil unabated. The mysteries of autotomy and autogeny would be sorely tested there, I thought to myself.

Barrier Island Birds

George Reiger (b. 1939)

We return to Cobb Island, where Frank Chapman described the exploita-
tion of the native birds. Now the humans have left, and the birds have returned. George Reiger is our guide and he takes us on an expedition to
band royal terns, which are thriving on the island, now part of a Nature
Conservancy Reserve. Like any good writer and naturalist, he expands on
the narrative to present his insights into the island's human and natural
history.

Reiger is a refugee from the New York City business world who has
spent thirty years on the Eastern Shore of Virginia advocating and living his
philosophy for the responsible sportsman and landowner. His columns in
Sports Afield have been collected into many books and provide a chronicle
of hands-on conservation. Reiger has little time for theoretical conservationists or animal rightsists. Real conservation is hard work, as he well
knows, for he has practiced it for years.

From *Wanderer on My Native Shore* (New York: Simon and Schuster, 1983)

Hurry!" called John Weske as he trotted close by. "We don't have much
time today. It's going to be a scorcher!"

Even as our group spread out and slowly began herding flightless baby
terns down the beach through the overwash area behind the low dunes and
toward the distant figure of John Buckalew by the holding pen, the sun's
ball levitated from the sea and struck us with the brutal force of its radiant
heat. A southerly breeze sprung up, but we knew it would offer us and the
seabirds scant relief if we didn't have them all banded and released by ten
o'clock.

A gang of about eighty terns tried to run through a break in the line two
hundred yards away. I dashed over to close the gap. Perspiration soon
formed in my eyebrows and dripped onto my glasses, and the glasses began
sliding off my nose. I signaled to the flank woman to move out and cover
my former zone down by the surf. She couldn't hear me for the roll of the

water, and I couldn't hear her for the screaming of adult terns diving close overhead, but she finally grasped the meaning of my frantic arm motions.

Wildlife research is glamorous stuff to read about in an armchair where such realities as heat, biting insects, grime, improvised food, and disappointment—the constant disappointment of missed opportunities and simple misjudgment—do not intrude on the coolly worded summaries. Nor do wildlife reports provide many clues to the years of grueling effort that sometimes go into a single insight.

The two researchers for whom we will band birds this sultry July dawn are John Weske and John Buckalew, both former employees of the U.S. Fish and Wildlife Service. Buckalew started banding birds in 1927, long before there was a Chincoteague National Wildlife Refuge for him to manage and near which he presently lives retired. By contrast, John Weske quit the service in mid-career when it sought to reassign him away from his beloved crested tern project—an effort he first began in the late 1960s. Now he continues the project, using his savings and odd-job money to finance the research, driving back and forth between the coast and his parents' home in suburban Washington, D.C., in an ancient automobile and towing a battered skiff and trailer.

Buckalew has banded almost 200,000 birds of about 180 species during the past half century. Although he is content to clamp an aluminum USFWS band around most any bird's leg, he is especially interested in the wanderings of the laughing gull. Weske, on the other hand, only began banding in 1959, and while he is willing to band other species, including helping Buckalew with his laughing-gull research, his priority—indeed, his obsession—is the second largest of all North American terns, the royal.

John Weske finds it difficult to explain how and why a boy born in Cleveland, Ohio, mostly reared in upstate New York, and who did graduate research at the inland University of Oklahoma should have developed such an abiding passion for a strictly saltwater species that nests on coastal islands from Mexico to southern Maryland. One reason, of course, may be that the royal is the most majestic of all the "sea swallows" or "strikers," as English-speaking watermen have called terns for centuries. Although the royal is not as large as the Caspian tern, the royal has a more deeply forked tail, less gull-like wings, and a less raucous cry than the Caspian. Furthermore, the royal eats only seafood (mostly small fishes of any available species and occasionally crustacea and squid) and does his own fishing, unlike the Caspian tern which commonly robs other terns of their fare as well as steals their eggs.

There are four North American species of terns with feathered crests on the backs of their heads: the Caspian, royal, sandwich, and the elegant, which looks very much like the royal tern and would cause considerable confusion among birders except that it is mostly found along the Pacific coast where the royal rarely strays. The sandwich tern has a distinctive "kirrik, kirrik" cry and normally fishes farther offshore than its larger royal and Caspian cousins. I have seen them twenty-five miles off the Virginia coast coursing over fifty-pound bluefin tuna, waiting for these pelagic predators to drive baitfish to the surface so the terns could dive for their share. The largest nesting colony of sandwich terns along the Atlantic coast is found on Ocracoke Island, North Carolina, which is, perhaps not coincidentally, closer to the Gulf Stream than any barrier stretch north of Florida's highly developed beaches—useless, of course, to nesting sandwich terns. This species is unique in having a bright yellow tip on the end of its slender black bill.

However tempting other members of the tern tribe may be, John Weske knows there are already people studying or who have studied the little tern—with a wingspan of only twenty inches, smallest of all North American terns; the Arctic, common, and roseate terns—which look generally alike except for bill color and which I'll leave the more detailed field guides to distinguish; the Forster's tern, which can only be easily distinguished from other similar-sized terns during the winter when it wears a narrow black eyepatch; the gull-billed tern, which, as its name suggests, looks like a small gull with a notched tail and is often seen hawking for insects over land; and such dark coastal visitors as the black tern—a tiny insect eater which breeds on freshwater marshes; the sooty tern, and the noddy tern— both of which snatch their prey from the surface rather than dive for it like other terns, and both of which breed along the U.S. Atlantic coast only on Dry Tortugas at the extreme end of the Florida Keys. Weske feels he would not be making as much of a contribution by reevaluating the work of other researchers as by getting afield himself and studying such a relatively unknown species as the royal tern. Surprisingly, before Weske began his work little more than a decade ago, no one had showed much scientific interest in the royal.

Ten years of more than a hundred juvenile roundups like the one we are on, of tracking down information stemming from the scant return of bands, of travel to remote islands to study the birds' wintering as well as breeding habits, and what has John learned about the royal tern?

He has discovered that royal terns are opportunistic colonizers, ready

". . . the screaming of adult terns diving close overhead." Royal Terns, B. Hines, from *Wanderer on My Native Shore*

to move into new areas for breeding rather than clinging stubbornly—and, therefore, disastrously—to former breeding islands overrun by the children of man and his dogs and cats. This explains why Cobb Island, Virginia— uninhabited today and where we will band nearly a thousand young royals—had no record of breeding royal terns at the turn of the century when it was a popular resort for wealthy Northerners.

The flexibility of royal terns in responding to changing barrier island conditions makes them analogous to the shad family of fishes which select breeding rivers sometimes far removed from their natal streams if those new rivers are more suitable for propagation than the old. Many other Atlantic seabirds are less flexible than the royal tern, and the alcids, which include puffins and dovekies, are analogous to Atlantic salmon in that once a puffin or a salmon loses its natal ground, the total population of puffins or salmon shrinks by that number of nonreproducing birds and fish unless their eggs or young are artificially introduced elsewhere.

Another important fact about royal terns is that they rarely nest before they are three years of age. In all the years of Weske's research, he has found only one two-year-old bird in a breeding colony and that one may only have been a voyeur to the nuptial proceedings. Furthermore, he suspects that the majority of royals may not begin breeding until they are four years of age. This obviously raises special problems for the management of such a species. Most birds, like the popularly hunted puddle ducks, breed the spring after they hatch. Barring such natural calamities as drought or severe winters, mallards are a cinch to manage if the objective of management is to ensure sufficient survival to maintain the same approximate number of breeding pairs year after year.

However, management difficulties increase with each additional spring it takes for a species to reach sexual maturity. That may be why certain diving ducks, which are two and three years old before they begin breeding, have such unstable populations in comparison with the mallard or pintail. Hunting regulations can only be established by the U.S. Fish and Wildlife Service in consultation with the Canadian Wildlife Service based on this year's crop of goldeneye, not what may happen to those species' breeding sites during the next two years.

That is also why the Atlantic sturgeon and most sharks—species which take well over a decade to mature—are well nigh impossible to manage for sustained yields, and why commercial fisheries for such species always have collapsed. Finally, that is why it is irresponsible to exploit any resource before we understand its life cycle and ecological requirements, and why—

although there is no longer a market for common tern wings and royal tern eggs as there once was along the Atlantic coast—the royal tern's population tends to fluctuate wildly, while the rapidly maturing common tern's numbers rise and fall more gradually. Of course, there is a kind of resilience built into the population dynamics of any species capable of reproducing many times before the individuals die. John Weske has recovered royal terns that were at least seventeen years of age, and older birds almost certainly exist, but bands sometimes fall off or their numbers become obliterated after longtime exposure to the marine environment.

Still, royal tern parents tend only one egg at a time. When they lose that one, they may make another nesting effort that season, but more often they do not. One year there may be more than five thousand successful breeding pairs of royal terns on Cobb Island; the next year, a summer storm over-washes the island and sweeps away every egg or chick. A significant portion of that entire species' year group has been lost, and four years down the road there will be a slump in reproduction even though breeding conditions seem ideal. Such slumps were once regarded as mysterious, but now are less so, thanks to John Weske's ongoing monitoring of the species.

For those who feel that security and "getting on" is what life is all about, John Weske has "wasted" his life. For those of us who feel that curiosity is a rare gift that should not be squandered doing what less gifted people can do, Weske's work takes on the quality of an odyssey, and each discovery becomes another small milestone in our longing to understand life.

After the terns were safely corralled, Weske gave me a carpenter's apron and a necklace of bands. I strapped on the apron and unclasped the necklace, sliding the bands into one of the apron's pockets. The other pocket contained a pliers for clasping the bands around the birds' legs.

"Any particular way you want this done?" I asked. "Right leg? Left leg? The band right side up?"

"I band all my birds' right legs. Other banders band the left. That's so we can tell our birds apart at a distance. Also, try to keep the band numbers up so we can read them later with a spotting scope."

"Can you really make out these tiny numbers on a free-flying bird?" I asked.

"Not flying, but free," interjected John Buckalew. "I get some of my best 'returns' on laughing gulls just sitting in my car in the Assateague parking lots with a pair of powerful glasses."

"Make sure you don't band any sandwich terns with the bands I gave you," said Weske. "They're strictly for royals. All baby terns look somewhat alike, so if you have any doubts, give John or me a shout."

Buckalew was already on his knees passing birds over the wire screen to three other volunteer assistants for banding. He managed to keep the volunteers supplied with terns and still band more birds than the rest of us combined.

"You seem to be experienced at this sort of thing," I said to Buckalew as I reached in for my first bird.

"You might say." Then with hardly a glance at the bird I was holding, he commented, "You better let me have that one. It's a sandwich tern."

As if in confirmation of the fact, as I passed the young bird to John, an adult sandwich tern swooped down between us. How had the parent picked its youngster out of the many hundreds of birds crowded in the corral?

Vocalization seems to be the key. Just as human parents can recognize the sound of their youngsters amid the din of a kindergarten, royal and sandwich terns can distinguish their young in the crèches into which the baby birds are herded and fed. Of course, there are subtle differences in coloring, and as John Buckalew could distinguish the pinkish baby sandwich tern bill and smaller bill and leg proportions from those of a baby royal tern with yellower bill, the parent terns probably identify equally subtle differences in plumage. However, such marks only confirm what their hearing has already told them: this chick is mine.

Buckalew quickly squeezed a smaller-sized band (3b) around the sandwich tern's leg and released it. The bird quickly trotted off across the sand with its parent hovering overhead and seeming to chide the youngster, as if it had somehow been responsible for the predicament of the past hour.

Cobb Island has a unique history that is at the same time typical of all Virginia's coastal islands which were settled early and abandoned in comparatively recent times as storm tides and the continually rising sea took their toll of human life and treasure. The next island north of Cobb Island, Hog Island, had a post office and daily mail service until Friday, February 15, 1941. Now only waterfowl hunters seasonally occupy a decommissioned Coast Guard station on the north end of the island, and sand blows through the broken windshields of vintage automobiles that once took summer visitors for Sunday-afternoon drives along the strand.

In 1833, Nathan Cobb, his wife, and their three sons sailed from Cape Cod to Virginia's Eastern Shore where Cobb bartered several hundred bags of salt boiled from a local seep for the barrier island that now bears his name. In those days, Cobb Island was nearly twice as large and considerably higher than it is today, and its southern end was more than half a mile east of its present location. Although our banding party had a half hour's boat run across Broadwater Bay to reach the island, back when the Cobb boys were courting local girls on the mainland, they had to sail more than half a day to reach Willis Wharf.

Eventually the boys returned to their father's island with their brides, and the extended family set up a successful market-gunning enterprise before the Civil War and then a luxury resort for triumphant Yankees after the war. Ducks, geese, swans, and shorebirds were shot for Northern food markets, and when the millinery trade took to using mounted whole terns and wings, the Cobbs cleverly charged their sporting guests a guide fee and a stiff price for shot and powder, and then the Cobbs sold the birds to schooner captains working up the coast. The most valuable tern was the tiny least, for which traders paid the Cobbs between 10 and 25 cents each, depending on condition and increasing scarcity. However, even common terns' wings were worth a few pennies since they could be styled into hats for ladies who could not afford to buy a chapeau with the whole mounted bird.

Cobb Island's relative distance from major fashion markets may have been the reason the Cobbs were not paid more for birds that sold for as much as $50 by the time they were converted into hats. Gunners on Long Island and in New Jersey received up to $1 a bird. Yet more modest prices for Southern birds did little to protect terns nesting along the Delmarva Peninsula. Upward of 40,000 terns were shipped from Cobb Island one summer, while farther north, according to ornithologist Frank Michler Chapman, Gull Island, Long Island, and Muskeget Island, Massachusetts, "are the only localities, from New Jersey to Maine, where the once abundant Common Tern, or Sea Swallow, can be found in any numbers." Every other colony had been blitzkrieged. "Now it is the Egret's turn," predicted Chapman.

Today, the Cobbs are long gone from the Virginia island named for them. Of all the grand buildings that once graced this strand, only a dilapidated Coast Guard station, an older life saving station, and a modern peregrine falcon hacking tower brave the periodic hurricanes. The last cemetery marker was sucked into the sea twenty-five years ago, and brown sharks now cruise over the site of the former resort's ballroom. The island has reverted to the wild, and the summer silences of the 1890s have been replaced by the cries of thousands of breeding birds.

Frank Chapman visited Cobb Island at least twice about the turn of the century and made museum history with specimens he collected there. Before 1900, mounted institutional wildlife was mostly displayed in dusty glass cases. While possibly useful to the specialist, bird collections were a bore to the general public. At last, the British Museum began experimenting with new display techniques, and an American sportsman and philanthropist, John L. Cadwalader, saw what the British were doing on one of his annual shooting trips to Scotland. He returned to America and offered Frank Chapman a generous sum of money if he could improve upon British efforts. In Chapman's own words:

"The result was the Cobb's Island, Virginia, group. It shows a section of beach six by 18 feet with its birds on their nests and in the air, and its vegetation so arranged to merge with a painted background of the ocean that, at a short distance, one cannot tell where the group itself ends and the painting begins. The desired illusion is, therefore, secured; the group conveys a feeling of the seashore and its life, and the birds, placed in their natural surroundings, can be studied in relation to their actual environment."

Chapman's more conservative and jealous colleagues hated the idea of mixing art and illusion with science and reality. They conspired to have the exhibit thrown out. However, Chapman's tenacity and the wisdom of a few senior board members of the American Museum of Natural History (including President Theodore Roosevelt) eventually swept the criticism aside, and this first wildlife group in diorama established a standard for museum displays imitated by institutions around the world to the present day.

Chapman was also an innovator in at least two other respects. In the 1900 edition of *Bird-Lore* (predecessor to today's *Audubon* and *American Birds*, published by the National Audubon Society), he proposed a "Christmas side hunt in the form of a Christmas bird census," to stand in contrast to the sporting side hunts that had gone out of fashion in which "everything in fur or feathers that crossed their path" were killed by local shooters. The concept caught on, and today about 125 million birds of several hundred different species are counted in more than 1140 count circles, 15 miles in diameter, from the Arctic to South America.

Chapman's other innovation was a bird identification guide for laymen. Ornithologist Elliott Coues (1842–1899) had created the first "keys" and "checklists" for North American birds beginning in 1872. However, these publications were for the already expert. Chapman's contribution was in recognizing the need for a manual to get the fledgling birder going.

In 1895, D. Appleton and Company published Chapman's *Handbook of*

Birds of Eastern North America, and within a decade the book had gone through six "editions," in those days meaning printings. In 1920, Chapman published *What Bird Is That?* subtitled "A Pocket Museum of the Land Birds of The Eastern United States Arranged According to Season." This book had a less successful publishing history, and some editors may have thought that the field guide phenomenon was over. However, a decade later, a young illustrator and amateur ornithologist by the name of Roger Tory Peterson thought he could refine Chapman's concept by focusing on distinguishing field marks in a genuinely portable book that would at the same time eliminate much of the background information on birds which Chapman had stressed, but which was more suitable to armchair reading than quick reference for identification in the field.

Peterson published his first *Field Guide to the Birds* in 1934. The book has subsequently gone through four major revisions with dozens of printings in between.

As a guide to general rules of observation, Chapman's *Handbook* still contains much to recommend it. For example, on page 80 of the seventh edition (1907), Chapman tells us that the quickest way to distinguish a distant tern on the wing from a gull is that "a Tern points its bill directly downward, and looks, as Coues says, like a big mosquito, while a Gull's bill points forward in the plane of its body." Unfortunately, neither Chapman nor any modern guide tells us exactly where the black skimmer fits in. This bird looks like a hybrid ternxgull, and indeed, it even flies like one, with its head pointing neither directly down nor "in the plane of its body." The skimmer is a colonial nester on the same barrier islands where royal terns and laughing gulls breed. Its nest or scrape, no more than a slight depression in the sand, is often found in overwash areas behind the dunes close to tern colonies, and the aggressive defensiveness of terns near their own scrapes and crèches probably helps protect the eggs and chicks of the more passive skimmer from marauding herring and great black-backed gulls, both of which are extending their breeding range south along the Atlantic coast at the expense of other gulls and terns.

Skimmers and certain terns, along with such disparate species as flamingos, common eiders, and emperor penguins, share the habit of herding newly hatched young into nurseries where only a few adults guard them while the rest of the adults are out getting food. This nursery or, more properly, crèche phase lasts the four to five weeks (in the case of terns and skimmers) it takes the young birds to fledge and fly. By the way, contrary to popular misuse of the word, fledglings can fly; it is nestlings—or in this case, crèchlings(!)—that cannot.

The black skimmer, scissor-bill, or flood gull, as local watermen call the bird, is one of three species worldwide in the separate scientific family Rynchopidae. Its large red and black-tipped bill is distinctive, and not in color alone. The skimmer is the only North American bird whose lower mandible is longer than its upper. As Chapman wrote, "opening the mouth, the bladelike lower mandible is dropped just beneath the surface of the water; then, flying rapidly, they may be said to literally 'plow the main' in search of their food of small aquatic animals."

Since the skimmer is a tactile rather than a visual feeder, this species is the most nocturnal of all coastal birds except the night herons. In the evening, the wind dies, and skimmers sail across the calm surface of darkened coves or beneath the blinking lights of channel markers and snap up young menhaden and silversides swept by on the incoming moon tides. When in small flocks working a particularly productive turning in the marsh or possibly one illuminated by marine lights which serve to draw baitfish close to the surface, the birds clack and quack incessantly while executing spectacular turns and glissades to avoid collisions. Their constant chatter doubtless keeps each skimmer informed as to the whereabouts of his feeding kin.

The banding was nearly over. Fewer than a hundred terns remained in the holding pen. It was nine o'clock. We'd be finished and back in the shade on the mainland long before the sun gave us the full effect of its furnace glare and heat. And we had not lost a single bird.

I stood to stretch my legs and saw John Weske coming across the overwash with a bird and a fisherman's landing net. John had left us ten minutes earlier to make sure that the fledglings being tended by adults south of our roundup area had already been banded. I met him halfway back to the corral.

"It's an adult royal tern with a broken wing," he explained. "I found it on the other side of the dunes. I know you have a federal salvage permit, and you know someone who rehabilitates injured wildlife. So I brought it back to you to make the choice."

The tern's left wing was broken in two places, and at one of the breaks, I felt splintered bone beneath the skin. Even if the wing was repaired with a splint, it would not mend so the bird could fly again. The bird would always be a cripple, and nature has no use for flightless or sightless terns. I held the bird's breast and began applying pressure on its lungs and heart with my thumb and forefinger.

The tern began to pant and tried to twist from my hand, but it quieted when I stroked its head with my free hand. Whether or not the bird was a breeder it had already shed the adult's black breeding cap, revealing the white feathered forehead which helps distinguish this tern through most of the year from the dark-foreheaded Caspian species.

"There is a man named Balram Pertab in Guyana," said John Weske, "who regularly reports band numbers from royal, roseate, and especially common terns. He apparently catches the birds for food. We'd like to discourage this practice, of course, but he says he has failed at everything else he has ever tried in life, except bird catching, and since there is no point in catching birds unless you eat them, we really shouldn't ask him to give up his livelihood. Since we naturally value the fact he is one of the few people in that part of the world to make the effort to report banded birds, we try to ignore what his numerous reports imply—especially when it comes to roseate terns which, because of their increasing scarcity, may become the first federally protected *Sterna* under the Endangered Species Act."

The royal tern's eyes had closed and its head lolled to one side. Alive, the bird had seemed larger and more substantial than its statistical eighteen-inch length. In death, the tern appeared smaller and strangely fragile.

I slipped off my shirt and carefully bound the tern's body to protect its plumage. I would mount the bird and give it to The Nature Conservancy which owns this island and most other islands in the Virginia barrier chain. Perhaps, one day a diorama of island life can be constructed at the mainland headquarters of the Virginia Coast Reserve, and people unable to visit the islands but curious to know about them will have a chance to see—and possibly to learn—something about coastal life-forms which no longer exist on islands that man can easily reach.

The Passion of Eels *and* Potomac: The Nation's Sewage Plant

Tom Horton (b. 1945)

Tom Horton is a columnist for the *Baltimore Sun* and a strong advocate for the restoration of the Chesapeake Bay. His book, *Bay Country*, won the Burroughs Medal in 1988, and is a worthy successor to the books of Klingel and Warner. Horton addresses conservation and restoration more than his predecessors. Like Warner, he has mastered the scientific work being done on the bay and is able to discuss it in a manner that is both enjoyable and understandable to the lay reader. His discussion of the reverse migration of eels is a fine example of this style.

He brings the same skill to his discussion of the Blue Plains Sewage Plant in the second selection. At the time, this plant was the most technologically advanced in the world and was a major factor in the early restoration of the bay. It may seem strange to some readers that we are including this piece in an anthology of natural history writing. The problems of pollution and habitat destruction have become integral to the natural environment; we believe that written discussion of such problems from this perspective can be considered natural history writing.

Both selections from *Bay Country* (Baltimore: Johns Hopkins University Press, 1987)

The Passion of Eels

AROUND THE Chesapeake Bay, our attention to autumn's migrations tends to be monopolized by wild geese returning. We scarcely notice the concurrent exodus of another creature from every rivulet in the estuary's 41-million-acre drainage basin, a journey that is still tinged with mystery more than twenty-three centuries after humanity began to wonder at it. It begins as it probably has begun for seventy million years, on October and November nights, always in the dark quarter of the moon, usually in the wake of a storm. Throughout the bay and throughout half the globe, the eels' hour has come. Only a few Marylanders anymore are attentive to the great departure for the spawning grounds. A handful of the bay's commercial watermen harvest the ocean-bound hordes of eels, chasing them down the bay until, miles off the Virginia capes, the migration drops over the lip of the continental shelf, a point beyond which no one has ever seen a spawning eel.

Even before the watermen, Tony Robucci has seen the migration coming. Robucci, of Hagerstown, is superintendent of Minor Power Stations for the Potomac Edison Power Company. Each fall the eels, moving down from Appalachian and Piedmont creeks high in the drainage of the Shennandoah [*sic*] and Potomac rivers, must be cleaned from the turbines in the utility's old but cost-efficient hydropower dams in Western Maryland. "I have seen 'em four-foot long and they can clog the water intakes some years," Robucci says. An eel that big may have spent nearly twenty years maturing, much of it in a stream no wider than you can jump across. Camouflaged by their grayish and muddy yellow coloration, and nocturnal in their activities, eels are such unobtrusive residents that people are surprised to find how abundant they are. With the possible exception of man, no species ever has colonized the bay's watershed more ubiquitously. A five-year study of sixteen streams across Maryland found eels the most abundant species in all cases—up to fifteen hundred per acre of water. In the bay proper, eels by the early 1980s had become the second-biggest commercial fin fishery in Maryland, at about one million and a half pounds, behind menhaden and ahead of rockfish. The record eel ever caught here was 42.2 inches long and weighed 5 pounds, 10 ounces.

No one knows what compels the eels' fall migration. Not all of them go in any given year, nor does their departure come at any particular age or size; but those chosen have been undergoing dramatic changes for some months to ready for the long—and presumably final—journey. Their digestive tracts have shrunk and, to facilitate navigation through the darkness and the intense pressures of ocean channels one hundred times deeper than the bay's, their eyes have grown to twice normal size and their swim bladders have toughened. The shape of their skulls has altered, and their coating of slime has thickened, armoring them against dehydration from the extreme salinities they will soon encounter. And such fine-looking armor! Gone are the drab colors matching the eel to its stream-bottom home; now it shimmers olive and bronze and metallic silver that glints pink, and almost purple in certain lights. The late Gilbert Klingel was the only person I have known to describe such an eel in its full glory. He wrote in *The Bay* of a dive one night, several decades ago, beneath the bay's surface: "In the depths of the Chesapeake, in its own environment, this great eel was a thing of exceeding grace . . . but its real beauty was in the hitherto unsuspected iridesençe of its soft, silken skin . . . of a soft lustrous glow, leaf green above and pearl pink below. This pink altered in tone as the eel moved its coils. One moment it flashed pale-lavender fire, next delicate and evanescent yellows." Alas, when taken from the water, the eel's glory fades as quickly as that of tropical fish.

What triggers the great change is as much a mystery as what guides the eel—which all its life in the bay never ranges more than a few miles—to rendezvous unerringly across half an ocean with every other migrating eel in North America and Europe. Eels do not appear to rely on odors, orientation to the sun and stars, salinity and temperature differences, or any other of the underwater guideposts that are thought to guide salmon, herring, and other anadromous (upstream) spawners from the oceans to the streams of their birth. The eel, whose migration goes just in reverse, is the bay's only catadromous spawner of any note. It may well be using subtle electrical fields created by water currents to navigate from its home streams to the continental edges, scientists think; but that is still a long way from where the eel must go, and, despite the considerable amount of fishing that has gone on for centuries in the Atlantic Ocean, no one has ever caught a migrating adult eel once it leaves the continental shelf. A few eels were found in the belly of a sperm whale harpooned off the Azores years ago; and a television camera lowered into the Straits of Florida once showed a silvery female snaking along the bottom nearly a half-mile below the surface. But that is all.

Apparently, their spawn (eggs) and milt (sperm) do not develop until the eels are well at sea. Thus, outside of laboratory experiments, it is still true what Aristotle, the first person to establish that eels moved downstream to the sea, wrote twenty-three centuries ago: "Nor was an eel ever found with either milt or spawn." (Wouldn't that be a gift for the person with everything, for the most jaded gourmet—caviar produced from eel roe, a dish no king has ever tasted?) This uncertainty about eels' spawning led to some wild versions of how they reproduced, including spontaneous generation from slime, or from horsehairs thrown into water. Oppian of Cilicia in A.D. 2 gave poetic expression to what until recent times remained the most widely held theory—that the eel mated with snakes:

[the eel] glowing with uncommon fires,
the Earth-bred Serpent's purfled curls admires;
He, no less kind, makes amorous returns.
With equal love the grateful serpent burns.

. . . His mate he calls with softly hissing sounds.
She joyful hears and from the ocean bounds.

Seamier details of this slimy affair abound in Oppian's *Aleuticon*. By 1684, a Tuscan nobleman, Francesco Redi, had confirmed that adult eels spawned in the sea. But no one had a clue as to where until just before the Civil War, when German scientists first identified as European eel larvae some transparent organisms the shape and size of willow leaves, found floating in the Strait of Messina. Nearly half a century more passed before the detective hunt for the birthing place of the eel began in earnest. A young Danish biologist and oceanographer, Johannes Schmidt, was charged by his government to crisscross the Atlantic, dragging a fine mesh net behind his ship, the *Thor*, until he found where the little willow leaves originated. For years the search spread—to the North Sea, the English Channel, the Faero Islands, the Azores, across to Newfoundland and down to the Antilles—twenty-three Danish ships were involved by now. Ever smaller *Leptocephali*, as the larval eels were called, kept turning up as Schmidt closed in on the location, finally announced in 1920. It turned out to be a place of super-saline, stagnant water where an estimated ten million pounds of seaweed in great clumps drifted timelessly in an area nearly the size of the continental United States.

"It might very well be," wrote Rachel Carson, "that some of the very weeds you would see if you visited the place today were seen by Columbus and his men." The place she spoke of, the birthplace and universal spawning ground of all the eels of two continents, was in the depths of the Sargasso Sea. The helpless, free-floating larvae, the little willow leaves, scientists would later show, are seized by great, slow, clockwise currents that many months, even years, later deliver the American and European eels near their respective seacoasts (their spawning areas are in slightly different parts of the Sargasso).

By the time they reach the coastal fringes, the eels have reached the "elver" stage, a few inches long, looking quite eel-like, and are able to swim on their own. And how. Up and up they go, up the bay, up the rivers, up the creeks, up the sheer walls of high concrete dams, up sewer pipes, even overland to ponds and wells more than a mile from flowing water. What urge impels them so toward fresh water, to bodies of water they could not possibly have prior knowledge of, is not understood, save that it is one of the more powerful motive forces on the planet. They surmount Great Falls on the Potomac in Washington, D.C., a barrier that historically has stopped even the great leaping spawners like the shad. Richard St. Pierre, a fisheries biologist with the federal government on the Susquehanna River, says he routinely gets reports of eels crushed as they slither across U.S. Route 1 where it traverses the top of the Conowingo Dam. Built in the 1920s, Conowingo is more than one hundred feet straight up.

Because the eel breathes quite nicely through its skin as long as it is moist, it can travel over land some distance if there is so much as a heavy dew on the ground. Sometimes, if it cannot climb a dam, it just goes around it. Eels returning from the Sargasso appear to have crossed even the eastern continental divide which runs through the far western third of Garrett County in Maryland. Traveling, perhaps, through inland waterways of the Potomac system, eels have somehow gotten into the Youghiogheny, the only river in Maryland that flows toward the Gulf of Mexico rather than the bay. Charles J. Hassel, Jr., a thirty-five-year plumbing veteran of New York City, tells of the time the water supply was cut off for an entire building at Third Avenue and Sixty-third Street. Blocking the main pipe was a healthy, thrashing, two-foot eel.

It is mostly female eels that seem to have the urge to push as far upstream as the water lasts, say John Foster and Robert Brody, the state biologists who have made a study of Maryland's eel population. Males, which never grow more than about 18 inches long, stay in brackish water and in the creeks along the ocean coast. Chincoteague National Wildlife Refuge takes advantage of the seaside elver run each spring by opening floodgates connecting fresh-water ponds with the ocean. The millions of elvers thus trapped in the ponds provide food for migrating wading birds and, indirectly, hearty fare for the tens of thousands of bird-watchers who flock to Chincoteague each spring. As you might expect of eels, they don't all follow the rules. I know one big old female that, for whatever reasons, never pushed farther upstream than Smith Island, where she has lived for years under the crab shanty of a man in Rhodes Point, who feeds her royally on dead soft crabs.

Foster and Brody know as much as most scientists about the habits of eels, but even they, in talking about where eels go to spawn and die, at depths far below our scrutiny, must always hedge. To recall Aristotle's writings, "nor was an eel ever found with either milt or spawn." Scientists have, however, calculated the calories of energy in the body of an adult eel and then estimated the energy that eel would have to expend on its spawning run to the Sargasso. It looks like they have a one-way ticket. It is easy to imagine their arrival on the spawning grounds, based on such one-way trips documented in some salmon species—flesh literally rotting, bones demineralized and spongy, all systems irreversibly shutting down, remaining energies all channeled into the organs of reproduction, a sad, ruined version of Klingel's glorious encounter beneath the Chesapeake. But what a way to end it all. Imagine billions of eels, each female bearing millions of eggs, silvery projectiles all converging on the dark, warm Sargassan womb (also tomb), literally disintegrating in a blast of superfecundation that covers thousands of square miles, only then sinking slowly into the cold abysses, even as a galaxy of tiny willow leaves starts drifting gently back toward the Chesapeake Bay.

Potomac: The Nation's Sewage Plant

Potomac River, September

In the way a space buff would thrill to strap into the command capsule of a moon rocket, and a horse-racing fan dreams of saddling the Derby winner for a gallop, I like to use the throne room here at the Blue Plains Regional Wastewater Treatment Plant. I like to hear the toilets flush, reverberating through the capacious tile and porcelain and chrome chambers with all the authority one would expect of the sewage plant that serves the capital of a world power and safeguards the health of the nation's river into which it discharges. No other sewage plant on earth combines the size and sophistication of Blue Plains. This is the Apollo Mission of water-pollution control, our thoroughbred champion in the high-stakes race to reclaim our rivers.

Now, if there are two things we nature lovers generally revile as the answers to environmental concerns, they are bigness and technological fixes. Both tend to ignore natural limits to growth and are all too capable of creating problems as bad as the ones they solve. Both reach perhaps their ultimate synthesis in Blue Plains on the Potomac. If there is anyplace where society's pursuit of progress at the peril of natural systems should be bumping up hard against the limits of big high-tech to prevent disaster, it ought to be here at Blue Plains.

It ought to be, but you won't find evidence of it in the definitive report on the state of the Chesapeake Bay and its tributaries that was issued by the EPA after six years of studying the region's most pressing water-quality problems. Almost lost in the EPA's overall message of system-wide decline was this: "parts of the Potomac River ... currently exhibit improving water quality." So dramatically had some types of aquatic life rebounded that professional bass guides had begun working out of marinas within the District of Columbia. The Potomac's condition was a clear testament to better sewage treatment undertaken after pollution turned the national river into a national embarrassment by the late 1960s. With marvelous understatement, the EPA report of 1983 concluded: "This policy, costing about a billion dollars, seems to have worked."

At the heart of the policy, having absorbed the lion's share of the billion in federal and state tax dollars, stands Blue Plains, the final defense interposed between the wastes from two million people and the Potomac, a Maginot line that works, that seems to say, for enough money, we *can* have our cake (rapid development) and eat it too (enjoy healthy rivers). There is a flaw in such comfortable assumptions, but environmentalists who hope to expose it by waiting for Blue Plains to reach its limits do not understand the nature and history of how our society controls its pollution. Blue Plains collects sewage from an area as large as the drainage basins of many bay rivers. Wastes that enter its arteries on a Tuesday evening out around Leesburg, Virginia, or in Damascus, almost in Frederick County, may not receive final processing at the main plant until the weekend. Sewage moves through Blue Plains at the rate of a third of a billion gallons a day, a capacity that virtually equals all the other sewage plants in Maryland combined. Of the nearly thirteen million people who live in the five-state watershed of the Chesapeake Bay, an area sprawling nearly from Vermont to North Carolina, around 15 percent are hooked to a single sewage-treatment works, Blue Plains.

The plant's beginnings—construction was completed in 1938 on a parcel of land originally called Blew Playne—did not bespeak the current, high level of faith in technology to overcome any sewage problem that might arise. Its location, on the Potomac's east shore below Bolling Air Force Base and not far above the Woodrow Wilson Bridge, was chosen on the simple premise that it could cast its effluent downstream beyond the ability of the tides to bring it back into sniffing distance of the District. Those early years were relatively quiet ones for Blue Plains, which only removed about 40 percent of the gross pollutants in the sewage then. "It looked like a college campus . . . beautifully landscaped," an old-time plant engineer recalled recently.

Now the plant, approaching its fiftieth anniversary, has become a small city, with its own quarterly news magazine. Scarcely a corner of the 154-acre site remains which is not devoted wholeheartedly to concrete and steel, working furiously to process the unrelenting river hurtling down upon Blue

Plains from its 725-square-mile catchment area. Rail spurs shuttle in the chemicals that Blue Plains gulps by the 55-ton tanker-car load in purifying its sewage, and a continuous stream of trucks flows in and out of the grounds to carry off the four million pounds of solid residues, or sludge, extracted every day from the waste water. The sizeable technocracy required to maintain the quality of the effluent that enters the Potomac is housed in a soaring, pyramid-like headquarters building, elegantly sheathed in bronze-gold reflecting glass. This last, along with the plant's near-billion-dollar price tag, have earned Blue Plains the sobriquet the "Craphouse Taj Mahal" in national sewer circles.

Blue Plains' state-of-the-art manipulation of sewage begins straightforwardly enough, where twin pipes, large enough to drive through in an eighteen-wheeler, feed the plant through a set of *bar screens*, mammoth grates of steel with inch-square openings. These pluck the grossest matter—tennis shoes, beer cans, condoms, small trees—from the raw sewage, which does not look so gross as you might imagine, because even at this point it is around 97 percent water, 3 percent solids. Visitors to sewage plants always have to make their quota of bad jokes and tasteless questions. I ask Ray Brown, a veteran of twenty-five years in the "primary treatment" section of Blue Plains, do they ever get dead or dismembered bodies off the bar screens? Oh, he says, he recalls a limb or two, probably amputated at hospitals; then, almost as an afterthought, "of course we used to get them . . . ah, them feces . . . " What does he mean, "feces"? What else would a sewage treatment plant get? "No, I mean . . . you know," he gropes for another word . . . "they mostly stopped after the Supreme Court"—he points vaguely uptown across the river—"after they made that abortion ruling. When we would used to get the little things on the bar screens we'd call the cops, give 'em a little burial."

Past the bar screens, the sewage races turbulently through deep, concrete header channels, where grit, sand, and gravel settles out. At this point, the color of the water is a dense, slatey, gray-green. At no point through the plant does it smell all that foul. Emerging into the sunlight, the sewage lingers in a series of placid, circular ponds, one hundred feet in diameter, where further settling of solid matter occurs. Great flocks of seagulls ride the arms of mechanical grease skimmers which revolve around the surface of each pond; frequently, a bird will hover and pluck something gray and rubbery-looking from the water. A cool autumn breeze whisks away odors, and a warm sun spangles the Potomac in the background and glances off the headquarters pyramid, set in golden splendor against a sky of bright, blue enamel. The ponds and seagulls are the final stages in the physical cleansing processes known as primary sewage treatment, which Blue Plains was doing by 1938, and which was as far as the big Patapsco treatment plant on Baltimore's harbor had advanced by 1983.

Next, biology and chemistry are unleashed on the sewage, by this point slightly more translucent than it looked in primary. Giant aerating pumps bring it to a rolling boil in dozens of long, narrow channels that cover several acres. This is where microbes that feed on oxygen and waste attack the subtler stuff, like coffee and other dissolved solids that remain after primary treatment. It sounds simpler than it is. Much care and thought are devoted here to the proper care and feeding of "the bugs," as the microbes are called. Keep them hungry, but don't starve them, and watch so that heavy rainstorm flows entering the plant don't wash them away.

Don't fall into the secondary treatment ponds, workers warn you. If you did, I joke, you'd smell for a week, huh? No, you'd be dead, they say. The sewage at this point is blown so full of air that, although it looks like water, it has the consistency of whipped cream. Even a champion swimmer would go to the bottom of those deep, murky channels like a stone. Next, the "bugs" having had their go at the sewage, it is treated by adding chemicals, ferric chloride and pickle liquor, to flocculate, or precipitate out, whatever escaped the gnawing bugs. Ferric gives you better "flocc," but pickle liquor, a by-product of steelmaking, is cheaper, a technician says. Blue Plains' use of pickle liquor represents a happy partnership between the treatment plant and Bethlehem Steel's giant Sparrows Point works. Blue Plains, whose growing needs at one point were straining Dupont's entire U.S. production capability for flocculating agents, was tickled to take it off Bethlehem's hands, and out of the steel company's polluted discharges to Baltimore's outer harbor.

To all this treatment, Blue Plains also adds chlorine, a disinfectant, in quantities that demand a rail car of the chemical every week. At this point, the sewage has been detoxified to a degree equaling, and usually exceeding, almost any large treatment plant in the world, but Blue Plains is only getting cranked up. Next the waste water flows into a section of the plant where it undergoes *nitrification*. Nitrification does not actually remove waste; rather it converts elements of it to more stable chemical forms, so that they will remain essentially inert and harmless to water quality after entering the Potomac. It is a term I have heard environmental officials toss around fairly glibly at meetings called to express concerns about putting more sewage into various rivers of the bay. Don't worry, they say, if it should turn out that the river can't take the additional pollution, they have left space to expand, they will just install nitrification. You should see what "just adding nitrification" means.

At Blue Plains the sewage to be nitrified is led through a dozen concrete ponds, each nearly the length of a football field, each divided into fifty-nine separate stages for treatment. To provide sufficient aeration so that special, nitrifying bacteria may do their work, the plant is underlain by tunnels containing miles of piping, eight feet in diameter. They carry oxygen pushed by five blowers of 4,000 horsepower each. It takes $500 of electricity to flick one on and off. To control precisely the oxygen, pH (acidity), and numerous other factors so that proper nitrification occurs, Blue Plains maintains a water-quality laboratory on a concrete island amid the acres of treatment ponds which would be the envy of many a state environmental health department. Nitrification takes up about half the space of all the treatment that has preceded it, and it costs more to operate than both primary and secondary.

After hours amid the churning of sewage and the howling of blower pumps, it is a relief to enter the cool serenity of the MultiMedia Filtration building, where sewage gets a final filip and polish before it meets the river. The waste water entering here looks clear as tap water, even before it is forced through the massive filters of two-foot-thick crushed anthracite, a foot of fine sand, and a layer of almanite. After each batch of waste water has been filtered, the filters are backwashed, and clouds of the purest black mud erupt from their every square inch. They remove nearly eight tons of additional solids here each day. Plant officials, I was told, occasionally drink the final product, although my guide said he wouldn't, possibly because he works back in primary. The discharge of water from Blue Plains adds about 4 percent to the Potomac's average flow at this point although, in the very driest of times, Blue Plains may amount to half of all the fresh water coming down from the river's 9-million-acre drainage basin. EPA officials sometimes get heated calls about the quality of the plant's discharge from congressmen flying into National Airport, just upstream and across the river. They call to report what looks like an oil slick emerging from the plant. There is nothing that can be done, they are informed. The old Potomac's waters will always form a turbid contrast to the glassy clear stuff coming out of Blue Plains.

Through the gray-tinted glass of the filtration building, which is constructed just like an airport control tower, except quieter and roomier, you have a fine view back over the whole of Blue Plains, and you begin to appreciate what the water-quality engineers mean when they explain their "linear approach" to problem solving. They proceed step-wise, solving the major or most pressing problem, then turning their attention to the problems that may arise from the solution, and so on. One problem at a time, the engineers like to say. And you realize—looking back over the bar screens, grit chambers, grease-skimmers, "bug" tanks, "flocc" tanks, nitrification, filtration—that for all its sophistication, Blue Plains arose from no grand design or vision, but from decades of adding-on, usually in response to crisis in the river. It is a testament to linear problem solving; and if it seems there is never a problem that Blue Plains cannot solve, then there also seems never to be a time without a problem in need of solution. The chlorination process, for example, has raised concerns about the effects on spring spawning runs of fish from the chlorine that does not get used up in disinfection; so Blue Plains is adding another chemical process to dechlorinate its discharge; and to take care of possibly undesirable by-products of dechlorination, the engineers may tack on yet another chemical addition of sulfur dioxide. Then there is the space reserved at the plant for denitrification, which in a nutshell is what you do if it turns out that even nitrification is not enough to maintain river quality. Some people are not even sure denitrification can be done, but it is generally agreed it would cost $600 million to try it. Ironically, nitrogen is not even a problem in the Potomac River around Blue Plains; but there is mounting evidence that it acts as a major pollutant when it reaches the different chemistry of the water in the open bay at the river's mouth.

If there is a single accomplishment of which the engineers at Blue Plains are justifiably proud, it is the big plant's supreme efficiency at removing phosphorus, the "candy" in sewage on which noxious algae that can choke the river's other life depend for growth. Blue Plains removes phosphorus at an efficiency that often approaches fifty times that of conventional modern plants. Thus, in the summer of 1983, the engineers were shocked when a massive algae bloom, reminiscent of the 1960s, covered portions of the river. After two years of study, scientists hypothesized that somehow Blue Plains may have altered the pH of the river enough to liberate extra phosphorus that had been locked up in the sediments of the Potomac's bottom. The likely solution will be to add another step in the treatment process to increase the alkalinity of the waste water.

Soon, Blue Plains is going to embark on a mammoth expansion, adding capacity to send another sixty-four million gallons daily into the Potomac. Can you really do that and maintain the quality of the treated sewage that goes to the river? I asked the engineers. No, they said, they plan to improve on it. If the money—a contemplated third of a billion dollars or so—is there, the technology will not be found wanting in the foreseeable future. Pass the cake and praise the linear approach to pollution problem solving. But before anyone praises it too much, they should look at what else is implied by an extra sixty-four million gallons of sewage besides a given quantity of waste water, and its impact on a certain point in a river. For starters, the added capacity for Blue Plains means that we will be able to accommodate development to house an additional half-million or so people, mostly in the Maryland suburbs of its service area. That amounts to adding about 10 percent to the state's population, which in turn translates to a number of impacts, which spread across the whole watershed like ripples from a stone thrown into the water.

Adding 10 percent to the population, assuming current trends in our demands on the region's resources, should add about 13,000 boats to traffic on the bay each summer weekend, about 30,000 people to the peak crowds that throng Ocean City's beach, an extra 300,000 automobiles to state highways, traveling an extra two billion miles annually; also an extra 90,000 fishermen competing for catches on the bay in an extra 218,000 fishing trips, and an extra 155,000 new dwelling units. The ripples will not stop there, of course. The extra housing should boost the state's usurpation of forest and farmland for development by about three-quarters of a square mile annually for several years; and because more people will want more air-conditioning, the likelihood of having to plunk another massive power plant somewhere around the bay's edge, where it can draw cooling water, will increase dramatically—likewise for the pressure to build a third bay bridge from rural Southern Maryland to the Eastern Shore, and to embark on another round of highway building.

I thought, driving home from Blue Plains, how the rapid growth of the Washington region has already begun to affect my friend Jimmy Hancock, who has lived all his life about twenty-five miles downstream from the plant, on a lovely little capillary of the Potomac system called Mattawoman Creek. On a canoe trip, Jimmy showed me his childhood swimming hole, where the current had scooped out a place near the bank—his father swam there before him; and he took me to the sand-bottomed slough where he brought his wife when they were younger to catch snapping turtles sunning in the clear shallows. We pushed through a dense cluster of giant water lilies, found nowhere else in Maryland. He used to lie on the gravelly creek bottom and breathe through their huge, hollow stalks. He showed me wood duck chicks and wild swamp roses in recesses of the creek, and told me about the ephemeral lilac scent of one special flower that bloomed only one week each year in one tiny pocket of the marsh, "and withers in five minutes if you dare to pick it." He used to spin tales for his young son of a magical community down on the creek, presided over by Old Judge Owl and by Old King Possum, who went about dressed in spats and a silk hat and was always fighting it out for control with Old King Coon. All day long on the creek, we did not see a soul.

Jimmy, a cobbler in LaPlata in Charles County, had gotten so fed up with local efforts to develop the land around the creek that he earned a law degree by correspondence to fight for preserving the Mattawoman. He won, too. The state is acquiring much of the land for a Natural Environment Area; so I was a little shocked to hear him say, recently, that the place had changed so that he didn't go down there nearly so much anymore. It wasn't land development or water quality, per se, he explained. It was all the big powerboats that had begun to throng the creek since they had begun building new marinas up the Potomac for all the people moving into the Washington area. They churned up the shallow bottom, muddied the clear waters, were killing off the aquatic grasses . . . the place just didn't seem to belong anymore to quiet canoers and sniffers of delicate marsh flowers.

I imagine the engineers up at Blue Plains will feel some sense of accomplishment, being able to accommodate even more human waste, while maintaining, maybe even improving, water quality in places like the Mattawoman. But there is a lot more to it than meeting the list of legal requirements on pollutant discharges in the federal permits for a sewage plant. It is a lesson that we are still learning, that there is a vast difference between keeping Maryland pollution-free and keeping it lovely and unique; between keeping it environmentally legal and keeping it eminently livable. Such considerations become more critical as Maryland and its neighbor states continue on a path that will, in the next few to several decades, see twice as many people living on the land in the bay's watershed, twice as many people desiring to enjoy its waters and its shorelines, its natural areas and its aquatic resources.

The linear approach of the sanitary engineer—add on a solution wherever you spot a problem—is the way we still approach a wide range of environmental problems. But you cannot bolt on equipment to redress the loss of a paved-over forest, or add another chemical process to take the powerboats off Mattawoman Creek, or make bay watermen competitive for fish and for dock space with hundreds of thousands of well-heeled sport fishermen and sailboaters. Because the sewer puts such a sharp focus, quantifiable almost to the quart and the pound, on the pollution we all inevitably generate, there is a powerful tendency to use it as the gauge of our success or failure in protecting our environment. Some see it, hopefully, as the bottleneck whose limits ultimately will undercut our abiding faith in big, high-tech solutions to the impacts of continued growth and development. Others look at the marvels already wrought by the engineers at Blue Plains and say it is proof that such faith is justified. Both sides need to realize we may well be seeing clean water in the Potomac long after the ripple effects of an expanding and well-sewered population have degraded natural systems and supplanted traditional cultures the length and breadth of the state.

There is preliminary evidence that such a realization is dawning. Something is happening along the shores of the Potomac and around the bay that has upset the land-development interests in Maryland as nothing has done in a long time, perhaps in part because it is such a nonlinear approach to safeguarding the environment. The state has passed a law designating a thousand-foot strip around the edges of the bay and its tidal tributaries as a Critical Area. It is complex, and its regulations fill a small book, but the heart of the law says that in all the remaining undeveloped areas of the shorefront, where we do not yet have severe environmental problems, we are going to dramatically restrict human activities, to try and insure that we never do have problems to solve there. It is a very, very controversial piece of legislation, and the next decade will undoubtedly see many attempts to repeal or chip away at the concept. However, many people are convinced it is a concept that must be expanded to the whole state, not just left to protect a thin fringe nearest the water, while progress as usual builds to the bursting point behind it. What we end up doing will make a better gauge of where Maryland is headed than any measurements of treated sewage: Will we admit to limits on having our cake and eating it too? Or will it simply prove too seductive to continue as Blue Plains, to just go with the flow?

Then and Now:
Thirty-five Years in Suburbia

John Terborgh (b. 1936)

John Terborgh is James B. Duke Professor of Environmental Science and director of the Center for Tropical Conservation at Duke University. He has written extensively on the fauna of the tropics, including problems affecting songbirds migrating from North America. In *Where Have All the Birds Gone?* he provides a comprehensive review of the possible causes for the decline in neotropical migrant songbirds. Like Rachel Carson in *Silent Spring*, he opens the book with an emotional portrayal of the effects of the problems under discussion. In "Then and Now," Terborgh describes the decline in birds and other wildlife he noted thirty-five years after his childhood in northern Virginia. The Washington area provides not only the immediate personal basis for Terborgh's concerns but also valuable evidence on which the scientific arguments are based. Bird censuses in Rock Creek Park and other Washington areas, begun in the 1940s, have been conducted annually ever since; they constitute a unique database in which the decline of songbirds has been fully documented.

From *Where Have All the Birds Gone?* (Princeton: Princeton University Press, 1989)

INSPIRED BY my uncle John, I became a birdwatcher in 1950 at age fourteen. At the time (and still today) my family lived on two acres of abandoned farmland in northern Virginia. The house fronted on a winding dirt lane that came to a dead end two doors down. Our mailbox was one of a cluster at the top of the hill where our lane met the paved road. From an upstairs window one could look across a sea of treetops to the distant spires of Georgetown University across the Potomac.

A narrow path led down behind the house to a quiet wooded stream and then continued for over a mile until ending on a high bluff overlooking the river. In all that distance, the path crossed but a single road and passed by only a single house.

These woods and the stream that ran through them were my childhood playground. As it happened, none of our few neighbors had any boys my age, so instead of playing football and baseball, as I otherwise might have done, I spent my days in the woods looking for snakes and salamanders or fishing in the river.

After Uncle John focused my attention on birds, I did what most bird-watchers do, I began to keep lists—a life list, a state of Virginia list, a list for the year, and of course a list for our own 2-acre homestead. We lived in the woods, and the birds that inhabited our domain reflected this. There was always a red-shouldered hawk in the estate across the lane, and yellow-billed cuckoos, scarlet tanagers, red-eyed vireos, peewees, hooded warblers, and other birds nested along the creek at the foot of the property. Although my list eventually grew to over 150 species, the house sparrow was not among them, and other denizens of suburbia, such as purple grackles, were mainly seen flying overhead. One of my fondest memories of the period was drifting off to sleep in the lingering twilight of early summer, being serenaded by a chorus of acadian flycatchers and whip-poor-wills.

Birds were not the only songsters to liven the evenings. There were frogs and toads along the stream, a succession of them that marked the passing of the season. Spring peepers and wood frogs heralded the approach of spring after the first warm rain of March. The next mild spell recruited toads and swamp cricket frogs to the cacophony. Shortly afterward the wood frogs fell silent, and the peepers began to sing with less ardor. By now it was April, a time when the weather in Virginia can do almost anything.

Suddenly one day the temperature would soar into the eighties, and the tune would change. That evening for the first time there would be green frogs and gray tree frogs. The last to add their voices, usually not until May, were the bullfrogs, whose dronings imparted a special flavor to the summer nights.

Far less evident in their presence, but infinitely more exciting to discover, were the snakes. Though they were never easy to find, even though one knew how to look for them, there were many species, some familiar to the average country dweller, such as pilot and racer blacksnakes, garter snakes, green snakes, and water snakes, while others had names that rarely appear in print: mole snake, queen snake, worm snake, DeKay's snake.

Of all the reptiles, the most abundant and conspicuous were the box turtles. There were dozens of them, so many that one was forever having to stop the lawnmower to put one out of the way. They were a special nuisance in the garden, where they directed their attentions to our tomatoes, systematically biting a chunk out of each one as it approached the peak of ripeness. One day my father became so exasperated by these depredations that he ordered a roundup. In less than an hour, three of us gathered half a bushel of them. The unwelcome tomato thieves were then driven ten miles into the country and unceremoniously dumped in the woods. After that, the situation in the garden was better, but only slightly so. There were still plenty of turtles to be found.

A Few Years Later

It would be impossible for a boy growing up in Arlington, Virginia, today to relive these experiences. The population of the county has increased tenfold, from twenty to two hundred thousand. The woods and fields of 1950 have been converted to housing developments, roadways, and shopping plazas. Through this transition, which was essentially complete by 1960, the citizens who served on the county board were not mindless of environmental values. They zoned against high-rise apartments and large business and reserved a generous allotment of woodland to create a park system that needs no apology. But even in these protected lands, the state of nature is not the same as it was in 1950.

I know this very well, because one of the county's largest parks includes the valley behind our property. There is still a path along the stream to the river, but now one passes a number of houses and crosses three roads. Nevertheless, the park is extensive, and the woods it protects have matured over the years. A wall of trees rises behind the orchard where our land adjoins the park. On the other three sides of the property, the changes have been drastic, but not atypical. The erstwhile dirt lane is now a major commuter thoroughfare. The seventeen-acre estate across the road has become a housing development. On either side there are houses and lawns where before there had been woods and brush.

In spite of these changes, the woods along the stream are still there, little modified from their former condition except that the trees are now taller. What about the wildlife? I wish I could report that it too is very much the same, but it is not. To make a tennis court, our neighbors across the stream filled in the little marsh where the frogs bred. Spring evenings since then have been silent except for the rush of passing cars. I haven't heard a frog there in twenty years. The snakes too have vanished, though I am less certain of the reasons why. Strollers in the park are unlikely to tolerate the sight of a basking serpent. There are more cats and dogs and small boys than there used to be. But I suspect that the most important factor is the increased density of roads. Snakes, especially the larger, more conspicuous ones, do not long survive the incursion of roads into their ranges. The same can be said of box turtles. A few still survive, but finding one nowadays is a rare event.

The amphibians and reptiles of our little valley, a community that once numbered more than twenty species, have been decimated. Only the occasional box turtle affords a lingering reminder of former times. Casual observations in other parks in the county indicate that the disappearances are general; the proximity of suburbia, for one reason or another, is inimical to the survival of these humble forms of life.

The loss of lower vertebrates, about which most people care little, may not be regarded as a particular cause for concern, but birds have a following. Have they proven any more adaptable to urban encroachment? Sad to say, they have not. Granted, there are still lots of them. Robins, mockingbirds, catbirds, house wrens, song sparrows, woodpeckers, chickadees, titmice, and the like still abound, and with all these it may be easy for some, especially newcomers to the neighborhood, to assume this is the way it always was. But the birds that breed around our property now are a different lot from those we observed in 1950. My thirty-five-year-old memory won't let me forget the thrushes, warblers, vireos, cuckoos, flycatchers, and tanagers that used to liven the woods along the stream. Now there are none of these, nor have there been for a long time.

Why not? What has happened? Draining the little marsh discouraged the green herons and kingfishers that used to visit from time to time, but the disappearance of warblers and tanagers must be attributed to something else. One is tempted to point to the encroachment of suburbia, with its roads, dogs, and small boys, but the causal linkage is obscure because the forest in the park remains very much as before. What has happened to our forest birds is something more subtle, something that does not meet the unaided eye, and that scientists are just beginning to debate in earnest.

All the answers are not yet in, and for that reason one might argue that my concern is premature. My reply is that things are going wrong with our environment, even the parts of it that are nominally protected. If we wait until all the answers are in, we may find ourselves in a much worse predicament than if we take notice of the problem earlier. By waiting, one risks being too late; on the other hand, there can be no such thing as being too early.

Make Room and They Will Come
and Leaving Earth to Save It

John P. Wiley Jr. (b. 1936)

We don't often think of downtown Washington as a home for wildlife, but it does happen. Jack Wiley's article about creating habitat in Bolivar Park and the Mall can open our eyes just as the National Park Service opened these areas to wildlife. In the second selection, Wiley extends his theme of nature abhorring a vacuum to cover the whole Earth. As the final selection in this book, it can be viewed as apocalyptic or optimistic, depending on one's values.

Wiley is the conservation editor for *Smithsonian Magazine* and he writes the column "Phenomena, comment and notes." Originally trained as an astronomer, he has covered topics ranging from light pollution of the night sky to the Smithsonian study area on Barro Colorado Island, Panama. *Natural High* is a collection of the best of his columns, many of which show that city dwellers, even today, can enjoy the natural world around them if they look for it.

Both selections from *Natural High* (Hanover, N.H.: University Press of New England, 1993)

Make Room and They Will Come

IT ALWAYS surprises me to walk into a brand-new restaurant and find it packed. Presumably all those people had managed to eat the day before. But there is a kind of life pressure that rushes into any new opening, fills any space, like water pouring over uneven terrain.

People produce the most tangible life pressure. Roads, houses, shopping centers, factories spill over natural habitats like an onrushing tide. Humans push the wild into smaller and smaller spaces, leaving only the occasional pocket as park or refuge. One envisions wildlife confined to islands in a sea of human development.

But this dominant, human pressure is not the only life force rushing in to fill openings. Lots of traffic moves the other way. The wild is all around us, and pushes in on us whenever and wherever it can. The wild is searching, circling, watching, waiting for a new opening even more intently than city dwellers look for new restaurants.

Like many a city dweller, I tend to head for those parks and refuges when I want a taste of the wild. But all I really have to do is raise my eyes. There have been summer evenings when I dragged home from a day in the marsh, only to find more action in the skies above the city rooftops than I had seen all day. The nighthawks had come out and were swooping through the dusky light after the insects I could not see. And there was a morning in a quintessentially urban environment, standing on a subway platform (at an aboveground station) in a crowd of commuters. I looked up from my paper to see what the hammering was and saw a pileated woodpecker, as big as a crow, all pterodactylous black triangles, red crest flashing as it worked an old tree in back of a caterer's establishment.

The wild sneaks in every time we blink. I walk down a wide concrete sidewalk between an eight-lane avenue and a row of concrete-and-glass government buildings. There is a government gardener, meticulously pouring poison into the expansion joints in the sidewalk, trying to kill the grasses that have taken root there. She may win the battle, but she will never win the war.

This life pressure can be seen best by deliberately creating new openings. A happy band of subversives in the National Park Service (NPS) has been doing just that here in Washington, with extraordinary results. They have taken a couple of architect's reflecting pools and converted them from algae-ridden trash pits to living ecosystems.

It all started in Bolivar Park, one of those little triangles that grace the city. The central feature is a concrete reflecting pool, set squarely in front of the Department of the Interior building across the street. As John Hoke of NPS relates the tale, the question arose as to whether there should not be a little life in a pond in front of the building that is headquarters for both the Park Service and Fish and Wildlife Service. The pond already cost money to manage: It had to be drained several times a year to get ride of algae and litter on the bottom.

After an extended discussion of the esthetics involved, Hoke and his colleagues—in the NPS Division of Resource Management and Visitor Protection and in the Ecological Services Lab—got the go-ahead. They planted cattails and water irises in boxes of swamp soil just under the water surface. They introduced enough floating vegetation to cover about a third of the

"Every year one or more broods of ducklings are hatched there." Mallard Duck with Ducklings, S. Finnegan

pond. They put in a large log and then turtles to climb out and bask on it. And best of all, they built an island, no more than six feet across.

A postage-stamp island in a concrete pool next to a busy intersection in a fair-size city would not have appeared very promising to me, but then perhaps my own life pressure is a little sluggish. Ducks had flown far enough into the city to spot the island, and then quickly made it their own. Every year one or more broods of ducklings are hatched there, feeding on the aquatic vegetation (and some judiciously spread trout meal) until they are ready to travel.

In the spring, office workers from Interior come out at lunchtime to watch drakes battle for breeding rights while resident hens band together to keep interloping hens out of the pool. The crowds of people are heavy enough so that the Park Service has had to replace the original lawn around the pool with a tougher fescue and downgrade its maintenance standards. Yet hardly any trash is thrown into the water anymore.

The same magic has been worked in the seven-acre pond in Constitution Gardens along the Mall. Designed and built strictly as a formal reflecting surface, the lake was seeded with submerged vegetation in underwater planters; the one tiny, wild island was immediately commandeered by breeding ducks.

Along the way, Hoke and his colleagues have found a secret ingredient that keeps their ponds in balance. They were still having trouble with algae, even after they resorted to an inert black dye that darkened the water enough to slow algal growth. So last July, when a particularly noxious bloom occurred, the Park Service took a pumper truck (the kind used to empty out septic tanks) to Kenilworth Aquatic Gardens, loaded up 500 gallons of bottom muck and inoculated Bolivar Pond with it, much like adding sour-dough starter mix to a batch of pancake batter. In weeks, algal growth stopped.

The same miracle muck has been added to the lake in Constitution Gardens and the Reflecting Pool that lies between the Lincoln Memorial and Washington Monument, with the same happy results. The accountants are happy, too. Where it had cost $2,000 to drain Bolivar Pond to get rid of the algae (sometimes that had to be done four times a season), it had cost $20,000 to drain the Reflecting Pool.

Hoke and his colleagues have a history of working with nature instead of trying to overcome it. Years ago, when a cluster of "temporary" Navy buildings were removed from the Mall, some Park Service managers were dismayed to find a low, soggy wet area that quickly became a depository for beverage cans and windblown newspapers—and a breeding ground for mosquitoes. It made no sense to install expensive drains, for the area was to be torn up again for the creation of Constitution Gardens.

So they went the other way. The area was trying to be a wetland: They would help it along. They scooped out a hole deep enough for fish life. Next they raided a natural swamp for cattails and water irises, water lettuce and duckweed, mosquito fish and bullfrogs. Dragonflies and water striders arrived on their own, as did, naturally, flotillas of wild ducks. For the price of a few hours work with a backhoe and one truck trip to a swamp, they turned a seep into a flourishing wetland that quickly became popular with noontime picnickers. That pond and swamp are long gone, but the philosophy behind them is still very much alive.

At the entrance of the Park Service's National Capital Region headquarters on Hains Point is a concrete pond where experimenters can try out new combinations of plants and pond organisms. Bass and bluegills live there, and it is not unknown during the lunch hour for a Park Service worker to step outside with a fly rod, let out some line in a few false casts, and drop a tempting tidbit next to a lily pad.

Bouncing along the Mall in his electric cart, Hoke laughs with pleasure at how fast life moves into every new space he manages to create. He wants to know more about why what he does works so well. He hopes that somewhere a graduate student will take on the mission of finding out exactly which herbivores and decomposers in that pond muck—which microorganisms, aquatic worms, and insect larvae—play the key roles.

He thinks about other wild creatures that circle our city islands, always looking for a new opening. Not long ago he was in London, trading information with the people who manage the Serpentine Lake in Hyde Park. As many as 50 species of unusual waterfowl are seen there in a year, he was told. And it is not clear to him why we cannot do better here. If John Hoke has his way, there will be a lot more traffic coming the other way.

February, 1984

Leaving Earth to Save It

A dark forest used to stand silent just inside the National Museum of Natural History, a growth of hemlocks 4 to 5 feet in diameter. Through the trees you could see a river, a wooded island on the right, and acres of wild rice to the left. No bridges crossed the river. It was the spot where Rock Creek empties into the Potomac River in Washington, and you were seeing it as the Indians saw it before Europeans arrived. Malls and memorials stand now where once the wild rice grew; a seawall keeps the river in its place.

When I walk the seawall, I try to see the river as it was. I do the same on Chesapeake Bay or along the Hudson River, remembering accounts of the extraordinarily abundant fish and wildlife found by the early explorers. And I wonder how well they might recover if we went away for a few centuries. Would hemlocks grow again in what is now a boathouse parking lot at Rock Creek?

To find out what would happen, one could consult the literature on plant succession, study abandoned highways, visit ruins in Mexico, travel to lost cities in Asia. Or one could make evacuating the entire Earth the premise for a science fiction story, and let the special-effects people fill in the details when the story is snapped up for a major motion picture. New York City 10,000 years after the last human left would be a new challenge for the model makers.

The scenario goes something like this: The time comes when, despite our best efforts, the only way left to save Earth is to leave it. Everybody. For a long time. So many species have been lost, so many ecosystems impoverished, that the whole biological life support system is close to collapse. The natural waste-removal systems, the recyclers, the air filters and water holders are being overwhelmed.

In this fantasy future, field biologists are the new elite. They are paid more than Congressmen, although less than basketball players. Biologists have been multiplying as fast as species have been disappearing. In 1980 one expert had told Congress that there were only 1,500 people in the world competent to identify tropical organisms; when brown leafhoppers destroyed several billion dollars worth of rice in Southeast Asia in the late 1970s, only a dozen people in the world could distinguish with certainty the 20,000 species that make up that insect group.

Now, decades later, armies of biologists carry on with a wartime intensity, desperate to learn more about how the natural systems work before they disappear. They need to know not only what should be saved first on Earth, but what should be added to the recycling systems on the space colonies and asteroid mines overhead, which, like most home aquariums, do not quite work as closed systems. By now humans live as far away as the moons of Jupiter, but all the secrets of life remain on Earth.

At some point it becomes clear that the race is being lost. True, human numbers are dropping. Heavy industry has moved into space. But so much tropical forest has already been cut, so many watersheds destroyed, so much topsoil washed away that the biological decline has unstoppable momentum. It is too late for management, no matter how wise. Thus a decision once made by bands and tribes, to pack up and move, is now made by the population of a planet. The actual mechanics are a little fuzzy in my fantasy, except that more and more people would move into space to build more and more colonies for more and more people to move into space.

With a little suspension of disbelief one can see the story unfold on the Earth they left behind. Grass appears in the boathouse parking lot. A small section of the seawall collapses and, with no one around to fix it, the river moves in like a silent bulldozer. The noblest experiment of all has begun. The story moves in fast-forward, time-lapse photography; we watch nature reclaim itself through the eyes of appropriate creatures. Early on we see city streets through the eyes of a rat; we follow the feral dogs and cats that roam the suburbs along with the raccoons and skunks. A century later a coyote hunts in the streets of Manhattan; five centuries after that a panther uses the pinnacle of a rubble pile to search for prey. A pigeon's eye view of a city changes to a falcon's.

Humans will not be able to leave the planet completely alone, of course, any more than an editor can pass on a manuscript without making a mark. The luckiest biologists of their generations will be landed at monitoring stations. Remote sensors will be maintained, camera lenses cleaned. A little crisis intervention might be allowed at first: aerial tankers putting out a fire about to destroy the last known stand of some special plant. But as far as humanly possible, the biologists would keep their hands off, acting only as passive receptors. Nature would be the protagonist and the star. A living Earth regenerating from the ruins. The miracle that struggles to happen in every vacant lot happening everywhere. All with appropriate inspirational music, of course.

Conflict for a story line should be easy. At the start the conflict would be over whether to leave; I could stoop to a line something like: "Gazing out into the dark—30 stories above the East River—after a day of hearing out the ecologists' deputations, the Secretary-General became biologically literate." Later the conflict over whether it was time to return would grow stronger. The latter argument would not sound entirely unfamiliar to anyone who follows today's debates over multiple use versus preserving wilderness areas unsullied. A writer might suffer the temptation to inject ideological harangues into the dialogue.

In the meantime, the miracle would be fact. The biological crisis would be past. Nothing would have returned from extinction, but the several million species left would be plenty to keep the bio in biosphere. An optimist would end the movie with humans returning to live in gentle coexistence. A pessimist might have us come back to ravish the Earth all over again. Something in between seems more reasonable.

I'm completely over my head in every part of this fantasy, of course. If we flew 100,000 people off this Earth every day, it would take 125 years to move the current population. I certainly don't know if hemlocks could or would ever grow again in that boathouse parking lot.

But I like the uniting of what are now inimical factions: the high technologists who believe the future of our species lies in space, and the environmentalists who fear we would foul the rest of the solar system just as we have fouled the planet. Environmentalists might be a little humbler if the spacers save the world. I also like the idea of a species, grown out of its infancy, given a second chance at husbanding a remarkable place to live. Possibly even the only place to live.

But the strongest appeal is really the vision I started with: Fish leaping in clear water, forests growing to the water's edge, swamps and marshes pulsating with life. The way things were here just five or six lifetimes ago.

To some people today, an environmentalist is a monomaniac. Worse, still, is a preservationist: an elitist unconcerned with people. Perhaps I am most unspeakable of all: a preservationist who not only wants to keep what we still have but would like to bring back what we once had. I don't feel antipeople at all. We people need the life support of the biosphere. The whole system is slowly failing, but still has the power to regenerate without any help from us. All we have to do is stand back. Now, if only that were somehow possible.

September 1982

Permissions

Index

This index comprises the names of persons, places, and natural features. Boldface page numbers indicate text devoted primarily to the subject of the entry.